The Transformation of Chinese Socialism

The Transformation
of Chinese Socialism

Lin Chun

Duke University Press

Durham and London

2006

© 2006 Duke University Press
All rights reserved
Printed in the United States of America on acid-free paper ∞
Designed by Heather Hensley
Typeset in Minion by Keystone Typesetting, Inc.
Library of Congress Cataloging-in-Publication Data
appear on the last printed page of this book.

To my parents,
idealist communists, who have taught me to be honest.

To my friends in China,
who have forgiven me for having not yet returned home
where we grew up socialists together.

To the memory of
Lin Wei, Li Shu, Wolfgang Stargardt and Robin Cohen:
mentors, friends, humanists and internationalists.

CONTENTS

PREFACE

This book took me many years to write. The long process of writing and revising motivated not only my constant effort to keep pace with China's profound and ever-puzzling changes but also a searching engagement with debates about those changes. My debt to the influence of many thinkers is acknowledged in the text and notes.

I remain most grateful to Michael Apple for his initial interest and trust. Maurice Meisner inspired a transformation in my own perspective despite any disagreements. I wish to thank him also for his persistent support, including hosting a fruitful workshop at the University of Wisconsin, Madison in 1997 to discuss an early draft of this book. My gratitude also goes to the workshop participants from afar for their invaluable responses: particularly Robert S. Cohen, Zhiyuan Cui, Katie Lynch, Tom Lutze, Carl Riskin, and Marilyn Young. I cannot possibly specify all of those who commented on my project at different stages, but I owe thanks for each instance of time and insight generously offered to me. As the work traveled from one publisher to another, Robin Blackburn, David Held, Michael Moran, and Reynolds Smith found rigorous and perceptive reviewers for me, whose constructive criticisms were truly beneficial.

At London School of Economics I was most fortunate to have four successive departmental conveners who supported my work in every possible way; this was remarkable especially because they did not necessarily share my views. Christopher Hood was a role model of high standards and scholarly rigor. Brendan O'Leary understood all matters involved, both personally and intellectually, in writing a critique of something in which one was brought up. So did Dominic Lieven, who took the trouble to read a rather messy early draft, and to meticulously make corrections and comments. George Philip graciously allowed me a year of special leave so that I could, though unexpectedly, carry out yet another round of revisions. Meanwhile, Meghnad Desai and Michael Yahuda separately read the entire manuscript and urged me, each in his distinct concern, to rethink certain sets of issues. Their warm encouragement was once again granted in spite of serious differences of opinion. My students, coming from many parts of the world, were often my best critics in the ways they were not aware, and I thank them, too, with hope.

Tani Barlow heroically went through several versions of the manuscript. Her extensive and thoughtful suggestions were greatly and gratefully appreciated. She, along with others, also pushed in terms of my writing (in a foreign language). Bernard Crick was irritated by the "dense and difficult" style of articulation and Dominic Lieven by the "Gucci handbag" of jargon. Lieven also correctly insisted on the need to treasure national and cultural traditions, an attitude toward the *longue duree* that my education was biased to overlook. As I struggled with grasping plain English I was lucky enough to be assisted by Debra Keats, Deborah Strod, and Jean Brady, whose intelligent and careful editing rescued the book. I certainly hope they will find the final product a substantial improvement. Reynolds Smith at Duke University Press has been both morally supportive and professionally demanding. I deeply admire his recognition of the topical importance of this book and his patience in bringing it to light. Justin Faerber and Sharon Torian, also at Duke Press, were sources of cheer and effective assistance. My academic affiliations with Boston University, Harvard University, and Northeastern University were of essential help in terms of intellectual exchange as well as library privileges, for which facilitation by James Coony, Laura Frader, Nancy Fraser, Roderick MacFarquhar, Elizabeth Perry, Libby Schweber, and Alfred Tauber will be appreciatively remembered. The devoted librarians at the Historical Studies–Social Science Library at the Institute for Advanced Study in Princeton provided the best services I could ever expect.

I was privileged as I undertook this project to have friends standing by me through thick and thin. These friends are simply too numerous to list by name, but each deserves my heartfelt gratitude. I nevertheless must specifically mention a few of those who lent a hand directly: my thanks to Marion Kozak for her willingness to discuss my writings and for providing me a home in a foreign land, and to Dorothy Wedderburn for much of the same—she and Marion also broadened my horizons with their astute questions about China and their memorable answers to my questions about the world. Thanks to Cui Zhiyuan for his critical reflections on the manuscript, his refreshing discussions over the years, and his selfless efforts in selecting and sharing information; to Wang Jin for her wise and principled advice on presentation at a time when political sensitivity was biased against "socialism"; to Wang Xiaoqiang for his extraordinary sense of duty and urgency, and for pressing me to put an end to this work while other tasks were waiting; to Evelyn Fox Keller for her daily check-up calls, at a crucial stage of the project, to ensure that I was working, and for the use of her Cambridge apartment as my refuge; to Sam Schweber for his kind help with books, computer issues, and photocopying while he, like Evelyn, had far more important things to do; and to Zhang Xiaodi for his noble deed of quietly taking care of my parents in Beijing so as to partially relieve me from the inflexible scheduling of family visits. Bob Cohen remains my first reader and I continue to rely on his guidance and judgment. Cao Tianyu, a political victim of communist repression yet a steadfast defender of the Chinese revolution and the Marxist outlook, for me as a constant reminder of conscience. As ever, this book was written also for Rosa, with my loving appreciation of her youthful passion for truth and justice; and for my sisters whose incredible generosity sustained me.

At the Princeton Institute I began and concluded the book. I still owe a debt to the early mentorship of Joan Scott and Michael Walzer, as well as Clifford Geertz and Albert Hirschman. Joan, in particular, was always there for me to turn to. The School of Social Science was a wonderful place to think, write, and argue, yet I missed my own country intensely. In the end, this work is unfinished, and better works are bound to follow. To all of those who played a role in what I managed to write here so far, I extend my grateful acknowledgment.

The Making and Remaking of the Chinese Model

CHINESE SOCIALISM CAN BEST BE GRASPED AS A MODERN PROJECT THAT has sought to develop by its own unique means into its own unique type, always conscious of the other possibilities it has refused to emulate: that is, Soviet-style bureaucratic socialism (and now Russian postcommunism) as well as diverse forms of peripheral capitalism. From the beginning, the Chinese communist revolution—the successor to and radical transformer of a republican revolution—was self-consciously an alternative to colonial modernity. The post-revolutionary Maoist experiment, in turn, aspired to create an alternative to the Stalinist model, which it considered both a failure and a betrayal of the project to construct a credible socialist society. Even when the post-1978 reforms as a socialist self-adjusting movement were set back by the logic of a market transition in the late 1980s and 1990s, the People's Republic of China (PRC) continued to search for a "socialist market" alternative to capitalist integration. Insofar as this collective effort has persisted, the chance of the Chinese model to succeed cannot be ruled out. As a country of 1.3 billion people and as an economy reaching $1.64 trillion in gross domestic product (GDP) in 2004 (the sixth largest economy in the world), and with an ambition of resisting subordination to global capitalism, China is at the epicenter of global transformation.

To conceptualize China's trajectory in these terms we must delve into the Chinese model of socialism as well as the Chinese model of reform. Both models synthesize contradictions; and Chinese alternative modernity is conceptually based on the continuities and discontinuities between the two. To seek a coherent interpretation of these contradictory developments we also need to clear the ground by rejecting a number of widespread myths about contemporary Chinese experiences. For example, liberal commentators at home and abroad assume that China began to modernize economically in a rational manner only after the market transition that was initiated in the late 1970s. This assumption amounts to a total dismissal of the formidable socioeconomic progress made during the Maoist period. By implication, it also blames the communist revolution for the inability of the country to "catch up" with the other modern nations. However, a comparison of uncontested historical evidence suggests that such assumptions are false. China, viewed as the "sick man of Asia" (a symptom and symbol of forced opium consumption) until 1949, when the Chinese people were declared to have stood up at the founding of the PRC, contrasts sharply with the new China as a proud national power prior to the reform. There is definite proof that neither the revolution nor the socialist attempt was a lengthy interruption of modernization. Rather, the communists, changing faces over time, had been effective modernizers in leading the "Chinese nation's great rejuvenation" (*zhonghua minzu de weida fuxingi*).[1]

Another example is seen in the view of neoliberal doctrine that China's remarkable economic successes since the 1980s are attributable to the opening of its market to foreign investors and joint ventures, manufacturing for export, measured privatization, and far-reaching decentralization. Yet careful studies have found other contributing factors that are equally (if not more) compelling than that of embracing globalization: the relatively strong "human capital" accumulated through decades (including during the pre-reform period) of investment in basic needs, public education, and health care; state and rural collective ownership of the land; the dominant public sector that retains the nation's strategic industries; government sponsorship of trade and technology transfers; state regulation of the movements of foreign capital, major financial transactions, and currency exchange; coordination between the center and provinces in fiscal and tax management, public spending, and developing regional comparative advantages; booming township and village enterprises (TVES); a countrywide increase in household incomes (including remittances sent home by migrant workers) and, therefore, a "consuming revolution" of a major increase in consumption. To be sure, the strengths of these determinants drastically declined in the 1990s, as typified in the hijacking of decentralization by privatization. It is also not always plausible to disentangle competing causes. Nevertheless, the two modes of explanation sketched out above provide different lessons for strategic and policy choices.

Yet another frequently repeated observation is that since the reform had not replaced the one-party rule, it was solely an economic matter—as though systemic shifts in the economy could be possible without thorough political changes, and as though glasnost were the only road to transition from state socialism. But politics surely comes first. The leadership succession in 1976–1978, followed by Deng Xiaoping's campaign for "liberating the mind" and extensive rehabilitation to rectify earlier purges, along with the party's democratic platform of its watershed plenary session (the third session of the eleventh congress), were each indispensable in paving the way for subsequent economic reforms. No less important was the institutional development—empowering the National People's Congresses (NPC), separating government from the party and administration from management, pursuing the rule of law, and opening public spaces for civic associations. When accompanied by broad political participation in deliberation and decision making, these institutional changes would be conducive to meaningful democratization even in the absence of multiparty elections.

Conversely, the degradation of common people, the abuses of labor rights, and the rising inequalities and mounting corruption were regressions from the democratic gains of China's century-long revolutionary and socialist struggle. These erosions indicated a wrongheaded agenda aimed at "market spontaneity," rather than a lack of direction as is often suggested.[2] The point, then, is that the party system may not be a primary gauge of regime type, and that a more fundamental issue is the purpose of a national state and, notably, the place of the citizenry in the power structure of a polity. To the Chinese eye, postcommunist Russia (not to mention the post-Tito war-torn Balkans) in particular demonstrated that "negative liberties" alone, and economic liberalization and electoral competitions alike, could not be the road to a functional democracy. Critics of authoritarianism are yet to note three extraordinary things about the PRC politics. First, by historical account the Chinese Communist Party (CCP), a massive and still aggressively recruiting organization with a membership of sixty-six million,[3] was neither the sole obstacle nor solely an obstacle to democracy. Second, the party had never been entirely unified while lacking formal factions (Mao was known to have cheerfully admitted "parties within the party"); and dedicated democrats were found as often within the party as without. Third, by virtue of an official ideological stance guaranteeing pressure for the norm, the party would be compelled to respond to public demands in one way or another, including deterring certain aspects of the (hardly democratic) process of globalization. In other words, as far as political reform is concerned, the CCP must be treated not only as part of the problem but also as carrying with it the needed sources of a solution. This is the case not least because having changed from within beyond recognition, the party remained the only institution powerful enough to shield national unity and to bring itself, for its own sake in accommodation with societal interests, to the authority of constitutionalism and legality.[4]

Yet another standard example of misconception about reforms in China can be noted when the contrast between the Chinese approach and postcommunist transitions is perceived as a contrast between incrementalism and "shock therapy." Superficially, the issues of China's transitional "dual-track" price system, its "rural first" strategy, and the political caution with formal democratization were indeed cases of gradualism. At the heart of the matter, however, China's nonconformity exceeded mere method. Despite a clear departure from conventional socialist ideologies and practices—above all the repudiation of egalitarianism—the CCP still could not abandon its constitution centered in the commitment to the working classes, which originated in the epic liberation endeavor of the Chinese people. Similarly, despite waves of "spontaneous privatization" in which corrupt managers and officials illegally embezzled public assets of state-owned enterprises (SOEs), the government had not allowed such embezzlement to seize the entire agenda of reforming the SOEs. In the end, we will understand transitional processes in different political economies only by comparing their respective reform objectives and policy orientations, rather than scale and pace of change. Moreover, we can appreciate the foundation or destruction of regime legitimacy only by recognizing specific national yearnings and social preferences. What was known as "double transition" to a free market and liberal democracy (or "triple transition," to include new nation-building) in the former Soviet bloc does not provide a yardstick for measuring the Chinese case. Policies in China might have been mistaken or confusing, but its long-term goals have so far not been defined in the similar terms of new Russian capitalism.

As self-identified with "primary-stage socialism,"[5] the priority that China gave to economic growth was in official discourse justified by the argument that such growth would improve general living conditions and prepare for socialist advance. The slogan "socialism with Chinese characteristics," defined by Deng as eliminating exploitation and attaining common wealth, was far from a cultural slogan about preserving traditional "Chineseness." Rather, it was a political program to develop the nation by appropriating market tools while rejecting capitalist vices.[6] This fit with China's modern path of searching for a modern alternative, which historically was marked by revolutionary modernity, socialist modernization, and a market economy evolving into an all-inclusive *xiaokang* (literally "moderate prosperity") society. The neoliberal turn after the Tiananmen event in 1989 was confirmed by the fourteenth party congress in 1992 and then boosted by the fifteenth party congress in 1997, which signaled a green light to further economic and financial deregulation. An unexpected degree of "marketification of political power" (*quanli shichanghua*) followed. Yet this major retreat from reform socialism did not yield a total reversal. If the pursuit of a socialist alternative, tricky and rocky as it has been and will still be, succeeded under compelling moral and rational impulses backed by a broad social consensus, it would challenge, and eventually contribute to transforming, capitalist modernity. This is the site of messages such as that stemming from the Cancun meeting in 2003 (the so-called G22 initiated by Brazil and India to mobilize a redress on farm subsidies for trade): when China is allied with other developing countries in multilateral negotiations, together they can begin to halt or revise the rules of globalization. If the reform course can be conveniently divided into a first decade (the 1980s) and a "long" second decade (1989 to 2003) (cf. C. Wang Chaohua 2003, "Introduction"), then a distinctive third decade seems to have embarked with a new team of leaders. The emergence of a "Beijing consensus," the introduction of a "green GDP," and the pledge of attaining "social harmony" by bettering the plight of peasants and migrant workers are among the signs of a resumption of reform socialism.[7]

Is there, then, a distinct and definable Chinese model in the making? Some argue that the reform is ultimately capable of creating something close to a "market socialism" or a "social market" in which public commitments to fundamental freedoms, profit sharing, and social justice could be incorporated in entrepreneurship and innovation (see, e.g., White 1996; Schweickart 1998, 7). Others depict a renewed phase of social-national development in China, a hybrid of state socialism and private capitalism (Amin 1998, 133–42; Therborn 2000, 151). Still others diagnose a repressive and pathological adventure of "bureaucratic capitalism" and "market Stalinism" that blends the worst elements of both worlds (Meisner 1996, 300–45; Nolan 1995, 160–67; Blecher 1997, 100–9, 204–6). Finally, the reform policies are viewed as no more than typically "third world" capitalist, a process geared to the demands of the global market and multinational corporations (Weil 1995; Huang 2003).[8] Many also observe a "Latin Americanization" of China, in the sense that the country seems to be slipping back to a semicolonial status in its increasing dependence on foreign capital and foreign trade and in its growing risks of debt accumulation and financial instability.[9] Each of these assessments is in part grounded in reality and meets the expectation of certain theoretical frameworks; but none has been decisively vindicated. Is it not too hasty to pass judgment on a still unfolding development that has been uneven, contested, and necessarily experimental?

The only thing we can be certain about is the political innovativeness of a Chinese alternative to the capitalist homogenization of the world, even though the "Chinese" identity itself cannot, and never did, imply internal homogeneity. The CCP's consecutive manifestos stated the party's determination on a socialist choice. They deserve to be taken seriously because national leadership is pivotal for any modernization effort; because ideology (de)legitimizes and creates reality; and because there are real power and social forces behind the decisions and rhetoric of the party. As a vast site of structured as well as contingent human activities, as long as it held together China would be too preoccupied with its wealth of heritages and enduring aspirations—however interpreted—to fall prey to any predictable models. As Carl Riskin notes: "Because Chinese history, culture, and revolutionary experience are exactly shared by no other people, the possibilities and constraints China faces in reconstructing its socioeconomic system are to a degree unique" (1982, 319). Yet, even a *sui generis* Chinese modernity cannot be comprehensible in an ethnocentric perspective, especially because the socialist outlook remains a defining element of the Chinese modern identity. In this sense, then, the crisis of Chinese socialism and its transformation is in part cultural, but it is essentially political and reflects the paradoxes of modernization in China and of modernity itself.

The search for a novel path that defies either Stalinist or free market logics is not unprecedented—other cases exist, for example, in the Nordic undertaking of social democracy, the European debates over a "socialized market" or a "caring economy," the development of a "welfare society" (as opposed to the welfare state) in East Asia, and the pioneering reform communism in Yugoslavia and Hungary. The task, however, is formidable for a country of continental scale with a population comprising one fifth of humanity. The continuation of the search in China was no accident, for it was, for reasons elaborated in the pages following, better positioned than most poor and transitional societies to navigate in unfamiliar waters with powerful countercurrents. The Chinese revolution had not only nurtured a public culture of equality and solidarity, but also a protective and regulative state. A sophisticated social organization of production and distribution for basic needs was arguably achieved under a "socialist developmental state" in the first thirty years of the PRC. With Mao Zedong's suspicion of Stalinist management, the Chinese loosened central planning in favor of decentralized local initiatives, thereby anticipating some of the post-reform development strategies. The reforms in turn accomplished some of the boldest missions of socialism in China, of which the gigantic antipoverty project (the so-called 8–7 plan) announced in 1994 was only one example. In the words of the United Nations Development Program, the project "constitutes a commitment, rare among the world's nations, to basically eliminate absolute poverty by the end of the century" (1998, 8). According to the World Bank, the number of Chinese subsisting on less than $1 a day had fallen from 490 million in 1981 to 88 million in 2003. Further, in 1977 there were 250 million—or 30.7 percent of the total rural population—who remained below China's own subsistence line, whereas in 2003 they reduced to 50 million, of whom around 30 million were rural and 20 million emerged as the new urban poor.[10] Overall in this period, China accounted for three-quarters of the global population lifted out of abject poverty.[11]

But more recently China had been losing rather than building up its advantages. The national political autonomy and economic independence needed to safeguard vital social interests—ranging from domestic producers and internal markets to financial security and fiscal stability—had been endangered by a single-minded open policy. Meanwhile, macro regulation and coordination of capital and resource allocation had been weakened by

profit-driven and short-sighted investment at the expense of general equilibrium. This situation intensified "overcapacity" relevant to undercon-
sumption directly linked with cheap labor, and with it came the threat of a
classical crisis of overproduction. Moreover, social welfare deteriorated as
nonprofit, inexpensive public services shrank while the private concentration of capital and wealth surged. Consequently, various inequalities and
disparities expanded along regional, sectoral, class, gender, ethnic, and
other lines, which resulted in sweeping protests of the likes seen only in the
doomed days of the Guomindang (GMD).[12] The Gini coefficient of household income jumped from 0.33 in 1980 to 0.454 in 2003, surpassing not only
most of the wealthy capitalist countries but also poor and transitional economies, including Russia. The government admitted in a report to the Asian
Development Bank conference in May 2002 that China had one of the
world's greatest wealth gaps.[13] Many county and township governments in
the poor regions, still overstaffed, went bankrupt after the center practically
withdrew from its financial obligations. The peasant households then had to
pay for a large portion of public expenditure, not least of which was in the
form of the local cadres' salaries.[14] The government began with provincial
experiments in late 2004 to remove agricultural taxes altogether, shaking
grassroots regimes at the same time.[15] Meanwhile, urban workers suffered
from layoffs, frequently without adequate compensation; and many entered
the private sector in which labor was even less protected. The official unemployment rate was said to have been kept below 4.5 percent, but the actual
figure, including unregistered job loss, could easily have been double or even
triple that amount, as was widely published in newspapers and research
reports. In fact, 25 million people working in the manufacturing industries
were deemed redundant, along with 300 million in the agricultural sector
(CASS 2003).

A decline in the universal provision of basic health care and education
had raised a serious public concern with what the market could and could
not do, and thus by implication what the government must take as its own
responsibility. The accelerating cost and dropping coverage of insurance in
a once publicly financed medical system threatened "a humanitarian disaster" that could undo what had been achieved in poverty alleviation—one of
the country's proudest successes (Lawrence 2002, 30–33). Indeed, the vulnerability of public health, especially in rural China, could wipe out what

was considered "perhaps the Chinese revolution's single most important achievement."[16] Many in the countryside, where a functioning rural cooperative arrangement had disappeared, remained, or became poor due to unaffordable hospital bills and untreated illness as a result. In education, the government claimed that its nine-year compulsory program reached an attendance rate of 91.22 percent in 2002 from 73 percent in 1998, and the gender ratio for primary school enrollment was equal.[17] These data, however, ignore the high dropout rate in poor regions and do not reflect the massive number of the children of migrant workers who faced all kinds of difficulties in attending schools, such as disputes in residential status and extra fees levied in discriminatory practices. Behind rising tuition fees in schools and universities, legal and illegal, was the idea of bringing education into the market (*jiaoyu chanyehua*). Astonishingly, China's state budget for education was lower than the 4 percent of GDP average found in the developing countries.

The boom of sweatshops, filled by migrants working long hours for low wages and in insecure working conditions, made a mockery of the Labor Law, the Law for Security in Production, and the requirements for environmental standards. Engels's description of the conditions of the working class in nineteenth-century England became applicable to Chinese workers in some coastal cities. It was widely felt among them, as reported by one labor scholar, that "if Marx could see Guangdong today he would die of anger."[18] Needless to say, these workers were scarcely organized, although a union branch membership of the state-sponsored All China Federation of Trade Unions (ACFTU) was a legal entitlement in both public and private sectors. The number of work-related accidents and deaths had rocketed since the 1990s due to mismanagement and neglect. This picture is encapsulated in an angry line in the poet Shao Yanxiang's "Mourning the Coal Miners": "Cheap labor, cheap lives"![19] The violation of labor rights in China was put before U.S. Congress in a petition to challenge "the *artificial* and *severe* reduction of China's labor costs below the baseline of comparative advantage defined by standard trade theory."[20] While public funds and private profits flow into pockets of the super rich, a significant portion of the population were impoverished.[21] The mistreatment of peasants, workers, migrants, and other marginalized social groups involved policy bias, urban exclusion, and rights abuses ranging from withholding or even denying wages to acts of police cruelty. As economic liberalization went on, ordinary citizens lived literally in a "risk society," where they had little means to fend for themselves.

In gradually switching sides from labor to capital, local communist authorities, in particular, often openly backed "capitalists" in suppressing labor unrest, perceiving the necessity of maintaining a "good investment environment." The thirst for foreign direct investment (FDI) had a structural and political explanation in a source of official corruption that officials took a share of any gains yielded—an appalling contributing factor to the legitimacy crisis of the regime (Yue and Chen 2003).[22] The term "regime" as used here needs to be differentiated not only from "government" but also from "system" (*zhidu*) in the Chinese political vocabulary. Government in the PRC changed through the NPC under the same communist regime, of which one might be more or less popular than the others. Regime performance was evaluated against the principles of a Chinese socialist system. A great deal of what was seen as the failing of official conduct and policies was precisely where the system (either despite of reforms or because of them) was believed to have once succeeded, or had the obligation and resources to succeed. Upholding national dignity, providing economic security, delivering public goods, and overcoming corruption were among the normative expectations. That is, once things had gone wrong, public anger would be directed more to the individuals than to the systemic fundamentals or the basic rules established after 1949. When a particular institution appeared questionable, it was expected to be repaired or replaced within the system. The target of inner-party criticisms and wider social protests was thus generally not the socialist system itself but rather state policies and the power holders who failed the norms of that system, of which the most memorable catchphrase had been "serving the people." The "systemic reform" (*tizhi gaige*) needed to transform a command economy and its accompanying institutions on the one hand, and retaining China's collective self-identity with reform socialism on the other, remained congruent.

Two major responses to the legitimacy crisis arose. One response was designed to push for further privatization to be carried out in a more fair and orderly manner along with other measures of deepening liberalization. The other response was to press for political reforms to resume the sovereign place of the people along with their socioeconomic rights and participation in policymaking. The latter, or the democratic solution, rather than the former, or the neoliberal solution, constituted a genuine challenge to the state (which could act at governmental, regime, or systemic level, depending on substance and context). Yet the democratic solution, more appealing to an active citizenship, might work only through reforming the establishment within the boundaries of a socialist vision and policy formally safeguarded by the PRC constitution. This latter consensus, a monumental project distinctive from democratizations elsewhere, should not be missed in the loud cry for global convergence. The changing Chinese self-image, in real socio-historical movements with great intellectual and popular energy, must be read carefully as struggles over reflecting and constructing the reform model.

Lacking cohesion and sufficient credibility, would the Chinese model in the making vanish even before it could be solidly made, by a "peaceful evolution," a revolutionary upheaval, a form of national disintegration, or an eruption of financial meltdown? To contemplate any such scenario is, of course, also to acknowledge the transformative power of capital. As soon as China's old political elite and new economic elites both, willingly or reluctantly, became the awkward agents of that power, globalization was no longer external to the Chinese existence. After having "delinked" and then "relinked" to the global market, the phrase "making global linkages" (*jie-gui*) became the country's household motto. Such linkages, ideally, should be democratically selected and controlled to ensure benefits and reduce risks, but that would require determined and intelligent strategy and policy choices yet to be taken. Membership in the World Trade Organization (WTO), for example, caused the immediate vulnerability of China's staple agricultural products and infant hi-tech industries, and threatened to elevate unemployment to an even greater degree.[23] Until China opens all of its sectors, the so-called transitional period—of steadily lowering import tariffs, benchmark quotas, and other limitations on foreign ownership/control in banking, insurance, securities, retailing, and so on—will end before 2010. While the other side of the coin could be the widened access to global markets, the opportunity is only premised on the perpetuation of an export-oriented development, which might not be sustainable in the long run and which would condemn the competing exporters (in the textile industry, for instance) mainly in the third world to a lose-lose situation of beating down prices and the employment rate. Also impaired, vitally, would be China's ability to handle budget deficits, national debt, capital flight, and fiscal liability to international financial turmoil.[24] As is now commonly acknowledged, China's nonconvertible capital account, as well as its foreign exchange controls, were decisive factors in limiting the impact to the country of the Asian financial crisis of 1997–1998, in contrast to a score of its devastated neighbors. Concessions to the U.S.-led demands during trade negotiations toward WTO accession turned out to be excessive and were made without public knowledge or consultation inside China using the Chinese language.[25] The Supreme Court even promised that wherever domestic laws contradict WTO statutes, the latter should take precedence.

In tracing developments in China since 1978, one observation to highlight is the mid-course turn of the reform; a turn that departed from its initial project of socialist self-adjustment as opposed to "revolution" in the style of Eastern Europe in 1989.[26] The obvious demarcation is the crackdown in Tiananmen Square that same year (and its aftermath in a world of crumbling communist states and united sanctions against China). The party had since deserted some core components of the original reform program. This allowed the reforms to derail, which ran counter to the preference of the general wage-earning strata (*gongxin jieceng*) of workers, managers, professionals, and intellectuals, as well as the peasants and the jobless people who, combined, constituted an overwhelming majority in China. The derailing, nevertheless, may not be irreversible.

An elaboration of this assessment will be presented in the following pages. Here, a four-fold argument needs to be advanced in order to understand the path of China's journey as well as its possible destination. First, Chinese socialism as one of the grandest modern projects of social emancipation—in spite of the destruction amid its colossal construction—cannot be dismissed. China's present crisis did not result from its incomplete market transition, as many argue, but rather from the reform's shattered promises of regaining socialism in terms of common prosperity, social justice, freedom, and democracy.

Second, the current transformation in China is bound to be open-ended despite the mighty power of globalization that everywhere keeps driving the process toward integration. Transforming China will not be a matter of wishful thinking but path-dependent on potent historical constraints.

However, the project could also be path-breaking, and breakthroughs may result from incorporating market dynamics and innovations into the socialist moral boundary. The Chinese alternative would be realistic if its "structure" and "agency" in dialectic interplay could progressively define and expand a space for such incorporation.

Third, the strength of this alternative is in its determination to redress development, of which the familiar pattern of industrial revolution (as wasteful, energy thirsty, and capital-reliant for socialist and capitalist alike) is morally and physically exhausted. Such exhaustion is judged both on human well-being and on ecological balance and the preservation of natural resources. It will be globally disastrous if there is no alternative to the traditional means of industrialization. For even as capitalism has declared victory, it has grossly failed in its destructive effects on a vast number of the world's people. The intrinsic inability of capitalist development to mend global competition over raw materials and to prevent environmental devastation, poverty, injustice, and conflict seems logically to necessitate an alternative: "socialism or barbarism," a discernible form of the latter would be fascism. What must be emphasized, then, is the type of states, both central and regional-local, and the line of leadership, variations in which can explain many of the differences in the extent and quality of development within the same capitalist epochal parameters.

Fourth and finally, any incompatibility that appears between social and market priorities beyond individual and communal agreement must be resolved by governments at all levels and by governmental authority directly conferred by the people. Precisely because of this indispensability of public power, only political and economic democracy can rescue the Chinese model by placing it, and the market society it fostered, under public scrutiny and control. Democracy, standing for the people and the social via legal and procedural arrangements, is a device of crisis management as much as a fundamental legitimating value for socialism and reform.

To sustain these theses, China's experiences will be situated against a macro-scale of "history" and accounted for in their inevitable complexities. The chance for China to eventually evade either an antisocialist "revolution," or another populist revolution of a similar nature as 1949, will depend on the renovation of its reform course. Indeed, the paradigm of globalization makes the very notion of "alternative" dubious. Has not deeper inte-

gration in the world market been proven to have reduced national autonomy, thereby causing any alternative to globalization to be less affordable?[27]

Taking shape in a fast-growing economy and facing challenges from all
directions, the reform model bears profound contradictions and uncertainties. On the one hand, socialist elements seemed to have been on an overall
retreat for quite some time, side by side with decays in public morale. On
the other hand, a changing China also looked remarkably vibrant and
reflective in economic activities, cultural production, civic organization,
intellectual debates, and political rethinking (Zhang 2001; H. Wang 2003;
Cao 2005). One of the great political effects of communication and information technology in China has been electronic online mobilization
through free Internet discussions and postings.[28] Support for vulnerable
social groups has thus found new channels of petitioning, dissent, and
critical journalism. The norm by which money and market values could not
dictate the lifeworld was resilient. This norm was not lost in youth culture
and popular culture, nor even in business circles, as it might have a bearing
in the traditional Chinese concern with "equal share" of the wealth (jun pin
fu). But it would not have been so strong without a profoundly educational
experience of revolutionary socialism in China. The socialist legacies, rather
than cheap labor racing locally and globally to the bottom for market
competitiveness, are central to China's real and sustainable "comparative
advantage" (Lin 2005). Only with such an advantage could the reformers,
initially blessed with a popular mandate, begin to regain public confidence.
The "fourth-generation leadership" since the NPC convention of 2003 has
signaled a willingness to change by reviving the party principle of "relying
on the people, ruling for the people" (yi min wei ben, zhizheng wei min). It
has vowed to fulfill the constitution, pursue social harmony and environmentally sustainable development, and tackle the problems of labor rights,
income gaps, and corruption. A crisis of governability is recognized as a
"life-and-death matter" for the party to survive.[29] Still, baffled by countless
obstacles, the full content of the reform project transcending conventional
models is yet to be determined, and its success or failure can only be judged
collectively by the Chinese people themselves, who are the ultimate arbiters,
even as victims, of their own endeavor.

This study intends to reflect on competing interpretations of the formation and transformation of Chinese socialism. In working with both history

and theory, it aims to provide a critical commentary on the historicity of the Chinese revolution, the reach and limit of China's post-revolutionary modernization, the ongoing reconstruction of the social contract along a turbulent reform course, and the contested legitimacy of each of these undertakings. The impending questions of the source and direction of China's journey, or "where from" and "where to," are probed in the context of the country's modern search for alternatives, chronically and logically, to colonial, bureaucratic, and capitalist modernity. And, along the way, the overriding concepts as precursors and organizers of these experiences will be clarified.

Chapter 1 situates China's modern change in its epochal conditions of imperialism and capitalism. The triad of nationalism, socialism, and developmentalism is the analytic framework in which I delineate China's socialist modernization. The unity of logic and history requires modernity to be taken as a starting point, and thus beginning with Chinese modernity, a subject matter assumed to be a valid and important social science case, which cannot be treated as a "deviation." China's large share of the world's land and population only makes it all the more persuasive that established assumptions and conceptions be duly tested by those trajectories contradicting the myth of the liberal capitalist universe.

Chapter 2 is an inquiry, through the lens of once-undisputed egalitarian ambition, into China's political economy. In this chapter I explain the nationalist footing of socialist modernization, the developmental imperative dictated by the predicament of "socialism and backwardness," and the impact of these structural conditions on class, ethnic, gender, and regional relations. A comparative assessment of the pre-reform and post-reform periods is ventured to illustrate some of the intrinsic contradictions of both Chinese socialism and its transformation.

In chapter 3 I examine the idea and exercise of "people's democracy"—a forbidden "outcast" in the received scholarship—in its intellectual, historical, and international circumstances. Here I consider the tensions between the moral and the institutional in the Mao and post-Mao era, both respectively and comparatively. I show that only by "bringing the people back in" can the foundation for democratization, locally perceived, be laid. This leads to the Chinese riddle, earlier in the revolutionary socialist period of liberation despising liberalism and later in the reform era liberalization undermining liberty and democracy (discussed in chapter 4). The clarifications attempted in this analysis also involve a reading of liberalism into socialism and vice versa; a reading that is mediated by the republican and humanist notions of legitimacy. Taken together, chapters 3 and 4 argue how in China the democratic solution might be chosen over the neoliberal one, and why only by honestly recognizing the banner of freedom of China's revolutionary and socialist traditions can the country's development be adequately and critically grasped.

The concluding chapter focuses on the making, unmaking, and remaking of the reform model. This effort is preceded by a discussion of the unfolding struggle between socialism and capitalism with Chinese characteristics—on the one hand in the context of a confusing relationship between the market and the bureaucracy, and on the other hand in light of the contested goals and role of the state. In reproaching the developmentalist impasse against a background of ever-greater demographic and ecological crises, I sketch the imperative and opportunities for China to carve out a fresh terrain of a politics of nature, work, time, and participation. The plausibility of "*xiaokang* socialism" beyond the official version is explored, along with a brief explanation of path-dependence and path-breaking specific to the PRC.[30]

Any illusions that the labels "China" and "Chinese" signify static, uniform entities will be dispelled by the narrative to follow, where unevenness, fragmentation, and diversities easily suppressed by generic terms will be in ample display. Although I do not intend for this book to add more "facts" to the immense amount of data already gathered over the years by dedicated scholars, I do draw extensively on empirical sources both old and new, while trying to limit the number of references from materials not available in English (which would be difficult for a nonspecialist to locate). Interested readers may find the notes helpful, for they contain information about evidence, statistics and references, and at times germane quotations as well.[31] But they may also be skipped as the text can be read as a reinterpretation of known events. I write for colleagues, students, and general readers, with hope and appreciation.

Chapter 1

China and Alternative Modernity

LOCATING CHINA, A COUNTRY OF "CONTINENTAL CHARACTER" (WEBER 1951, 100), in relation to the spatio-temporal notions of "modernity" and "modernization" is no easy task.[1] This is especially the case because the concept of "history" itself has come to be so contested. The construal of history is now more than ever loaded with epistemological, methodological, and ideological controversies (cf. Dirlik 2000). Writers who mount a contemporary defense of attainable objectivity and "truth telling" gesture toward three main schools of twentieth-century historical interpretation—Marxism, the French *Annales,* and U.S. modernization theory—which share a conviction of the scientific nature and universal applicability of their respective theories. This shared conviction "helped foster a Western history that aimed to homogenize the study of all other places and times into general Western models of historical development" (Appleby, Hunt, and Jacob 1994, 78–79). Without engaging the relevant debates, here I will posit the minimal intellectual need to sustain a "grand narrative" constituting elements of each of these schools while bearing in mind their constant internal tensions. Such a narrative is indispensable, for within the limit of conceptual tools presently at our disposal, no specific trajectory could otherwise be intelligibly counted. The notion of modernity is itself a profoundly universal generalization premised on a broad understanding of historical movements. But the price of accepting (as critically as we may try to do) a "master scale" of European origin that has dominated thinking and communicating elsewhere (and everywhere) is, of course, that non-European histories are made compliant with the teleology of modernization.

This metahistorical paradigm has been a problem, politically and psychologically, for modern thinkers in the Global South since long before postcolonial theory or multiculturalism became fashionable. Many of those involved in national liberation lived with the paradox of being at once revolutionary nationalists and devoted learners of Western modernity.[2] Chinese development is not free of the modern teleology, yet what distinguishes it from its counterparts in most third world societies is the way in which it presents an alternative to capitalist development on the one hand, and to capitalist or noncapitalist underdevelopment on the other. This alternative, in the mold of the Bolshevik revolution but also a deviation from Stalinist statism, breaks down the received equation between third world modernization and capitalism, thereby liberating the meaning of modernity in the peripheries from the interpretive confines of a false Eurocentric universality. The use of such common terms as "developed" and "underdeveloped" (and "first" and "third"; "advanced" and "backward") requires an awareness of their ideologically charged implications. Dependency theorists, for example, insist on a causality between the developed core of the world system and "the development of underdevelopment" in the subordinate zones, pinning down global exploitation through unequal accumulation and exchange.[3] But if a time-bound developmental perspective projected spatially is nothing but a "colonial representation,"[4] to discard it would first entail normative socioeconomic and political-institutional measurements established in the capitalist West being redefined and reclaimed—if not altogether replaced.

I begin my argument by situating China's modern path in the epochal conditions created by international capitalism. In so doing I critique the notion of singular modernity, and I clarify Eurocentrism in an open perspective of history. In stressing that the globally transformative power of capital cannot be limitless, I next trace China's twentieth-century revolutions in their nationalist resistance to imperialist impingement as a manifestation of the fragmentation of the "totality" of capitalism. It is, however, the political and social dimensions of the communist revolution that set China apart from its neighbors undergoing capitalist colonial or conservative modernization. In the final pages of this chapter I briefly discuss the problematic discourse of "Asia," which ignores these differences.

Globalization and Noncapitalist Development

Capitalism, emanating from Europe, is intrinsically globalist in its drive to conquer new markets. In its earlier stages this conquest took the form of direct colonization; later, other forms of globalization came into play. The world's present political, economic, and financial order (as well as a great deal of cultural production) has been largely shaped by global capitalism and various responses to its expansion. Indeed, as noted by Marx, "world history" began with the epoch of capitalism. This "epoch" has been characterized by an unprecedented amount of communication and interaction, dictated by market forces and their ideology of free trade, which no longer preserves any "Chinese walls" or permits effective "delinking" by regions from the globe. The continuities between domestic affairs, on the one hand, and external, "epochally specific transnational parameters" on the other increasingly outweigh traditionally sustained discontinuities.[5] The impact of world capitalism on any sizable human societies as both political-economic units and sites of cognitive-cultural trends is inescapable to the degree that long-term isolated development becomes impossible. Consequently, in the "age of capital," postindustrial problems intertwine with problems of industrialization while at the same time there is a lessening of the many previously rigid demarcations that had been understood to mark different developmental stages in culture, imagination, and identity.

That said, capitalism is not stable and cannot homogenize the globe despite its ability to convert, absorb, or eliminate dissent. It has, rather, evolved and reformed through triumphs and crises, and has itself been in flux or hybridism at its expanding frontiers. Globalization, if taken as the incorporation of the global market into national and regional communities (not a new phenomenon), is a two-way movement. Local-global interactions have been instruments of change for both parties. Individual states and societies as willing or reluctant participants, if led by a legitimate regime with determination and public support, may retain their specific goals and identities. In such cases, the agenda and consequences of globalization are modified by local conditions. World history, locally based and accommodating, encompasses "localized spaces, globalized places" (Luke 1997), and is at most a "paradoxical unity, a unity of disunity" (Berman 1983, 15). Capitalism with inherent contradictions never was, and still cannot be, a monolith. It splits not least between a welfare democracy gradually nurturing a "social model" (as germinated in the European Union) and a structural North-South divide, a divide that is often also internal to rich and poor nations alike. The newly industrialized countries (NICs) scattered here and there are strictly comparable to neither form. Meanwhile, commercial standardization and the universalization of the distribution of knowledge in the media or social sciences also breed opposition. The Forum on the Global South, the Forum World for Alternatives, and the World Social Forum are examples of mobilization from below against the neoliberal push for globalization.[6]

Capitalism, Eurocentrism, and Open History

The local maneuverability of globalized norms is even more likely in vast and unevenly developed countries. As the Chinese saying goes (as quoted by Mao Zedong to explain the elastic space for guerrilla movement), "If there isn't light in the east, the west must be bright; if darkness shrouds the south, let's go to the north."[7] In defiance of any defeatism in the face of powerful enemies, the sense here of subjective capacity and contingency in a flexible reaction to shifting balances of power is beyond military strategy. China (and, for that matter, many other large countries) is one country but many worlds. Its increasingly fluid outer borders and formidable internal boundaries have encouraged a deconstructivist treatment of "China" as a "false unity" of analysis. This critical tendency features a "bifurcation of linear [national] histories" through provincial narratives (Duara 1995, 51), the reconceptualization of local-central-global relations (e.g., Goodman and Segal 1994), and the dubious discourses of cross-border "Chinese networks" and "greater China" (Hamilton 1999; Harding 1993). But this treatment is at most about plural or multiple capitalisms, leaving possible alternatives to capitalism uncounted. Yet history does not end—rather there exist historical limits to capitalism as a particular mode of material and spiritual production as much as a global epoch, hence its rise and fall.

Debates over Eurocentrism, apart from an obviously valid assessment of its "original sin" of despising non-European "peoples without history," and its failure to appreciate the initial contributions by other cultures to European achievements, are relevant to my argument only insofar as the Eurocentric outlook permits a conflation between modernity and capitalism. This conflation, however, is feeble, even though industrialism's (and lately a knowledge economy) and liberalism's fin de siècle paradigm of formal liberal democracy, the hallmarks of modernity, were indeed first successfully advanced in the capitalist market. These benchmarks of economic modernization and political democratization have been insisted on (and with condescension) in non-Western societies, and this repetition has been with extraordinary confidence seen to reaffirm the fabricated universality of European precedence. Indeed, the "West is now everywhere, within the West and outside: in structures and minds" (Nandy 1983, xii). So long as developments are measured and compared on the scale of modernity, anti-Eurocentrism—as antimodern, not anticapitalist—is ultimately a losing battle.

If Eurocentrism has been under fire from critics in both conservative political science and radical social theory and cultural studies, these critics have thus far failed to come up with any systematic alternatives to Euro-genetic "universal goods."[8] To be sure, the commitments to humane compassion, impartial fairness, personal dignity, and moral authority are by no means specifically European and are evident in Islam, Buddhism, Confucianism, and other non-European traditions. But certain other values do have their roots in the epoch-making events following the European scientific revolution—the Renaissance, the Reformation, and the Enlightenment; the Dutch and English industrial transformation; and the French and American revolutions.[9] At the forefront of such values are those of economic and technological advancement for the well-being of humans, scientific rationality, constitutionalism and representative democracy, and individually based human rights. Each value may indeed be subject to moral and intellectual challenges or institutional modification from a variety of viewpoints; but none, so far, have been solidly overturned and still do not seem to be replaceable. Even the powerful ecological rejection of the concept of "conquering nature" will not succeed until and unless development per se can be forsaken without impeding new modes of production and consumption that can satisfactorily support a growing global population.[10] This may explain why, despite extensive emotion and energy, critiques of Eurocentrism have achieved little beyond the recognition of major influences from outside geographical Europe on the construction of modern values.[11] Such values have spread and been reinterpreted in and by their new settings, mostly and ironically through decolonization, reforms, and revolutions. But they are nonetheless shared legacies of a human civilization. In referring to universal rights and speaking to cultural relativists, David Harvey argues that "to turn our backs on such universals at this stage in our history, however fraught or even tainted, is to turn our backs on all manner of prospects for progressive political action" (2000, 94). After all, "historical capitalism" is not the only thing of European nature, nor is it merely toxic.[12] If the Enlightenment "is the line both of destruction and of civilization" (Horkheimer and Adorno 1972, 92), "Europe" also represents struggles for freedom, equality, and fraternity as much as it does imperialism, colonialism, and capitalism.

"Eurocentrism" is thus a confusing label when applied in the absence of a distinction between "modern" and "capitalist" development outside the terrain of Europe (e.g., Negri and Hardt 2000, 81–82). Lost in the confusion is not only the reality that capitalism is not required for a society to be or become modern (that is, as it implies industrialism, nationalism, secularism in the public sphere, education and literacy, stratification and specialization, and so on); also lost is the space for alternative structures. Yet "capitalism" cannot be held responsible for everything modern, neither for the undeniable social achievements of anticapitalist regimes nor for the equally visible noncapitalist forms of exploitation, repression, and destruction. As such, it is modernization within the parameters of global capitalism, not the capitalist method of modernization, that is inescapable if we agree that the invention of modernity and globality has virtually eliminated their outsiders. Still, this invention does not put a hold on time but "opens itself up to the novelty of the future" (Habermas 2000, 5). Indeed, the pressure of time only intensifies internal tensions and contradictions in the realm of the modern, making it transitory while making the present historical. By marking time globally and transculturally, and thereby universalizing temporal identities across spatial entities, modernity has otherwise come to be a neutral signifier in the Weberian horizon.

Encountering a radical Eurocentrist is a rare experience these days.[13] But Eurocentric errors and bias have endured far more effectively in those critics who argue for the discovery of culturally defined "multiple modernities" (Eisenstadt 2000) that allow no distinction between development and capitalism, or between modernization and capitalist transformation. No doubt, capitalist development itself varies in types and shapes. Timing, circumstances, elite choices, and collective action may all function to yield "one system, many models" (cf. Coates 2000; Hall and Soskice 2000). But a real turnaround in the debate would only come when steps were taken to separate modernity and capitalism, even taking into account the end of historical communism, whatever judgment might be passed on its many versions and dimensions. That there is a seemingly superior model that is of Western origin and at once capitalist, developed, modern, and dominant, cannot obliterate other modern projects, certainly not that of socialist development as consciously modern and deliberately anticapitalist. Whether that project remains a viable alternative within the epochal conditions of global capitalism (where it has been from the outset), and whether it can transcend those conditions, is another issue. Dipesh Chakrabarty calls the Eurocentric discourse "history 1" (European modernity), which suppresses the experiences of "history 2s" or colonial modernity, as vividly narrated in his Indian and Bengali cases (2000). But there must also, then, be "history 3s" in the same terms of capital or culture: those revolutionary and socialist modernities that intend to break free of the teleological genealogy of Europe and its colonial extensions. In so doing, these new "histories" will also transform the existing paradigm of modernity itself.

However, neither multiple modernities nor multiple histories are capable of generating an alternative theory of world development in its logical and conceptual totality, a world which culminated in global capitalism. The political and intellectual price paid for refusing to distinguish between modernity and capitalism, or reducing capitalism to a matter of cultural Eurocentrism, has been high. The Eurocentric positions, now refined and adjusted to more pluralist and multicultural perspectives, are stronger than ever before. Ethnocentric and cultural relativist demands gain ground only in forms of "inverted Eurocentrism" (Amin 1989, 136, 147). What is bypassed in the entire discourse is a sustained critique of capitalism that is intrinsic to typical Euro-American prejudice. Also missing are genuine alternatives, past, present, and future, to capitalist development, and therefore an alternative political sociology of global evolution to account for the historicity and transformation of capitalism. These are issues of irony and hypocrisy most strikingly manifested in the gulf between capital accumulation and concentration in the northern zones of the globe and the typical Eurocentric demand of impoverished nations to "catch up" with those ahead in the game. Capitalism, in reality, continues to destroy the myth of Eurocentrism, and it does so by depriving non-Western societies of the means to modernize in the approved combination of free market and democratic institutions. Pockets of "late development" do not alter the picture. What alone speaks volumes about the self-contradiction of prevalent ideologies is the fact that the core countries, through international financial and lending institutions, collect from their former colonies billions of dollars annually in debt repayment.

Modern European socialist thought is echoed in many non-European political cultures. Marxism in particular took root in foreign soil, including China. Socialism opposes capitalist exploitation and alienation, but it has no quarrel, neither morally nor epistemologically, with the modern norms of freedom and equality, democracy and development. Rather, it stands for these principles, and it is believed among groups and communities of people to be the only rational system true to, and capable of, their full realization. Likewise, socialist development, however costly, was conceived in communist Russia and China as not only the fastest but also the only way to achieve national sovereignty and to transform backward and unjust social relations. Where capitalism is resisted in other efforts at modernization, it is not because capitalism is able to develop an economy with due social benefits but rather precisely because of its failure to do so.

"Modernization" is thus also destined for postcolonial and socialist programs, and certain "Eurocentric" assumptions are indispensable for a continued critical understanding of world history. The gaps as mirrored in the European models may be amenable by unconventional agents and methods, depending on political will and innovation. I will return to this point in the concluding chapter when I use it as an additional argument for an open historical conception in which both traditional and modern bondages are to be transcended.

The Dialectic of Backwardness

The dilemma of "socialism and backwardness" to be overcome marked the Leninist predicament first encountered by the Russian revolutionaries who broke the weak link of capitalism in the eastern periphery of Europe. Before Lenin, the anti-tsarist Narodniks had a more optimistic intuition about being backward as a paradoxical advantage for national revitalization; as noted in their 1861 populist manifesto: "We are a belated nation and precisely in this consists our salvation."[14] The populists inspired Marx to wonder about the viability of preserving the collectivist village *mir* and whether it could be equipped by industrial technologies so as to make a leap from precapitalism to communism in the event that a Russian-triggered European revolution would take place.[15] The "privilege of backwardness" was taken up by self-conscious history makers (in the double sense of actors in history and historians) from Leon Trotsky to the Chinese Marxists (cf. Dirlik 1978, 1994, 20–36). Trotsky conceived of a developmental pattern in which "the privilege of historic backwardness . . . permits, or rather compels, the adoption of whatever is ready in advance of any specified date, skipping a whole series of intermediate stages" (1959, 3, and ch. 1; cf. Rosenberg 1996). Without even paying attention to the controversial "stage theory" in Marxist historiography, Mao famously declared that the more backward the economy, the easier the transition to socialism.

The practical implication of this thesis for contemporary socialists lies in the possibility of bypassing capitalism for an alternative future and not in reviving any romanticized national pasts. The rationale here is straightforward: beside and despite the accomplishments of welfare democracy, capitalist modernity has a record of sweatshops and crushed unions, violence and injustice, and imperialist wars. Instead, industrialization and democratization should and can be achieved via a path that avoids the familiar methods of development that abuse workers, polarize society, damage the environment, and push colonial extraction. The idea, thus, is that less-developed societies tend to enjoy more flexibility and adaptability, which allows them to absorb scientific and material accomplishments from the heartland of capitalism. Backwardness could then be removed, provided that revolutionary changes in international relations and trade structures convert developmental weaknesses into opportunity and strength. As a conception of history more than a strategy for growth, the lost language of the "privilege of backwardness" has little to do with the Ricardian doctrine of "comparative advantage" in development economics.

There is nothing obscure in this proposition, which has found ample support in historical evidence about uneven development and compressed "leaps" (e.g., the move of China's Buyi or Hezhe ethnic groups from a "primitive" to "socialist" society). Latecomers and global or regional peripheries have repeatedly surpassed their more advanced counterparts: consider Bismarck's Germany and Meiji Japan in the nineteenth century, the emergence of an "American century" since Roosevelt's New Deal, and so on.[16] The swift and impressive post–World War II reconstruction in Germany and Japan was due not only to heavy U.S. aid and engineering, but also to these countries' own creative and effective absorption of advanced organizational tools and technologies, and the sheer necessity that comes from starting from scratch. This is indeed the gist of Mao's saying (1958) about the "blank sheet" on which "the newest and most beautiful symbols and pictures can be drawn" (though he was apparently putting aside the issue of China's rich cultural inheritance). Further (and even grandiose) in history, the "rise of Europe"—or, from a different perspective, the "decline of Asia"—around 1800 is another case in point with contemporary echoes. The success of the NICs in turning themselves into manufacturing and technological vanguards confirms, once again, the possibility of rapid "industrialization through learning" (Amsden 1989). China's open policy is precisely premised on this latent potential, as a privilege of backwardness, which may be combined with its comparative advantages in market competition.

As persuasive as this line of argument is in many respects, it is easy to overlook the necessary conditions for such privilege and advantages to be materialized, and the possible expenses or unintended consequences involved. There are also important internal and external constraints. Progress is always accompanied by destruction. Even where upward appropriation and assimilation do happen, there are no certain benefits, let alone the guarantee that such benefits will be spread fairly among the population. Standing in the way might be harsh conditionality attached to loans, the transfer of outdated or polluting technologies, or poor allocation or mismanagement of borrowed resources. In particular, countries often make structural adaptations defensively, and a given regime may not accept its social responsibilities while seeking growth. Indeed, the human social as well as eco-environmental costs could also be tremendous and irreversible. Mao's self-reliance was a heroic response to the isolation imposed by the cold war. Deng's desire to "make use of foreign capital, technology and managerial skills" had to be jealously guarded against the counter forces of subordinating China to international capitalism. The privilege of backwardness is only relative and conditional, and absolute inferiority may persist. The dependency theorists are at least partially correct when they insist that unequal exchange, low wages or cheap labor, and the deprived ability of surplus retention are what keep poor people poor. Moreover, capitalist powers use their financial, military, and other weapons to coerce a global order in their own favor. With a profound sense of the tragedy of under-development, Harold Isaacs sees China's tormented modern experience since the opium wars as rooted in the country's desperate struggle to compress developmental tasks (1951, chapter 1).

It is worth noting that there existed a "socialist market" before the collapse of the Soviet bloc and its Council for Mutual Economic Assistance. Further, albeit to a lesser extent, China also took part in ambitious aid and trading programs for target countries in Asia, Africa, and Latin America. That market cracked as the two communist giants split partly over the issue of whether the trade engaged was sufficiently socialist and internationalist to live up to its claims. The existence of an international market indepen-dent of the capitalist global network nevertheless did fragment the capitalist system. Arguably, the defeat of the anticipated chain of revolutionary changes leading to the globalization of socialism (a hypothesis of commu-nist thinkers since Marx) and, in particular, the disappearance of an alter-native market, have banished the prospect for late development to be ac-tively assisted by the developed world. The way forward seems cleared, rather, for the latest push of globalization which endures polarization and injustice on a global scale.

Three general assumptions thus follow: First, a cooperative and aid-gratuitous relationship between rich and poor countries is generally un-likely. Instead of a "privilege," the latter are vulnerable to dependency, debt crises, and civil strife (among other dangers). Yet, second, global interde-pendence would eventually give rise to a shared impulse on a rational basis to minimize inequalities between and among regions and peoples on dif-ferent developmental levels and pathways. Third, there is a salient but somehow unspoken conjecture that any privilege of backwardness actually requires a revolutionary rupture, in one form or another, to effectuate. All considered, economically backward societies may develop, against the odds, with leadership skills and institutional incentives falling into place. The case of difficulties in national development should not be exaggerated as only an "illusion" because of international competition being more than ever a zero-sum game. More convincing is the strategic proposal to overturn this game by "overloading" the system both locally and globally—and thereby dismantling capitalism itself, bit by bit—through political mobilization and economic redistribution wherever it is possible (Wallerstein 1991b, 123–24, 168).[17] Bubbles, downturns, and—uncertainty notwithstanding—synchronic developments have proven neither rare nor accidental, as demonstrated by both centrally planned and market economies. Hasty state-led modernization is a hallmark of historical communism. Giovanni Arrighi is certainly correct in his belief that peripheral development is often arduous and costly, especially in regard to the toleration of foreign exploitation. But his assertion that "developmentalism" has failed, and that this failure also explains the downfall of communism, seems overstated (2001, 22–55). Maurice Meisner more eloquently remarks that the greatest failure of state socialism (in China) was not economic but political (1999, 246), thereby separating the two aspects rhetorically.

History is full of twists and breaks. Turning backwardness into a developmental privilege is a marvelous collective feat that disregards and compresses conventionally designated "stages." Consequently, even the perception of "skipping over" (capitalism) is mistaken insofar that it presupposes a normal, linear course of evolutionary progress. Appeal is frequently made to such a course by the revisionist theorization of "socialism and backwardness" in reformist China in an effort to revive the myth about the inevitability of a capitalist stage of societal evolution and to justify a retreat from socialism. By contrast, the thesis of the "privilege of backwardness" speaks for concrete and deliberate trajectories within the epochal totality of capitalism but without a predetermined phase, or destination (in dominant social theory today), of capitalism for poor nations. If "weak links" of the world system can still be broken, there are opportunities for ready-made models unfit for local wants and needs to be transcended. In the end, earlier developments may not be repeatable, nor may they be appropriate to serve others as an image of their own future.[18]

Transcending Singular Modernity

To seek the place from which a society has evolved, as well as its potential direction, is to engage in a conversation between many facets of its past, present, and future. The language of that conversation has to be at once modern (hence universal) and particular (be it traditional or otherwise). The past is not passed, in part, because of a modern awareness of the past's anachronistic residuals in the present, but also because there is a persistent authority of certain traditions as legitimate sources of invention for the future. "Historical treasures" continue to be considered relevant in enduring civilizations. Although the idea of modernity is itself premised on the transformation of whatever is deemed premodern, the thresholds on that rocky continuum are necessarily mobile, relative, and "reflexive."[19] Indeed, the coexistence of conditions traditional and modern—or, in most non-Western societies, indigenous and Westernized—is part of modern life. The customary dichotomies oversimplify these interplays to the extent of missing out on the tensions and contradictions within modernity. To historicize the boundaries between developmental stages is thus to dispute the current ideology of the modern that endorses spatial displacement of the temporal at least in the division between the (post)modern Euro-American core and the premodern or less-modern non-Western peripheries.[20] "Modernity," as a social construct involving specific power relations, whose paradoxes are embedded in the predominance of "modernization" and "globalization" premised on capitalism, calls for critical responses to its supposed legitimacy. This critical stance should apply to modernity both as an idea and a project, as a set of values and socioeconomic-legal institutions.

In comparing state-making in Europe and China, Bin Wong observes that certain "modern" ideas and institutions in the West are simply not "modern" in China once it is made clear "how recently some of the traits we label generally 'modern' " appeared in Europe only long after their Chinese possession (1997, 101, 194–97). As is well known, China's highly sophisticated bureaucracy was already "extraordinary in its scope, capabilities, and 'modernity' " before modern times; and it has survived since 1949, through imperial, Soviet, and Western influences (Lieberthal 1995, xvi, 12). It has also adapted a notable degree of the communist war-time military style of command and the technocratic leverage of the East Asian developmental state. By compressing traditional and modern developments in its body politic, the PRC government may look simultaneously moralistic (in the Confucian sense of "rule by virtue") and pragmatic, patrimonial and professional, and patriarchal and socialist.[21]

There are many examples of the ways in which China's traditional social organization continues to be not only politically and economically efficacious but also significantly engaged in issues of development. To take one such example: The ancient competition between producers and tax collectors (and often between local and central authorities) over who controls an agricultural surplus remains a contemporary struggle, and one that has long been mediated by low-level officials. When such officials are deemed to be out of control, the state seeks rectification by allying itself with the peasants. Beijing's campaign, begun in the late 1990s, to "reduce farmers' burdens," specifically targeted arbitrary local extraction. It was thus, in this respect, a replay of the age-old, three-layered dynamic set against the background of cycles of rural rebellion that frequently forced policy, and indeed dynastic, changes.[22] The Chinese communists carried out a land revolution; they accommodated themselves to many precommunist mechanisms of local governance so as to secure a relatively adequate level of taxation and welfare. During the war years, the success of sustaining supplies was "attributable in large measure to the communists' skill in building upon traditional cooperative practices within the familiar village context" (Selden 1971, 266). The party also made sensible concessions to peasant ways of living and coordinating, thereby winning rural support for collectivization in the 1950s (Shue 1980). The "traditional world" of rural society was shown to be especially resourceful for community revitalization in the reform era, from voluntary service to mutual help (cf. cases in Hunan, Zhang 2003). The experiences of self-management and collective action of the Chinese peasantry are yet to be incorporated within theoretical reflections in the acclaimed moral economy literature.[23] In fact, the modern concept of market socialism—which goes beyond the growth-centered official version (and which I will discuss later)—would rely on a creative recapturing of certain traditions. Together they could achieve a radical reorganization of economy and society toward needs-oriented and nature-friendly production, consumption, and nurture.

Nevertheless, any inquiry into the historical location of "China" must also compare it with other countries and other trajectories among multiple paths of modernization. This multiplicity can be expansive to the extent of allowing epochal parameters to be reshaped, destabilizing the modern scale of measurement itself. Weighty players with alternative proposals, such as the Chinese attempt at a "socialist market," may, over time, have a decisive input in the rules and laws of the international order. Transition in China, in the long run, could well bypass bizarre mixtures of Samuel Huntington's depiction of "political disorder" and Jürgen Habermas's "social patholo-gies" caused by the sudden uprooting, disparity, and disintegration charac-teristic of rapid modernization. A hybrid process does not have to be paren-thetical or pathological if it opens an unprecedented terrain of possible new social formations. What at the moment seems transient or deviant viewed in light of familiar models may eventually acquire novel substance and stable qualities through trial and error. The outcome, then, will call for conceptual articulations in our intellectual lexicon to revise or redefine established norms and expectations. The overused and misused notion of "hybridity" should not overshadow the insight of a "third space" that "dis-places the histories that constitute it, and sets up new structures of author-ity, new political initiatives, which are inadequately understood through received wisdom" (Bhabha 1990, 211).

The ownership of township and village enterprises, for instance, is equivocal in that owners are not clearly identifiable. Responsibilities, bene-fits, and risks were shared among managers, local governments, surround-ing communities and workers in shareholding cooperatives. Even privately run enterprises tended to bend to the communal pressures for social obliga-tions, such as fair distribution of employment and regular donation to local public service facilities. Such practice by "stake-holders" left the textbook requirement for a "mature" structure of property rights without any appar-ent urgency or justification (Nee 1992; Weitzman and Xu 1994). Yet TVES underwent a sweeping transition from a collective "Sunan model" to a privatized "Wenzhou model" in the late 1990s, which seemingly proved the transitory nature of intermediate "local state corporatism" (Oi 1995, 1999; Walder 1994; Oi and Walder 1999). Without evaluating China's controver-sial rural industrialization, suffice it to note here that the change was guided less by any intrinsic need of privatization than it was forced by artifi-cial engineering under a mounting market ideology.[24] Consequently, this aborted experiment with collective-corporate managerial and productive relations should neither falsify its useful lessons nor verify the requirement for "complete clarification of property rights." After all, what had funda-mentally enabled the entire episode of TVES was the institutional fact that land in China was publicly owned, or socialized, with use rights granted by the state to rural households, and thus it could be socially used to reward the population involved without the obstacle of private ownership (Pei

2002). In a similar vein, the unusual makeup of China's inexperienced stockmarket prioritized state shares and public property through limited internal trading of listed state-owned enterprises and nonstate legal persons. The distinction between "A" shares that are confined to Chinese citizens in Chinese currency and the foreign "B" shares was designed to protect the local capital market. The central supervisory body, a target of frequent public criticism for policy mistakes and lack of professionalism, was nevertheless open to innovative structures and technicalities, and acted as if to preserve the possibility of generating funds for strategic national industries, and to curb the potential disturbance of speculative private tycoons (cf. Green 2003).

But the largely closed knowledge systems of political sociology and social science lingua franca are incapable of accounting for such unconventional formations. The preoccupation with "a single history and a singular modernity," as Michael Walzer, among the earliest critics of modernization theory, puts it, is still held by "the characteristic naiveté of writers who make the contemporary and familiar into something superhistorical."[25] The end of the cold war, won by American capitalism (rather than European social democracy), has only fortified the conception of privileged Western trajectories. But to insist on such a conception is to misread history, misjudge modern processes elsewhere, and miss modernity's other expressions. Ideological opponents, like historical materialism and conservative modernization theory, do not part over a "necessary" forward march of capitalism, leaving noncapitalist yet modern (i.e., not precapitalist) developments uncounted.[26] Barrington Moore's classical yet now-deserted typology of diverse routes to the modern world is exceptional—bourgeois revolutions leading to the Western forms of democracy, "iron and rye" revolutions from above leading to fascism, and peasant revolutions leading to communism; also exceptional is his keen awareness that the "methods of modernization chosen in one country change the dimension of the problem for the next countries who take the step" with the "advantages of backwardness" (1966, 414). In other words, independent of any moral choice, earlier methods may simply not be repeatable in changed circumstances. And Moore's willingness is, logically, restricted to accommodate alternative modernities rather than alternatives to modernity.

A qualification must be made to the notion of "alternative modernities" so as to exclude religious or other regressive "alternatives to modernity" insofar as the "normative" and "modern" are effectively synonymous. Rationalist and humanist arguments, for example, are often put forward to counter antiegalitarian, antidemocratic, and quasi-racist representations of a supposed cultural incommensurability of either "Western" or "Eastern" supremacy. Seeing modernity as relative to local, specific epistemological and material contexts is one thing; treating different polities as culturally incompatible is another. That certain modern values may find echoes in a particular tradition grants additional legitimacy to a modern-minded, purposeful cultural conservatism against national nihilism in a given society. But this is quite different from playing conservative culturalism in the vested interest of power (as demonstrated by the debate over "Asian values" when twisted by both dismissive liberals and opportunistic authoritarian rulers). The multicultural celebration of "multiple modernities" cannot be sustained if the very notion of "modern" is not defended against the essentialist claim that modernity acquires meaning only in locally particularistic terms. Any "national modernity" or national road to modernization, then, should be justified not by ethnocentric appeals to culture, but rather by that culture's positive association with modern values. Indeed socialist modernization deserves attention not because it is something superiorly "Eastern," or "Chinese," but because it strives to surmount capitalism.

There is no doubt, however, that the feelings of cultural pride and confidence, or else fear and anxiety, are always crucial in understanding politics. Even matters deemed universal must require reworking for local applicability. The "sinification of Marxism" is an outstanding example of how something initially foreign can be successfully transplanted through an injection of native intellectual and institutional sources. For a Chinese socialism that is faithful to its modern roots and ambitions, there is nothing glorious in its country's past repressions. The rejection of repression was thus deliberately done by a proud people rising to the modern challenge over a century ago, and it found expression in the May 4th (1919) movement's slogan of "science and democracy." Striking a balance as the party campaigned in Yan'an, led by "Marxists from the mountain valley" against Moscow-trained "dogmatists," modernizing China was taken as a twofold revolutionary task. It aimed to defeat imperialism while selectively appropriating capitalist accomplishments, and also remove domestic "feudal"[27] obstacles without discarding the treasured heritage of national culture.[28] This story disproves any belief in a Chinese immunity to foreign values or to comparative external scrutiny. If it is an exaggeration to speak of the Chinese revolution as a movement "against the west to join the west" (Levenson 1970, 8), the phrase nevertheless captures the momentum of making China an equal with other modern nations.[29] If it is an overstatement to say that China's revolutionary modernity represents not the destruction of an old civilization but rather its reformation, the statement still sheds light on the persistence of "Chinese" identities as plural in many possible ways. However inward-looking China might have been, it was never culturally closed to outside influences: Buddhism is one example of this and Marxism is another. The ability to make the alien indigenous is what has rendered "China" and the "Chinese" inherently multicultural in the first place.[30]

With an external border of tens of thousands of kilometers in length; with equally far-reaching, and sometimes tension-laden, interior frontiers; and with the advance and popularization of information technologies, Chinese society has become ever more open, both extensively and intensively, to foreign cultural and material imports as well as to internal diversities. As such, culturalist expectations cannot be fulfilled because they rely on a concept of "China" as a uniform, singular entity that does not really exist. The internalization, here and there, of the exogenous is all the more destabilizing because it blurs demarcations between outside and inside. Only the event of the interaction and interpenetration between the general and specific, or the universal and particular, is where China can best be situated as the global in the local as much as the local in the global, and where a search can be made for its explanations. The Chinese case illustrates the extent to which plural modernities can take place within a nation-state, especially when enabled by uneven development. The mutual embeddedness of global and national, central and provincial relations, parallels the direct interaction between transnational firms/agencies and subnational locales, bypassing the central government. Hence, the slogans "one country, two (or more) systems," "one system, many cultures," and "one China, multiple paths" may seem to fit the playful postmodern imaginary of modern fragments floating free. This is beside the point, however; at issue here are local capacity and initiatives. To speculate on socialism in one country, or in one county for that matter, is no more utopian than sustaining capitalism in one region—especially in light of how European social democracy has pushed back free-market doctrines, leaving the American model on the defensive. In post-reform China, side by side with the special economic zones of "contained capitalism," cases of "socialism in one village" also developed.[31] Scattered communist and socialist local governments and communities have long been noted as auspicious within the world system. To explore, Charles Taylor contends, "the full gamut of alternative modernities," or for that matter alternative histories, is "the most important task of social sciences in our day" (1999, 165).

Oddly enough, there is little dispute about communism's function, through industrialization and progressive social policies, as a vehicle of modernization in Russia or China. Yet socialism, often straitjacketed into soviet statism, is also viewed as either pseudo modern or insufficiently modern relative to its capitalist counterparts. Postcommunist transition is thus single-mindedly expected to foster Western-style changes and thereby to complete modernization as global integration. If, however, indigenous communist revolutions only succeeded where capitalism failed to develop a society both economically and politically, then is not there a hidden causal linkage between capitalism and underdevelopment and, further, between capitalist failures and socialist alternatives? By the same token, has not the revolutionary causation between "socialism and development" permanently transformed, albeit in a limited fashion, the predicament of "socialism and backwardness"?

Revolutionary and Socialist Modernity

Modernization and nationalist projects have been integrated in China ever since the encounter with Western imperialism in the mid-nineteenth century, a time when the country, itself an empire, was suffering a recent internal decay. That is, modern Chinese nationalism could not be a matter of the cultural preservation of an old civilization but rather of the political renovation for nation building. An elite consensus here gained ground around the turn of the twentieth century, in preparation for the republican revolution, which was that for the multiethnic Chinese nation (*zhonghua minzu*) to repel foreign domination and survive—and prosper—in the modern world, much of imperial China's traditional encumbrances had to be cast off. This position was crucial not because the Han high culture was unsuccessful, nor because modernization in China would not find abundant native sources, but because the focus of the New Culture and May 4th movements of the first decades of the twentieth century was to change the cultural obstacles to modernity. Anything that stood for the *ancien regime* and repressive traditional society was to be removed (Schwarcz 1986).

Cultural China and Political Nationalism

While China was not fully colonized during the period known as "a hundred years of accumulated weaknesses" (*bainian jiruo*), it was utterly humiliated by the Western and Japanese colonial powers through political and military defeats, unequal treaties, and forced reparations and foreign concessions. It began with the first of the Opium Wars (1839–1842), and continued through the loss of the entire imperial navy to Japan in 1895 and the invasion of the Euro-American Eight Allied Forces of 1900. In the same period the Qing state managed to put down the Taiping peasant rebellion (1851–1864) and to crush the constitutional reform movement of 1898 that was closely followed by the doomed Boxer uprising. Long at the brink of collapse, the imperial court's ability to defend even its most immediate holdings went up in flames as the magnificent Royal Gardens in Beijing were destroyed in the course of weeks of burning and looting by the Anglo-French Allied Armies in 1860. The slow yet catastrophic disintegration was so profound that, for China's radical modernizers who were in contact with Western ideas such as social Darwinism, nothing less than a revolution could "rescue the Chinese race"; a total crisis required a totalistic response (Tang 1988, xxxv).

The race rhetoric invoked by China's first generation of modernizers is distinct from the language of the Han-Manchu conflict of the previous two hundred years. The earlier ethnocentric conception of the Han people battling against alien rulers (cf. Dikotter 1992) was replaced by the idea of a unified race, which marked an "awakening" of China and the emergence of a modern Chinese nationalism. Sun Zhongshan (Yat-Sen) adopted the term "Chinese race" to signify modern citizenship in a nation-state that embraces, or neglects, internal ethnic differences and frees traditional tribute payers along its external borders. This line of argument utilized the earlier imperial tactic of legitimation through universal inclusion, but without imperialism and thus incomparable to racial supremacy as it occurred in colonial conquest. Sun's ideology of nationalism, along with democracy and the livelihood of the people—known as "land to the tillers" and "keeping capital under control"—constituted the "three principles of the people," confirming universal human values to be fulfilled by a future cosmopolitanism (Fitzgerald 1996, 86, 121–22). But, more to the point, the formation of Chinese nationalism was intimately linked to the rising national consciousness of colonized and oppressed peoples. This linkage found an expression in Sun's "greater Asianism" (despite Japanese colonialism—Japan, after all, served as a most important base where Sun and his followers prepared for revolution in China) as a "shared world stage" on which "Chinese intellectuals aspired to launch China" (Karl 2002, 17, 198). Ernest Gellner's logic of nationalism, requiring cultural and political boundaries to be congruent, could replay only paradoxically in China, where a common national identity formed not through the breakup of an empire but through the republican integration of a cross-ethnic "Chinese people."[32] Such a unique route of transforming empire into a nation both in consciousness and in history rendered that identity simultaneously (and resolutely) nationalist and transnational with a civilization-wide sense of solidarity (cf. H. Wang 1999). As 1911 was a belated response to the mounting blows struck from the outside, the foreigners themselves spoke of their encounter with China in terms of race (Lin 1979, 62).

The humiliation of the Middle Kingdom by the "barbarians" was a shock, and it proved to be devastating for the ruling order. Revolutionary nationalism in China, on the other hand, had to fight concurrently the Western-Japanese "slicing of the Chinese melon" and the indigenous "old society" blocking of national renewal. This nationalism sought a developmental alternative to what was termed in the language of the Communist Party as "comprador-feudal and bureaucratic capitalism" peculiar to semicolonial conditions. As such, Chinese nationalism fundamentally differed from the nationalism that arose earlier in Europe, as it likewise did from the forms of European state-building extended in many colonies. Its unprecedented goal was to make China exemplary among the world's wealthy and weighty powers; its modern political theater had been preoccupied by ambitions of a "progressive and strong" nation. Both the republican and communist revolutions gathered momentum from the promise of national revival and greatness and it is this fact, more than any element of either an "oriental despotic" tradition or a communist totalitarian tendency, that explains the predominance of a specific variant of statism in contemporary Chinese polity. Not surprisingly, nationalism and modern statehood in the PRC were, from the outset, a matter of collectively redeeming humiliation and restoring honor, not infrequently with claims to status and territory reminiscent of the empire (Yahuda 2000).

The remarkable structural continuities between the imperial and the national state in China have permitted two rival narratives of Chinese identity since the republican revolution, one imperial-cultural and the other political-national. This ambiguity alone undermines any anachronistic "world history" that relies on a strict dichotomy between modernity and premodernity, as well as on other linear breaks between nation and civilization, progress and stagnation, democracy and autocracy, and Europe and Asia (Wang Hui 2004, "Introduction"). The perception of "cultural China" had often confused assessments of China's relation to modernity. As traceable to the Enlightenment imagining without credible or sufficient information of a far-away continent, that perception of "cultural China" (along with cultural India, and so on) persisted. It found echoes also in Max Weber's notion of Germany needing political maturity in terms of national identity, cohesion, and unity by his conceptual identification between modernization and national legitimacy. Sinological studies that distinguish Chinese from Western nationalism see the former as inadequate by the infusion of either centripetal or centrifugal identities not deemed properly "national." But the scrutiny of a sinocentric political culture, however useful, can be misguided when "culturalist" prejudices, themselves highly political, are led to the denial of the civic, as opposed to ethnic, nature of nationalism in China (and in most non-Western societies).[33] An exemplary verdict, as succinctly put by Lucien Pye, is that China remains "a civilization pretending to be a nation-state" (1992, 1162).[34] For Pye, if there were a premodern Chinese collective self of any sort encoded in Confucianism, or in the emperors' jurisdiction over all that is *tianxia* ("under heaven"), it has not been renovated by China's twentieth-century revolutions and post-1949 nation-building.[35] As Pye further notes: "Much of what is usually thought of as Chinese nationalism are really powerful sentiments of racial and cultural identity and not feelings about the nation as a state" (1968, 230). In contrasting China with Western norms, such an identity is more accurately to be associated with ethnic "Han chauvinism" or the "Middle Kingdom complex" than with modern political development. Cultural nationalism and modernization are thus "essentially antagonistic forces" (Pye 1996, 91).

The analysis takes an odd twist when semicoloniality (unfavorably compared with full colonization) and its revolutionary eradication are explicitly declared (though not verbally) as new China's birth defect. And thus is Pye's complaint, shared by others, that Chinese intellectuals were so vulnerable to the dictates of their country's leaders that a compelling "patriotic complex" "paralyze[d] their critical faculties." The lack of individuality, or the "logic of dependency," entails a patriotism without nationalism and is judged indicative of China's inability to modernize. The missing modern subjectivity, according to this social psychoanalysis, is rooted in the ancient giant's misfortune of not having had enough colonialism to achieve sufficient socialization as an infant in the modern world. The "identity crisis" that is indispensable for non-Western peoples to complete the transitional stage toward "world adulthood" was skipped over by China due to its incomplete colonial penetration (otherwise read as a successful revolution)—a penetration that could have equipped it with superior modern consciousness and institutions (1985, 193 and chapter 7; cf. Barlow 1997). Similarly, David Landes blames "a self-defeating escapism" of Chinese "xenophobia" against capitalist investment, ownership, and cultural influence for the setbacks of modernization during the Mao period (1998, 345).

Capitalist colonialism, or forced globalization, however, was invariably often a history of violence against native societies that had included deprivation and genocide. Ignoring that history, the not-enough-colonialism thesis is just another, cruder, confession of the West's civilizing mission. Free trade is one thing, but colonial exploitation and repression are quite another. Marx laid out this notion long ago in his controversial dual judgment on British rule in India: Colonial modernity, being instrumental for destroying the economic foundation of closed and vegetative social structures and therefore producing "the only *social* revolution ever heard of in Asia," was but a page written "in the annals of mankind in letters of blood and fire" (1969 [1853], 93).[36] But even Marx leaves no space to question whether colonies might have developed differently, and in better ways, without fatal interruptions by foreign intervention. Neither did he foresee the many long-term, disastrous social consequences of colonialism, as later witnessed in the Middle East and South Asia, and in the "African tragedy" (Leys 1994).[37] It is a lavish lie to "forget" imperialist crimes and the sufferings of the people involved, and thereby ignore the ultimate historical explanation and moral justification for national liberation movements in the third world. As Tani Barlow points out, "when you erase a mark what you have is an erasure" (1997, 373).

If we refuse the misrecognition of "cultural China," we can proceed to take a self-conscious national collectivity as a distinctly modern phenomenon that is powerfully demonstrated in China's post-imperial history with extraordinary clarity. Modern nationalism had motivated Chinese political actors, within or without national power, ever since the days of republican agitation that made the empire obsolete. The Chinese revolution, in both its republican and communist phases, was first national and then social, and could not be otherwise. The communists postponed their "maximum program" (unlike their internationalist counterparts in the Soviet Union, but like their nationalist compatriots), and they had a firm conviction that if social interest conflicted with national interest, the social must yield to the national. This was, as John Fitzgerald notes, "an axiom of the revolution" (1996, 176),[38] which recognized the Chinese nation's "class" position in an imperialist international system.[39] Being first and foremost liberators, defenders, and modernizers of the nation, they were thereby nationalist even "in an internationalist ideological sense" (Levenson 1967, 269). The revolutionaries worked on every front to cultivate a national consciousness in both urban elites and rural masses. Fundamental strategic shifts accommodated by the warring parties during the Japanese invasion, both the CCP's "united front" and the GMD's suspension of civil war, exemplified a common nationalist priority. The PRC state has no doubt frantically defended its constitutional sovereignty and self-determination in its foreign relations according to the modern norm. It is prejudicial to compare an overwhelmingly cultural China with the political definitions of modern nations, as though whatever is "Chinese" must be antithetical to "modern" in its incompatible ethos.

This is why the modern character of the communist system in China has to be insisted on, an insistence that neither overlooks historical continuities nor denies inevitable ambiguities. More conceptual precision would allow an appreciation of modern alternatives to capitalist modernity. A barrier here is the failure to see through the assumptions of current social sciences, which define nationalism and capitalism as the parallel pillars of the modern world. These "two forces grew up side by side, spread around the globe, and penetrated every aspect of contemporary life" (Smith 1998, 47), fundamentally delimiting both the context and content of "modern development."[40] However, the fact that the organizational complexes of nation-state and systematic capitalist production first emerged in the West, and that they are the "two great transformative agencies" of modernity (Giddens 1990, 174), cannot form the ahistorical premise that has long been revised by the Western powers themselves. National liberation movements in largely agrarian colonies, for one thing, have pushed the paradigm of nationalist-capitalist unity into the background.

The point is not whether there could already be forms of proto-collective self-awareness of national belonging before nationalist agitation in these societies, nor is it about the collaboration between the metropolitan and local elites required for stable colonial domination. Regardless, it is still the case that "nationalism comes before nations" (Hobsbawm 1990, 10) and that, as an essential fact downplayed in the core literature on nationalism, imperialist expansion catalyzed nationalist resistance against capitalism itself. Intellectual honesty, with obvious political implications, obliges us to acknowledge not only the artificiality of postcolonial borders but also all forms of modern nationalism and state and nation building even where they are noncapitalist or anticapitalist. Surely, China attained its modern national identity and pursued modernization not through a typically capitalist economy—an option closed by the imperialist international order at least until after the cold war—but through its revolutionary and socialist attempts to break free from that order. Cases of fully fledged new nations born of national liberation struggles without significant capitalist development simply bear too much weight to be neglected by any sound theorization of modern nationalism.

The Chinese Revolution

The Communist Party and its followers sought to unite and modernize China on a nationalist platform as well as a social (not yet socialist) platform. This unorthodox blending of communism and nationalism was an outcome of semicolonial conditions in which the ruling class either associated itself with imperialist interests or was too weak to lead a resistance to them. After the 1911 revolution, which capped ten years of intellectual and political campaigning (Meisner 1967; Dirlik 1989), local Marxist groups formed the Communist Party in 1921—with help from representatives of the Comintern who were preoccupied with the "Eastern question" (Van de Ven 1991). The party went on to organize workers and peasants and, after the GMD broke the alliance with the communists in 1927, established an armed force in the countryside (Schwartz 1958; Eastman 1974; Hartford and Goldstein 1989). In the aftermath of the republican revolution, and in the absence of a developed, mature national bourgeoisie, a "new democratic revolution" was supposed to require a communist leadership. Conditioned on such a leadership, in the "new democracy" scheme, a "certain development of national capitalism should replace the repression of foreign imperialism and domestic feudalism."[41] Thus the Chinese revolution was distinguished from that of the Bolsheviks in that it included, rather than targeted, the bourgeois class which, in the economically deprived (semi-)colonies, was known as a "national bourgeoisie." Furthermore, a communist revolution in an agrarian society could not truly be proletarian in nature, even if its vanguards did adopt a Marxist formulation and drew cadres, and loyalty, from industrial workers. Instead, the party forged a broad coalition of social forces based on the lower and middle classes and turned "the political periphery into the political center" (Womack 1982, 195). While the GMD and CCP shared a Leninist organizational style, they were fundamentally different in their respective composition, ideology, and ambition. Unlike the GMD, which leaned to colonial capitalism and therefore to a bureaucratic-comprador network that included reactionary landowners, the CCP appealed to the urban and rural poor, to progressive intellectuals, and to sympathetic "patriotic democrats" in the business circles. From then on, nationalist and class struggle, national liberation and social revolution, and, ultimately, nationalism and socialism coincided in the Chinese communist revolution.

For those who classify revolutions into the categories of "liberal democratic" (French and American), "socialist developmental" (interwar European and Russian), and "peripheral nationalist" (Chinese, Vietnamese, Cuban, and so on), China is a case worth reconsidering for its cross-typological characteristics. It may be defined, for example, between "Western" and "Eastern" types or, specifically, as more of a French type compared with typical third world revolutions (cf. Huntington 1968, chapter 5; Skocpol 1979, 41–42).[42]

Perceiving the revolution as one that to a large extent was aimed at solving the land problem, the communists, long before taking national power, began to destroy the rural infrastructure of the old regime. They carried out massive and painstaking work in land reform, and they engaged grassroots mobilization through working with popular organizations such as those for peasants and for women. They ran local governments in their base areas, in the midst of military operations, while reconciling themselves with—and even taking advantage of—certain traditional organizational forms and methods. Land reform was the issue that decisively changed the balance of power between the communist and the nationalist forces during the civil war: millions of those who had recently gained land joined the People's Liberation Army (PLA) or its logistic networks. The communists promulgated a land constitution in 1947 that, in William Hinton's view, "played the same role as did Lincoln's Manifesto of Liberating Black Slaves during the American civil war" (1972, 7).

Recent research into economic relations of the late Qing period has moved away from an oversimplified class analysis. It has revealed that during much of the nineteenth century the state's land tax was low while famine relief efficacy was high (a fact that provides an explanation for the continuous demographic expansion), and that large land holdings in northern China became rare by the mid-twentieth century. Nationwide rural poverty since the turn of the twentieth century, then, was the result not solely, or even mainly, of heavy rent, but rather from deprivations due jointly to unequal land ownership, bureaucratic-financial capital, usury, and commercial monopolies (cf. Huang 1991, 1995). Moreover, revolutionary success could not end with the elimination of landlordism; it would have to dismantle the concomitant power of the old system controlled by central, local, and village autocrats (*tuhao lieshen*). Land reform was vital to that task en route to communist state building (Du 1998, 782). Historically, peasant rebellions were mostly caused by overextraction experienced as "tyranny that is fiercer than a tiger" (*kezheng meng yu hu*), referring to the regimes either of landlords or of taxation that the state failed to regulate. Hence, "encircling the cities from the countryside" was not merely a creative strategy in defying Moscow but an enormously difficult and far-reaching project of political and socioeconomic transformation. The revolutionary process built, from its grassroots, "a state in a state" of communist local governments before 1949 (Tsou 2000). On the eve of the founding of the PRC, the communists had made themselves China's most unbeatable nation builders; they had "clarity of national purpose, a charismatic leader at the helm, and the identification of the international positive and negative reference groups" (Dittmer and Kim 1993, 258). This, in turn, helped legitimize the transition of the CCP from a revolutionary party to a ruling one and gave it the moral confidence and practical authority indispensable for post-revolutionary construction.

Yet, the resolution of the land problem remained one of the greatest achievements of the Chinese revolution. This achievement can be appreciated from several related angles. First, the post-revolutionary regime was able to claim (though not without controversy) for the first time at least since the late Qing period that it had succeeded to feed one fifth of the world's population on only 7 percent of the world's cultivable land (Riskin 1991b). Another angle is that the capitalist global system, by contrast, had not been able to sustain the basic food supply worldwide, thereby failing about half of humanity in rural poverty and urban shantytowns. Despite its unprecedented productive capacity and wealth, capitalism also produces an immensely vast reserve army of unemployed individuals, along with cycles of crises of overproduction relative to insufficient demand resulting from low wages and impoverished income, not only in the poor countries but in some rich ones as well. This scene is, unfortunately, also emerging in China following the privatization phase of market reforms. Moreover, there has been a worsening trend of land loss (apart from that through industrial use and abuse and desertification among forms of ecological destruction) by farmers in recent years to land seizure by private developers that was allowed by local officials for short-term profits. Many of the forty million farmers who lost their land were left deprived of their basic means of living because there were no proper procedures or means of compensation for the seizures, and because double-level management, designed for peasant welfare in the early 1980s after decollectivization, was never solidly in place.[43] The now precariously loosened protection of land rights threatened to undo the vital social dimension of the revolution that guaranteed equal access to land.

New China, as only the second large socialist country after the Russian revolution (along with smaller communist regimes) briefly followed the lead of the Soviet Union. But China, in part due to the path it had traveled toward revolutionary victory, soon turned to reliance on its own vision and resources, which later were justified in the CCP's polemical documents of the 1960s known as the "nine commentaries" or *jiuping* (Gittings 1968). After winning the civil war in 1949, the party began a heavy-handed process of political consolidation, including such measures as the "oppression of counter-revolutionaries" as well as the rapid economic recovery that had been achieved by the time of China's stalemate with the Americans in the Korean war (1950–1953). During the first five-year plan (1953–1957), labor and other resources for capital accumulation, investment, and technological build-up were mobilized both locally and nationally. Skipping the "new democracy," the government rushed to nationalize industry, handicrafts, and commerce (1953–1956) and to collectivize agriculture (1955–1958). These moves, labeled a "socialist transformation of the national economy," were followed by the disastrous Great Leap Forward that simultaneously pursued centrally imposed, impracticable targets and discarded functional planning mechanisms. Having recovered from the most severe famine of the twentieth century (1959–1961), the country now found itself in a series of political campaigns that led to the Cultural Revolution. Exhaustion from this period's ideological extremism, political turbulence, and social chaos brought the pragmatists back to power in the mid-1970s.

Returning to the question of where the Chinese revolution fits within the rubric of the "modern," we must take a long-term historical perspective. Has it really transformed the old society and broken with the dark side of tradition? Is the communist rule virtually another dynastic cycle of China's lasting despotic and bureaucratic politics? Can the country's modern revolutionary movements be interpreted as part of a sequence of regime alternations (the CCP defeats the GMD, then is crushed by Mao's fanatic "continuing revolution," which in turn loses to Deng's reign of "market Stalinism") that have not made for fundamental changes in the nature of state power? Is it only this latest undertaking that finally promises economic modernization, demonstrating (as the cliché goes) that socialism is only a long detour to capitalism? Or are even the post-Deng administrations, which are committed to liberalization, nevertheless doomed insofar as the one-party dominance remains unshaken? Repeating a convention from the perspective of the "free world," S. E. Finer writes with authority that the pattern of the Chinese state since the first imperial unification (221BC) under the emperor of Qin had been "centralized, unitary, bureaucratic, paternalistic, authoritarian, and even despotic," and that the "entire subsequent course of Chinese government is nothing but the development of this [pattern]" (1999, 526–27). A totalizing and tyrannical Chinese past is seen to be so weighty a burden that "even a historical event of such magnitude as a revolution appears to have accomplished little more than scratch the surface of a society hardened into immutability" (Dirlik and Meisner 1989, 17).

The latest revisionist scholarship has expanded its critical horizon from the French and Russian revolutions to include an assault on the Chinese revolution. With or without the familiar cold war overtone, the best of these works are empirically impressive, containing extensively documented and researched materials. The work done within the PRC commonly laments a lost "new democracy." Across a scholarly feast of sorts is the discovery of abundant evidence of historical "civil societies" in China, sometimes compared to the East European "golden past" (though this nostalgia is expressed elsewhere more than locally). It is said that when the communists took power, they wiped out significant liberal reforms and civic developments that preexisted the revolutions. Business associations and guilds are one focus; folk religions and secret societies serving spiritual and commercial needs are another; and social-political networking and protesting yet another. Yet the enthusiasm becomes suspect when it goes so far that, as Dirlik complains, even the late Qing gentry and merchants are made to appear more progressive than the subsequent social transformers (1996, 50). Indeed, it is highly problematic, even within the terms of this analysis, not to count certain organizations and their activities as an organic part of the revolutionary process itself, and hence those organizers as themselves "civil society" campaigners (cf. Strand 1989; Wasserstrom, 1991). The social transformers have instead been denounced for their political radicalism, ranging from Liang Qichao, who made a "wrong" anti-reformist choice after the aborted "hundred days of reform," to Mao, who was determined to launch land redistribution and guerrilla warfare. "Radicalism" is diagnosed as China's "[twentieth-]century disease" (cf. Li and Liu 1995).[44] Even opium, a never-disputed symbol of the ills of imperialist trade and invasion, now comes to be deemed a "medical panacea" rather than anything physically or politically harmful (Dikotter et al. 2004). The fact that post-revolutionary Chinese society has been neither liberal nor democratic by Western-turned-universal standards certainly feeds these bitter reflections. As Jonathan Mirsky thus declared, on the occasion of PRC's fiftieth anniversary, there is "nothing to celebrate" (1999).

Another revisionist move is to call for the "collapse of the 1949 wall," a reevaluation of the Republican era that acknowledges a historically "consensual Chinese agenda" shared by the CCP and GMD in the context of Chinese nationalism (and the remarkable modernization achieved later in Taiwan as well). This gesture is intended to bridge the socioeconomic construction during the "Nanjing decade" (1927–1937) and the communist effort to modernize China without the conventional perception of a gulf (Oksenberg 1993, 315; Wang Gungwu 1996; Fitzgerald 1999, 5; Wakeman and Edmonds 1999; Kirby 2000a; Cohen 2003, 30–31). Entailed here is either an evolutionist paradigm of modernization or an unbroken narrative of continuous revolution in modern Chinese history. Both marginalize the demarcation of 1949, hence the communist breakthrough, and the two coincide when modernization and revolution are conceptualized such that they explain one another. In a similar vein, two counterfactual questions have been raised: Might Sun Zhongshan's three people's principles have been better for China's modern development (cf. Gregor 1995)? Was the "new democracy"—constituted of a mixed economy, a coalition government, and a national-popular culture (Mao 1940; 1949)—a missed opportunity? These questions can be conceived in an integrated manner given the fact that the communists initially took pride in Sun, considering "the minimum program of communism and the political tenets of the Three People's Principles [to be] basically in agreement" (Mao 1945, 122–23, 134). The commonality is so compelling that it is inscribed on the monument to the people's heroes in Tiananmen Square, which honors China's revolutionary martyrs from 1840 onward, crossing the divide not only of 1949 but also of 1911. Yet the fundamental distinctions between the communist system and the previous regimes are simply categorical, even conclusive. Moreover, in the aftermath of the civil war, a new identity for the PRC was necessary—not least for it to renounce the unequal treaties imposed on old China, which required a complete discontinuity from the old regimes along with their respective international bearings. After all, a new state had emerged, geared toward the party's "maximum program" of a socialist revolution, carrying with it many fresh policies.

No doubt the groundwork for the construction of a modern republic prior to 1949 should not be underestimated, which included state-sponsored projects and autonomous social movements for important goals ranging from political representation, power devolution, and universal suffrage to literacy and gender equality. The credits to the GMD, however, cannot compensate for its failure to reform its state apparatus against corruption and repression, or to carry out land redistribution, which it did not pursue until having retreated from the mainland. These failures were what enabled its communist competitor to win popular support and national power. In the end, however shaky the "1949 wall" might become in the fashionable language of Chinese modernity, it is much harder for the collective memory of noble, popular struggles to replace an old society with a new one to disappear, especially at a time when aspects of the old and rejected are beginning to return. However, economic and political liberalization, aided by reform communism's partial repudiation of the revolution's long-held beliefs, does erode revolutionary legitimacy. But if such a transition from communism is ever justifiable, what was the point of taking a socialist path in the first place? What was there to justify the enormous cost of, and sacrifices for, that choice? Even if a successful capitalist transformation lies ahead, it could only bring the "wall" down in logical, not historical, reasoning. For the Chinese were historically robbed of the option of liberal capitalism. And the total, urgent crisis, both national and social, "precluded the possibility of piecemeal, incremental reforms" as it also became obvious that none of China's fundamental problems could be solved without a new, sovereign, and centralized state (Tsou 1988, 327).

The questions posed about China are very similar to those about the October revolution: Was a liberal democratic viability open to the Russians in February 1917 (if not 1905, cf. Hobsbawm 1997; Pretty 1998)? Were it not for the Bolshevik takeover, could much of the bloodshed over ideology and political power in twentieth-century Russia, if not the world, have been avoided? Whether or not a consensus is achievable, it is worth noting that Chinese Marxism was Marxist enough to hold that capitalism would progress from feudal and patriarchal structures and that socialism would not be possible without sufficient material bases. As the national bourgeoisie, small and fragile, was at the time squeezed between and dependent on foreign capital, bureaucratic compradors, and landlordism while struggling to survive wars and turmoil, what a cruel joke it was that China (among countries in a similar position) would be expected to repeat a "normal" capitalist path! With much of their wealth and freedom taken away, where could the colonies turn to for their own "primitive accumulation"? China was not ever given a chance to "refuse" any golden opportunity for the development of private capitalism; rather only the "new democracy" style of state capitalism, as found on the communist agenda, was perhaps pursuable.[45] Chinese Marxist historians thus have reason to believe that imperialism was a fatal interruption of China's "natural" development, however dubious may be the notion of anything natural in history.

The point here remains plain and simple: national development is premised on national independence. That is, revolution was the only option and, as a matter of reality, it was not until the PRC consolidated its sovereign state power that it gained the strength to opt between self-reliance and the negotiation of foreign investment and technologies. As far as modernization is concerned, therefore, meaningful comparisons for China would not be with typical capitalist democracies but rather with peripheral forms of capitalism for which underdevelopment is the norm. In other words, to modernize backward, largely agrarian societies, certain revolutionary changes might be indispensable. A thorough-going land reform, for example, has proven crucial for economic growth and human capital in most NICs. By the same token, the absence of such a reform and accompanying improvement in productivity and changes in social structure, as social scientists broadly agree, explains major developmental difficulties in South Asia and in Latin America. Cases exist of industrialization in which land reform is bypassed, but they are rare because redistributive measures are generally desirable, or even necessary, for addressing rural (and, in turn, also urban) problems of poverty and polarization. Land reform is often the first step toward the democratization of productive and social relations.

Structural and nonvoluntarist interpretations that deny the explanatory role of conscious actions in the making of a revolution are nowhere more erroneous than when applied to the Chinese communist revolution.[46]

Among Joseph Esherick's "ten theses" highly skeptical of that revolution, at least one is entirely sound: "The determination, sacrifice, and commitment of individual communist revolutionaries—the subjective elements of the revolutionary dialectic—were both essential to the revolution's success and critical in shaping its nature" (in Wasserstrom 2003, 50). The incredible personal faith and the supreme courage it took to fight against overwhelming odds did not come without a rational cause. Deliberately chosen and paid for by unimaginable hardships and by numerous heroic lives, the revolution was a driving force of modern changes in China. Modernization theory rightly takes an independent, unified, and strong national government as the principal achievement in third world striving. "The measure of how successful a revolution is is the authority and stability of the institutions to which it gives birth" (and "the measure of how revolutionary a revolution is is the rapidity and the scope of the expansion of political participation") (Huntington 1968, 266). Similarly emphasized are "the accomplishments of revolutionary regimes in such areas as maintaining political order during the course of economic transformation" (Skocpol 1994, 281). In this mode of reasoning, in sharp contrast to democracy's prestige and priority in current ideological discourse, civil liberties and democracy come after the political institutionalization best suited for national development. Revolution enables and enhances modernization above all by creating a "developmental state." The national autonomy and territorial integrity of the PRC (mainland), its organizational capacity, and the public management of basic welfare were the factors that began to remake the world's largest poor country. These qualities also ensured that the regime was better grounded in support, consensus, or conformity than in force.

It is true that the Mao years, in particular, also suffered grave institutional defects that often resulted in social and economic destruction. The Great Leap led to a great famine. The Cultural Revolution turned into a decade of ideological purification that produced a cultural wasteland. Endless political campaigns subjugated persons, abused the constitution, and set back modernization. These movements, however, were attempts to perpetuate the revolution and safeguard socialism; they were not altogether irrational or unjustifiable. More remarkably still, political upheavals did not stop China's GNP from growing an average annual rate of 6.2 percent between 1952 and 1978.[47] The industrial sector outperformed most other developing economies. Although rural revitalization was seriously impeded by urban bias, the quality of life was "not merely improved but transformed" throughout rural towns and villages. Decades behind the economically developed world, China was, before the spectacular post-reform growth, already "on a par with middle-income countries" in human and social development (Bramall 1993, 335). Except for extraordinary times, such as the period between 1959 and 1961, the population was mostly fed and healthy, albeit at a basic level. As Aiguo Lu and Manuel Montes note: "Measured by social indicators such as life expectancy, infant mortality and educational attainment, China forged way ahead of most market economies at similar income levels and surpassed a number of countries with per capita incomes many times greater" (2002, 8–9). This overriding fact, as John Gurley commented at the twentieth anniversary of the PRC, is "so basic, so fundamentally important, that they completely dominate China's economic picture, even if one grants all of the erratic and irrational policies alleged by her numerous critics" (1969, 345; cf. Eckstein 1977; Rawski 1980; Riskin 1987). Developmental momentum surely has precedents elsewhere, but China's development was a vast and distinct experiment with production for needs. Broad social objectives, side by side with national independence and pride, such as workers' beneficiary status, women's participation, equality of nationalities, universal public education, and a government-financed health care system leaning to preventive medicine against epidemics, transformed the country and economy in less than three decades. Only the degree, not the essence, of this assessment might be disputed.

Equally true, however, is that one of the unintended consequences of the communist revolution was its unfulfilled promises in liberty and democracy against hierarchy and bureaucracy, a grave problem exposed foremost by the socialist principles of freedom and equality themselves. Inherent in a long-fought, armed revolution are classical dilemmas, again and again, over means and ends and the collective and the individual. Rosa Luxemburg is torn while writing: "Determined revolutionary activity coupled with a deep feeling for humanity, that alone is the real essence of socialism"; and, further, an unjust world must be overturned, "but every tear that flows and might have been staunched is an accusation; and a man hurrying to a great deed who knocks down a child out of unfeeling carelessness commits a crime" (quoted in Cohen 1965, 9). In rising to the modern challenge, however, revolutionary methods were not desired, but propelled by concrete historical constraints—above all terror and violence from powerful enemies.

Thus now, at a moment when revolutionary legacies have seemingly vanished, it is time to ask whether the revolution was, with all its costs, necessary in light of what it accomplished (Cumings 1997; Gregor 2000, 7). Any attempt to answer this question has to begin with the revolution's historicity and rationality. Rather than a utopian liberal capitalism blocked by external imperialism and an internal ancien régime, the revolution was inspired by the realistic prospect, as understood then, of new democracy and socialism. The actual fruits of the revolution are compelling. It has built into the Chinese nation the soul and bones of modern existence measured in terms both of national identity and international standing. The symbolic power of legendary struggles, as exemplified by the Long March (1934–1935), has become part and parcel of the Chinese culture. Looking back, it was all too clear that a proud People's Republic had left behind itself the ruins of war, foreign domination, extensive and extreme poverty, and old forms of social injustice (Friedman 1974; cf. Dunn 1989, 70–76). Thus the Chinese communist victory, and the socioeconomic development that followed it, must be deemed one of the century's greatest achievements—if only because, as Meisner explains it, "with an acute and painful awareness of all the horrors and crimes that accompanied the revolution" or were performed in its name, "few events in world history have done more to better the lives of more people" (1999a, 1, 12). Ultimately, the historical justification for the Chinese revolution (as for profound social revolutions elsewhere) lies in the revolution's purposeful transformation of the social conditions in which human suffering is both an unbearable reality and the causal link to revolt.

Comparative Modernities and "Asia"

The revolutionary Chinese model contrasts sharply with colonial and conservative modernity elsewhere in the non-Western world.[48] Without doubt, freedom has to be fought for and won with or without a revolution (Fanon 1967). Democracy is not something simply handed to a nation—as in the case of India, despite what is inherited from former colonizers: "No historical explanation can be complete unless it takes the 'agency' of India's freedom movement into account" (Vashney 1988, 38).[49] However, crucial statistics, including those provided by authoritative international sources such as the United Nations and the World Bank, consistently support the appraisal that China has been faster and more advanced in terms of social and human development than most states in the global South, of which many are seen as liberal capitalist and formally democratic.[50]

Nonetheless, there has been a more recent, damaging trend in China toward increasing inequalities and declining public services. A rural health crisis pressed China's ranking by the World Health Organization down to the near bottom in 2000, well behind India and several other countries with a lower GDP (Wang Shaoguang 2003). Thus it is here where a turn toward the social logic of democracy should work, if democracy is taken as "a political system in which the members regard one another as political equals, are collectively sovereign, and possess all the capacities, resources, and institutions they need in order to govern themselves" (Dahl 1989, 311). Such is a rather tall order, and one that possibly is not achievable without fundamental socioeconomic transformations. Why has modernization in a large part of the postcolonial world been crippled? According to Moore, the answer must be found in the absence of "*a revolutionary break with the past* and of any strong movement in this direction," which explains prolonged backwardness and governing difficulties in countries like India (1966, 431). The Machiavellian thesis that revolutionary baptism is required for a new order should not, of course, be taken absolutely.[51] Yet it seems evident that post-revolutionary nation- and state-building shines in comparison with colonial modernity in transforming societies that are large, poor, agrarian, illiterate, and patriarchal. Revolutions have generally "given birth to nations whose power and autonomy markedly surpassed their own pre-revolutionary pasts and outstripped other countries in similar circumstances" (Skocpol 1979, 3). Different national experiences notwithstanding, an effective public-serving state power is, everywhere, a key to development.

The contrast between revolutionary and colonial modernity is also manifest in the difference between a deliberate and active reversal of the course of imperialism and colonialism, on the one hand, and societal passivity along colonial paths on the other. That is, among non-European peoples, some have been brought into modernization by the liberation movements, while others "entered history not as subjects but as objects of the transformative powers of capitalism" (Dirlik 1994, 22).[52] The role of a vanguard Communist

Party cannot be taken to negate the role of popular participation from below that completely differs from elite arrangements negotiated between the metropolitan colonizers and the domestic rulers. Consequently, postrevolutionary states are more likely to seek the reconfiguration of global capitalism, even though China in its current integration fervor seemed to present the opposite.

Revolutionary and colonial modernity diverge further in that the former does not usually transplant democratic institutions from the West, while the latter is easily seen to be an extension of European history. Political authority in each case relies on its own institutional foundations, with state capacity tending to be much stronger in post-revolutionary societies. There are no doubt subvariants across typological borders, but the point here is that twentieth-century revolutions (as both historical events and myths) stand for alternative modernity in the sense that they are evoked by, and mobilized for, the desire to transform capitalism. As such their destination becomes modernity's culmination.[53] A revolution leading to socialist modernization is thus a path with a hope to transcend the "anguish of backwardness" as much as escaping "the tragedy of development" (Berman 1983, 175).

The indiscriminate genealogy of "third world modernization" that does not distinguish models of modernity is therefore only of limited use. Likewise, arguments that consider development to be "the last and failed attempt to complete the Enlightenment in Asia, Africa, and Latin America" (Escobar 1995, 221) overlook large exceptions, especially socialist ones, in these regions. Furthermore, the Chinese trajectory of compressed development, while sharing many colonial and postcolonial constraints with others within the same epochal parameters, also curbs global hegemonic relations. Modernity cannot be terminally capitalist if only because the communist revolutionaries were bound to transform themselves into ruthless modernizers. If their visions and projects have fallen apart here and there, they cannot for that reason be written off the grand modernist narrative. In breaking free of the "law" of capitalist development, Chinese revolutionary and socialist undertakings at their best amounted to a vindication of the greatest "privilege of backwardness" in modern history, the opportunity of which colonial modernity was deprived. In other words, instead of unequal development, or indeed underdevelopment as the violent working of world political economy (Nairn 1997, 335–40), China has taken a developmental path to its own advantage.

Revolutionary modernity sets China apart from not only colonial modernization but also conservative "revolution from above" (Trimberger 1977, 1978), exemplified by the Japanese-style "alternative modernity" (Jameson 1993; Feenberg 1995). While not denying similarities in the actualization of the latent privileges of late, state-led development aided by bureaucratic and authoritarian instruments, the revolutionary model remains radically different from the historically specific routes and aspirations of conservative modernization. Moreover, as Japanese military expansion and colonization in Asia exploited an anti-Western ideology of the "greater East Asian co-prosperity sphere," the language of "Asia" was tainted for peoples in affected countries. The postwar U.S. occupation, which engineered a constitutional democracy replete with a naked dose of racism for geopolitical purposes (or what John Dower calls a "neocolonial revolution" [1999, 203]), could not have much local appeal either. Yet, a "capitalist developmental state" characteristic of productive and bureaucratic efficiency (Johnson 1995) has turned Japan into not only an economic giant but also a corporate welfare society (as opposed to welfare state) rich in human capital.[54] As originally a part of the Sino-magnetic zone before the Meiji reform, Japan thus becomes a fantastic example of compression and synthesis, a superb reproducer of the "West" as much as a formidable innovator of "a modernized society which remains wholly non-Occidental in its cultural traditions and forms of life" (Gray 1995, 83, 168). The complexities of this case are instructive in understanding the contested identities of "West" and "East" and "Europe" and "Asia."

Modern Asia, as a regional entity, is the product of joint and competing forces among "oriental" civilizations, Western empires and their protectorates, and intra-Asian cooperation and conflicts (in imperial networks, colonial conquests, wars, and revolutions). Its geography is structured with many political, socioeconomic, and cultural spaces in which the temporal notion of "modern" acquires both shared and locally distinct meanings. Not an innocent concept, the term "Asiatic" is a Western construction in opposition to, and defined by, things "European"—contrasted by Hegel as the difference between the beginning and the end of history—and hence between the "people without history" and the historical peoples. China, in particular, is "the oldest state and yet [has] no past," it is "a state which exists today as we know it to have been in ancient times. To that extent China has no history" (quoted in Wright 1960, 245).[55] The rise of an industrialized and democratic Japan undermines this Europe-Asia antithesis; less noted, however, is how even greater a Chinese negation has been forged.

If comparisons between China and Europe tend to bypass Asia, critical and comparative Asian studies may rectify that habitual narrowness of intellectual imagination by engaging different Asias, for each is a separate historical formation subject to conceptual analysis. There are countries that do not fit cleanly into received notions of existing entities such as "Pacific" or "Confucian Asia," or the Far East (as projected from Europe, of course) in an East Asia–centered discourse about "Asia"; notions that suppress the impact of liberation nationalism and developmental socialism. The huge differences between revolutionary, colonial, conservative nationalist, and other (secular or religious) models of modernity must not be buried in these loaded generalizations. Treating China, due to its imperial heritage, as a cultural realm unto itself is to forget that the country's search for reconnection with, or reposition in, both its indigenous traditions and surrounding world is based on, rather than free from, the revolutionary changes it has achieved. Rejecting the colonial modernity that had been partially experienced in China was among such changes, from which lessons about developmental strategy can be drawn. Similarly, the lumping together of imperialist and resistant nationalism into a generic conception is not only morally but also analytically crooked. Their respective versions of internationalism are a striking contrast between capitalist global domination and socialist revolution perceived in the language of overcoming "socialism and backwardness." In this connection, superficial and fictional notions of the "Asian way" or "Asian values" engender more confusion than clarification, and may even aid residuals of expansionist ultranationalism that are all too familiar in the region.

Any Asian narrative, as an object of intellectual fascination, will have to be sufficiently sensitive to the frontiers inside the continent and inside regional entities. To see a single capitalist world market as being embedded in, and dictatorial to, development everywhere still cannot imply similar outcomes in all times and places. While the Chinese revolution's international effect remains debatable, its domestic impacts have set China's trajectory permanently apart from that of most other Asian states. This distinction persists even in the postcommunist era in which Chinese participation in globalization alters the terms of struggle, if not yet the basic rules of the game. To refute any illusion of Asian totality is not merely to admit political, geographical, and cultural divisions inside Asia. More to the point is never to see Asia as a group of latecomers striving to catch up with world historical time of the modern at a standstill ("the end of history") in the global North (of which the myth of Western singularity is also increasingly difficult to hold). Confident modern societies, like those of Chinese socialism, Indian democracy, or Japanese corporatism, at once share commonalities and striking individualities. Their specific historical situations emit locally unique opportunities and limitations.

The Chinese search for an alternative to the "master course" of teleological progress defies the dominant ideologies of modernity and modernization. This search has been outlined in this chapter as a revolutionary alternative to colonial modernity, a socialist alternative to Stalinist statism, and a reformist alternative to capitalist integration. The Chinese model has thus modified the "world time" of globalization by instituting an alternative national history.[56] This argument has less to do with whatever may be seen as "Chinese characteristics" in cultural terms than how and why China took the paths it did and what causal links might explain the still-to-be-defined nature and future of its transformations today.

If modern alternatives to capitalism can still be viable, it is not because (as pluralist and cultural nationalist arguments often entail) any variant of non-European ethnocentrism is persuasive, or that traditional values can be revived to counter modern destruction, or that the West-rest divide must be perpetuated. If the teleology of capitalism as the linear route and sole form of modernity is unacceptable, the rational humanist norms, for which anti-Eurocentrism has so far offered little coherent and comparable substitutes, are also largely uncontestable. Any normatively sustainable departure from the Euro-universal framing of the modern would therefore at best still be "post-Eurocentric" (cf. Dirlik 2000, 63). To affirm modernity while rejecting the monopolizing and homogenizing tendencies of capitalism is not a question of plurality of values or multiculturalism. It is rather to identify those developments that (potentially) defy the hegemonic global ideologies and the Euro-parochial images of the modern world. In other words, if the false universality of capitalism is yet to be replaced by a novel theorization of an alternative universalist paradigm—in which cultural diversities would surely flourish—such a paradigm cannot conceptually depend on the particularities of any culture.

China, as we study it, exemplifies these subtleties. Anti-imperialism did not ally itself with conservative traditionalism; nor did the enlightenment stance against Confucian authoritarianism uncritically embrace Westernization. The dialectical union of "Chinese modernity," to be attained through revolutionary nationalism and socialism, was a collective response to a national and social crisis triggered by the invading foreign powers. The modern inspiration for China's transformed self-perception culminated in radical moments to favor nationalism over traditionalism, Marxism over liberalism (which was allied with imperialism), and revolution over reform. "Modernity," after all, cannot be an abstract gauge of meanings for diverse historical experiences. In China it concretely signified national salvation for an oppressed people determined to throw off the shackles of both external imperialism and internal premodernity. Thus the obvious logical conclusion here is that national liberation was the precondition not only for modernization, but also for any future creation of a multinational "civilization-nation" or federation. A sovereign and unified state capable of defending and developing the nation was an indispensable modern norm of legitimation. Once again, what China has sought is an alternative to capitalist imposition, not to socioeconomic development or any other normative objectives of modernity, such as a desirable pathway to global integration that is in line with international justice and developmental sustainability. Chinese socialism, ideally, is committed to a higher form of modern society, an alternative civilization, in which nations and their knowledge systems can be reordered to better serve the need of all peoples as equals (Ye 2000; Xian 2001, 14–15).

If there is no chance for any particular modern path to bypass epochal parameters, local performances still differ greatly from site to site. Capitalist expansion has not been a one-way business; its ideological and physical edges do not move across borders with immunity. Globalization is simultaneously localization through translation and adaptation; autonomy and interests are locally defined and yet cannot be treated outside of their global connections and contexts. The reach of capital has neither the same meaning nor consequences in different and complicated situations. The dynamics between constraints and choices, trends and contingency, generate both the promise of a development with expected liberating effects and the predicament of tensions between identity and transformation, continuity and change. The Chinese reform model, a continuation more than a replacement of the Chinese socialist model, has, with a considerable amount of luck, ridden globalization without conclusively losing either its promise or its control over predicaments. This tenacity distinguishes China from the rest of Asia, for which modernity signifies different meanings and of which countries inevitably face different problems and follow different solutions. The fact that ideologies of a Western origin can be creatively adapted to Asian minds and localities—such as Marxism in China and other communist states, or liberalism (variously) in India and Japan—must be a reason why Asia is not the West's singular "Other," and why ethnocentric prejudices cannot counter Eurocentric ones.

Chapter 2

Chinese Socialism

CHINA'S POST-REVOLUTIONARY PROJECT OF SOCIALIST MODERNIZA-
tion can be analyzed in a social-national-developmental framework. This
framework also fundamentally explains both the maintenance and breakdown of social cohesion and political consensus in the PRC. Nationalism
denotes national unity, sovereignty, and autonomy; socialism stands for
equality and social justice; and developmentalism implies a determination
to overcome backwardness. Together, national pride, socialist ambition,
and economic drive underlay the Chinese desire for distinction and international recognition. Because of their intrinsic interconnection, the potential conflicts among these three dimensions can be reconciled in principle
and can be dealt with through strategic adjustment insofar as China remains defiant to capitalist subordination. These forces are tied to each other
but also are in competition, and as such inform policy negotiations and
decisions. Their meanings and structural equilibrium, however, have not
been fixed but rather are constantly contested in varying domestic and
external conditions over the past more than half a century since 1949.

Looking at the triad of Chinese development more closely, the issue of
nationalism—finding expression in territorial claims, foreign relations, nationality management, and so on—appeared in its overall function to be
more independent than socialism and developmentalism. Consequently,
nationalist considerations often had the greatest weight in the state power.
That power was extraordinary in its range and depth under Mao, and it
gradually receded during the reforms when privatization had overtaken
decentralization in the 1990s. Yet the PRC state had remained the arbiter of
social interactions, the controller of the economy, and the defender of
national interests. On the other hand, policies promoting market forces
indicated retreats not only from socialism but also nationalism, leading to
development priorities over government's social obligations as well as cer-

tain nationalist concerns. As I discuss in chapter 1, socioeconomic development had always been a preoccupation for Chinese modernity, from the imminent task of nation building to the ideological belief of socialist superiority. What has changed is that development now becomes imperative for regime legitimacy when there is a shortage of other sources of legitimation. The growing imbalance, however, with socialism being overwhelmed by nationalism and especially developmentalism, simultaneously hurts national security and developmental capabilities as it undermines the three-dimensional foundation of the PRC on which the country's political and social stability has also depended. In particular, if socialist development is premised on an anticapitalist conviction, the marginalization of socialism inevitably delegitimizes the Chinese revolution and the whole project of China's alternative modernity.

In this chapter I will first construe a state-centered analytical framework of nationalism, socialism, and developmentalism for investigation and assessment. The interdependence and changing balance among these pillars of the PRC state and society are shown to be vital in both the forward and backward movements of the country. Next, I discuss class politics in the context of an externally imposed "internal accumulation," which had to be pursued by a centrally commanded quasi-war economy of concentrating capital and human and natural resources. Social mobilization and control, urban (and in fact also rural) bias, and the plight of the national bourgeoisie are my main focuses. I then move to the "nationality question" and the "woman question" by examining the situations of ethnic and gender equality respectively. Comparisons between the socialist and postsocialist conditions of existence for major social classes, national minorities, and women are made against the ideological background of egalitarianism and broad social justice. I also look at central-local relations and the parallels of regional-ethnic patterns in terms of spatial politics. Finally, I will sum up the arguments over the primacy of the socialist state in national development and in arbitrating cleavaged social processes. The closely related topics of bureaucracy and political campaigns of "class struggle" will be addressed in chapter 3.

Socialism, Nationalism, and Developmentalism

In considering what might be leveled to critically retain in the paradigm of Western impact and Chinese response in sinological studies, nothing is more important in the causality of the irreversible modern turn of Chinese history than foreign invasion—by military means as much as commerce and culture. Here an international perspective is necessary because, at least for a good part of the nineteenth century and the entire twentieth century, "everything important had an international dimension" (Kirby 2000b, 179). Indeed, the Chinese domestic situation had, since the 1840s, been strongly affected by world politics, especially by competitions among the United States, Russia, and Japan. The various influences of each of these countries, and later of the Soviet Union, were also powerful. Discussing "America's failure in China," Tang Tsou considers, for example, the U.S. policy of nonintervention—and hence not restraining Japanese expansion in Asia after World War I—to be partly responsible for the consequent development in China leading to the communist victory (1963).

The International Dimension

The blockade of the PRC was at the heart of the American strategy to contain Asian communism after "losing China." From the Korean War (1950–1953) and the Taiwan Strait crisis (1955–1957) to China's exclusion from the United Nations (until 1971) and the U.S.-led diplomatic boycott and military threats, the policies of the "free world" continued to fuel nationalist sentiment in China.[1] This fact was nowhere more evident than in the Chinese involvement in Korea: no other event in the People's Republic had ever matched the "intense concentration of military action, domestic mobilization, and popular emotion" during the war (Townsend 1992, 119–20). It was thus political realism that compelled the new regime in the early 1950s to opt for Soviet support, "leaning to one side," as Mao famously declared.[2] Later the reversion of that stance, seemingly irrational in view of China's painful isolation, also had its own logic. Dogmatic rigidity and miscalculation notwithstanding, Mao's anti-revisionist campaign from 1960 onward reflected the CCP's ideological (or "genuine Marxist") and moral conviction as well as its *realpolitik* of maneuvering between the two superpowers.[3] Despite changes in foreign relations, Beijing was remarkably consistent in its nationalist positioning. That is, China's collective self-consciousness of struggling in the predicaments of "socialism in one country" (after the "betrayal" of the Soviet Union) might have been misguided, but not false.[4] Yet, it should be noted that the Sino-Soviet split had not only worsened the developmental conditions inside China but also cut deep into the international communist movement. For all its faults, the Soviet superpower was the only brake on (American) imperialist hegemony and aggression. Without that split it is not unthinkable that the movement could have fought out a different outcome of the cold war.

The systematic threats and constraints generated by global capitalism created a harsh situation of "dictatorship over needs" (see chapter 3). However effective the regime intended to be in order to impose the needed social transformation, its strategic and policy options were circumscribed by external forces. Fred Halliday is not exaggerating when he asserts that while "the capacities of the revolutionary states were most evident *internally,* it was *internationally* that they were most challenged and these very domestic capacities undermined" (1999, 261–62). Such challenges also caused a fear of subversion and decay in the communist mentality. A more-imminent menace in the 1960s even forced China to prepare for nuclear attacks. The enormously costly defense industry and "third-line" construction in the mountain areas of the Chinese hinterland seriously diverted the country's national income from productive and welfare spending (Naughton 1988, 1991). As Chris Bramall notes, "Consumption grew slowly in Maoist China primarily because of the American threat . . . China could only have avoided this fate by surrendering her sovereignty" (1993, 336).[5]

In the end, external pressure took a heavy toll at home, not the least of which was seen in the ravages of policy blunders, material hardships, and political upheavals. China never completely severed its foreign trade, yet its difficulties in achieving economic self-sufficiency were intensified by outside hostility. Not until the 1970s did the PRC gain a seat in the U.N. Security Council while normalizing relations with the United States, Japan, and a dozen former foes. However, this repositioning on the international chessboard, though ending the blockade against China, was more a triumph for the United States than for China, with the subsequent Chinese support for American foreign engagements and puppets wherever they were anti-Soviet. Many were angered when Mao received Nixon, whose government had waged the war in Vietnam.[6] In the post-Mao period China has restored links with the world market, thereby releasing itself from the impasse caused by the joint effects of internal and external pressures. In the past twenty-five years, the process of national development steadily shedding its socialist core was the same process in which an inward-looking pattern of economic autarky and political secrecy broke down.

In China, the official and the popular, and the Han and the minority ethnic nationalisms were not always distinguishable. In their integration Chinese nationalism was essentially a response to, and in that sense also determined by, foreign threat. Historically, Chinese nationalism was both revolutionary resistance against imperialism and a modern alternative to the Eurocentric assumption about capitalist universality. As such it was also simultaneously socialist—hence the paired formulation of "Chinese socialism." Chinese socialism was in turn itself a developmental project that aimed to rise above national backwardness without capitalist distortions, thus the coherence of revolution and modernization. In prescribing and embracing one another, nationalism, socialism, and developmentalism constituted an overriding consensus and legitimating discourse in the PRC. Together they clarified the purpose of a liberated people and their government: nationalism for national greatness, socialism for social justice, development for public welfare. The more-culturalist reading of Chinese nationalism into tradition-centered Chineseness had in recent years revived when ideologies and policies traditionally related to socialism declined, leaving the national rather than the social to dominate the interpretation of "socialism with Chinese characteristics." The "civilization" rhetoric (*huaxia-wenming*) in the party's patriotic education had even born an unwelcome air of imperial nostalgia. But to strip the Chinese model of its alternative modern character is only to misread history in which legitimation and delegitimation of the Maoist and reformist regimes took place.

Special attention should be paid to the fact that socialist modernization might be impressive, but it was also much more difficult than "dependent development" in the capitalist peripheries. In sharp contrast to the PRC, most NICs in Asia had benefited substantially from the geopolitics of anticommunism. Japan, South Korea, and Taiwan all had had a huge inflow of dollars in aid as well as an open U.S. market (which was by no means accessible to many other countries) for their exports, which provided a key stimulus to their respective economic takeoffs.[7] Now that the cold war blocs were unraveling and China had committed itself to market integration, old tensions became loosened. Nevertheless, the communist giant—regardless of its sheer size and all that may imply—by virtue of retaining its independence in the name of socialism continued to be greeted with suspicion and "containment" in a global order that was not only capitalist but also postcommunist. As long as defending national independence and integrity were perceived to be the same thing as guarding the country's socialist system constitutive of a Chinese identity, and as long as nationalist and socialist goals both depended on growth, the national-social-developmental triad would endure.

Mao was a master of the dialectic of the possibility of turning a disadvantage into an advantage. His confidence lay in the Chinese Marxist conviction in the developmental superiority of revolutionary socialism and a voluntarist notion about the abilities of the party and people. In a truly sober state of mind he wrote about the need, in the spirit of development with honor, of learning from those countries "with a high scientific and technological level," even though they "are overblown with arrogance." The Chinese could thus "strive to wipe out China's economic, scientific and cultural backwardness within a few decades and rapidly get abreast of the most advanced nations in the world" (1956, 306; cf. Schram 1989, 114). His optimism, however, missed what later proved an insurmountable exogenous barrier that, reinforced by mistaken adventures at home, prevented China from gaining substantial outside assistance. Consequently, the national paths to socialist modernization had to be redrawn.

Here the adjective "socialist" is used with an awareness of postsocialist confusions. Socialism is classically qualified as a system or mode of production for needs as contrasted to production for profits under capitalism, which makes basic sense. But in the Chinese political vocabulary, socialism more concretely also implies public ownership and redistributive justice ("to each according to his/her labor") overseen by the state as a "public good regime."[8] This straightforward understanding was not a problem in the Mao years before a profit-driven economy emerged. The "purpose of socialist production," as heatedly debated (as late as) in the early 1980s, was believed to satisfy broad social needs from the viewpoint of equality. Today, as the topic no longer appealed to the economists and politicians in China (as elsewhere), the word "socialism" is increasingly hollow. Yet it should still be treated as a searching sign in the Chinese project of making "a socialist market."

The Imperative of "Internal Accumulation"

As early as 1942, during the "big production movement" in the base area around Yan'an, Mao realized that publicly managed enterprises could be "an extremely great accomplishment." It was "a new model for the national economy." "This new form is neither the old Bismarckian national economy nor the Soviet Union's newest national economy; rather it is a New Democratic or Three People's Principles' national economy" (quoted in Selden 1971, 265). Merely a decade later, the Yan'an model of relying on internal resources and wartime organization was seen on a national scale. The Chinese communists in power, emerging fresh from a three-year recovery after the end of the civil war in 1949 and the Korean armistice in 1953, began to push for a "socialist transformation," discarding the moderate program of new democracy. Socialist industrialization was, then, not only to support national strength and workers' well-being, but also to minimize China's economic dependency, including that on the Soviet Union.

What stood out in terms of internal constraints was, above all, the primitive accumulation of capital through sacrificing rural development and exploiting the peasantry. This was the case fundamentally because the socialist state possessed neither colonies along with a global trade network (in contrast to early capitalist development in Europe) nor the means to borrow from the advanced economies.[9] Thus, in order to sustain an internally generated high accumulation rate, wages and consumption had to be suppressed and the countryside subordinated to urban demands. The so-called socialist primitive accumulation, though missing colonial extractions, did not radically differ from classical capitalism in its equally exploitative method toward the countryside. But it was carried out without a choice. In Soviet Russia, "socialist accumulation" or "internal accumulation" was originally formulated to justify "grain requisition" (not only from the *kulaks*). Such methods of what Bukharin called "extra-economic compulsion" were seen by Lenin as necessary in the nearly impossible circumstances for the transition from capitalism to socialism, so as to safeguard the world's first and only workers' state. The Bukharin debate in the 1920s did not settle the matter. The more moderate proposal for gradual industrialization based on fair and balanced exchanges between industrial and agricultural sectors—hence also a solid worker-peasant alliance—was not given a chance to be verified or falsified in practice.[10] The civil war and foreign intervention after the 1917 revolution were too soon followed by the antifascist war of 1941–1945 reaching far on the Soviet soil. This episode of history proves the "law" that socialism in one country, sabotaged by economic and military capitalism, would be defeated without speedily strengthening and arming itself.

In theory, by the time of the founding of the PRC, socialism had taken over two big countries, and China initially obtained from the Soviet Union generous aid indispensable for its economic recovery and regime consolidation. Agricultural collectivization in China also went relatively smoothly with considerable consent from the peasants without Stalinist atrocities (as discussed in the next section). Mao's immediate reaction to Khrushchev's secret report in the twentieth party congress was a highly original analysis of the "ten major relationships" to be rationally handled between industry and agriculture, among others, and also between heavy industry and light industry for consumer goods (1956, 23–30). Yet attempts to boost rural interests were unsuccessful, and the terms of trade between the two sectors eventually resembled the pattern of the unequal "scissors price" (of artificially cheapened agricultural products in exchange with artificially more expensive industrial goods) that earlier in Russia had led to peasant revolts and the "scissors crisis" of 1923 (Carr 1966). China did not in the end escape the developmental strategy and tragedy that caused rural impoverishment, for which later the great famine was an ultimate price.

The Chinese government until the early 1980s imposed near state monopoly over the purchase and marketing of grain, cotton, and other main agricultural products and permitted a quasi-segregation system between urban and rural residents. By administratively categorizing and confining people into those who consumed commodity grain and those who produced it while keeping the rest for self-consumption, the system enabled a rapid process of industrial growth and the construction of cities. The agrarian surplus was squeezed by the state to finance industry and other investment priorities. Urban bias is no doubt a common developmental headache, but here it was pushed through by a socialist state even more forcefully, despite the CCP's traditional roots in the peasant population. This was among the worst of the unintended consequences of the Chinese revolution that, after all, had marched to power from the countryside.

The state-led, intensive process of accumulation in the name of socialism and the nation yielded contradictory results. On the one hand, in attempting an alternative to excessive centralism, China's command economy was more decentralized and the state sector proportionately smaller than in the Soviet Union. Centralization and decentralization took turns partly in reflection of the balance of power between central and local authorities (cf. the timeline in Wang and Hu 1999, 172). Much less rigid, central planning in China at times fell into a "crippled hybrid" (Riskin 1991, 136). On the other hand, certain statist fundamentals adopted during local state building in the base areas stayed strong, displaying instrumental rationality as well as institutional defects. Many of the economic disasters during the periods of policy adventurism, in the forms of mobilized or spontaneous mass movements, were attributable to the lack or deliberate neglect of planning rather than to its normal functions. Comparisons between a command and a market system would therefore make little sense without taking into account their concrete timings and situations.

Moreover, socialist development—hence publicly committed and relatively insulated development—is not readily comparable with the beneficiaries of the capitalist world order or with countries far less burdened by either public service obligations or defense expenditures. Nowhere else could the constraints on development be more pronounced than in the conditions of an antagonistic milieu resulting in the obsession with internal unity and self-reliance. That is, China's external relations with global and regional cold war contenders must participate in explaining its alternating cycles of stability and disruption, and liberalization and repression, no matter how the nature of the regime is labeled. The contrasts between a socialist accumulation structure and a capitalist developmental state are many, and are all played out in China against a background of the greater adversities confronted by socialist accumulation in a world dominated by capitalist political, economic, financial, military, and cultural institutions.

Already engaged in a daunting task of freeing itself from the predicament of "socialism and backwardness," the Chinese project was all the more difficult because it aspired to be an alternative not only to underdevelopment and dependent development but also to the statist approaches to development. Being itself state directed, there was an inherent limit to Chinese socialism's ambition to follow a more democratic path. The barriers on that path may not have been historically and structurally surmountable—precluding serious counterfactual contemplation such as Liu Shaoqi's proposal on "consolidating new democracy" (for ten to twenty years before the socialist transformation). As the communists were in charge of creating an alternative path to socialist modernization, any other developmental goals and strategies, if at all possible, were also ruled out.

It might be plausible to argue that the completion of the socialist accumulation in China (measured by industrial output having exceeded 50 percent of the GDP and by the establishment of a solid infrastructural groundwork) objectively marked the end of the Maoist model (cf. Hunt 1988, chapter 8; Prime 1989). But it is also the case that the reform agenda became feasible in the first place and proceeded to rely on many prereform achievements only because of the existence of an economic basis prepared for further development. This factor helps to explain the relative smoothness of leadership succession and policy reorientation in the late 1970s. The economic logic alone, however, is insufficient to understand the particular conjuncture of the reform initiative if, as Barry Naughton notes, "despite its deep-seated problems, the economy had clearly not exhausted its growth potential under the old system" (1995, 60). In fact, according to Dwight Perkins, the economy during the decade of the cultural revolution performed "deceptively" well (1986, 39–42). It was Mao's death in 1976 that allowed the changes to happen, and new leaders took the groundbreaking decision to reform Chinese socialism via market tools. They were able to do so in the aftermath of the massively destructive campaign politics of the Mao era, beginning with political rehabilitation and limited liberalization, and improving living standards along the way. Coincidental detente in China's international position provided the country with an unprecedented incentive to open itself to foreign investment, trade, and technologies. "Relinking" with the world market soon turned out to be the order of the day, anticipating nothing close to a consequential crisis of the socialist state to come.

National Development as a State Project

In retrospect, the extraordinary effectiveness of "internal accumulation" in China without massive discontent or terror was phenomenal and only possible in a post-revolutionary and centralized state. There we see a site of "history 3" (see chapter 1) in which people were thoroughly mobilized and society organized on a quasi-war economy footing, and a popular leadership committed itself to national development. The party, in particular, was in absolute control while incorporating useful elements of traditions, such as those socially cohesive forms of grassroots self-management. Central planning operated side by side with personal directives as well as local initiatives. Governmental agencies formed a "vertical-horizontal matrix" of the provincial and lower-level bureaus of state ministries answerable also to local party chiefs (Lieberthal and Oksenberg 1988). A participatory society based on political education and organization ensured compliance with the state's developmental objectives, aided by the ideological encouragement of collective conformity and personal sacrifice. No ordinary developmental state could ever imitate similar measures or reach a comparable extent of command. In fact the NICs, being strategic players of the cold war geopolitical game backed by the capitalist powers, did not really need a dictatorship for capital accumulation. Their regimes were often dictatorial for other reasons such as countercommunist "security" concerns.

There is nothing new about national development, and late development in particular, being a state project. Not only had industrialization always been state-sponsored as in Europe and later in the other continents,[11] but also nationalist and modernizing projects normally conjoined each other (cf. Gerschenkron 1962; Wilber parts 5 and 6). The novelty of socialist development lay in both its historical origin of revolutionary modernity and its post-revolutionary mission of overcoming backwardness. As such, the Chinese socialist state was perceived as representative of the best public interests and the natural agent of development. What distinguished the PRC state from its noncommunist counterparts in the third world was not so much its autonomy from as its penetration in the societal infrastructure and its monopoly of power. This ability of erasing any state-society demarcation might merit some cultural interpretations, but it owed more to a societal consensus, a social contract, furnished by the revolution and the party's long-term mobilization work at the grassroots. Not only was the party-state morally obliged by the revolutionary tradition to lead and serve the people, but it also possessed the necessary organizational and ideological apparatus to do so.

It is at this point that two tempting comparative references surface: the "national socialist" ferment in interwar Europe; and the postwar NICs in Asia (for their historical-cultural connections to China) and in Latin America (for their comparable developmental experiences with China).[12] The obvious incompatibility between communism and fascism makes the comparison odd but not illegitimate. When François Furet sees in the "three tyrannies" of the twentieth century—Russia, Germany, and Italy—a shared history, he overlooks the moral and political distinction of revolutionary socialism that characterized at least the earlier Soviet undertaking. But he has a valid point in depicting the reduced ideological distance between them "as Communism became increasingly national and Fascism increasingly social" (1999, 208). Both were built on the widespread socioeconomic desperation and destruction of war and defeat, and both were modern and, in different ways, popular responses to the capitalist crisis.[13] However, the communist forces everywhere engaged themselves in antifascist struggle and made an essential, monumental contribution to the allied victory in 1945. The categorical differences between the two ideologies and movements are no less than the following three points: first, the right-wing populist parties did not have a program even remotely compatible with what the communists envisioned and began to pursue in their idealist phases—abolishing private exploitation and creating a classless society with free associations of free producers.[14] In this case, *pace* Furet (in explaining Elie Halevy and clarifying two kinds of tyranny including Bolshevism), "dictatorship was a provisional stage on the political state's path to liberty, whereas tyranny lacked that horizon" (1999, 207–8). Second, such core communist preoccupations as egalitarianism and internationalism were nowhere found in the fascist ideologies. Despite its anticapitalist rhetoric and selective union links, "national socialism" was no more than a peculiar variant of capitalism.[15] Third, as Charles Lindblom observes, "while fascist indoctrination appealed to unconscious, irrational motives, a preceptoral system appeals to the conscious and rational" (1977, 59).[16] The term "preceptoral" refers to communist socialization in order precisely for it to be distinguished from fanaticism. This leads, finally, to the case of the Nazis being not only anticommunist and anti-liberal, but also committed to racial genocide and military conquest. The Stalin regime at its worst (the great purge, Gulag, anti-Semitism, and deportation of the minorities) was beyond meaningful comparison.

The paradigm of the developmental state based primarily on the empirical studies of late development in East Asia, on the other hand, offers genuine comparative attractions. This paradigm is remarkably nuanced in its methodological pluralism against established ideologies. The main insight of these studies, unshaken by the Asian financial crisis of 1997–1998, is about the indispensability of a strong and dedicated state capable of "governing the market."[17] It is the state's "infrastructural capacity" and its functions of protection and promotion that may ensure sustained national growth, basic financial stability, optimal foreign investment and trade, needed technological transfers, and relative equity in social policies. At issue is not the amount or size of government but its policy objectives and effectiveness. Sharing important features in such a model, the capitalist developmental state is nevertheless not a ready analogy for the socialist accumulation regime. Disciplining both labor and capital was indeed also a reality in the "workers' state" without private capitalism, where the government, too, intervenes to "get the prices wrong" so as to manipulate the profits while keeping wages low, consumption repressed, and union activities contained (cf. Amsden 1989). However, the communist regimes were legitimized on an ideological commitment to labor and public welfare and, once again, needed even greater state autonomy to achieve control and guidance in a hostile international environment. The fact that for decades the United States did not permit "free trade" or Japanese-style neomercantilism anywhere beyond the cold war coalition in Asia ensured that the PRC would not open up.

Developmental advantages and disadvantages for the PRC also especially differed from those of the democratic postindependence states that followed a path of colonial modernity. The contrast between the earlier paths predictably had a lasting effect on their respective subsequent developments. Indeed, public expectation of what the government ought to deliver was much higher in China than in most developing countries; and, furthermore, socialist industrialization in the Chinese context generated its own set of problems and solutions due to its specific internal and external constraints. An India-China comparison reveals that "liberal democracy in India may actually have reduced pressures for more far-reaching reforms" beneficial to the population, such as a land reform (Randall 1997, 216). A higher and more equitable growth, an "unusual compatibility," may not be achievable without the power of state authority and public action more available in China but "more difficult to implement in democratic and liberal economies like that of India" (Bhalla 1995, 292).

It is unsettled as to whether a developmental state has to be authoritarian in social science modeling; or, further, whether a socialist developmental state can be democratic (cf. White 1988; Robinson and White 1998). What matters for development, Adrian Leftwich argues, "is not the system of government, or regime type . . . but the type of *state*" (1996, 5; 1995). A misjudgment of the Asian crisis comes in faulting the model altogether for the damages; in so doing the real issue is missed as to whether such a state can be democratized while maintaining its developmental abilities of surplus retention and income redistribution.[18] Is there a democratic model for the developing countries to surmount "development of underdevelopment" or "dependent development"? (Frank 1969; Evans 1979). The "trade-off" thesis—between economic satisfaction and political freedom, growth and democracy—is rightly rejected, even though democratization has actually been resisted or postponed in the perceived interest of development in many places. The reason for this lag might be the actual discord between democracy taken as a mere introduction of multiparty elections and as popular demands for equal citizenship and government accountability. If the "democratic transition" as in Eastern Europe or electoral "bureaucratic authoritarianism" as in Latin America (O'Donnell and Schmitter 1986) could not improve the quality of ordinary lives, as was the case in large parts of these regions, then why should similar changes be imitated elsewhere?

It was the extraordinary degree of state autonomy, authority, and governability that enabled China to first pursue self-reliance and later take the risk of "relinking." Neither of these strategies would have worked without a powerful socialist state. It remains hopeful for the reform project that by retaining such a state even the private marketplace could be socially managed through rational devices, and even the dynamics of profit making could be channeled to satisfy public needs. It had been believed from the beginning that authoritarianism in the name of either a "people's democratic dictatorship" or a "socialism with Chinese characteristics" was a price to pay for the necessity of surmounting the contradiction of "socialism and backwardness." The paradox, however, is that once the state took control over societal (and personal) affairs for the perceived public good, it also undermined a vital aspect of the revolution's emancipatory ideal. The logic of statism overtaking nationalism in nation-building is the same as that of statism hijacking socialism in development.

Thus is the dilemma of the social-national-developmental configuration of China's alternative modernity, a dilemma beneath the ups and downs and interactions of each and all the forces involved. Nationalism's persistent strength had found diverse expressions in the reform period—from the "patriotic" student movement in protest against official corruption and mismanagement in 1989 to the popular support for the government's opposition to the NATO bombing in Belgrade in 1999 or to the U.S.-Taiwan arms trade and the U.S.-Japanese defense treaties. Even the eager "globalizers" in the post-Deng leadership dared not lower the Chinese nationalist banner. Nationalism thus continued to set limits on, provide the ground for, and align otherwise divided groups in political discourse and actions. The communist ideologues had also appealed to Confucian ethics in an awkward "civilization" rhetoric as an attempted antidote to social disillusionment and political apathy. Developmentalism meanwhile was dictating the order of the day, competing with nationalism as the regime's soundest remaining source of legitimation. In the place of Mao's "politics in command" was the economy with Deng's motto that "development is a hard truth." This nonnegotiable principle of growth over social and ecological considerations resulted in a mindless developmental priority.[19] It pushed developmentalism to such an extreme that significant rectification must be called for if only to deter the mounting adversaries for the regime to survive by rebalancing the triadic foundation of the Chinese model.

After all, development and socialism are mutually required in coherence in the original articulation. If development separates itself from socialism, much of what the revolution fought for and what the post-revolutionary public-good regime achieved would be reversed. The weakening of socialism understood in its Chinese context threatens collapse of the Chinese model itself because socialism is the key link of China's alternative modernity. By losing it the Chinese project would cease to be an alternative and would lose its greatest credibility as compared with either Stalinist socialism or third world capitalism.

Egalitarianism's Predicament: The Politics of Class

In Chinese communist terminology, especially the reform discourse, one version of "egalitarianism" (*pingjun zhuyi*) has born a peculiarly negative connotation associated with the traditional petty peasant aspiration (rather than a designated proletarian outlook) for small holdings of the land and for equity in land distribution.[20] This notion was also less congenial to the arguments advanced by the contemporary egalitarians than to what was warned against in the Tocquevillean perception of equality being over-stretched to hamper liberty (1968, 258ff) or in the Nietzschean cry for meritorious recognition (instead of the flat and identical last men). In finding analogous Marx's conception of the French peasantry as "sacks of potatoes" needing a despot to "represent" them, "egalitarianism" became a standard target of criticism by the post-Mao critics of "agrarian socialism" and the "ultra-left" ideological zest of the Cultural Revolution; so much so that "egalitarian" tendency was related to the "feudal tyranny" and there-fore not only was theoretically but also politically unacceptable.[21] The self-awareness of the Chinese revolution's agrarian origin meant that its ideol-ogy was especially sensitive to anything deemed less than adequate by the modern working-class criteria. In fact the premodern idea of small-scale farming, and with it the sentiment of equal sharing under heaven, were rejected in communist political education.[22]

Political Equality and Class Struggle

The Maoist bid to equalize society had an impact yet to be digested in development thinking. It included goals as grand as "eliminating the three great distinctions" between industry and agriculture, town and country, and manual and mental labor; replacing centralized bureaucracy with self-managed people's communes; and dismantling the rigid division of labor. These goals were the subject of many experiments but did not succeed overall. The urban-rural divide was sophisticatedly institutionalized in a way that deprived the rural population of any fundamental freedom of upward mobility toward city life. Although the developmental gap between the coastal and inland provinces was narrowed through deliberate policies as well as by otherwise hugely wasteful "third line" industries, regional cleavages persisted. Class-based income inequalities, sectoral disparity, and rural poverty remained outstanding while the standards of living either stagnated or declined in the late Mao period (Riskin 1987, chapter 6, 1990; Selden 1988). The system was to exhaust its moral glamor as the post-revolutionary promises on both welfare provision and democracy were unfulfilled.

By the early 1980s, as noted by the editors of a collection of reappraisals of the Cultural Revolution, "the failure of the egalitarianism of the Cultural Revolution to motivate higher levels of productivity underlay the resurgence of elite and mass support for 'letting a few people get rich first' " (Joseph et al. 1991, 14); the new approach thus openly encouraged significant inequalities. That "support," however, was limited as it was later withdrawn in the face of the widespread polarization between the rich and poor. Along the way, not only did the reform ideology repudiate the socialist principle of equality by confusing it with a backward-looking "egalitarianism," it also in effect legitimized inequalities. Strangely enough, the language of class was abandoned, and class consciousness was repressed, precisely at a time when economic classes and class conflicts reemerged. To understand the political economy of the PRC before the reform—and then the reform itself in its two phases—a quick look at the history of Maoist class politics is in order.

If class analysis had always been engaged in an oversimplified fashion in the Chinese revolution (e.g., during the land reform campaigns), class definition became all the more problematic after the completion of nationalization and collectivization. Other than occupational difference, social class now had to be determined without an actual basis in economic relations. It was thus done "objectively" by a given person or group's previous class identity and/or family origin, and "subjectively" by the political stand and behavior of the subject in question (Schram 1989, 166). In the specific post-1949 context, "class enemies" referred to the remnants of the old exploitative and reactionary classes as well as elements allegedly associated with the subversive forces abroad and in Taiwan. This latter dimension was in the background against which such quasi-class categories as "spies," "counterrevolutionaries," and "rightists" could be decoded (Kraus 1977; Watson 1984). In addition, according to Mao, since the transformation of productive relations alone was insufficient and the battleground rather concentrated in the superstructure, class struggle must be waged at the political and ideological level through mass movements against the bureaucrats and a "bourgeoisie born anew" within the communist party. The inner-party "two-line opposition" thus mirrored intensified class struggle in the long transitional period (Dittmer 1977).

The CCP's eighth national congress in 1956 resolved that class-based, large-scale political movements should come to an end and the party must focus its effort on economic construction; for no longer was the "basic contradiction" of Chinese society class conflict, but rather conflict between its backward productive forces and advanced relations of production. Mao, alarmed by Khrushchev's de-Stalinization in the Soviet Union and the uprisings in Hungary and Poland, personally reversed that resolution in 1957. His message of "never forget class struggle" defined as "between the proletariat and the bourgeoisie, between the socialist road and the capitalist road" became a national slogan (1962, 492), and it took the country more than two decades to return to the 1956 line in the post-Mao 1978 party plenary session. In hindsight this was a detour, yet it is worth asking why Mao was able to gain the sufficient degree of elite consensus and especially the mass following that he apparently enjoyed in the following storms of popular mobilization. The purges, mainly of intellectuals in the "anti-rightist" campaign (1957), of party officials committed to "rightist opportunism" (1959–1960), and of corrupt local cadres in a "socialist education" movement (1964–1965), were accompanied by massive denunciations of "revisionism" and "bourgeois humanism and individualism" (which peaked in 1962–1965). The nationwide campaign of "learning from the PLA" and the model soldier Lei Feng since 1964 was of a different nature, which popularized one of the PRC's most seductive axioms, "serving the people," and was later remembered with nostalgia as part of the post-reform "Mao fever." These events were preludes to the Cultural Revolution launched in 1966 that, as common perception has it after the fact, was a nightmare of political catastrophe for the regime itself (see chapter 3). The Cultural Revolution interrupted the optimistic developments of the country recovering from the famine and, most remarkably, testing its first atomic bomb in 1964 and repaying its entire domestic and foreign debt the following year.

In the socialist theory, social equality is not in conflict with class struggle because socialism aims at eliminating inequalities as the results of class exploitation and oppression. The actual taking of class struggle as the "key link" in China without a ground in the economic relations, however, undermined equality as a culture and policy principle of socialism. On the one hand, socialism was deemed a transitional stage toward classlessness that demanded steps not only to abolish class divisions but also toward the withering away of the state. Mao thus compares the CCP and "the political parties of the bourgeoisie" as follows: "They are afraid to speak of the extinction of classes, state power and parties. We, on the contrary, declare openly that we are striving hard to create the very conditions which will bring about their extinction." In a dialectical twist, he states that the "leadership of the Communist Party and the state power of the people's dictatorship are such conditions" (1949, 411). On the other hand, he also believes that "contradictions among the people" can be correctly handled only in the larger context of clashes between the people and their enemies, clashes that inevitably intensify during the long transitional period from capitalism to communism (1957). Here as Wang Ruoshui argues, Mao mistook social relations and interests, which as an institutional matter should be regulated through the democratic means within the legal bound, for a question of epistemology and ruling method, thus paving the way for arbitrary politics (1998). While rejecting the "revisionist fallacy" of denying class contradictions in the conception of an all-inclusive state and party of Soviet society, Mao's "philosophy of struggle" ended up devastating the Chinese project not so much by slowing down the economy as by splitting the citizenry and victimizing innocent individuals.

The history of the PRC shows that the state acted as the supreme arbiter within the given social structure but above social classes however defined. That state was not the agent for any specific class (as compared to the latest case of state sponsorship for entrepreneurship of which any conceptualization is as yet immature) in a cross-class agenda of national development. Being instrumental for "socialist modernization," the PRC state was certainly very far from symbolizing the political rule of the working class. In other words, at once socialist, nationalist, and developmentalist, the Chinese model had to be class blind despite its intense language and episodes of "class struggle" in the Mao years. The level of simultaneous state autonomy from, and embeddedness in, society was so high that the state effectively dictated classes and class structure, ideologically, culturally, and administratively.[23] Not surprisingly, the knowledge production of the meanings of class in the processes of class formation and reformation was as inventive and ad hoc as it was confusing.[24]

The Urban-Rural Divide

The sweeping yet step-by-step rural collectivization in China began soon after the land reform under the CCP's "general line for the transition to socialism" proclaimed in 1953. It took on four incrementally upgraded organizational forms in a short timespan of six years: mutual aid groups, primitive cooperatives, advanced cooperatives, and people's communes. This was an organic part of the socialist economic transformation and the first five-year plan, reaching the apex in the Great Leap Forward in 1958.[25] The project, researchers agree, proceeded largely on a voluntary basis "with neither the violence nor the massive sabotage characteristic of Soviet collectivization" (Selden 1982, 85); it was a "miracle of miracles" (Friedman 1982, 205). The contrast, as explained by Barry Naughton, lay in the experience of the Chinese agrarian revolution as well as in the party's carefully steered moves to organize collective farms; collectivization "was carried out smoothly primarily because, unlike their Soviet predecessors, the Chinese had already established a network of state-controlled institutions in the countryside" (1991, 230).[26] There was also something running deeper. The urgent need to reorganize a scattered and primitive agricultural sector arose from the nearly impossible task of financing industry (as discussed above) and, equally pressing, from the fear, with signs visible, of rural polarization. A new regime that came into existence through a peasant revolution would not be able to afford another revolutionary situation in the countryside. The first test of a crucial worker-peasant alliance would be the relationship between the communist government and the agrarian population. As Liu Shaoqi sees it, "the future of socialism relies on not only a proletarian state and a big industry but also cooperatives"; and meanwhile agriculture cannot grow healthily without the support of a developed industrial sector (1993, 54). Yet in the end the internal accumulation process prevented the collectives from retaining wealth for their members. The communes at the eve of the reform were poor with a low level of productivity, income, and work incentives. Even William Hinton (1994), the ardent defender of Maoist communal socialism, admits that 70 percent of the communes had failed or stagnated by the 1970s.[27]

The household registration (*hukou*) system, a main institutional expression of socialist urban bias, was set up in China in 1955. For the next three decades it secured a virtual urban-rural segregation. Controls over mobility from agricultural to nonagricultural sectors were tight. Rural residents did not have the same access to important goods available to city dwellers, such as employment with retirement and fringe benefits. Subsidized food and housing, guaranteed schooling, and health service were urban privileges. This arrangement amounted to a rigid quasi-caste division in which the peasants were second-class citizens. The result was a "dual society" of one country, two worlds, a construct that "decisively shaped China's collectivist socialism by creating a spatial hierarchy of urban places and prioritizing the city over the countryside" (Cheng and Selden 1994, 645). This structural inequality was poison to the party's image and alienated the revolution's historical constituency; and in the long run it eroded the moral foundation of Chinese socialism. Mao and his colleagues knew the predicament only too well: As Mao stated, "The Soviet Union has adopted measures which squeeze the peasants very hard. It takes away too much from the peasants at too low a price . . . This method of capital accumulation has seriously dampened the peasants' enthusiasm for production" (1956, 291). In spite of such criticism, however, they were unable to translate their words into an alternative policy. For, as Naughton points out, maintaining an "absolute level of profitability of industry" through urban priorities and the price scissors was unavoidable for big-push industrialization, which was "precisely what the Chinese economy needed." Abstract morality makes little sense: there was "simply no other adequate source of savings" (1991, 231–32).[28]

It would be a mistake, however, to view the nature of the state-peasant relationship in communist China as antagonistic and coercive, not least because collectivization enjoyed some genuine enthusiasm from below. Collectively arranged welfare even partially substituted for government provisions (cf. Selden 1988, 210). Schools and clinics in the villages were mostly free of charge, with formally trained as well as "barefoot" teachers and doctors. The grassroots women's federations fought the patriarchal tradition in its rural strongholds with help from local government authorities. Developed from the mass campaigns in the 1950s to enforce sanitation and disease-prevention measures to eliminating epidemics, China had accomplished a successful "public health revolution," institutionalized in the countryside by village-based cooperative medical care alongside more advanced urban medical service.[29] Together the national system achieved coverage by the late 1970s of "nearly the entire urban and 85 percent of the rural population, an unrivaled achievement among low-income countries" (World Bank 1993, 210–11; 1994, 1–17). In addition to basic collective welfare, the Chinese peasantry, perhaps the least dependent class in the PRC, allowed themselves a measured degree of internalization of certain communist ideas and organizational patterns. The integrated social-national-developmental project endured a mechanism of hardship bearing and sharing, at least for a great portion of the Mao period. Subtly and uniquely, much of the suffering was blamed on the extrinsic factors and even "compensated" by a deliberate politics of recognition and dignity that glorified "poor and lower-middle peasants" in their constitutional alliance with the workers.

This helps explain how government monopoly and manipulation over rural surplus could succeed even at the expense of the regime's own legitimating basis. Nowhere was the reach of the communist power—which must have carried with it the inertia of the moral appeal of the communist revolution—more revealing than in the willful policies of the Great Leap, which led to the great famine.[30] As Brantly Womack remarks, "Only a government that had been built from the countryside and had the self-confidence of popular support could have been strong enough to cause a disaster of such magnitude" (1991, 75). His point drives home the extraordinary degree of revolutionary legitimacy in China, given the ancient Chinese tradition of peasant rebellions provoked by food shortage or excessive grain seizure. While during the famine a number of provincial borders in the disaster regions were patrolled by police, this fact cannot explain the absence of revolt. A more convincing reason might be the lack of peasant associations, but rural protests are frequent occurrences today in spite of the nonexistence of any such large and independent organizations. Thus it appears that the "three-year period of difficulties" was not attributed to the party, but rather the blame was channeled from domestic policies to natural calamities and foreign hostility.

Just as the results of collectivization were mixed, decollectivization, as measured by its own objectives, was also marked by multifaceted results. For all its deficiencies, rural reforms in the early 1980s raised prices for farm products, eased restrictions on migration, and nurtured a free-wheeling development of TVEs.[31] Rural industrialization was not new but rather "a central pillar of Mao's developmental strategy" (Wong 1991, 183). Still, it was of a different nature in an autarkic economy and no match to the TVEs in scale.[32] Major post-reform gains came in the efforts to dismantle the sectoral and occupational discrimination embedded in the resident registration system, to remove class labels against the landless "landlords" and no richer "rich peasants," and so create legislation for village elections. Considered a huge success, the expansion of rural industries from their rudimentary basis in the Great Leap and Cultural Revolution reduced various disparities and absorbed a large number of superfluous rural laborers. The peasant-turned-workers now produced mainly for the market—local, national, and frequently also international—and provided China with its second largest labor market (Wang Fei-Ling 1998, chapter 4). Sociologists describe China in the 1990s as an "industrializing country, peasant society," where a rural, while mobile, population still made up 70 percent of the national total, but among them at least a third were engaged in nonagricultural activities. The flourishing TVEs brought employment and cash income to the locals as well as to migrants, and for quite a while they tended to be community-oriented in their public functions (in terms of productive or educational infrastructure and cultural entertainment) due to traditional collectivist ties, both kinship and communal. The rationale behind the support for the TVEs declined later as the problems of losing precious cropland, and of increased pollution and poor labor conditions, worsened. Many enterprises also became productively wasteful in competition with better-equipped and better-managed firms in the urban sector, and the waves of their closures or privatization in the late 1990s set back the already daunting level of collectivity in extensively affected areas.

After an initial liberalizing effect, the dissolution of communes turned out to be disastrous wherever the collective networks of maintenance and welfare collapsed. The initial innovation was a system of self-governing "double-level management" that combined individual household farming and organized social support. Such support was to include government and cooperative assistance in production, finance (e.g., credit co-ops), marketing, technology, infrastructural work, and information, consultation, and other logistic services, as well as basic provision of education, health care, and poverty relief.[33] In many localities the double-level design simply did not materialize, leaving a single level of unorganized peasants unprotected in the face of fluctuating natural and market environments, deficient investment and subsidies, and overtaxation. It is notable that some of these problems were similar to the conditions that earlier gave rise to the dynamics of the collectivization movements. Further, such problems also had a grave consequence, as became all too evident later. As John Burns notes: "If peasant interest articulation is widespread, but not institutionalized, instability is a likely result" (1984, 126). Another imminent effect of the failure of double-level management was China's lack of preparation for its World Trade Organization membership. Potential opportunities for technological improvement and quality control notwithstanding, the country would be unable to compete with agricultural imports flowing in with weak barriers. The "triple problem" of farming, farmland, and farmers (*sannong wenti*) loomed large on China's developmental horizon.

Returning to the question of class, if peasant spontaneity catalyzed the dissolution of communes, and in the process turned the party leadership into a "followship," the move also paved the way for rural class reformation. The (re)making of classes and the resumption of class conflicts had, however, been thus far contained by political intervention from above. In theory, the socialist state is the vehicle for society to achieve equality, classlessness, and eventually self-management without bureaucracy. In reality, the PRC state first institutionalized the urban-rural divide and later allowed the old forms of class inequalities to be restored in the marketplace. Both sets of policies addressed China's developmental imperative and can be comprehended in their respective contexts of constraints and stimulus. Yet, the pending task of seeking an alternative that does not subordinate socialism to a developmental or nationalist mandate still awaits an answer. Clearly the reform did not stop the exploitation of peasants; in fact, it added to the familiar ways of state extraction not only a swelling layer of local bureaucrats but also private appropriators. The picture still largely revolved around the rural surplus in line with the insight of moral economy.[34]

"Work Unit Socialism"

The cities, too, had undergone a sea change featured by industrial restructuring, the fragmentation of workers, and the inflow of rural immigrants. In the 1990s an urban underclass appeared, which was composed of laid-off workers, migrants looking for jobs, and low-paid laborers in privately owned manufacturing and service industries. Thus a "floating population" joined the reserve army of the unemployed in fluctuating proportions at an annual size of approximately 100 million as estimated in 2004. Individuals in this "floating" category were often treated as outcasts in terms of lacking residential and related entitlements, such as getting essential licences and sending their children to schools without extra fees or enrollment restrictions (Solinger 1999). A large number of small- and medium-sized state-owned enterprises (SOEs) dismissed their employees while selling themselves often at a reduced price to their former managers. Giant SOEs in their transformation into joint-stock corporations also cut loose from public control and adopted streamlining for efficiency. Between 1998 and 2002, employment in the state sector fell by nearly a third, for a total of 26.8 million job losses, and the reemployment rate was no more than 15 to 20 percent (CASS 2003). Side by side with the shortage of work numerous sweatshops mushroomed, none of which, by definition, met the minimal legal requirements for labor conditions and environmental regulations. As workers' unrest erupted from one place to another, a 2001 report by the party's central organization department acknowledged that "an outstanding feature of the current contradictions among the people is the increase of their antagonistic tendencies."[35]

Although the existence of workers' representation in factory assemblies was legally binding on paper,[36] workers were not independently organized in the SOEs and were scarcely unionized in the private sector and in migrant labor. Of China's 350 million waged employees in 2003, only 130 million were union members (Li 2003). While nonstate enterprises hit 2.97 million and grew from producing 10 percent of GDP in 1989 to 50 percent in 2003,[37] many of their 25 million workers were not even aware of their legal and organizational rights. However, it is confusing to state that the issue was the banning of independent unions, for it ignores the fact that in China's public sectors, at least, it was still the state itself that symbolized organized labor and labor protection. The All China Federation of Trade Unions (ACFTU) did not exist politically, because as an official extension of the workers' state it logically could not function, and did not need to, in any real sense of class politics. Only the dismantling of such a state, as was slowly happening and reflected in formal ideology, rationalized independent unions. Limited union reforms had been underway for twenty years, while cadres, researchers, and activists were learning the new concepts from "collective bargaining" to "labor-capital partnership" and "co-management."[38] Worth noting is the fact that the idea of industrial democracy in the Maoist legacy is restated in the Labor Law (1994), alongside protective measures against abuses in employment contracts, minimum wages, workplace safety, and work hours and benefits. A typical circular, issued from the center in June 2002, further instructed "making enterprise affairs known to the public via workers' supervision," and called for labor participation—through activating workers' assemblies and delegations—in major managerial decisions over production, operation, finance, and work contracting.[39] The implementation of these laws and regulations had been worse than problematic, yet they were significant in what must be seen as a continuous collective striving to preserve the basic norms of socialism.

An adequate assessment of the pre-reform experiences must be sought in light of the radical changes in the distribution of power and wealth both within and outside of the workforce in China. A view common to both the Chinese mainstream and foreign commentators is that state-sector employees enjoyed a status of quasi-labor aristocracy especially during the Mao period, which curbed work incentive and productivity. This easy verdict, however, deserves a threefold critical response. First, contrary to the widespread belief that the state sector is bound to be inefficient, in China that sector remained the chief contributor, with substantial productive gains, to the nation's fast-growing economy. From 1995 to 2002, the number of industrial SOEs fell from 77,600 to about 42,000, while their total profit surged by 163.6 percent. By 2000, the state sector still accounted for 47 percent of China's industrial assets, 34 percent of the national annual output, about half of government revenue, and a third of urban employment. The 474 flagship SOEs reported a 42.1 percent profit growth in the first seven months of 2004.[40] Many "solutions" to the unexamined problems based on the dogma of a deficient and burdensome state sector are in need of critical scrutiny (Nolan 1996; Lo 1997, 1999). Those SOEs that indeed lost money and operated by borrowing from government banks did so for complicated reasons, including, in particular, unequal competition in a "distorted" market by deliberate policies in which SOEs were burdened by much higher income and value-added tax rates than were foreign joint and private companies who enjoyed tax breaks during the transition. Experts reckon that the actual tax burden for SOEs and other domestic firms is at a rate of 22 percent as contrasted with 11 percent for foreign companies (Zuo 2005). Also apparent is the unfair calculation in the existing accounting system in which enterprise-based welfare spending implied higher labor cost. Nation-wide, large SOEs still ran tens of thousands of nurseries, schools, hospitals, and service centers today. Some of these enterprises actually increased factor productivity by technological and technical improvements, yet could not maintain profitability at a socially responsible employment and welfare level. Others sometimes were also pressed to produce unprofitable products for national considerations beyond the interest of individual enterprises (cf. Lardy 1998a).

Second, it should be reasonable to argue that there is nothing wrong with job security and other such benefits for workers, not only from a socialist moral point of view but also in view of incentive-based economic rationality.[41] The dignity and well-being of labor, morally and institutionally built into a self-conscious socialist state, was a magnificent accomplishment of the Chinese revolution and cannot be coherently repudiated by any such state. What was indeed wrong about the state payroll were its privileges—the provision schemes were stratified and (partially) excluded the collective, contracted, and agricultural sectors—and their socio-psychological consequences of hierarchy and dependency. The reform, by the market logic, instead of working toward sustainability and universalization of public welfare, had been driven by smashing the "iron rice bowl" as an obstacle to work incentives and a drag on efficiency. It pursued changes as though security, coupled with political-social esteem, did not and would not yield dedication, creativity, and responsible performance. To clarify, factors other than material benefits must also be taken into account here, from general social relations and working environment to personal and collective reciprocity, solidarity, and pride. These factors certainly changed from the revolutionary or mobilizational times to "normal" or routine ones. High morale might not always be expectable, but nor was it accountable only for material attributes (cf. Riskin 1973; Walder 1982, 221–27; Frazier 2002).

That is, the demise of an "iron bowl" system of work units (*danwei*) would have a greater impact on society than what unemployment and forced early retirement already implied. The *danwei* model that covered productive and service enterprises (*qiye danwei*) as well as administrative and other government institutions (*shiye danwei*) was successful in its triple function for both the state and individuals involved in managing labor, organizing and protecting social and individual life, and maintaining control (cf. Shaw 1996; Lu and Perry 1997; Gu 1998). Apart from public provision and services (e.g., the large units often ran their own clinics and schools, as mentioned above), the socialist workplace was designed also to nurture collective spirit and work-related identities. To be sure, without "wage labor" in a typical capitalist labor market of the free selling and free movement of labor, security-loyalty came with a "feudal" element of immobility and hierarchical attachment-conformity. Yet precisely here, on both accounts, losing *danwei* meant more than the loss of a means of living. What could not be compensated by any safety net or alternative sources of income was social exclusion and alienation in the form of being cut off from the connections of belonging. At the macromanagement level, "work unit socialism" was the building block of China's political economy, and most assuredly it "distinguish[ed] everyday Chinese politics and society from the west" (Womack 1991a, 324). To indiscriminately discredit the model is to neglect history and the transaction cost of "market rationalization," a cost that might be unaffordable if the pain and destruction could not be mitigated. Entrepreneurial restructuring and administrative downsizing would have to reinvent, rather than discard, the socially beneficial aspects of the old system (cf. Saich 1984; Lee 1998).

Third, although special care for the state-sector should be negated only on the grounds that the subsidies were limited to a minority of the workforce, thereby permitting state-sanctioned structural inequalities and statist efficacy, the old privileges were born by a nominal doctrine of workers as the "leading class" in a socialist polity. The workers were protected and glorified without enjoying the actual power of ruling or self-governing, and they were at once socially honored and politically subordinated. In the end, preferential treatment and abstract esteem could not be a tradeoff for democratic leadership and citizenship. Since those on state payrolls (and their families) relied on much of what was unavailable to the majority of the population (and hence became dependent on the system) they hardly developed a vision of self-mastery or the means to it. By allowing themselves to be indirectly "represented" by the party-state, industrial workers in particular were not in a class position as a "class-in-itself" in the Hegelian-Marxian sense of a distinctive class consciousness, and were disciplined under the supreme command of national development.

The transition from "low wage, full employment" (in the urban section and with hidden forms of unemployment and underemployment) to a free labor market has altered the moral and institutional foundation of Chinese society. Yet as the vital social-national-developmental endeavor is not viable without active workers' participation, they remain as much the backbone of today's market economy as they were in the days of socialist planning. Even an incoming "knowledge economy" in an information age, or Deng's revisionist wisdom of counting intellectuals (and now, semiofficially, the entrepreneurs for their "managerial labor" as well) as "part of the working class," would not reduce the weight of workers. Although capital grabs power in the marketplace, the status and plight of labor is a determinant as much as an indicator of the popular mandate in China, of which the constitutional identification remains one with "primary-stage socialism." Hu Jintao and his colleagues had little choice but to repeatedly reaffirm "the pioneering position of the Chinese working class."[42]

The founding legitimacy of the PRC was no longer intact in the face of the peripheralization and degradation of workers in the public sphere. Their latent political strength can be traced to the great revolutionary tradition in which it gathered momentum in the powerful strikes and uprisings in Guangdong and Shanghai against imperialism in the 1920s and the massive surges of factory agitation against the GMD regime in the 1940s. Most striking was the dual nature of labor unrest in the 1990s onwards as both a positive confirmation of the socialist reform and a resistance to the "rational virtue" of capitalist degeneration. The fact that workers were enraged more by fraud than by lost jobs or unpaid wages and pensions, which stripped labor of its rewards, speaks loudly about where the reform path had taken a wrong turn. By opposing corrupt cadres, incompetent managers, and especially outright robbers of public assets through illegal privatization (in the peculiar forms of "insider deals" or "management buyouts") a renewed, nascent labor movement had declared its devotion to public property and its faith, however lingering, in a workers' state. Meanwhile, the peculiarity of the politics of labor in China was such that the state for its part still had to side with labor on fundamental issues and in formal gesture, even though too often the government, especially at local levels, became pro-money and pro-business at the expense of labor's interests.[43] The stance of workers was a testimony to the vitality of socialism and its weighty bearing in China. Moreover, the opposition to privatization and polarization had been winning broad social support, both urban and rural, including support from some previously freemarket leaning liberals, as shown in the resurgent popularity of the Chinese language of "social justice" at the beginning of the twenty-first century.

Three Lives of the National Bourgeoisie

The favored position of business classes, replacing workers, in a reformed, market-facilitating state, contradicted the communist ideology at its core. China's new economic elite of industrial, financial, and commercial entrepreneurs, however, constituted no ordinary class and possessed no unified identity. The continuities of class character between such elites and their pre-1956 predecessors were detectable but patchy. Yet only by obtaining an overview of a native capitalism's evolution in modern Chinese history can we put the current market transition in perspective. This is so also because despite a standard category of the national bourgeoisie elaborated in the theories of the new democratic revolution, the united front, and noncapitalist development, the historical experience and role of that class was distant and contorted in the Chinese collective memory.

The birth of a national bourgeoisie around the Qing reformers' "Westernization movement" (*yangwu yundong*) in the second part of the nineteenth century was a product of China's modern crisis culminated by foreign stimulation vis-à-vis a dying dynasty at home. China, with its people harmed, territory invaded, and architecture and cultural treasures destroyed or looted, was made to pay an astronomical sum in silver for the destruction to the invaders (including the Britain of the opium wars, the number one "drug country" in modern world history). Financially devastated by the reparations, the country, once believed the wealthiest on earth, found itself in poverty and despair by the early twentieth century. The slowly growing Chinese bourgeoisie was politically and economically crippled by a weak state, a gentry bureaucracy, and multiple imperialist powers. But it also in many ways tied in with these forces, not least in terms of investment and trade. Historically, as Barrington Moore notes, "China, like Russia, entered the modern era with a numerically small and politically dependent middle class. This stratum did not develop an independent ideology of its own as it did in Western Europe" (1966, 177). Nevertheless, it formed political groupings and contributed to the dissolution of the mandarin ruling class. The fact that the national bourgeoisie bypassed state power in the wake of the republican revolution explained its persistent weakness. Vacillating between rival political forces, this bourgeois class by and large allied itself with the communists in a nationalist revolution to remove what was popularly known as the "three big mountains of imperialism, bureaucratic capitalism and feudalism" that lay like a dead weight on its own growth.[44]

In the theory first formulated in Moscow and later translated into the Chinese context, the underdeveloped national bourgeoisie in the east, wavering and timid, would be incapable of revolutionary leadership comparable to its classical Western counterparts in the age of transition from feudalism to capitalism.[45] The "new democratic revolution," as discussed in chapter 1, was a historical as much as a conceptual invention. It had distinct goals of an initial mixture of limited capitalism and experimental socialism, and subsequently socialist rather than capitalist development. The communist leadership and state power were thought to be the guarantee for such a direction. The revolution indeed paved the way for China's socialist modernization, which was rapid, uneven, and costly and did not exactly follow the steps projected for it. Beginning with the 1953 "general line," the capitalist sector was abolished from the economy by sweeping nationalization and socialization in a mere three years. The process, though peaceful and in parallel with the agricultural cooperative movements, was radical enough to abort the short-lived program of "new democracy" considered one of the party's "brilliant successes" (CCP 1981, 588). The innovative scheme of property redemption was an outstanding alternative to the violent Soviet method of confiscation.[46]

A reason for this haste, despite a shared, sober acknowledgment that it would be "sheer utopian" to "want to build socialism on the semi-colonial and semi-feudal ruins" without a stage of new democratic mediation, was the surge in capitalist activities. The young regime felt uneasy and threatened (while also under the pressure of war in Korea). It launched a campaign in 1952 against the "sinister five" (bribery, tax evasion, theft of public property, cheating on government contracts, and stealing state economic information) allegedly committed by private businessmen (Gardner 1969). This campaign was preceded by a rectification campaign of the "three evils" of corruption, waste, and bureaucratic work style within the ranks of party and government cadres. Mao already spoke about class struggle in the early 1950s involving the revolution's former ally. The departure from new democracy had been viewed by many throughout the succeeding course as a lost opportunity, a mistaken and premature rush to socialism.

Whatever the disagreements, it is uncontroversial that the primary outcome of the socialist transformation was the state itself taking the role of capital accumulation and surplus extraction. Such a supreme position of the state, reminiscent of Lenin's state capitalism of new economic policy (NEP), had been rationalized long before the developmental state model came into fashion. The subordination not only of an indigenous capitalist class but also of the working classes was desirable as a consequence. A further peculiarity was that the size of the former was far smaller than the latter because the number and organizational power of workers also grew around foreign capital before 1949. After 1956, moreover, no longer with any actual means of production and circulation, the feeble national bourgeoisie still had to undergo "ideological remolding" to make itself fit in a new society. It was a bizarre scene (though not entirely unique in the post World War II socialist bloc) that the industrialists, traders, financiers, and their intellectual fellow travelers of earlier times were loosely associated in their "patriotic and democratic parties" within the communist united front.

The completion of the socialization of the national economy in 1956 was a turning point for the PRC. The energy of the political campaigns afterward was mainly geared to targeting the "capitalist tendencies" and "bourgeois ideologies." Thanks to the united-front tradition, China's national bourgeoisie was not demonized until uncontrolled red guard attacks on former capitalists took place in the Cultural Revolution. As a class symbolically represented and recognized in the PRC's constitution, its individual members were given credit for their contribution to the revolution and to economic nationalism. The record of China's "red capitalists" (a phrase used by Chairman Liu Shaoqi, who was later duly denounced in the Cultural Revolution as "the chief capitalist roader") showed that they shielded underground communists, donated aircraft to the Chinese volunteers in Korea, and devoted themselves to the nation's development even after losing their own properties. In the reform era, along with individuals from overseas who wished to help their (ancestors') homeland to modernize, private "capitalists" inside China had been promoted to become "socialist entrepreneurs." With approval as well as suspicion, they found themselves nationalist, even publicly spirited, while participating in the "Glorious Project" to invest in the poor regions, or in the "Hope Project" to aid schools for rural children, as well as numerous other charity and community works.[47] The perceived need to revive the dead fostered a reconstructed tradition of the Chinese national bourgeoisie that ignored past greed, cruelty, exploitation, and injustice. Those who ran sweatshops with the aid of foreign investors, tainting the tag of "made in China," could be conveniently and even convincingly separated from this tradition.

The national bourgeoisie, viewed as a whole, had had its career interrupted time and again into three stages. It came into existence during China's first modernization effort since the 1860s (Skinner 1977; Chan 1977); showed "some definite signs of emerging from official influence and domination" around 1910 (Moore 1966, 177); and then, in relative terms, flourished in the early republican era. Next, it briefly functioned between 1949 and 1953 in a new democracy pact, playing a major part in China's economic rehabilitation and political consolidation. Finally, with a fresh face it returned as a market economy designed to accommodate the useful tools of global capitalism. Arguably stronger than ever before in modern Chinese history, its space and potential of development would be complicated by a "bureaucratic bourgeoisie" (see the concluding chapter).

If the national bourgeoisie had a hard time in China, it was not because of any unfavorable cultural tradition but rather the specific historical conditions shaped by imperialism and revolution. Trying to develop a modern economy, China's first business generation battled between crooked officials, stingy landowners (though it was common for conservative traders and bankers also to own land), and disruptive warlords. But above all they also had to fight Western and Japanese competitors who were backed by what the Chinese described as "solid ships and powerful cannons" in control of China's foreign concessions and treaty ports (Dernberger 1975; Murphey 1977). The environment in which they strove to progress featured rural deprivation, urban chaos, and territorial and political disunity of the country and all that followed. While the absence of intervention by a monarchy or a centralized state might have been a blessing by allowing business activities to peak (stimulated by WWI) in 1914–1925, their subsequent decline also confirmed two related points. First, if peace, stability, and legal protection are given necessities, the GMD-style bureaucracy was certainly not helpful in normal market operation. The money and networks of the "big families" directly related to the government penetrated the economic and political world. Commenting on the missing "Prussian road" since Manchu China, Marie-Claire Bergere blames the "bureaucratic" choice by the late-Qing Westernizers and especially the Nanjing regime: "China's failure in this respect must be laid at the door of the Chinese state" (1989, 25; cf. Mann 1987). Second, this judgment on the state's failure rather than bureaucratic involvement per se serves as a historical justification for the Chinese revolution's state-building effort. In the same vein, any successful state project of national development had to be nationalist more than statist in the sense that the project is held above the self-interests of the rulers.

Culturalist explanations for the historical underdevelopment of capitalism and capitalist classes in China may have a point in the Chinese tradition of occupational preference based on state monopoly over commerce. But such explanations cannot stand the tests of either the recent expansion of China's market economy and its "cosmopolitan capitalists" or centuries of business success among members of the Chinese diaspora (Hamilton 1999). Instead, it has been forcefully argued that Confucian ethics, for example, may be either conducive or adverse to a particular business culture tied to a given political economy; and a similar culture may be (in)hospitable to different socioeconomic systems (cf. Redding 1990; Ong and Nonini 1997). As a matter of history, it is also true that China's political elites, from nationalists to communists and reform communists, did not attempt to take a free market "option," which was not always, if ever, actually available. There seemed to be a consensus among national developers, and that consensus became itself, so to speak, a cultural tradition. Sun, the foremost spokesman of an earlier national bourgeoisie in China, believed in the necessity and morality of "restricting capital," anticipating a tenet in contemporary thinking about the developmental state. The idea has had a vast resonance in Taiwan's path to modernization.

Comparative Assessments

In terms of the politics of class, the socialist alternative in China would not be defensible if in general practice it violated the very principles that defined the transition to socialism itself, such as eliminating exploitation and promoting equality. The Chinese experiences, however, were in a fundamental way bound to be self-contradictory and more subtle than can be expressed in any superficially totalistic appraisals. This should apply to both Maoist and reformist experiments and both the formation and reformation of the reform model.

Rural reforms in the late 1970s pioneered the process of dismantling state monopoly over sectoral exchange, mobility, the surplus, investment, and public service expenditure, all of which were conditioned on the need to facilitate industrialization at the cost of rural development. Against this background the removal of the fatal stigma of "agricultural" was immensely liberating for hundreds of millions of peasants once literally "locked" wherever they were born. Indeed, it put an end to a unique institution of developmental priority and social segregation, painful as well as poisoning to a socialist accumulation regime. In the first half of the 1980s, as the government raised the prices for grain and cotton and stimulated the growth of the TVES, average household income surged and poverty decreased (cf. data in Kelliher 1992; Yu 1997; Lu 2001).[48] The improvement of material life for a billion people across China's vast countryside was no trivial matter. Yet, it must be stressed that the work of the Maoist strategy was not in vain, not only in view of the country's industrial and accompanying achievements, but also because an infrastructural foundation was laid in the Mao years for future developments, without which many fruitful reform measures would not have been possible. Even as regards the rural sector, Peter Nolan was able to conclude that "over the long term China's collective farms did not perform disastrously. A great deal was achieved in relieving local poverty and constructing a rudimentary rural welfare system, and farm output was able to keep up with China's fast-growing population." More controversial was his opinion that apart from the many shortcomings of the people's communes, inefficiencies arose from "the managerial diseconomies of large-scale production," which showed that collective farming would be "not, usually, a useful institutional form for poor countries" (1988, 4–5). China, at least, found itself in a specific historical situation (as noted above) that rationalized the cooperative movement, if not one for the "bigger and more public" (*yi da er gong*) communes. Without seeking a general agreement, it should be reasonable to argue that the reform initially altered the typical course of capital accumulation through rural deprivation in classical capitalism as well as state socialism. Changes in the economy also had an obvious and significant political impact. It was not until the late 1980s that the positive trend slowed to a halt and living standards and local governance deteriorated in many regions. The old problems and limitations of vulnerable small-scale production had returned to haunt the reformers.

Prior to the reversal of the gains in dissolving communal socialism, Martin Whyte observes that despite the widening of inter- and intracommunity income differentials, the post-Mao reforms brought about greater equality overall among the Chinese people. The skeptics were thus mistaken in their "Maoist egalitarians versus Dengist inegalitarians" analysis. As Whyte states, "Market-oriented reforms may not, in some circumstances, promote inequality, but may instead help correct some inequalities fostered by a bureaucratic distribution system" (1986, 119). Similarly, Edward Friedman considered the reforms to have done "much better than Maoism in helping the poorest of the poor" (1987, 409). While noting the gain of "accelerated rural development and a reduction in the sharpest sectoral divisions underlying the social structure," Mark Selden warned that possible "new and potentially antagonistic social classes" would undermine these gains (1988, 180). This fear unfortunately came to pass in the subsequent polarization between the new poor, rural and urban, and the new rich; and, once again, the disparities also simultaneously developed along the urban-rural divide. By the early 1990s, grain farming was not profitable due to falling prices for staple crops relative to the prices of chemical fertilizers and water, electricity, and other industrial services. The government, soon trapped in fiscal austerity and deflation, was unable to formulate an adequate policy on subsidies and failed to intervene so as to rectify insufficient demand and below-cost prices of agricultural products for both state purchases and market retailing. On top of these difficulties, irregular land seizure by private developers through public offices became a frequent occurrence, as did overextraction (rather than agricultural subsidies) imposed by country and township authorities starving for funds.

The initially equalizing effect of reforms was thus overtaken not only by the decline in upward mobility of the low-income population but also by the groups newly impoverished by unemployment, sweatshops, the loss of hitherto free or inexpensive public provisions and services, and, in the case of mistreated migrant workers, uprooting and new forms of exploitation and urban bias. Meanwhile, the 1990s witnessed an increasing concentration of wealth in the hands of those who could grab public wealth or market profits, or both. China, of course, was not alone in its market transition, its confusing process of market allocation replacing state redistribution and bureaucracy appropriating the market, and its reinvention of equality or inequalities in many layers (Nee 1989, 1991; Nee and Liedka 1997). Certain changes initially in favor of a more equal society in some other transitional economies also diminished by the privatization of the state apparatus itself (Rona-Tas, 1994). Without lumping together China's two reform phases with the reform agenda of others, by now few would deny the fact that class polarization in China was a consequence of its derailed reform course. It was evident that the old lines that divided China into separate worlds had been preserved or redrawn along with the new ones.

Within a class-centered debate, some query whether it is the Maoist or the Dengist model that is more relevant to socialism. If socialism is about the absence of class exploitation, then both models lose out for different reasons. In the case of the Maoist experiments, an internally exploitative regime of capital accumulation had a fundamental class dimension, and the politics of class struggle in the PRC had victimized arbitrarily designated enemies (see chapter 3). In the case of the Dengist reform, the market economy re-created economic classes and conflicting class interests that had not been contained by socially more justifiable public policies. If socialism is about eliminating the "three great distinctions," the Maoist effort was most pronounced, yet it stood in stark contradiction to the institutionalization of urban bias. The reform pounded at those distinctions, only to quickly find itself defeated by their forceful resumption, a more recent expression of which was an abused citizenship for rural migrants in the cities. A typical picture would be the sad, dirty, and gritty faces of construction workers who could never even dream of moving into the buildings they built for a meager wage and miserable working conditions.[49] If socialism, finally, is about freedom from all forms of exploitation and oppression, and from hunger, illiteracy, and alienation, then the two models are in tight competition, for each has a mixed and contradictory record, respectively, in its practical movement toward or back from those ideals. Taking socialist modernity in China as a developmental alternative to capitalist injustice and inequality as well as to statist bureaucracy, the tortuous Mao era deserved credibility not least for its investment in human capital and aspiration for a people's democracy. The reforms must in turn be evaluated for their ability or inability not only to surmount past errors and failures but also to achieve socialist modernization in a different environment in which many past developmental constraints had receded.

The comparisons made in the 1980s in favor of post-Mao changes, though overtaken by the downturns of the 1990s, are highly relevant and contain enticing arguments that can be used to understand the structure and contingency of reform. Did Maoist socialism subordinate economic rationalism to utopian egalitarianism, whereas post-Mao leaders sacrificed equality and justice for efficiency? Was the second phase of reform inclined to the neoliberal global trend inevitable by market logic? Was the crisis of the reform caused by the incompleteness of the market where the only way out would be further privatization and global linking? An explicit premise in the debates around these questions is that efficiency and equality, development and social justice, are mutually exclusive goals; we cannot have both worlds. What is forgotten is that Deng's project aimed and had begun to succeed precisely in resolving that alleged incompatibility (of which a satiric expression of the cultural revolutionary ferment was "choosing socialist poverty rather than capitalist prosperity"). Also forgotten is the long-held conviction that the dilemma of "socialism and backwardness" in China can be overcome only by socialist development. This clarification is necessary for the rehabilitation of reform as originally a socialist self-adjusting movement. As the historical materialist wisdom has it, social existence determines social consciousness and, as the emptiness of "socialist spiritual civilization" shows, material problems still require material solutions (Dirlik 1982). But it is no less a matter of dialectical materialism to realize that social consciousness, reflexive and discursive, also actively participates in the destruction, deconstruction, and construction of social existence. For the "losers" in China's marketplace—the working poor, the unemployed, and the marginalized,—if "socialism" means anything, that meaning is concrete and urgent.

Industrialization in China's severely constrained circumstances required an extraordinary degree of mobilization and control, discipline and obedience, devotion and self-sacrifice. The institutional fit that the Chinese created was a distinguished corporatist citizenship in which the state managed class and other social cleavages. Egalitarianism's predicament is not about rational choices between efficiency and equality, as misconceived in the reform ideology that "a premature pursuit of equality may do great damage to development by undermining incentives to work" (Selden and Lippit 1982, 26). Nor is it, regarding urban bias, derived from orthodox Marxist hostility toward the peasantry. The Chinese revolution's rural roots have obliged rather than deterred the party in fulfilling its commitment to transforming peasant China, past and present; as millions, now freed from the land, are yet to be liberated from displacement, poverty, and discrimination. Rather, the predicament is about the economic and moral imperative to surmount "*capitalism* and backwardness." As political philosophers continue to debate whether equality, if indeed appealing, is ever possible and in what sense or in which spheres, at issue in China is the resumption of state arbitration among social interests and forces in the new context of rising class-based conflicts and injustice. But to do so the state itself has to be democratized and "class" must be revived as a pivotal concept for understanding and changing the Chinese world. What is conspicuously missing in the language of reform is no longer dispensable when the class nature of the experiences of market transition and the politics of resistance can no longer be concealed.

Egalitarianism's Battle: Ethnicity, Locality, and Citizenship

Along with the inquiry about the impact of reform on class relations is the question of whether the changes had widened or narrowed regional and ethnic disparities. Compared with the political campaigns of "class struggle" in the pre-reform years and the class polarization in the post-reform era, did the regional and ethnic aspects appear less dismal with regard to both periods? To be sure, these two aspects are far from being identical or entailing the same political and policy questions, but in China "ethnicity" and "region" often overlap geographically as well as conceptually because they frequently share temporal (e.g., "primitive," "backward") and spatial (e.g., "peripheral," "frontal") identities. The Chinese Muslims are topographically connected mainly with China's western inland and Central Asian borders, as signified in the name of their primary homeland, "Xinjiang," translated as the "new frontier" (to the Qing empire in the eighteenth century). The Yi people inhabiting the mountain areas in the south-west province of Sichuan—along with dozens of other minority groups, as told in Chinese history textbooks—had "skipped" the intermediate stages to be embraced into socialism directly from a tribal society (Harrell 1990). What made developmental gaps between regions politically sensitive was that they were often coupled with ethnic differences, especially between the Han majority and the national minorities residing mostly in the country's hinterland—a generally poor area yet one with greater resources in terms of oil, minerals, and forests, as well as strategically critical border locations. In 2001 the size of the provincial economy of Guangdong, one of the richest provinces in China, was 1,000 billion yuan (about $120 billion) in contrast to that of only 13.9 billion for the Tibetan Autonomous Region, the latter being much larger in territory and much smaller in population. The effects of economic reforms on the minority regions varied, looming large wher-ever cross-ethnic equality increased or decreased by a correlated regional trend (in e.g., educational opportunity; cf. Postiglione 1992).

Still, the obvious distinction between the categories of "ethnicity" and "locality" must be observed for their respective attributes and correspond-ing policy options. Ideologically speaking, equality among nationalities is a normative and legal principle in the PRC; while regional inequalities, seen as both a problem in itself and a drag on inter-ethnic solidarity, are nev-ertheless more expected ("uneven and compressed development") and tol-erable in formal rules of national coodination.

The Nationality Question

The ethnic issue is vital and highly sensitive to the sovereignty and legit-imacy of the People's Republic as a multinational state, which is recorded in the 2001 census as having fifty-five constitutionally designated minority nationalities making up over 100 million members or 8.41 percent of the total population and 60 percent of the country's territory. Whether or not such an entity can be properly called a nation-state is a matter of conceptual preference, but either way the PRC is a fully fledged sovereign multinational state on a par with the other nations in the contemporary international system.[50] Chinese "civic" nationalism (as discussed in chapter 1), which developed politically only in the twentieth-century revolutionary move-ments, has been one side of the same coin of which the other is generally underdeveloped ethnic nationalism in China (except for Tibetan nationalism). Even the majority Han nationality, with or without an *ethnie* (Smith 1999) in history, was a recent invention in the republican struggle against the Manchu rule. The gradual formation of the Muslim identities in China proper was similarly convenient, contingent, and fluid (Gladney 1991; Lipman 1997). Most remarkably, the multinational nation of China, or *zhonghua minzu*, had historically nurtured a self-perception of racial unity. As John King Fairbank remarks, regarding "racial stock the Chinese have a deceptive homogeneity" (1979, 10). Instead of assimilation by a dominant Han culture, the official conception of Chineseness "would represent an amalgamation (*ronghe*) of [China's] component cultures" (Dreyer 1999, 591). This conception was surely owed to anti-imperialist nationalism, of which an outcome and the strongest institutional expression is the state of the PRC. This state in turn presupposes multiethnicity and carries with it not only what is taken as a sacred duty of enhancing political unity and social cohesion across ethnic boundaries but also a realistic recognition of national diversities. Tensions between the generic Chinese identity and the distinctive minority nationalities are not denied but are believed manageable within the socialist framework.

Socialist nationality theory, based on Marxist internationalism and the Leninist principle of national self-determination, has been radically "sinicized" by the Chinese communists. Marx believed that "no nation can be free if it oppresses other nations," and Lenin, in his seminal piece "The Right of Nations to Self-Determination" (1914), epitomizes the Marxist position.[51] Ironically, it was precisely this distinction between oppressor and oppressed nations that translated a "class dimension" from revolutionary nationalism into the official nationalism of the PRC, thereby conveniently overlooking the Chinese state's own imperial tradition. The fact that China, as an empire and a republic, had been an oppressed rather than an oppressor "class nation" since it suffered foreign invasions and colonial domination left little room for minority assertions. By the same token, so-called bourgeois and separatist nationalisms could be legitimately crashed. The Soviet model is thus only partially adopted in the PRC constitution, specifically without the minority right to secession: as stated in Article 4: "All nationalities in the People's Republic of China are equal. The state protects the lawful rights and interests of the minority nationalities and upholds and develops a relationship of equality, unity and mutual assistance among all of China's nationalities." Prohibited are both discrimination and acts of disunity. Mao, however, recommended in his famous analysis of the ten major relationships in 1956 that the emphasis be placed on opposing Han chauvinism. Although averting formal federalism, China has nevertheless also established five provincial-level autonomous regions and dozens of autonomous prefectures and counties for minority administration. According to Articles 115 and 116 of the constitution, in these areas local states via the local people's congresses "have the power to enact regulations on the exercise of autonomy and other separate regulations in the light of the political, economic and cultural characteristics" of the given units. Even though "Hanification" in terms of *ronghe* more than *tonghua* or assimilation had arguably been an unbroken traditional creed of ruling in China, a consistent policy was maintained to preserve minority languages, customs, and values as well as to assist their socioeconomic development (a need no doubt defined only by the socialist state) (Heberer 1979; Mackerras 1994).[52] The growing social inequalities in the reform period were certainly not ethnic specific but rather were formed along the west/inland versus east/coastal divisions where the regional and ethnic coincided.

Apart from the more contested case of Tibet, the project of national integration and modernization on the one hand and limited subnational minority autonomy on the other has been for decades relatively successful. The first few years of the Cultural Revolution passed as an unexpected and hugely damaging interruption. But, generally speaking, social gains for China's minorities since 1949 in education, poverty alleviation, population growth, and public welfare were real. These gains had been systematically underreported or dismissed in the international media due to fierce propaganda wars between Beijing and its critics. Until at least the early 1990s, there had been few large-scale incidents of ethnic conflict. Even in the Xinjiang Uigur Autonomous Region, where ethnic relations had soured under the influence of newly independent post-Soviet Central Asian republics, the Islamic militants found it difficult to recruit among the locals. It was only the armed East Turkic revivalist movement, in spite of its origin in historical injustice, that created a "Xinjiang question" after nearly half a century of overall ethnic peace in the region disturbed, but not overwhelmed, by adverse events (such as in Yili where nearly a quarter million people defected to the Soviet Union) (Ferdinand 1994; Karmel 2000). The communist regime at least had maintained minimal intergroup harmony and stability without recourse to terror. Soldiers were not a constant presence anywhere outside of Lhasa and a small number of border towns ridden by violence or arms trade.

Various explanations surface for the slow coming of ethnic nationalism in the PRC, and these explanations speak to something deep in the strengths and weaknesses of Chinese socialism. The politicization of ethnic consciousness and tendencies to national disintegration might have spread everywhere after the events of Tiananmen and the Berlin Wall in 1989, but the notion of equality among nationalities and equal citizenship across ethnic lines had not been disputed in China's otherwise diluted ideology. This situation stood in contrast to the reform's ideological and policy shift over a class-coded egalitarianism. As the institutional build-up of transferring funds, skills, and technologies went on to improve the living standards and infrastructure in the underdeveloped minority areas, ethnic issues in China remained by and large "predicated on the socialist state's moral hegemony" (Bulag 2000, 178).

On the other hand, there were also signs of change for the worse in the wake of what had torn apart the former USSR and Yugoslavia, in spite of— or because of—their federalist structures and more liberal stands on the nationality question. From the mid-1990s onward, Beijing's nationality policy "acquired a marked Great-Han chauvinist cast" (C. Wang 2005, 94), seen especially in the new approach of pushing for economic expansion, hence increasing Han immigration into the minority regions. Yet the "real threat to [Xinjiang's] harmonious relations with China," as viewed by Peter Ferdinand, "stems not from economics, but from politics," with reference to rising resentment over "past colonization" triggered by current escalation of repression (1994, 284). The influx of Han immigrants, including uniformed professionals, had for years changed the regional demographic bases of nationalities. According to Walker Connor, by the early 1980s in China "a policy of extensive gerrymandering and migration has made the titular national group a certain minority in four of the five autonomous regions and a most probable minority in the other" (1984, 329; 1994, 273–76). Colin Mackerras, using China's official census data, shows that in Xinjiang of the total population of 19.05 million in the end of 2002, the Uigurs made up 45.2 percent, the Han 40.6 percent, and the Muslim Kazakhs 6.7 percent, as contrasted with 4.33 million in total population in 1949, of which 75.9 percent were Uighurs, 10.2 percent Kazakhs, and only 6.7 percent Han.[53] For the Tibetans, a very large portion of what they perceived to be "greater Tibet" in parts of the neighboring provinces on the Qinghai-Xizang Plateau was not incorporated into the jurisdiction of the Tibetan Autonomous Region. As a result the 2.29 million residents (in 2002) of the region were neither all Tibetans (who made up about three quarters of the population) nor included all of the major Tibetan communities (claimed to be 6 million by the Dalai Lama). Although at least 70 percent of local officials were required to be of ethnic Tibetan origin, including that of the regional governor, Han cadres were usually more powerful and occupied the post of party secretary. At the central level, national minorities had been always underrepresented in the legislative and governmental bodies. The military and police forces were also far from being sufficiently mixed in their ethnic composition.

Tibet had been the only major case of "occupation" (by the PLA) since 1952. In regular life, however, tensions between local Tibetans and the Han "personnel assisting Tibet" (*yuanzang-renyuan*) were not commonly confrontational (Hessler 1999). Since the 1951 "peaceful settlement" negotiated between the Tibetan elites and Beijing, life expectancy had increased from thirty-six years to sixty-seven years in 2003, and infant mortality and absolute poverty steadily declined. Roads, factories, schools, hospitals, and, above all, modern conceptions of equality and citizenship, however undemocratic they might still be, had transformed the land of snows where the cruelty and hardship of an ancient serfdom had been evident.[54] During the Cultural Revolution, of which Tibetan culture was not the only victim, temples were destroyed, monks were humiliated, and Buddhist believers were forced to convert to atheist socialism, even as a new religion. While the institutionalized social benefits brought to the mass of former serfs now remained in place, the effects of a characteristic communist paternalism were either diminishing or increasingly counterproductive. The enormous economic and financial aid packages committed on a yearly basis to Tibetan progress were constitutive of an ambitious "socialist civilizing mission" not free of Han chauvinism. Unilateralism in such a mission despised the idea of autonomy and self-determination, by which the minorities had the right to lead their own lives. Given the chance, they might well have chosen not to modernize if modernization implied imposition and alienation, and if development were not separable from Chinese nationalism and socialism in the country's triad modern project.

The practical problem with this quasi-colonial approach was that it neither attempted a thorough social revolution that would mobilize the lower strata to remove the old ruling class nor, alternatively, a compromise that would tolerate an utterly unjust and anachronistic system, and seek a bilateral treaty for peaceful coexistence. The communists neither completed a military conquest nor withdrew their troops and other apparatus of occupation. Tibetan Buddhism would perhaps never give in to Chinese secularism, but it is not entirely inconceivable that an indigenous revolution could transform Tibet nationalism into a more socialist, accommodating culture of society in the interest of local needs. Much of the confusion on the part of the Tibetan poor was caused by the contradiction of their communist "liberators" forging an alliance with their lords and chiefs in the "feudal" hierarchy (Grunfeld 1987, 220; L. Wang 2002). On the whole, Beijing thoroughly underestimated the power of religion along with the persistence of the Tibetan social structure in which the aristocrats had a powerful and lasting influence on society. In the end, the communists failed to win over a people by respecting their beliefs, identities and choices more than by providing material aids. The "democratic reform" after the 1959 uprising was involuntary in terms of participation from below, and it was also incomplete, leaving the core of a militant opposition intact. The present impasse—seen in the recurrent turmoil since the late 1980s—also had a source in the nearly universal support for Tibetan nationalism morally voiced and politically and militarily organized from abroad. For radical Tibetan nationalists, the Dalai Lama's middle way of demanding genuine autonomy and cultural self-preservation within the PRC through non-violent resistance was just too moderate (Goldstein 1998; Karmel 1995–96). As direct talks between Beijing and the exile government resumed in 2002 after a ten-year interval, cautious optimism surfaced, inspired also by a steady improvement in the Sino-Indian relationship. Yet anything short of independence would be unlikely to satisfy a future post-Dalai elite; and anything considered to violate China's "inalienable territories" would be resolutely rejected by the central state.

Whether or not the damage of a cultural revolution without cultural sensitivities was beyond repair, the memories could not be erased and were recycled for political use (cf. L. Wang 2002). There were also plenty of other sources for a resurgent Tibetan consciousness, just as there were for a similarly radicalized Islamic one. The communist regime had indeed committed very serious strategic and policy errors inconsistent with its own ideologies and codes of conduct. But some of the problems at hand might also be inherently insoluble, such as the perpetual external threat to Chinese unity and a unitary Chinese state. Political inexperience in managing multinationality by that state was rooted in a polity caught between an imperial tradition of a multicultural empire and a republican tradition of modern nationalism; and between a socialist nationalism as opposed to foreign powers and an internationalist socialism of equality and solidarity among nations. In the background was ethnic nationalism surging on a global scale. This particular dimension of globalization had produced a self-fulfilling prophecy in a potent discourse that was not only reflective but also creative as both a part and an initiator of reality. That reality had been gradually also felt in a China no longer isolated from the outside world. The ethno-religious complex of Tibet thereby serves as a primary example of the ultimate limitation of internalist and class-confined analyses. On this note, Tsering Shakya's disturbing reporting, accurate or not, is starkly honest: "The Tibetan Rebellion was a national one, supported by all classes. In fact, the bulk of the protests came from ordinary people and the poor, resentful not only of the Chinese but also of what they saw as the Tibetan ruling class's surrender of the interests of the nation" (2002, 53).

Spatial Politics

The "localist turn" in China studies has fruitfully channeled attention to local particularities and regional inequalities in relation to but also cut across class and other social cleavages. China's coastal-inland dualism has been a prolonged structural feature, with "coastal bias" as a special manifestation of urban bias. Efforts had been made to reduce such unevenness since the early 1950s throughout the pre-reform and post-reform eras. The Maoist developmental strategy was in part a hard choice of sacrificing growth in certain areas in exchange for improving national fiscal and redistributive balances (Lardy 1975). The cases of Sichuan and Guizhou illustrated how China's "subsystems within the political whole" negotiated their independence and flexibility through a national-local "dual rule" with the center, as done during the Great Leap experiments (Goodman 1986, chapter 5). As the reforms fostered growth, although general economic conditions improved in all regions in absolute terms after 1978, marked disparities along regional lines persisted or even enlarged in relative terms (Wang and Hu 1999).[55] Research findings at the World Bank about global income distribution in 1988–1993 showed "rapidly widening output and income differences between urban China on the one hand, and rural China and rural India on the other." Reaffirming state capacity as a foremost variable, Wang Shaoguang and Hu Angang insist that there is nothing "natural" in such disparities—labor migration, capital movement, and technology diffusion are determined as much, if not more, by political as by market forces (1999, 5, 35; cf. Wade 2001).

The same pattern was seen in the cyclical alteration of decentralization and recentralization, accompanied by ever-fiercer inter- and intraprovincial competition over resources, revenue retention, and budget allocation.[56] Decentralization went deep and far during the Great Leap and Cultural Revolution, which anticipated subsequent recentralizing efforts. The cycles of *fang* (liberalization) and *shou* (control) were clearly visible, and the reform itself could be seen as a grand adventure to decentralize through economic as well as political liberalization. The "political logic of reform," as Susan Shirk observes, led to a rehabilitation of regionalism that resulted from bargaining between and among national and subnational leaders via both old and nontraditional institutions (1998). As such, central-local relations in China did not have to be a zero-sum game, and the opening up of the country would not create breakaway provinces, at least not in the Han-concentrated areas (Li 1998). This was the centrifugal politics for "economic federalism" as a healthy structural development (Montinola et al. 1995). "Local state corporatism" flourished for a while in the counties and townships, where the petty bureaucrats supported and benefited from the market and TVEs without actual privatization or rampant rent seeking behaviors (Oi 1995, 170–75; 1999, 2–3, 19). These optimistic observations on local dynamism and flexibility suggest a possible third space, one fundamentally public, between conventional governmental spheres and the marketplace of private profits.

In the expanding scholarship on regional differences, "ethnicity" is sometimes used as a geographic and social category without invoking formal ethnic identities. The Han people, in this view, are constituted of multiple "ethnic" groups recognizable by localities, dialects, religions, or customs. "Internal peripheralization" and strifes have taken place within communities, near and far, sometimes with serious political repercussions: migrant workers in the cities, "unsophisticated" *subei* people among arrogant Shanghaiese, or distrust between the *tujia* natives and the *kejia* (Hakkas) late arrivals (cf. Friedman 1995, chapters 3, 5, 6; Hershatter et al. 1996; Safran 1998). This is only one of several contentions of a controversial intellectual enterprise of "deconstructing the nation" or capturing how "China deconstructs" (Duara 1995, chapters 5, 6; Goodman and Segal 1994). By looking inward at the cultural and spatial makeup of the country, it is demonstrated that there is no one China to be essentialized, that the PRC (or for that matter any other state) cannot be an inherently coherent unit of analysis, and that any "national" project must not be taken for granted.

Another dimension of redrawing the hard and soft boundaries of China focuses on its elastic borderlines in the aftermath of national isolation. A changing economic geography is one contributing factor; the repossession of Hong Kong (1997) and Macao (1999) as "special administrative regions" is another. As the coastal and other border areas developed external links of trade, with investment (both inflow and outflow) and labor migration easily bypassing central and even local governments, the PRC found itself steadily integrating into the Asian and Eurasian regional economic zones across national borders (Fujita et al. 1999).[57] It is remarkable that over a third of FDI in China had come from overseas Chinese, an enviable situation for most other transitional and developing societies. Economic ties between the mainland and Taiwan were hoped also to have a politically stabilizing effect. The proposal of "one country, two systems" and any other future framing along the way would involve further redefinitions of the outer and inner demarcations and frontiers of "China." It had always been the case that the interactions of social conditions across such frontiers "set the rhythm of the pulse" of (Asian and European) geopolitics (Lattimore 1951, xlvii-xlviii). Meanwhile, hitherto severed or hidden kinship ties and feelings of kinship between overseas and mainland Chinese societies were re(dis)covered in the elusive (and provocative) concepts of "cultural China" and "greater China." "Chinese nationalism" was then problemized by the even more elusive notion of Chineseness, not least because of the challenge of Taiwan's democratization to the status quo of a cross-strait relationship at a time when "democracy" was a global ideological gauge for defining nations.

Spatial ramification was nowhere felt more as an everyday experience in China than in the migration flows that were inconceivable twenty years ago under the *hukou* system of residence control. With a vast floating population inside the country, along with guest workers crossing national borders constantly and the "fever of going abroad" (*chuguo re*) among students and (traditionally) southern coast inhabitants, China appeared to be the largest site of today's phenomenal global emigration and immigration. As David Harvey comments, "State boundaries are less porous for people and for labor than they are for capital, but they are still porous enough" (2000, 46). A unique dimension of the Chinese politics of migration is related to the government's "westward" move embarked in 2000. This move was intended to develop the heartland and minority regions by reallocating financial, human, and technological resources still possible in a mixed system of central planning encompassing market mechanisms to redeem developmental unevenness. Modernization, however, is a double-edged sword, as it may improve the living standards (set in the metropolitans) for the locals but also harm their cultures as well as their often less wasteful and polluting ways of life. In Tibet, fear and hostility rose as trade and communication grew in the waves of non-Tibetan settlers arriving to boost business. If it were never a deliberate policy of "sending in" Han people to change Tibetan demography, a "free market" was now doing the job ruthlessly. Such a market invaded a resistant society, bringing with it not only the horrifying prospect of commercial homogenization but also actual market inequalities. Although the Tibetan heritage and the multicultural traditions in Xinjiang and elsewhere were officially "national treasures," little concern was leveled in the exploring-the-west strategy against what would be locally seen as invasive by ignoring the political risks of provoking ethnically and religiously incited resistance.[58]

Thinking about what Harvey describes as "geographical reorderings and restructurings, spatial strategies and geopolitical elements" from a "historical-geographical materialist" point of view, what people and places and their multidimensional relations undergo are indeed "tangible trans-formations" (2000, 31, 191). That is, in any political community at any level, where certain (national, local, regional, etc.) groups of citizens are margin-alized or excluded, or there is the marginality of citizenship itself, the poli-tics of space offers a perspective in which political imagination is also an institutional challenge. The shifting lines between, among, and cutting across state, society, groups, and individuals are manifestations of the po-tential practicality of Harvey's "dialectical spatiotemporal utopianism." "Future Chinas," by whatever names, will have to rely on democratic plural-ism and consensus-building among segments of a territorially and/or cul-turally differentiated population. The process would create new spaces on new scales through globally embedded yet locally constructed identities, national or otherwise (cf. White and Li 1993 on the cases of Guangdong, Hong Kong, and Taiwan). The idea of one country embracing multiple systems is yet to be creatively rethought and developed to include formulas that may depart from its current premises. After all, political and national borders, let alone ethno-cultural divisions, are never fixed but artificially drawn and redrawn, and they do not even necessarily enjoy historical legit-imacy (Desai 1990; Wallerstein 1991, 131). The authority of history is not always accessible to be used to arbitrate conflicting memories and claims in the organization and reorganization of political spaces. By taking "nation" as a practical category rather than a substantial entity (Brubaker 1996), nationhood becomes a source of openness as well as inclusion and toler-ance. Cultural blending enriches rather than impoverishes collective pride. The fault line between cultural preservation against assimilation (as in the Tibetan case) and amalgamation (as in multiethnic accommodation in China's many other autonomous regions) must be carefully worked out.

The predicament of Taiwan is obviously different from, or goes beyond, issues concerning culture or homeland. This is because it had moved to create a position that contradicted not only the nationalist principle that "the political and the national unit should be congruent" (Gellner 1983, 1) but also the Chinese social-national-developmental integration by splitting nationalist loyalty. Moreover, as soon as liberal democracy participated in defining the entity of Taiwan and a new Taiwanese nationalism (Gold 1993; Wachman 1994), a crack appeared in the notion of a shared motherland with the mainland and in speculation on unification. Among a range of fiercely contested perceptions, rapidly declining was the one that considered Taiwan to be a part of the Republic of China in which younger generations literally "imagined" a Chinese nation still "mapped in" not only the mainland but also Outer Mongolia. On the rise was the view of the island being on a par with the PRC, a separate "community of common destiny" with its own multilayered Taiwanese identity, in the form of either an independent state or an autonomous subnational region (Hughes 2000, 67, 76).[59] But if independence would lead to military conflict, the crisis could be total in the breakdown of China's triadic balance: from socialist and developmentalist propositions a war must be opposed, but such positions would be rejected by the nationalist defense of the sovereignty and territorial integrity of whole China. To avoid disasters, the PRC must seek alternative conceptual and institutional formulas from federalist or confederalist to any other forms appropriate to best settle disputed spatial identities. Extensive and reconciliational dialogues across the strait could be themselves constructive for democratization in line with the Wilsonian and Leninist axiom of national self-determination by which China had formally supported autonomous jurisdictions for its national minorities.

Indeed there was never a monolithic Confucian China and the imperial Chinese terrain was always multiethnic and multicultural. Still, and more significantly, we might ask if Chinese socialism had achieved relative peace and solidarity among its nationalities, then how did managing different ethnic groups come to be such a problem? Economic and ideological globalization certainly played a part in reducing the magnetic scope of the nation; the U.S. interventionist policy fueled the Taiwan crisis with arms trade. The "waves" of democratic transition involving Taiwan further complicated the matter, even though ever since the Three People's Principles and "new democracy" there is nothing new to China's modern consciousness about the mutual indispensability between democracy and nationhood.

The Chinese communists had all along been squarely criticized for their handling of spatially implicated ethnic and religious matters, not only by the human rights lobby in the West but also by their estranged counterparts in the former Soviet bloc and by the Left in the West in general. How and why such handling had evolved, however, is less understood. One of the "ten great demands" of the Chinese revolution was to "unify China and recognize . . . national self-determination," declared the CCP in 1928. The document did not specify whether "national self-determination" referred to the minorities as well until 1931 when the issue was clarified in terms of the model of the USSR. The party stated that wherever the majority of the population belonged to non-Han nationalities, "the toiling masses of these nations shall have the right to determine for themselves whether they wish to leave the Chinese Soviet Republic and create their own independent state, or whether they wish to join the Union of Soviet Republics, or form an autonomous area inside the Chinese Soviet Republic."[60] Later again, the 1945 party congress envisioned a new democratic "federal republic based on the free union of all nationalities," which would strive to realize peace and progress throughout the world. The communists on the road to power, however, had not been consistent in creating a list of ethnic nationalities to be included in such a federation, and after 1949 they swiftly abandoned the minority right to secede.[61]

This bizarre spectacle of Chinese revolutionary nationalism exemplified "the victory of political over cultural nationalists" within third world revolutions (Wallerstein 1999, 151) while reclaiming culturally non-Chinese territories in the old imperial tradition. It was colonial wars, destruction, and extraction in the soil of this empire that in turn defined foreign imperialism (Anderson 2001, 37). Granting a wide range of constitutional rights (except for secession) to the minorities, the 1954 constitution proclaimed that "the PRC is a single, multinational state." Accordingly, "acts which undermine the unity of the nationalities are prohibited," and the "national autonomous areas are inalienable parts of the PRC." This statement remained intact in each of the subsequent constitutional amendments. "Unlike the Soviets," Connor remarks, "the CCP dropped the doctrine of self-determination immediately upon assuming power, and has subsequently denied any right of secession not just in 'content' (as have the Soviets), but in 'form' as well" (1984, 88). The geopolitics of the cold war in East Asia, especially the anticommunist treaties between the United States and its Asian allies helped to keep nationalism strong in China. Similarly, by the logic of Chinese isolation, the CCP also reacted to the crisis of the communist world from 1956 onward in a nationalist more than a Marxist manner.

Might the globalized fashion of self-determination and the Chinese inclination for corporatist management combine to encompass certain useful "bourgeois" institutions? Might such institutions, of which elements were introduced into China's first-ever federalist movement in the 1920s, be incorporated in a novel space of a socialist democratic state representing a free association of self-governing ethnic and cultural communities? It was notable that the movement for self-government for allied provinces in south China around 1922 supported Sun Zhongshan's centralism in opposition to the feudal warlords (Spence 1999, 315; Chesneaux 1969; Waldron 1990). It was also remarkable that Sun's elaboration of a "greater Asianism" of democratic national co-ruling (*gongzhi*) in 1924 was beyond the concept of nation-state and close to the contemporary model of the European Union. His dual scheme of constitutional heterogeneity as well as homogeneity was simultaneously a self-critical reflection on China's own historical imperialism and a consociational response to Western encroachment (cf. H. Wang 2002). These experiences and the earlier communist legacies are instructive. For China, an unprecedented institutional configuration that guarantees autonomy, equality, and solidarity of individual units within a multicentered unity of shared sovereignty and universal citizenship is not yet in sight, but neither is it inconceivable.[62]

Speaking of spatial politics, Michael Mann's economic, political, military, and ideological sources of power complemented by geography and demography (including ecology) come to the fore (Lieven 2000, 415). The theoretical attention paid to the production of space and fusion of spatiotemporal differences resonates the macrohistorical thesis of uneven development. But it also sheds light on the micro level developments of fresh ideas, methods, and patterns of public affairs as well as personal and household management. Achieving ethnic and regional developmental equity can not be a static goal, and it is politico-culturally and economically contestable. Yet compression and leaps will still be sought in the peripheries insofar as they do not intend to be closed to other parts of the world, and as far as enhancing the quality of life, including political participation, is locally desirable. For China in its generic Chineseness and in its many local entities and identities, developmental unevenness is not only a problem but also a potential shortcut to redeeming underdevelopment. The rise of China's "great northwest" on the horizon could be one example; the "peaceful ascendance" of China itself is already another, assuming violent disintegration of the PRC state would be avoidable (cf. Goodman 1997, 4–6). Beneath the optimism and simplicity of the "privilege of backwardness" is inevitably a structure of feelings of both hope and despair—the actual historical extent of development is widely open.

Egalitarianism's Pride and Price: Gender Equality

If class relations represented the weakest link of Chinese socialism in terms of equality, the gender front was much stronger in comparison, even though the two realms overlapped. Women's liberation had been highlighted in the communist agenda from the outset and, in that sense, the Chinese revolution was simultaneously a women's revolution, and Chinese socialism a women's cause (Kristeva 1974). This is an overriding factor with policy implications and social-cultural effects, and it should be a point of departure for any investigation into changing gender relations in the PRC. Feminist critics in the West dispute this assertion, stressing that women's interests in modern Chinese history were secondary to national liberation, class struggle, or developmental priorities (Stacey 1983; Wolfe 1985). This criticism has a point, for, like "class," "gender" was also subordinated to the national project of revolutionary and socialist modernity. But, then, could women's liberation succeed alone without the independence and development of an oppressed people, for which women devoted themselves to the struggle?

Revolutionary Women and State Feminism

The struggles for women's rights were constitutive of the Chinese modern consciousness that rejected semicolonial domination as well as "feudal" bondages at home. For radical reformers and revolutionaries, China's deepening crisis since the mid-nineteenth century was essentially attributable to a conservative and repressive traditional society. Confucian patriarchal relations, a rigid gender division of labor, and the morality that held women collectively as an inferior class were features of the tradition. In rebellion, progressive intellectuals found inspiration in classical liberalism, utopian socialism, European anarchism, American pragmatism, Western feminism, and above all Marxism via the Russian revolution and Japanese translations (cf. Barlow 1993; Liu 1995; Wang Zheng 2000). The iconoclastic May 4th stance was debated in China throughout the twentieth century and into the twenty-first, and any positive evaluation of the Confucian conceptions about women and care (de Bary 1998; Tao 2000; Chan 2003) still hardly found a receptive audience in the mainland.

If the outstanding female republicans cherished a future world of harmony among and between men and women, they were still few in number. If the New Culture movement spread ideas of equal rights and free love, it was still largely an urban and elitist one. If the early CCP's spokesmen and leading cadres were committed to "woman-work," they were still compliant with male chauvinism within the party's body politic. But by the time of the general strikes of 1925–1926, and especially the land revolution in the decade after 1927, the communist consciousness-raising efforts and political agitation developed into mass mobilization at the grassroots of both sexes. Many women assumed leadership of women's organizations, which in turn established an important party tradition (Davin 1976; Johnson 1983). An important Chinese contribution to modern world history was making the transformation of gender relations part and parcel of a revolutionary enterprise, of which "feudalism," standing for an old, dark, and unjust society, was a main target. The term adapted to the Chinese communist vocabulary signified what Mao famously analogized as "four thick ropes" to throw off: the old political regime, clan patriarchy, superstition, and the male authority of the father and husband (1991 [1927], 31). As women's oppression was implicated in each of these interdependent powers, it was only logical that the revolution had to be intrinsically feminist in its appeal to, and involvement of, women. By participating in the revolutionary transformation of society before and after the founding of the PRC, women had also transformed their own place within and outside of the family. As the foundation of patriarchal kinship shattered, they began to redefine gender roles, even though the change was not easy, and the party had to sometimes yield to peasant conservatism. Worth mentioning here also is the groundwork done under the GMD regime to legalize political parity between the sexes: foot binding was prohibited and a civil code was enacted to allow women to vote; indeed, "Chinese women achieved suffrage and extensive legal rights— on paper at least—years before their counterparts in the Catholic countries of Western Europe" (Gilmartin 1995, 11).

Communism in power, first locally and then nationally, moved faster and farther from what had been done for women during the Guangzhou years (the CCP-GMD alliance), the Nanjing decade (the GMD rule), and the Yan'an period (Young 1973; Croll 1983). Through legal and policy instruments the communists effectively banned foot binding, child-bride marriages, and forced widowhood chastity. Mercenary and arranged marriages without the consent of the individuals concerned were outlawed, so was the trafficking of women and wife beating. Although such practices persisted to various extents in the countryside, they were seen as "dated," "wrong," and "illegal," which made a real difference. The influence of the landmark Marriage Law (1950), which also set up the moral standard for a new society, reached to the remotest rural villages. The law was revised in 1980, mainly to ease divorce disputes. In 2001, after three years of consideration by the National People's Congress, it was further revised to have women (and children) more effectively protected against the backlash of market transition that witnessed rich men's polygamy and underpaid female labor. The deliberation process of the draft revision was open and attracted public attention, involving in particular feminist scholars and women lawyers. Other relevant civil and criminal laws including the inheritance law were also adopted to ensure women's rights and interests.

The legal component of state feminism in the PRC was supported by social components. The word "feminism" was translated into Chinese to mean the rights and power of women (*nuquan zhuyi*), while also rejected, in the official discourse, for its "bourgeois" origin and flavor. Women's studies developed since the early 1980s preferred an alternative translation of *nuxing zhuyi* that simply coded as "womenism," an idea about and for women. The evolution of the meaning of "woman" from presocialist *nuren* to socialist *funu* and then to postsocialist *nuxing* (which was also a return to the "new woman" or *xin nuxing* of the May 4th era) is itself highly interesting (Barlow 2004, 49–63). The importance of that evolution can only be appreciated in the context of the arduous search for the female subject and subjectivity (Li 1995). The notion of "state feminism," on the other hand, is a Nordic creation (Hernes 1987) to be borrowed for the cases of state socialism. For the sake of convenience, I freely use in this discussion both "feminism" and "state feminism" (of which the connotations will be qualified).

Before the more recent surge of unemployment, which affected women more than men, the overwhelming majority of urban women had a job with a salary comparable, for equal work, to their male counterparts. The remaining wage gaps mostly resulted from occupational differences. State-sector employees, of whom 40 percent were female, were entitled to paid maternity leave, for a period between three to six months, along with a generous set of fringe benefits. In rural communes, women were encouraged to work in collective teams in return for rewards calculated and accumulated in work points. Joining the workforce in massive numbers, women earned an income and enjoyed a degree of economic independence, freedom from home confinement, and increased self-esteem and social recognition.[63] They also participated in political and other public activities, even though voting rights were nominal beyond the level of an individual's immediate working or residential units. While the female population was vastly underrepresented in legislative and governmental bodies (except for a short period when a quota of one third for female positions was demanded by the Cultural Revolution), a women-friendly state dominated by male leaders was entrusted to articulate and represent women's interests. Without a change in formal policies, the radical phase of reforms had a negative impact on gender relations. Female enrollment in primary education, for example, dropped sharply despite a compulsory national nine-year schooling program; the decrease is attributed to rising fees, falling expectations, and the rolling back of institutional instruments against gender discrimination. Further, according to official media reports since the late 1990s, the dropout rate was as high as over 30 percent in many poor villages involving mostly girls; and female illiteracy stayed around 15 percent higher than that of males.

Despite these trends of reversing past gains, the PRC was recognized as exemplary regarding gender equality among the developing countries, notably because of its significantly improved women's conditions in spite of its large rural population and low per capita GDP. This assessment had been statistically confirmed on an annual basis by the HDI values and "gender-related development indexes," though the country came out rather poorly in terms of equality in political participation by the "gender empowerment measurement" applied since 1996 (UNDP 2000, 161–68). Amartya Sen, for example, repeatedly acknowledges "China's excellent achievements" in raising the quality of life for women in education, health, employment, and other aspects of gender equality, which also decisively lowered its fertility rate (2000, 17). The record of the PRC, as I noted in chapter 1, was markedly better than that of the rest of the third world, with very few exceptions (one being the Indian state of Kerala, which is extensively discussed by Sen). In certain aspects the Chinese performance was also comparable to, or better than, that of some of the first world countries, in areas such as urban female employment, the gender division of labor, equal pay for equal work, and provisions for childcare, maternity, and sick leave (in the state sector). Indeed, unlike most places elsewhere, the "grand gender narrative" of "women's liberation" (Edwards 2000) in terms of female participation and gender parity was neither abstract nor fictional. It went so deep in China's social commitment that it had become a "public reason" as a universally validated and internalized notion of justice (cf. Rawls 1993).

Within such a notion, women in the PRC were normatively expected to be free from systematic subordination to male dominance at home, in the workplace, and in society at large. As long as the ideology and accompanying legislation, policies, and institutions were upheld to sustain the norm, women could fight for themselves against any violation. And, at least in theory, they would be backed by their communities, the courts, the media, the women's federations, and other governmental and now also nongovernmental women's organizations. Many such nongovernmental organizations (NGOs) were only comfortably semiautonomous, with official ties needed not least for financial reasons. The ambiguities also reflected the weakened state-sponsored network of support for women in the process of economic and political liberalization. Claiming to be an NGO since the UN World's Congress in Beijing in 1995, the All China Women's Federations (ACWF) remained a chief state actor in the politics of gender, but some of its local branches had ceased functioning or even disappeared in the neglected rural areas (cf. Howell 1996). The bold restoration of some "old society" biases and practices against women must be seen negatively as a vindication of the precious advances of women's liberation project safeguarded by a socialist state. As human traffic, domestic violence, forced prostitution, and commodified "femininity" spread, women in China were torn between market freedom and state protection. If seeking "absolute autonomy" in feminist activism was problematic in sections of the third world women's movements (Molyneux 1998), it would be an outright mistake in China.

The contradictory trajectory of women's liberation in China was felt most intensely in the changing social contract. The pro-women public policies that energetically promoted gender equality also at the same time cultivated a mentality of dependency among those who benefited the most in the state sector. Collectively, women did not enjoy a full and democratic

citizenship—nor did their male compatriots. The reform, even as it mitigated some of the problems associated with communist paternalism, also
reversed some earlier progresses and allowed the conditions of gender
equality to deteriorate. As the public spaces expanded for women's studies
and associations to develop within and without the state, the market forces
also at every possible step curbed the new freedom attained in this development. Taking into consideration both sides of the story, before and after the
reform, women in China were carving out their way to reform rather than
reject a women-friendly state so easily (as seen in some of the ex-socialist
states). For that state in its ideology and infrastructure put behind it the
fundamentals of what the previous generations bitterly experienced in a
traditional society. It also stood in opposition to many refashioned obstacles to female advancement brought into being by market greed, deception,
and prejudice.

It should be stressed that "women" or "Chinese women" as a collective
identity cannot be presupposed as homogeneous. Interior cleavages along
socioeconomic, personal (religious, political, relational, sexual, and so on),
and other lines were all too obvious, and attitudes toward the gender question were divided.[64] It is, however, intellectually and analytically justifiable
to preserve needed sociological categories, relatively stable, of groups and
their members. This is so also because, rather uniquely, women in the PRC
shared a great deal in their gender-specific relationships with the state, the
nation, and the modernization project, as opposed to their relationship
with men in the public and private spheres. Divisions among women still
could not override the truly generalizable factors about gender equalities
and inequalities, gendered perspectives on power and resistance, and the
powerful rhetoric of socialist feminism.

The "Public Patriarchy"

Another tempting phrase for state feminism as a contradictory legacy of
revolutionary socialism in China would be "public patriarchy" marked by
the following attributes: first, a socialist state obliged itself to a women-
friendly ideological, legal, and policy system in an openly paternalistic manner. Women's organizations were accordingly incorporated in the governmental structure, and the interest articulation for women was done in
statist more than democratic terms. Among the most striking outcomes of

this corporatist arrangement were not only group dependency but also institutionalized inequality within the group (e.g., between urban and rural women). Second, women's beneficial participation in the labor force and in social life in general was negatively compensated by their socially neglected "double burden." Third, the legitimization of public intervention in the private sphere of sexual and family relations simultaneously opened a leeway for depriving individuals of their privacy and personal autonomy. Fourth, the ideology of gender equality was compliant with hidden male standards.

The use of the word "patriarchy" for state feminism is also relevant here because of the astonishingly low percentage of women in state offices. Throughout PRC history only about 5 percent of minister posts have been occupied by women. Since 1983 the number of female deputies to the NPC never exceeded much more than 20 percent of the total, and the female share of seats in its standing committee only reached 25 percent in 1975 and had dropped to around 10 percent since 1998. In the party central committee the female share peaked at 10 percent in 1973 and then fell to 5 percent in 1997 and even less thereafter. Moreover, rarely have there been any women sitting on China's most powerful decision-making body, the Politbureau (cf. Woo 2003, 80).

The limitations on the Chinese socialist ambition of liberating women were not merely a matter of urban-rural disparity and the apparent gulfs between the norms and practices or the law and its enforcement. They were, first and foremost, a problem of the state itself—a state that was at once protective and repressive, liberating and intruding. The protection of women was grounded on the assumption that historically they had been not only socially, but also "naturally," victimized. While the "bourgeois rights" of equal opportunity were denounced and the equality of actual outcomes was sought, the rationale for the preferential treatment of women was epistemologically based on their supposedly weak sexual particularities. Regulations on physical work being periodically and individually adjusted in accordance with menstruation, pregnancy, and nursing, for instance, were justified by the perceived physiological need of a "weaker" sex with inborn disabilities. That is, women's equal worth and equal capabilities as fellow humans were inadequately encoded in policy thinking rooted in some pseudoscientific assumptions (Evans 1995).

The nonexistence of the term "gender" in the Chinese language might help explain the ironic misconception about the female body. This "useful category" (Scott 1988; Duggan 1989) was not until the early 1990s introduced in academic terminology, in the simple translation "social sex" (*shehui xingbie*), to counter the notion of naturally fixed sexual roles and identities.[65] Such a linguistic accident seemed to perpetuate ignorance on the part of feminist generations in China (whatever label they might think suitable for themselves) about the extent to which "men" and "women" were constructed in their social conditions. Li Xiaojiang, a pioneer theorist in post-reform "new enlightenment feminism," forcefully rejects "gender" as not only useless in China but also as an example of foreign worshiping and Western hegemony. She correctly notes that the Chinese word for "sex" encompasses two subtexts: *xing* or sex, and *xingbie* or sexual differentiation (of people), where the latter already contains a social dimension (2005, 4–5). The purpose, consistent in her influential writings, is to retain and cultivate the biologically distinctive feminine subject as a deliberate political act of "separation" against integration paradoxically embedded in the socialist universalism of equality. No doubt social constructivism as a feminist strategy could go too far, and be too utopian, if only the cultural transformation of gender relations would find its ultimate barriers beyond culture. But debate in China is yet to pick up the nuances of these contested conceptions and to position itself where biological reductionism left women deprived of their desired subjectivity.

The second limit to women's liberation in China was the shared "civilizational" constraint that no modern society had yet surpassed. The male-headed household remained the basic institution of social organization not only alongside, but also constitutive, of the communes and work units. For example, frequently only the father or husband was entitled to public housing distribution, excluding women either married or single. Moreover, the enduring gender division of labor ensured a "double burden" for working women. The effort to socialize housework and childcare in the unit-communal setting yielded some tremendously helpful results, but was far from sufficient in coverage and provision. Instead of further socialization, the reform wiped out many of its achievements as profit-making methods prevailed. Millions of female rural migrants, scarcely organized in unions, moved to work in the cities and county towns as domestic maids, reviving a traditional occupation within the host family yet without the family of one's own, a typical site of mixing gender and class inequalities. Although the "democratic household" (as the Chinese popular saying goes) of sharing not only housework but also family decisions was by no means uncommon, the age-old gender roles had not been transformed. The shift of labor away from agriculture—113 million or 23.6 percent of the rural labor force by 2000[66]—might have not been gender specific (Jin 2000); in some villages younger men sought work elsewhere, and in others women left while the children were cared for by grandparents. In most cases it was still women who attended to all kinds of work outside the home in addition to duties in caregiving and housekeeping. The sociological and psychological implications of the displaced life of rural women (and men) are yet to be grasped (cf. Gao 1994; Jacka 1997). China, like other modern societies, had not learned to treat housework as socially necessary and honorable as paid jobs. As largely and "naturally" carried out by women in isolation, housework remained unfulfilling and unrewarding.

Social "history" becomes "nature" in habits and customs, as Pierre Bourdieu argues, through knowledge production and communication that turn what is historically contingent into a solid present, a present that looks or feels extraordinarily ordinary. Every established order tends to naturalize its own arbitrariness. "Symbolic violence" has to be detected through an "objective archaeology of our own unconscious" structure or "habitus" (1977, 164; 1998). Thus, to delegitimize the Weberian authority of history in the case of women's double burden, it would not be enough to advance homemaking technologies and public services. Nor would the traditional kin network of nurture alone be dependable, even with voluntary or compulsory gender parity. Even shortening the work week and redefining wage-earning employment would be less than adequate. The foundation of a possible new civilization of work and life cannot be laid until the "habitus" is transformed in the three structurally interconnected institutions: family, state, and market. The work toward this goal will also be a mental, emotional and educational process, both personal and interpersonal. That is, the construction and reconstruction of the gendered self and gender relations are not confined to the private domain, and the public-private distinction is always contextual. The change, above all, will not come easily—hence Juliet Mitchell's powerful title *Women: The Longest Revolution* (1984)—as long as legitimation still appeals to "conventions" or "culture" that have become indistinguishable from nature (Rousseau 1947, 8).

The third limitation of communist feminism in the PRC is derived from the country's developmentalist impulse. Such an impulse placed gender equality at a lower order than other predominant state goals deemed more compelling or universal. This ordering was half-concealed during the Mao period, when labor mobilization coincided with female participation in support of both economic growth and women's liberation. Sheer developmental priorities were the feature of reform that forced people out of secured jobs and tolerated discriminative practices against women in hiring and firing. Female workers became the most vulnerable under the pressure of "economic rationalization" in the labor market where protective laws and rules regarding women were openly believed to hinder efficiency.[67] Meanwhile, sweatshops in illegal, appalling conditions relied on cheap female (and child) labor in abundant supply.

Finally, feminism in China, as elsewhere, was limited by the "equality versus difference" dilemma. Equality was either pursued through "sameness," as in the Mao years, or candidly given up in consumerism that celebrated "traditional" as well as commercialized images of femininity. The best-known Chinese expression of gender equality was the notion that "women can do whatever men can do"; it exemplified how male supremacy could be rejected only by projecting a "universal" benchmark in men's work and world (insofar as certain work was considered specifically masculine). Finding no way to transcend the essential, biologically determined confinement of the "natural woman," what socialism had done (perhaps the best way possible within the scope of a paternalistic state feminism) was to treat women as worker-citizens—they should "hold up half the sky" and their contribution be duly recognized and rewarded. Women's formal rights and perceived interests were nevertheless premised on the misrecognition of a weaker sex.

The puzzle of equality versus difference is of course not just a feminist one (Phillips 1997), but it can be strategically more pressing for women's movements everywhere. As women ask to be treated as men's equals, they also act as a group to invoke their sexually distinct identification and qualities. They seek to erase the very distinctions that, at the same time, are what they also must rely on for articulating their demands. This "'undecidability' of sexual difference," as Joan Scott puts it, drives self-conscious feminists to admit, in the words of the French revolutionary Olympe de Gouges, that they have "only paradoxes to offer" (1996, x-xi; cf. 1988). In China women's liberation, with all of its political, legislative, ideological, educational, and socioeconomic achievements, did not overcome the paradox; it was a non-question in the mindset of state feminism. The socialist state, unaware or incapable of solving many policy contradictions in its arbitration of gender (and class, etc.) relations, overlooked inequalities other than those related to the "vestiges of old society." The head-on conflict between the ideology of sameness and the "science" of a weaker sex did not appear to be a problem for theorists and policymakers.

This brings us back to "epistemological naturalism" which can be undermined by obvious commonsense analogies. If the differences between men and women are biologically determined, so would be "racial" and other more or less physiologically based variations among humans: the elderly, sick, "disabled," and "abnormal" of any sort. Fixed naturalness could then be taken as "social" categories with or without bodily references, such as rural-born individuals (as in China's *hukou* system) or those of foreign birth (as in global migration) or those born the untouchable or Dalis (as in India) and so on. Such a second "nature" produces corresponding (self-)identities. These identities in turn become preordained, stereotypical, and insurmountable; and their accompanying stigmas and disadvantages are difficult to address socially only in a deceptive language of "nature" detached from its social texture and context.

It does not follow, however, that objective natural differences, innate and adapted alike, have to be denied to achieve equality, or are inescapable obstacles to it. They may not be removable, but there may also not be any credible reason for them to be removed. The liberation of women cannot be a matter of biogenetic mutation, although new technologies have greatly improved individual self-control over the body and reproduction. In fact the notion of "equality" makes sense only because it is asserted among nonequals; and that is where public action is called for and contested. People are always different in their attributes as deep as their similarities in a historically specific yet shared "human nature." This fundamental complement is the only possible basis for communication and organization, in which "human rights" or "human emancipation" acquire comprehensible meanings. In other words, repudiating differences beyond the fallacious tendencies of biological determinism, sexual or otherwise, is neither sound nor constructive in the quest for equality. Women and men, as in any other physically divisible social groups, by the same principle of individual worth and autonomy should have similar as well as different desires, abilities, and attainments.[68] These similarities and differences also evolve over time with endless variations among individuals and situations. There is no need for societal authorities to contest the self-realization of individual and collective accomplishments, gendered or genderless, within observed social norms.

China's gender policies were marked by a unique perspective, taking sexual differences for granted in which women's disadvantageous position was either physiologically inherent (hence irremediable) or historically imposed (hence needing correction). In this perspective, government intervention, amounting to a public patriarchy, comes to be accepted both by the political and intellectual elites and by the larger population. A top-down approach was viewed as not only comparable to, but also farther reaching than, quotas and other measures of positive discrimination in many other countries. If feminist politics is about overturning the place of women in a male-centered civilization, then a women-friendly state was perhaps the most powerful and last transformative instrument to be captured, democratically, rather than discarded. Here I cannot discuss the weighty issues of family planning and reproductive rights, which merit separate treatises; but it is worth noting that the feminist stance in China is generally supportive of the one-child policy in light of its beneficial effects on women's health and social mobility. Yet feminists have also been critical of the excess in implementing the policy and have expressed concern about the lack of a long-term strategy regarding an aging population and the issue of an asymmetrical sexual ratio with the sociological upshot on demographic sustainability (cf. Croll et al. 1985; Milwertz 1997). They also have pointed out grave gender bias especially in abortion and schooling in many rural areas where not only did a male-centered tradition remain strong but social security was also little provided. Population control could otherwise be seen as another example of the "rational" subordination of individual preferences to those of society, justified on the ground that the latter incorporated the former, though in this case the coherence was indeed not lacking.

Women's Liberation and Modern Consciousness

The question posed earlier about class and ethnicity can similarly be asked in terms of gender; that is, whether equality had been achieved to a greater or lesser extent under the reform regime than under the Maoist one. Both periods, again, were full of contradictions. Whereas much of what the revolution aspired to carry on had been relinquished in the marketplace, thus taking away many of women's special benefits in public provision and social security, the turn to "reform and open up" was a fundamental gain. Rural industry and urbanization provided another blow to the remaining rigidity of domestic gender relations, as female farmers and housewives became cash-earning workers. But, more often than men, women were placed in low-grade jobs or suffered old and new forms of discrimination. Some traditionally patriarchal organizations came back in the vacuum created by the dissolution of communes. In political spaces the relaxation of central control had boosted feminist activism through state-sponsored channels as well as autonomous associations, and at both the elite level (the ACWF and its research arm, academia, professional networking, and journalism) and the grassroots. In response to policy needs or failures in protecting and promoting women, public debates occurred on such issues as sexually disproportionate unemployment, workplace safety and equity for women workers, human trafficking and domestic violence, bias against girls in schooling and other opportunities, as well as extramarital and lesbian relations. The spreading locus of women's and gender studies in workshops and conference rooms, in family kitchens and neighborhood committees, in books, journals, and newspapers, and in government offices and the NPC sessions expressed their urgency and popularity. The extent of feminist critiques and proposals certainly showed relative to other "marginalized interests" in the PRC, and women's interests continued to be viewed as legitimate and articulated most freely. In contrast, for the sake of regime and social stability, labor concerns were regarded as too sensitive and thus had centered on women workers (Howell 2004, 154–55). The "woman question" and also more recently the "peasant question," rather than the hitherto hidden "worker question," could be addressed in unison from above and below and in the media.[69] As a moral consensus more than a party ideology, and with its institutional backing in both state and society, the gender project, for all its weaknesses, has been a bright mark of Chinese modernity.

A twofold argument would give equal weight to the upward movements of women's self-liberation and to liberating women through top-down approaches. The difference between the two, and between private and public choices, was obvious but not absolute. On the one hand, waning egalitarianism was not paralleled with a decline in the demand of gender equality; the demand was reasserted, in a twist, by a postcultural revolutionary "individualist turn" to personal (and sexual) freedoms. Old egalitarian and new liberal sources in combination produced a more fresh, searching, and theoretically ambitious agenda for Chinese feminism. On the other hand, equality and justice in social relations, gender or otherwise, depended on corresponding legal and other public institutions. A committed, accountable, and resourceful state could be recaptured in a globalizing market as a necessary vehicle for women to accomplish greater equality, better life chances, and fuller citizenship. Between lost protection and gained freedom, it would be mistaken to forsake rather than democratize and reform state feminism (Lin 2002).

Gender equality comes out most positively for Chinese socialism in a comparison of the role of the state regarding women and of that role in terms of class, ethnic, and spatial politics. This credit, however, is seriously discounted as soon as other categories are brought in to intervene. If rural and urban China were two different worlds; and if poor women shared their lot with their fellow men in a particular social class or geo-ethnic location rather than with their privileged female counterparts in the state sector or the group of the new rich, then "gender equality" would be in part a myth. Surely equality cannot be the equal sharing of poverty and inequalities. Socialist urban bias and market polarization were both testimonies to the fallacy of an integrated and classless identity of "women." Likewise, neither sex had been politically free and equal in the PRC: men and women were merely equal in their limited formal rights. In light of these factors, a pressing question is whether gender equality can really be an isolated goal of feminism, and whether women (and men) can be truly liberated without universal social emancipation. For those in the "third" and "transitional" worlds, winning freedom and equality also requires a transformation of the disadvantaged position of their countries in the global distribution of power and wealth. Feminism therefore cannot limit itself to gender concerns. It has no way to advance without either governmental actions or allies in the other social movements.

It was the antipatriarchal Chinese revolution and state feminism that generated an unusually close relationship between feminism and socialism in China (Croll 1978; Honig 1985). Such a relationship, contrary to an impressionist view on communist totalitarianism, also inherited a liberal individualist legacy. Although the "patriarchal gender system" proved somehow enduring, the dedication to freedoms including "modern" marriage and free love among first-generation communists was as strong as a radical subculture (Gilmartin 1995, 3). Such a subculture in the tradition of enlightenment liberalism, in contrast with the puritanical repression of the Cultural Revolution, survived in certain forms and circles peripheral to the anti-liberal ideological indoctrination after 1949. The language of women's liberation did not necessarily silence various voices of female individualism but it overwhelmed them in the Chinese modern consciousness of modernization and national development. Like it or not, gender in the PRC "is not just 'about' women and men, but is about the state, the nation, socialism, and capitalism" (Rofel 1999, 20). In tracing the roots of these bonds in China's social-national-developmental trajectory, a feminist-nationalist alliance stood out. The "nationalist resolution of the woman question" might be common in the colonial and postcolonial world of a compelling intersection of women's subordination with imperialist, racist, class, regional, and religious forces of oppression (Chatterjee 1989; Jayawardena 1986; Mohanty et al. 1991). But there was no shortage of national regimes that oppressed women, and wherever this was the case it only supports the insistence that the cause of women is inevitably intertwined with those of others in the liberation struggle. Wherever such interconnected struggles overlap they would logically reinforce each other. It was the overarching socialist mandate that most powerfully endorsed a state feminism in China.

The "feminism" that is both embedded in and constructive of socialism is thus a greater signifier than what is customarily denoted by the term. More than female empowerment to counter male dominance, women's liberation was not separated from Chinese nationalism and modernization, which was the source of contention over marginalization of feminist concerns. But the meaning of "liberation" is itself contestable, as is "equality"; and both entail hard measurements as well as soft values and sensitivities. Paternalistic socialism had suffered deficiencies from the outset, and it became obsolete as the "woman question" evolved in the changing circumstances. Yet the public attitude in China had been broadly defensive of the proudest achievements of the revolution and of state feminism in the face of their destruction. Between a retreating state and a forward-marching market, between protection coupled with dependency and autonomy accompanied by insecurity, there must be room for synthetic rearticulations and institutionalization of socialist feminism. The ability of such a feminism to curb unchecked power in the private sector and in domestic spheres as well as to pressure and check on government policies would be a main indicator of the next phase yet to be defined of Chinese alternative modernity embracing gender equality. The "social" realm, a democratic antithesis of both state and market fetishism, would be where women's rights are fought and gender norms exposed, challenged and transformed. It would be also where the conditions of female existence transcend their gender boundary into the "human condition." Women's future in China physically and symbolically depends on how well the lessons of state feminism can be digested in the transition that also involves unprecedented information and bioengineering technologies. The impressive impact of the popularity of cell phones and, to a lesser extent, the Internet on the lifestyle and outlook of younger women is just a beginning.

Socialism, nationalism, and developmentalism as ideologies and processes were integrated into, and restrained by, one another. Their equilibrium relied on the willingness and capacity of the state. "Developmentalism" thereby applies to a constitutive dimension of the Chinese project in its specific historical and international contexts—the developmental imperative in line with China's national purpose and social goals. As such it is subject to critical scrutiny but is not limited to and may not always confirm the term's narrow and negative usage in the slow-to-come Chinese debate over sustainable development. Keeping this in mind, it should be clear that the tripartite foundation of the Chinese model has been structurally requisite for the country's basic political consensus, economic stability, and social cohesion; any unilateral change would disable or destabilize the model and threaten a systemic breakdown. The Cultural Revolution, to be discussed in the next chapter, is one example, in view of its feverish "revolution over production"; the Taiwan crisis is another example in terms of the Chinese nationalist dilemma. But the largest-ever case in point is the fading of Chinese socialism itself as a modern alternative in the teeth of a state-led market integration toward global capitalism. The immediate transaction cost already seemed quite unaffordable as the sense spread of "too many people having too much to lose."

No longer representing a national road to socialism in the conventional wisdom of public ownership, central planning, and an "iron rice bowl," the PRC state would continue to be central to China's development and the direction of that development. It has so far been the only capable agent—with multiple and at times even incoherent layers and constituents—to lead the change in the least-possible chaotic manner while coordinating efforts to accommodate conflicts and difficulties. Moreover, the socialist state's traditional duty and conscience has not vanished: the consistent push for poverty alleviation echoed the national campaigns in human development against epidemic diseases and illiteracy earlier launched by the communists fresh in power. Compelled to relieve social tensions, compensatory efforts, according to Dorothy Salinger, "have preoccupied much of the energy of the labor, social security, and of the civil affairs bureaucracies," of which the huge, government-funded reemployment program is only one example.[70] The creed of governing since "liberation" (the term used in everyday Chinese to refer to 1949) for public good and national dignity is retained in the sources of regime legitimacy. It was this creed that had nurtured a dedicated labor force and a compliant population, and set a standard for public policies and bureaucratic behavior to be evaluated.

As revolution was replaced by reform, the Chinese working classes had to reposition themselves in a class struggle that, unlike Maoist "key link" politics, began to engage itself in the real battleground of the global market. Compared with ethnic or gender relations that were by no means harmonious, class inequalities were still where Chinese socialism's greatest failure and predicament had to be identified. The image of a revolutionary ruling class had never been actualized, as workers became "gears and screws" of the socialist train driven by the party toward a destination so objectively or scientifically desirable that it did not need popular approval. The gulfs between rural and urban societies, between the Han and minority regions, and between ordinary citizens and privileged cadres, along with the repression of political dissent, contradicted an egalitarian ideology and the promised land of emancipation. This was the background against which the reform initiatives, respectively, in liberating the mind, the productive forces, and the rural poor, made every sense. The partial reversal of these developments in turn gave rise to mounting social crises and protests.

If social scientists, then and now, must "confront the fact that class tensions are a primary determinant of the nature of the Chinese state" (Kraus 1983, 145), it is also true that the communist state had manipulated class identification, identities, and relations. As a result, social classes in China and the concept "class" itself were scarcely independent and less "organic" than the cases elsewhere. It was not the leadership of the proletariat, nor the power of a worker-peasant alliance, but the state project of national development that had been the foremost preoccupation of Chinese socialism. By the same token, just as economically definable classes arose, the language of class was "tabooed." The regime, from its revolutionary upbringing, knew only too well what class agitation and organization would mean and, understandably, "stability" should be a catch-all word in a one party system. Liberal commentators also avoided any class rhetoric in a worldview of capitalist globalism. Incidentally, the intellectuals in the PRC cannot be treated as a class for reasons more than the millennial tradition of state assimilation. In Mao's famous skin-hair metaphor, they may be attached to any class contingent on where they stand as groups or individuals politically. The fact that the communist movement in China had an intellectual rather than a working-class origin did not strike the party as a note of inadequacy in its relevant ideological and policy formulations; and the Gramscian concept of "organic intellectuals" never accessed the CCP discourse. State arbitration and regulation in the relationships between and among China's nationalities, regions, religions, and genders also had an appealing as well as disturbing record. A telling example was that of paternalistic feminism, which, seemingly contradictory in terms, was nevertheless a coherent policy principle of the socialist state in firm opposition to traditional patriarchy. Managing ethnicity was a less-successful story, but what had been minimally established followed a formal commitment to ethnic equality and solidarity must not be trivialized.

What was phenomenal about the 1990s was the advance of a neoliberal tendency to integrate China without a remedy for its bureaucratic power buttressed by privatization. If globalization endangered national autonomy and rivaled state ability, it only propelled individual states to shoulder more, not less, security and welfare responsibilities to their peoples as long as national polities and economies remained the basic units of operation. The indispensability of a "right" state has been reaffirmed, again and again, to show what matters is not the scope but the nature of the state.

The socialist state standing aloof from the cleavages of society is resonant with the capitalist developmental state that seeks partnership with, but is also in control of, the private sector in a cross-class scheme of national development. The two models resemble each other to certain degree in their otherwise highly distinguishable corporatist structure and political culture, such as a collective- and duty-leaning conception of citizenship. As the consistency and performance of the state was the single most important institutional test of continuities and discontinuities between the pre- and post-reform eras, as well as between the first and second reform decades, it would be so also for the third, and especially critical, phase of the reform—critical because the crises since 1989 have to be addressed and because the reform model of a socialist market will finally be taking shape. To fulfill these tasks, both the state and market, politics and the economy, will have to be thoroughly democratized—not only formally for the pressure of a global ideology, but in the actual interests of the Chinese people in their infinite diversities. The democratic idea and ideal inherited in the Chinese revolution and in socialism will be an invaluable asset for a locally credible perspective in this endeavor. It is to the political puzzle involved that we now turn.

Chapter 3

People's Democracy?

THE NOW MOSTLY FORGOTTEN AND REJECTED CONCEPT OF "PEOPLE'S democracy" was employed in the Soviet satellites from the end of World War II until the last years of the cold war, and in the PRC before the end of the Cultural Revolution. But perhaps with a few small exceptions, only in Chinese socialism did the concept find a receptive setting as an elaborate and popularized ideology. The concept, associated with the purges, chaos, and destruction of, notably, the Cultural Revolution, was not directly denounced but simply erased from the official vocabulary after 1978. The theory and practice of people's democracy, however, have not been systematically and critically studied, nor has any consensus beyond superficial statements ever been reached on related experiences. Yet as polarization deepened and corruption mounted, the past public commitment to the power of the people became a surging undercurrent in the People's Republic where the government and political economy alienated the people. This implies something very specific about China: a common perception of people's democracy in the world's most populous country did not conform to the ideological and institutional packages on offer from the latest global wave of democratization, insofar as these packages did not address China's locally defined problems.

Democracy philologically means rule by the people. The Chinese translation *min-zhu* (demo-cracy) is a two-character term that literally links the subject noun with a predicate verb or noun to mean "people decide" or "people's rule." The standard Chinese one-phrase elaboration is *renmin dangjia zuozhu*, or "people in control of their own affairs." Although "people's democracy" (*renmin minzhu*) is thereby verbally redundant, it makes sense in the Chinese mind, especially because it is distinguished linguistically and politically from the contentious notion of "bourgeois democracy," which is believed to be a sham. As a vast episode of modern history that involved, in the PRC alone, one fifth of humanity, people's democracy is beyond the pale of the mainstream democracy discourse limited to the trajectories and conceptions around contemporary liberal societies. To examine "people's democracy" in China seriously is thus to recognize the tremendous weight of Chinese development in the modern age, something weighty yet "alien," and as valid as any "normal" cases that demand an explanation in political science.[1] Refusing to vanish in history, the attempt at people's democracy cannot be dismissed even minimally by the paradoxical conviction of liberal pluralism. As Max Weber famously puts it, "the highest ideals, which move us most forcefully, are always formed only in the struggle with other ideals which are just as sacred to others as ours are to us."[2]

I begin this chapter with the symbolic meaning of the concept of "people's sovereignty," and I critically trace "people's democracy" in both its Maoist theorization and its actual course within the Chinese communist revolution. In the second section I aim to clear the clouds overshadowing a discredited "people's democratic dictatorship" tied to post-revolutionary consolidation of power and bureaucratization along with a traditionally congenial totalitarian populism. The so-called grand democracy that had inspired a population of many millions to seek personal freedom and collective empowerment was a puzzle of participation in conflation with mobilization. In the third section I offer a comparative analysis of citizenship between the politics before and after market reforms. In so doing I contrast between the moral assertion of the sovereign place of the people and its distorted institutionalization in the former period, and between the dismantling of that morality and the construction of laws and legal procedures in the latter; and, further, simultaneously between these two sets of contradictions. I then proceed to argue that democratization cannot be achieved without the rightful position of the people and the supremacy of their will being reclaimed and materialized from above and below. Finally, I probe the conception of "Chinese democracy."

Revolution and Democracy

Like the Americans, the Chinese embraced "we the people" only through a social revolution en route to a new nation (Young 1993). *Min-quan,* as Sun

Zhongshan chose to label it among his three "people's principles," designated people's rights and power. Lenin spoke of Sun as an "enlightened spokesman of militant and victorious Chinese democracy," a "truly great ideology of a truly great people" (1912, 163–65). In the wake of Asia's first republic, the May 4th slogan of "science and democracy" represented extensive and intense searches into an array of Western schools of thought by China's modern-minded democrats. The communist revolution was conceived in the party's minimum program in terms of "new democracy." These movements against colonial domination and "feudal" and other anti-democratic forces at home made democracy a continuing and shared aspiration for China's successive revolutionary generations. If nationalism was what defined the continuity between the republicans and the communists, there must be something intrinsically democratic about that nationalism, for the liberation and self-determination of an oppressed people, and hence national sovereignty, would be prerequisite for any nationally assumed democratic government.

A democracy-centered narrative can neither be construed nor dismissed out of context. The communist revolution, in particular, contained in itself tensions between the goals of individual/societal freedom and nation-state building in order to defeat foreign powers. This tension was keenly felt by China's political and intellectual elites throughout the twentieth century. As such, imperialism certainly contributed to "totalitarian" tendencies in revolutionary Chinese politics in the same way as colonialism did for formalist democracies in colonial modernity elsewhere. Above all, the revolution took a violent path and adopted the means that violated its own democratic ends. Not only was the CCP forced to engage in military operations in the countryside after the massacre of communists and sympathizers in 1927 (Isaacs 1951), but it also endured internal slaughter in perilous situations.[3] It is a profound "modern tragedy," to borrow from Raymond Williams, because "we have . . . to see the actual liberation as part of the same process as the terror" (1979, 81–82). Yet there is the obvious distinction between "a slave-owner who through cunning and violence shackles a slave in chains, and a slave who through cunning or violence breaks the chains" (Trotsky 1966, 33). The revolutionary processes have to be thoroughly historicized in order for us to critically understand terror or war in justified response to unjust terror or war (Walzer 1977; Mayer 2000). It is for justice's sake that in the United Nations' Universal Declaration on Human Rights, law and order are justifiable only "if man is not to be compelled to have recourse, as a last resort, to rebellion against tyranny and oppression" ("Preamble," 5). An analogy between the Chinese and American revolutions (including the American Civil War) is telling when neglected parallels are seen in their nationalist, populist, and egalitarian impulses as much as in revolutionary violence.

We the People

A monumental achievement of the Chinese revolution was that for the first time in one of the world's oldest and largest civilizations the notion of "subjects" had been replaced with that of the "people." The revolution, rationalized and clarified in terms of new democracy, enabled massive participation by ordinary men and women learning to take control over their own destinies. At issue is more than "liberating" a people, which might be done in very different ways such as by foreign intervention (e.g., the occupation of Germany, Japan, or, for that matter, Tibet) and by native movements led by future dictators (as in parts of the postcolonial world). The point, rather, is about people creating history while changing themselves. Quoting Condorcet, Hannah Arendt reaffirms that the essence of a revolution worthy of its name has to be freedom—those who "had always lived in darkness and subjection to whatever powers there were, should rise and become the supreme sovereigns of the land" (1963, 21). The sovereignty derived from revolutions is democratic in nature for their participants; and nothing can be more earthshaking than "we the people" finding an institutional expression of national power.

In other words, modern revolutions—communist included—as precursors and markers of modernity cannot logically be democracy's antithesis. The event of bypassing Western-style institutions of political participation and competition was not an indication of bypassing democracy as such. The Chinese revolution initially legitimized the communist rule in the belief in people's sovereignty (*renmin zhuquan*), which in turn kept generating pressures on the regime. People's democracy is, then, normatively defined by the principle of the people being sovereign and the ultimate source and judge of the political authority. Their collective subject position is the foundation of the new state of a people's republic, of which the government, set up to serve its natural constituency, must be of, for, and thus by the people. To be sure, all types of modern states obtain legitimacy by invoking in one way or another the name of the people. But the PRC identity is so tied to that name that (tauto)logically the state and the people become one along with the conflation of national and people's sovereignty (cf. Rupnik 1999). Together, more than formal democracies, people's democracy self-consciously carries enormous moral significance as a sacred and inviolable power entity. In reality, written in the constitution, penetrating in the ideology, formalized in the people's congresses, and substantiated in relevant social policies with regard to meeting basic needs and promoting participation, the "sovereignty of the people" was not a mere deception. The NPC, as constitutionally the "highest organ of state power," was the basic form of a socialist representative democracy with elected deputies entrusted to exercise that power. It was thus theoretically an institutional alternative to classical as well as modern capitalist democracies. To be sure, revolutionary democracy decayed over time. But it would still explain something profoundly real in the support, consent, and obedience in a communist China not ruled by force. Wherever the People's Republic failed the people, it turned out not to be because it defied the Western models of government and their colonial extension, but because it departed from its own visionary inspiration and promises of democracy.

More specifically, the legacies of an armed revolution and the social-national-developmental imperative allowed the state to quickly insulate itself from the people in a process of transforming a revolutionary party into a ruling position. As the party-state began to swallow society in a top-down corporatist manner, state power representing both national sovereignty and internal order grew without the people themselves being empowered in their supposed sovereign capacity. The latter turned out to be an illusion as the conviction of a self-determining citizenry dissolved in the assurance of representation. Surely the bearer of sovereignty in a leviathan has to be unbound and absolute, be it the king, the court, the parliament, or the government of the people (Hobbes in McClelland 1996, 193–96). And social revolutions, "belying the liberal or democratic hopes of many of their participants . . . have led to stronger—more centralized, bureaucratic, and coercive—national states than the old regimes they replaced" (Skocpol 1994, 20). Yet we should not overlook how in the case of the Chinese revolution something unprecedented in the country's autocratic history also emerged. The cliché that the revolution was no more than another round of a sinological dynastic cycle of despotism is superficial. The historical depth of the revolutionary episode in China may be appreciated only if we look at the scope of its mobilization in a "people's war" and in the mass movements, and at the specific social conditions in which one revolution fermented could engender another. The communist state displayed complex qualities in engaging but also manipulating popular demands. As Marc Blecher observes, "while most authoritarian states seek to insulate themselves from society by repressing it into quiescence, the Maoist state chose instead to rule by activating society . . . It wanted believers, not subjects" (1997, 220).

The Chinese version of people's democracy also has two other problems—both of which I will later address in full; suffice it here to note their extent. The question, at the start, of who "the people" are could almost be specifically a Chinese one, which is different from defining the boundary of a political community in democracy theories (cf. Dahl 1989, 193ff, on "the problem of the unit"; and Habermas 2001, 1–25, on "what is a people?"). Putting aside the noun's Greek or Roman origins, the secular subject *demos* or *populus* as political equals being collectively sovereign was an invention of modern revolutions. The liberal democratic disposition, however, has compromised popular sovereignty for individual autonomy in opposition to absolutism.[4] The term "people" in "people's democracy," by contrast, is understood in a way more faithful to an originally populist project. Yet this understanding is discounted by two complications. On the one hand, the meaning of the term is socially broader than that of the "proletariat" in the Soviet concept of "proletarian democracy." In theory, the "people" is more inclusive while signifying where the power should be derived and possessed. It highlights the peasantry (in alliance with the working class) in a reflection of China's industrial underdevelopment and gestures to the party's willingness to preserve a multiclass and multiparty united front. On the other hand, the line was drawn in practice between the people and their enemies in "class" and "line" struggles. As the categories of enemy inside and outside the party wildly expanded, many people were excluded from "democracy" and subjected to persecution by a "people's democratic dictatorship." Such exclusion violently damaged what was hoped to be a democratic alternative to both "bourgeois democracy" and "proletarian dictatorship" (even though the latter label was adopted when the carefully theorized distinction between a *proletariat* and the *people* as regime identity disappeared after Mao's 1962 warning against class struggle being forgotten).

The other problem for which the claim for a people's democracy became dubious was the monopoly of power by a vanguard party. If that power was briefly challenged at the beginning of the Cultural Revolution, the challenge was still incited by Mao's personal appeal from above. The elitist undertone was the loudest, ironically, in a mass-line politics in which the party and leaders were assumed to know better in a downward pattern of command. Although political education was perceived a two-way process that required educators themselves to be educated, policymaking was concentrated at the top and mostly lacked transparency. Participation and voices from below only had limited impact on government, resulting in local and popular preferences being obscure or ignored. There is, however, no outstanding theoretical obstacle to reconciling the vanguard and the masses in the communist mind. People's democracy does not dispense with either leadership or "scientific social engineering." The state structure must mediate interplays between the two layers of the polity, and the ideal relationship between the party and the people, to use Mao's metaphor, is like fish and water. Indeed the populist thrust remained pressing throughout the revolution and Maoist socialism, paralleling the all-powerful CCP. It was not until the post-Mao repudiation of cultural revolutionary ideologies that "people's democracy" was dropped from the official rhetoric.

The Trajectory of an Idea

The vicissitude of the idea of a "people's democracy" serves as a vantage point in examining the ideologically charged politics of Chinese socialism. The persistent relevance of this idea is also evident in China's present legitimacy crisis revolving around social change. If democracy is part of what fundamentally legitimized the revolution, it would also come to the revolution's defense. The ultimate premise is that democratic and socialist undertakings are congruous if, as argued, the entire Chinese modern project can be grasped as an attempted alternative to colonial modernity, Soviet statism, and global capitalism. Each of these historical paradigms seen in a negative light—foreign oppression, bureaucratic domination, and market coercion—is rejected as democracy's antithesis.

The Marxian model of direct democracy is built on the Paris Commune's fullest possible promise. In that projected model, rather than the actual Commune, public servants of a "social republic," a free-unit association, are selected through universal suffrage and/or rotation by volunteering or drawing lots. They are supervised, and can be recalled at any time, by their immediate constituents. Instead of "deciding once in three or six years which member of the ruling class was to misrepresent the people in parliament," the municipal council, which is simultaneously legislative and executive, exemplifies an empowered people beginning to dismantle the state. Meanwhile, the political logic of the model also points to the need for abolishing private property and accompanying productive relations; and the necessity of "smashing" an existing state apparatus supportive of class exploitation and oppression. For Marx, the Paris Commune represented rational self-government and was thus "a Revolution not against this or that, legitimate, constitutional, republican or imperialist form of State Power. It was a Revolution against the State itself." Since the state must be seen as a "supernaturalist abortion of society," the revolution can only be "resumption by the people for the people of its own social life." The language of the people uneasily coexists with that of the "dictatorship of the proletariat" cited by the Commune, in the sense of class rule by workers against a counterrevolutionary bourgeoisie (1871 part 3; 1875 chapter 4; cf. 1852, chapter 3). Democracy and dictatorship are thus compatible as " 'outward dictatorship' employing violence against the minority of the former oppressors is an 'internal democracy' for the majority" (Sartori 1987, 470–71). But in Marx, the dictatorship of the proletariat is one of a class, not the state; and a "proletarian state" would be a contradiction in terms. The question is not so much whether the state should be regarded as the instrument of the ruling class as it is how to resolve the ambiguity of the nature and institutions of a proletarian dictatorship after the old state machinery is smashed. When this question is translated into the Maoist doctrine of a "people's democratic dictatorship" to imply a state system being democratic for the people while dictatorial over the enemies of the people, the Marxist rejection of the state as such is conveniently lost.

Along with Marx, Lenin envisioned a democracy thought to be immediately applicable to socialist Russia after the war. Such a vision needs neither a standing army, nor a police force, nor a bureaucracy, as ordinary citizens join in the administration of public affairs. "All power to the so-viets," councils of deputies run by workers and soldiers, became the banner of the October revolution. The Leninist conception of proletarian dictator-ship en route to a classless and stateless society is thus class-centered, transi-tional, and affirming the institutional potentials celebrated in Marx's Paris Commune. The leadership of the revolutionary vanguard party notwith-standing, Lenin's blueprint for soviet politics aspires to be "a thousand times more democratic" than capitalist democracies. Whatever might be written about Soviet history,[5] the communist state in China surely found no way even to prepare for itself to wither away, which left the idea of people's democracy with insurmountable contradictions.

But the strand of power from below in Marxism also echoed some native Chinese traditions.[6] The volumes *The Civil War in France* (1871) and *The State and Revolution* (1918), within streams of Marxist as well as anarchist, socialist, and liberal classics, made their way to a progressive Chinese read-ership via Japan and Russia in the early twentieth century. A "Parisian connection," as Elizabeth Perry describes it in the context of workers' agi-tation in Shanghai (1999) was resumed most loudly and proudly in the imitated cultural revolutionary "communes" in the Chinese metropolises (Starr 1972; 1979, chapter 5) and, though only vaguely, in the political imagi-nation of the Tiananmen protest of 1989. Seeing affinities between the populist, antibureaucratic inclination of Mao and what is highlighted in Marx's reading of the events of 1871, Meisner shows how an arresting histor-ical moment was reinvented in a distant time and space. The struggle in China to prevent the revolution from degenerating "made the Marxian concept of the Commune (and the revolutionary imagery it conveyed) *really* historically significant and a truly dynamic factor in Chinese Com-munist thought and politics" (1982, 140).

It may be tempting to draw a parallel between the aspirations of "peo-ple's sovereignty" in the tradition of "natural rights" in the Enlightenment and of "people-based governance" in the civic Confucian creed of "people-rootedness" (*minben*) as opposed to religion. The Mencian interpretation of Confucianism depicts the ideal polity as following the demand "first of its people, then its divinities, then its ruler." For that is heaven's order, as "heaven sees as the people see, heaven hears as the people hear." The pri-ority of the populace over the king is given on the grounds that their well-being is the duty as well as a test of ruling legitimacy. Accordingly, the unity of the rulers and the ruled is the basis of a virtuous and sustainable reign (Bloom 1998; Judge 1998, 194). The author of the three people's principles regards Mencius as "the ancestor of our democratic ideas" (Sun quoted in Jiang 1998, 215). Even the iconoclastic communists breaking with the old political culture could not disclaim their debt to the past (Schram 1987). Against orthodox Marxism within the CCP, Mao recommended "discarding the dross and selecting the cream" in the indigenous heritage "from Confucius to Sun Zhongshan." Modern people's democracy could borrow from the traditional wisdom of governing from *minben* to harmony of interests. Like Mencius' "heaven" being the voices of the commoners, Mao's "god" is straightforwardly the people. Telling a story about how "the foolish old man removed the mountains," he sees the work of the party as a matter of "touching God's heart" or the heart of "the masses of the Chinese people" (1991 [1945b], 1102). In contrast to the operation of liberal democracies with interest groups as the core, a regime is perceived to be democratic in China less when it is open to influence by the people divided in such groups than when it serves what is considered the people's collective and higher interests (Nathan 1985, 228). Consequently, constructing democracy is intimately related to, and conditioned by, the "more fundamental problems" of reorganizing the economy and society for people's livelihood and social justice.[7] A regime may not be fully legitimized by pursuing land reform, providing free health care, raising literacy levels and so on (Fukuyama 1993, 10), but neither should it be legitimized by mere free elections. Democracy cannot go very far when it is separated from social issues, especially in a third world country; and it also must be clarified as to whose legitimacy is at work.

The continuity of secular egalitarianism in an otherwise hierarchical and patriarchal tradition also had a particular cultural and psychological bearing on China's modern consciousness. Confucianism, Taoism, Monism, and even Buddhism functioned mostly as philosophies, natural religions, or folk superstitions. Without powerful churches they did not in any way curb state power, and Confucianism even became a state ideology itself. Meanwhile the factors of birth (except for gender bias) and of faith in China's bureaucratic recruitment and social status were not as decisive as in many religious societies or in European and Japanese aristocratic feudalism. Whatever Weber has to say about Chinese "religions," the fact that at least

Han high culture was essentially atheist and nonteleological helped explain the Maoist this-worldly confidence in the people and their self-salvation.[8] It was no accident that for the majority for whom there was "no god," communism played a spiritual role in defining a social outlook and an ethical code, "converting" nonbelievers, and making devotion and sacrifice bearable, even noble. As recent as Tiananman in 1989, the protest generation still embraced the *Internationale* for its overtone of self-liberation: "No one will give us deliverance; no god, no czar, no hero; we'll arrive at our freedom only by ourselves" (cf. Calhoun 1994). An ideological system might be functionally religious as a major source of power, yet the "political messianism" of self-emancipation in China was without prophecy and redemption.

While certain Chinese traditional and modern values might be complementary to each other (cf. Hu 2000, chapters 1–2), the incompatibility between the Confucian and communist cosmic orders is also obvious. To begin with, the replacement of the emperor's "subjects" with a sovereign "people" was a paradigmatic shift in social consciousness. However splendid and humane the passages of thought discovered in the tradition may be, that tradition is on the whole undemocratic and, furthermore, cannot be modernized simply through wishful reinterpretations such as those attempted by earnest scholars in contemporary neo-Confucianism. Above all, the notion of democratic citizenship is completely alien to the "ancient constitutionalism" of *minben,* and revolutionary mobilization fundamentally contradicts the "patrimonial rulership with a human face" (McCarmic 1990, 195–96) dependent on subordination. The revolution was to create a new politics based on active and extensive participation from "the masters of society" who were previously repressed by and excluded from the state. These conflicting tendencies were both present in the actual political development of the PRC.

The idea of democracy in China owes its genesis to important elements in a variety of traditions: from Marxist and anarchist antistate reasoning to socialist and liberal thinking of collective and individual rights; from the American, French, and Russian revolutions to the indigenous teachings about government and rebellion. But the strongest source of people's democracy is the Chinese communist revolution. This revolution comprised decades of revolutionary struggle, urban and rural, that first built up local institutions of a people's democracy to be taken over nationally. And it was the moral—more than political—authority of the people that injected in an extremely arduous cause the necessary optimism and pride among its participants.

The "Mass Line"

Mao's "mass line," or "from the masses, to the masses," featured what was epitomized as the "Yan'an way" of revolutionary China. It was an ideological conviction as well as a working method, and a concept of leadership as well as organizational techniques (Lewis 1963, chapter 3; Townsend 1967, chapter 4). In its classical design, the party takes the scattered ideas of the people, turns them into concentrated and systematic ideas, and then returns them to the people to use as guide for their actions. This process—of "pooling the wisdom of the masses" through soliciting views and educating the viewers, of interest articulation and aggregation, and of testing and adjusting decisions—repeats itself over and again in an "endless spiral." It aims at allowing the government to arrive at sound policies while minimizing mistakes and maximizing its power base (Mao 1964, 854). An analogy is the processing industry, in which good finished products depend on the workers (cadres) to process raw materials (gathered from the masses) in adequate quantity and quality—a task that requires informed, honest, and competent performances.

But unlike any mere material production, the mass line was about producing collective knowledge and consciousness-raising through words, songs, speeches, "telling bitterness" (*suku*), and many other forms of communication. The ideology had to be translated into an institution of discourse that could in turn penetrate daily practices of identity formation, subjective cultivation, and shared thinking and acting (e.g., "speaking Bolshevik" in Kotkin 1995). This translation had a further task in China, where Marxism traveled from the West not just to the East but all the way to the East's remote "mountain valleys." Involved was thus not only the sinification but also the ruralization of something originating in urban Europe. Mao elaborated the task in an address to Yan'an's literature and art circles, calling for the engendering of local and popular channels of transmitting political messages effectively in the folk media and peasant dialects. Revolutionary China thereby became "a mobilization space" filled with "the power of symbolic capital." As such, Chinese communism had enriched itself as a political movement by also being a sophisticated "discourse community," which strengthened loyalties and generated a powerful momentum to change the course of history (Apter and Saich 1994, 66–67, 300). The discursive dimension also extended to the self-correcting and self-limiting measures on the part of the party members, such as "criticisms and self-criticisms." The CCP, claiming to have "no special interests of its own apart from the interests of the working class and the broadest masses of the people," must "wholeheartedly" serve the people. "While it does all things for the masses, it also relies on all things from the masses. As the party springs from the masses, it must return to the fold" (restated in the CCP constitution 1992; see Lieberthal 1995, 386–87).

The mass line was also based on pragmatic considerations related to control. There was a shared Chinese wisdom of ruling, past and present, that reads the signs of popular discontent in order to evade social calamity. As "water holds the boat, but can turn it over too," those in power should be rationally motivated to allow room for criticisms before they would accumulate into revolts.[9] Beyond the tacit sanction of rulership, Mao was earnestly self-critical of the Great Leap disaster: "If there is no democracy we cannot possibly summarize experience correctly. . . . If ideas are not coming from the masses, it is impossible to establish a good line, good general as well as specific policies and methods." Stressing the necessary responsiveness of government to the needs and demands of the population, he went on in 1962 to tell seven thousand of the country's ministers and local governors that "without democracy, you have no understanding of what is happening down below; the situation will be unclear; you will be unable to collect sufficient opinions from all sides" (1996 [1962], 16). The conception of democracy here did not specify a free press or free association; it referred rather to the necessity of a close relationship between the leaders and the led, and a reliable reporting system to ensure government accountability at all levels with regard to policy formulation and adjustment. The background to this was that the center, misled by inaccurate information provided by local officials eager to please their superiors, failed to act promptly on preventing the famine from spreading. This point confirms Amartya Sen's thesis (1990; qualified in chapter 1) that famine does not happen in democracies.

The mass line was taken as "functionally essential" for the party's operation and applied to a desired inner-party democracy. Three particular functions were identified as follows: nurturing loyalty and creativity of individuals and localities of the party; strengthening ties between the party and the masses so to combat "subjectivism" and "bureaucratism"; and permitting flexible handling of specific local problems (Schurmann 1960, 54–55). The Chinese adaptation of Soviet "democratic centralism" was in effect a replication of "from the masses" (democracy) and "to the masses" (centralism) (White 1983, 35–36; Schurmann 1968). In following rather than departing from the Leninist organizational principle of the individual being subordinated to the organization, the minority to the majority, the lower to the higher levels of command, and the party to its central committee, the constitution of the CCP grants its members certain important rights. They may disagree with or criticize any party decisions and reserve their dissenting views, for example, provided that they obey a resolution while it is in force (Article 4). Such rights in reality tended to be merely formal and had been denied exercise during political campaigns. The inherent difficulty in holding a balance between freedom and discipline gave rise to a vicious circle of chaos ("too much democracy") and stifling ("too much control") in the party and the country at large. For Deng and his successors it remained complicated in the era after mass line to manage tensions between liberalization and stabilization. For the practical benefits of democratic devices, the rhetoric of "socialist democracy" had been preserved but interpreted in far less mass-oriented and more legalistic terms. Solicitation, deliberation, consensus building, and "reciprocal accountability" continued among power holders at different units of government. David Lampton (1987) has made the "bargaining treadmill" a well-known characterization of policy processes in the PRC, which explains why endless meetings of Chinese cadres may not be seen as merely bureaucratic routines without meaningful outcomes (Shirk 1993).

For those who look back with some nostalgia at the successes of revolutionary mobilization—from the land reform through collectivization and urban transformation—the mass line was the lodestar of a prototype popular democracy. That democracy, or "revolutionary incrementalism" (Goodman 2000), first flourished in the wartime base areas with peasant participation and later offered the sole standard by which one could "gauge the course of the transition to socialism" in China (Selden 1988, 100). As the mass line is about party/mass, leaders/rank-and-file relations, actual strains between guidance and spontaneity or between elitism and populism did not pose a serious theoretical challenge (cf. Worseley 1969). If the peasantry was traditionally a conservative class "by itself," then, as expected, in China too the "rise of a popular, participatory politics was not spontaneous" (Blecher 1989, 203). It took painstaking effort on the part of party workers in educating, mobilizing, and cultivating mostly illiterate activists at the grassroots. As detailed in scholarly accounts, they stayed with peasant families; visited the locals and networked among them; set up discussion meetings and workshops; organized militia, youth, and women's groups as well as literacy classes and agitation teams, and so on (Burns 1988; Blecher 1991). Indeed, even the extraordinary organizational ability and adaptability that the Chinese communists developed would not be a guarantee for overcoming the many formidable barriers to generating support. After all, populism "is not a peasant ideology, but a protest ideology of intellectuals speaking for what they perceive to be the interests of the rural masses" (Meisner 1982, 112).

Mao, for all his populist inclination, saw China as a "blank sheet" for socialism to write on and to paint (cf. Starr 1979, 278).[10] At issue was not the weight of tradition, be it a great burden or treasure; but the recognition that socialism had to be constructed on a thin basis of material preparation. Yet Maoist socialism contained a distinctly non-Leninist, anti-elitist, and even anti-intellectual tendency of revolutionary voluntarism. This inconsistency invites critical reflections on a range of questions within Marxist thinking, such as the acquisition and evolution of class consciousness. Yet the mass line is not self-contradictory in "relying on the masses" while needing a vanguard party, for it is essentially a party line. Peter Moody argues that compared with Soviet statism, mass line politics "is a technique of control, and its superiority over the bureaucratic method is in its effectiveness, not its democracy per se": in fact only a self-appointed elite could refer to fellow human beings as "masses" (1977, 13). What Moody overlooks, however, are not only similar demarcations in advanced democracies but also the gist of the mass line as a deliberate striving to ever overcome such demarcations. The assumption of the mass line is precisely the nonseparation of interests between political elite and ordinary people; Mao's "serving the people," initially written in honor of a soldier in 1945, was an exemplary statement as such. At issue is less about any correct meaning of democracy than the historicity and morality of revolutionary populism itself. That is, to historicize Chinese communism is not to take its slogans and theories at face value but to look into the complexities of its intention and experiences. Detecting in the mass line an attitude of persuasion as indoctrination, Charles Lindblom nevertheless insists on not dismissing the "humane elements" of what he calls a "perceptoral" approach to social organization. For the evident emphasis placed on autonomy and creativity of the people is "among the great visions of man in the history of human aspirations" (1977, 54–55. 62; cf. Gurley 1969, 332–33).

The mass line represented one of the most inventive features of the Chinese revolution. Mao's seemingly boundless faith in the people (despite the ambiguity resulting from vanguardism or his tolerance of a personality cult) stretched so far that at times it fell into outright voluntarism, running counter to the elementary tenets of historical materialism.[11] His radical conception of "history from below" centered on the laborers and commoners while removing the "emperors, ministers and generals" who occupied conventional historiography. A popular saying during the Cultural Revolution, which inspired a generation of cultural rebels, is that "the lowly are the smartest and the nobles the most ignorant." Without a similar notion of "interest groups" but with a keen sense of the need to articulate and regulate interests in society, Mao treated "contradictions among the people" seriously. Divisions among the people between left, center, and right would persist "ten thousand years." It was the confusion between these "internal" differences on the one hand and conflicts between the people and their enemies on the other that had driven the PRC into waves of political victimization. Moreover, Mao's revolutionary romanticist belief in the collective power of the people to get rid of old and new ruling classes found its ultimate limit in the CCP itself as the ruling party. Although the party never formally abandoned the mass line, the nature of communist politics profoundly changed when the proposed power of the people was overwhelmed by, rather than translated and actualized in, state power.

The mass line model in its ideal type is manifestly democratic notably because it is designed to encourage popular participation and deliberation for articulating and aggregating interests and preferences. In the liberal democratic tradition, citizenship as participation in civil life is a highly treasured attainment. It is also a form of public education and socialization, as John Stuart Mill and others elaborate it, and hence good in itself (cf. Crick 1962, 15–22). Contemporary theorists of political institutions do not deny the democratic nature of popularly participated aggregative processes. In such processes "the will of the people is discovered through political campaigns and bargaining" and "through deliberation by reasoning citizens and rulers seeking to find the general welfare within a context of shared social values" (March and Olsen 1989, 118). The idea of leadership following a mass line especially stresses inputs from below or the majority of the population. This conviction, together with the notion of seeking truth from facts and the impact of the political, economic, and military realities of the war years, "led Mao to advocate increasingly moderate polities in many areas," which "contributed greatly to the Party's ability to win over ever-larger numbers of the masses" (Tsou 1988, 270). It is not surprising that the "celebrated Chinese 'mass line,' " despite all its distinctiveness and limitations, should have been acknowledged in the liberal world as "a form of democracy" (Lindblom 1977, 262).

Institutional Infrastructure

To sustain its extraordinary ability and resourcefulness in generating popular support, the CCP created an institutional framework of intermediate "mass-incorporating state organizations" (Skocpol 1979, 112), such as trade unions, women's federations, and youth leagues, all with branches extending to the working communities and often also to the residential communities. Conspicuously missing was a peasant association, which no longer existed after the communists came to power. These organizations had a broad membership but were overseen by the party and formally embodied in the state or party hierarchies. Each represented a fairly clear-cut constituency and mediated bottom-up demands as well as top-down instructions. The channels they provided were both vertical and horizontal, in correspondence with the administrative matrix, and across social groups as well. They also functioned alongside work units, playing a dual role as agents of state control and instruments for social cohesion. The two systems, mass organizations and work units, were networked together as part of the party's operational infrastructure for transmission of opinions and manipulation of interests.

Though not analogous to either interest groups or civic associations in the studies of democracy and social capital, the "transmission belt" organizations still put some checks, and much pressure, on the government. They might be viewed as a far-flung extension of the state, but it would be just as plausible to say that they were a far-flung extension of society. Women's federations in the villages, or unions in factory floors—however dependent or "apolitical" in their relationship with the state—negated the already blurred state-society division by constantly repositioning themselves in shifting contexts between speaking for universal goals and representing identity-specific interests. It was reported that, during the Mao years, "structural channels for articulation are . . . extensive, and they carry a large volume of popular political debate and discussion" (Townsend 1974, 226–27; Falkenheim 1978). The feasibility of utilizing such channels again "was premised on the notion that a harmony of interests prevailed in a socialist state" between the government and the governed, organizers and organized, management and workers (Unger and Chan 1995, 37). This notion, on which a social contract could be forged under a socialist public-good regime, was not questioned until more recently after market reforms paved the way for exploitative classes to reemerge and hitherto protected interests to be marginalized. The political turn of trade unions became inevitable as "dual legitimacy" faded in a state no longer even nominally that of the workers. The official theory of the "three represents" prioritizes the "advanced productive forces" of capital and management. In response to this shift, the democratization of China's mass organizations was on the agenda, partly under the influence of global social movements and transnational NGOs (cf. Christiansen 1994, 156–64).[12]

"Institutional corporatism" is a useful concept for both the pre- and post-reform periods, and arguably there had been a gradual movement from "state corporatism" to "societal corporatism" (categorizations borrowed from Schmitter 1974). The former pattern features state supervised and socially penetrating organizations that enjoy a near representational monopoly and preempt autonomous associations. The latter, incorporating independent and voluntary engagements, "entails a form of interest-group politics." The Chinese development also kept the possibility open for a "democratized state corporatist system" or "socialist corporatism" that would promote workers' welfare and prevent social upheavals vulnerable to postcommunist transitions.[13] Related conceptualizations are "local state corporatism" wider than its original application to TVES and "civil society." Bureaucratic professionalization in Chinese politics after mass line did not close down all the old channels of two-way communication and mediation. The irony, most strikingly, was rather the apathy brought about by liberalization. If autonomous civic engagements were gains from the point of view of democratization, they were also discounted by rising social exclusion and political passivity. As long as democracy still must have something to do with popular participation, the mass line cannot be discarded, as it offers important lessons.

Another institutional component of people's democracy was the "united front" inherited from the organizational structure of the revolution. The term "masses" was not exactly the same as the "people," since the latter also included intellectual professionals and the "patriotic democratic personages" of nonlaboring classes including the former capitalist class. The four small stars on the PRC's national flag represented the four classes designated to be constitutive of the Chinese people: workers, peasants, intellectuals, and the national bourgeoisie. It is doubtful as to whether the Chinese People's Political Consultative Conference (CPPCC)—the umbrella organization of the CCP's united front, containing eight small "democratic parties" and independent nonparty "friends"—ever played a role in China's actual politics.[14] On the other hand, the historical relationship between the Communist Party and its noncommunist allies did affect the self-perception, hence behavior, of the regime in a way far from trivial. The party had carefully preserved such allies throughout with a strategic commitment to "long term co-existence and mutual supervision." Chinese communism thus had a different policy identity from that of Bolshevism, and later it was able to utilize that particular resource to boost reforms in China.

The united front was first formed during Sun Zhongshan's Three Great Policies (1924) of allying the GMD with Soviet Russia, the CCP, and labor, which joined forces in the Northern Expedition against the warlords (1926–1927). Seizing the opportunity, the communists accepted dual party membership within the GMD until Jiang Jieshi "purified" his party in 1927. Civil war followed until the next round of alliance, compelled by the Japanese invasion, when the Comintern's antifascist strategy also called for compromise. The CCP in the Yan'an period implemented a "three-thirds system" in the base areas, restricting communists to no more than a third of the official positions in local governments. As Mao explained, the nationalist united front was not a one-class domination of either the proletariat or the bourgeoisie, rather, "all those who stand for resistance to Japan and for democracy are qualified to share this political power, regardless of their party affiliations" (cf. Selden 1971, 161–71). This culminated into the party manifesto on new democracy and the coalition government in 1945. The communists respected their united front tradition as one of the revolution's "three magic weapons" (along with armed struggle and party building).

Though far from an equal partnership, the CCP maintained a friendly relationship with the other parties after 1949. The CPPCC provided a "seat" for each of the noncommunist parties and "patriotic democrats." Largely symbolic, but at times also vocal, these parties had survived and slowly expanded. History even witnessed an open debate between Mao and Liang Shuming, a distinguished and independent educator, over agricultural policy in 1953 (which resulted, not surprisingly, in Liang's disgrace). In recent years, members of the CPPCC frequently petitioned the CCP central committee on socioeconomic, educational, and environmental issues. In 2003, the eight democratic parties had 600,000 members, of whom more than 140,000 had been elected deputies to the people's congresses at various levels and more than 8,000 held leading posts in governmental and judicial departments above the county level. Seven vice presidents of the NPC were noncommunists.[15] The concept of coalition rather than their being opposition parties was the political basis of the constitutional principle of "political consultation and multiparty cooperation" under the communist leadership (Seymour 1987; Mazur 1997). By this principle the CCP is obliged to consult the other parties on all major policy issues. Although the CPPCC and the NPC cannot be more apart in their formal status and actual functions, annual national conventions of both bodies (*lianghui*) in Beijing at the same time have raised the status and stake of the CPPCC. This framework was among those institutional and ideological characteristics that distinguished the PRC (and other communist regimes born of a popular front) from the Soviet state. There is no reason why China's unique model of limited political pluralism may not benefit the country's future democratic institutions.

Self-Management and Economic Democracy

Another dimension of people's democracy was seen in the experiments with community and workplace self-management, which again had an origin in the locally diverse revolutionary processes of state-building. According to Hans van de Ven, "Communist organizations evolved out of local society, adapted themselves to it, and were enmeshed in it." The communist project may even be presented as "multiple revolutions" and, as "regional diversity was one of its hallmarks," the notion of the CCP as a hierarchical, centrally controlled organization is questionable (Saich and van de Ven 1995, xiii–xix). Not overstating the point, the localization of the revolution was more mirrored in the mass line and the grassroots regimes committed to social reconstruction, entailing interplay of powers from above and below. Traditional village self-rule—mostly by clan/gentry patriarchy (e.g., through an organizational *baojia* system and a communal compact or *xiangyue*) as part of the imperial ruling structure—was of low transaction cost but undemocratic.[16] The communist reworking of tradition had to dismantle the power of a landed elite in the first place.[17] Mao's "communal socialism" then became a pillar of self-reliance and an institutional expression of the ambition of eliminating the "three great distinctions." The more or less self-contained communal living would combine at the same time the functions of industry, agriculture, trade, education, and defense (people's militia). This was hoped to be a model not only practically suitable at a time when China confronted perceived external threats of war, but also as an innovative step toward a free association of direct producers without the rigid division of labor, as cherished in the Communist manifesto.[18]

"Communal socialism" was a utopian alternative to statism, bureaucracy, and alienation. The actual movement was far from what was intended, but neither was it entirely separable from the intention. It had evolved with adjusted and additional policies from resettling city residents in the countryside to organizing urban communes. Rural networks below the county administration were particularly important where the household, work team, production brigade, and the commune itself coordinated production, distribution, and collective social life. As a result, urban bias in Mao's China, both heavy-handed and counterbalanced by an ideological "rural bias," did not lead to widespread rural despair or a swelling underclass in the cities (also aided by *hukou* control) typical of the third world. Public policies concerning poverty, disaster relief, and collective welfare, inadequate as they were, were in place and implemented with the help from task forces regularly dispatched to localities at the lowest level. If capitalist primitive accumulation "is nothing else than the historical process of divorcing the producer from the means of production" (Marx 1864, 874–75), China's communal socialism was a unique effort to run a different course, even though it was in the end unsuccessful. With the land owned and cultivated by the collectives and with sideline production as well as local industries, the Chinese peasantry was not "proletarianized." What an ironic contrast between then and now as regards the plight of today's "floating population," of which a large portion was created in the aftermath of the dissolution of communes.

The communal socialist model has been squarely criticized in relation to "agrarian socialism" (chapter 2), not least for its allegedly backward-looking romanticization of a closed, small-scale, and self-sufficient mode of production and for its egalitarian impulse at the cost of liberty. However, self-management through direct participation in community affairs embedded in the model is not only democratically valuable but also socio-economically (and perhaps ecologically) desirable for coordinated allocation and utility of local resources. Herein lies the lasting significance of an unfinished project for communal autonomy and decentralized decision-making, and hence checks and balances on central control and planning in a rational political economy. Communization in theory thus posed a real challenge to the existing bureaucracies. Had the communes actually developed in the manner as envisioned, "centralized political power in China would have been fundamentally undermined—much in the way in which Marx had attributed to the Paris Commune the potential to restore to the producers those social powers which had been usurped by the state" (Meisner 1986, 241).

Urban residence–based communes mostly performed service-centered, nonproductive social functions, though some also managed small collective enterprises. These communes were outlived by neighborhood committees, which were active first in political surveillance and later in community welfare. Novel experiment with self-management was phenomenal in large state firms, in which participatory and flexible approaches were introduced as an alternative to Soviet "one-man command" and Taylorism.[19] The famous "Angang constitution" (1960), inspired by the practices initiated in several small factories and then adopted in the nation's largest steelworks institutionalized a short-lived yet far-reaching managerial system. Known as "two participations, one reform, and three combinations," the system required managers to participate in production, workers to participate in management, and technicians to participate in both processes. It dictated that office workers undertake manual labor; that elections of leaders be held in productive units; and that effective channels of communication and cooperation be established. It aspired to achieve equality and shared responsibility, which would in turn improve morale and efficiency. In seeking a structure of industrial democracy, the scheme was to "create rules and regulations . . . without making workers the permanent inferiors of a techno-bureaucratic elite" (Andors 1977, 129, 228–30). Unlike the Soviet planners and factory bosses, cadres in China were not supposed to reach decisions simply by studying incoming statistics, reports, and printouts. Instead they were to seek "a non-bureaucratic attitude to data collection and policy formation," and were to "go out into the field to collect information by personal observation" (Ellman 1979, 29–30; cf. Robinson 1972; Bettelheim 1974).

The Angang constitution was only a part of the effort to decentralize and "bring enthusiasm at every level into play." China must "walk on two legs," as Mao's metaphor went, mobilizing both center and localities, officials and masses, industry and agriculture, heavy and light industries, and so on. The centrality of human agencies and the vitality of local societies were pushed far, with special attention given to sectoral equilibrium and the shared interests of the state, the collective, and the individual. Over time Mao became increasingly impatient with socialism's "concession to the bourgeoisie" in such forms as the eight-tier wage hierarchy and the so-called bourgeois right in general, in favor rather of the earlier needs-based "free supply" arrangement within the communist ranks (1990 [1974], 413–15; Schram 1989, 178, 199). In the same spirit, Mao insisted on knowledge production being an independent undertaking by ordinary people. "Red and expert" and production and education must combine to transcend "feudal" and bourgeois cultural powers. Schools and universities should reach out beyond the campus to employ practitioners in order for textbooks to be applicable to scientific or productive enterprises. Only those on the ground of practice might be qualified educators, regardless of the amount of their formal education. Dogmatic and closed examinations treating students as enemies while giving no credible indication of their actual qualities should be eliminated. Needless to say, the affinities between the Maoist call for an "educational revolution" and Michel Foucault's thesis of "knowledge/power" were obvious (cf. Fraser 1971; Price 1970).

Mao's critiques of the Soviet political economy (1959) offers a background footnote to these developments and to his own growing anxiety over the future of socialism. He argued unambiguously for a democratic alternative to bureaucracy, one-sided material incentives, and alienated labor. Convinced that human creativity and socialist consciousness were stifled in the Stalinist system, he sought to rescue them in a Chinese version of socialism. Any honest assessment here would not miss the word "democracy" as most appropriate for the desire conveyed by this set of criticisms. What Mao failed to see, however, was the logic of the "normalization" of politics, by which—among other consequences—revolutionary idealism as a time-honored passion yielded to the apparent rationality of material incentives. The impracticability and technical absurdity of certain aspects of the Angang experiment must also be registered in its proper historical context.[20] It goes without saying that economic democracy in whichever forms cannot substitute for a political democracy in which a government is popularly elected and policies influenced by citizens.

Conversely, it is also the case that any democracy is incomplete without a democratic management of the workplace, followed by justice in profit sharing and income distribution (cf. Dahl 1985). This might be pursued through different approaches, such as capital-labor codetermination (as in Germany), self-managed public enterprises (as in the former Yugoslavia), and empowerment of workers' representative councils (on trial in many places, including China). If economic democracy is taken to mean the power of citizens as producers and consumers at both macro- and micro-levels of governance, then economic and political democracy has to be integrated with separate but mutually enhancing institutions (Cui 1997, 365–72). The problem of traditional socialism that the Maoist project sought to overcome was the conflict between two equally vital objectives—workers' management and central planning (Dahl 1986, 75 and chapter 3). It is notable that the post-Mao "socialist market economy" curtailed central command without promoting workplace democracy. Legal requirements for workers' assemblies or transparency in bookkeeping in the ongoing industrial restructuring still fell short of participatory management.[21] Political democratization was no more than tentative and fundamentally limited, despite the major fact that the party itself had been radically changed to the extent that its communist identity became increasingly irrelevant. As democratization is often confused with marketification under globalizing pressures, it is worth noting, however, that the latter can be pushed through (and often had to be) by undemocratic means. In this light, as the mass line style of participation left little trace in the wake of repudiating Maoism, gone with the Mao era were not only some extremist tendencies but also ideas and exercises with genuine democratic appeal. "Economic democracy," dear to many market socialists inside and outside China, is yet to be rehabilitated in the reformist course and discourse.

Finally, it should be noted that local institutions of self-rule, based either residentially or in the workplace, may not necessarily be democratic; and, even when they are indeed democratic or so viewed, an impact on national politics may continue to be lacking. This fact has been amply demonstrated in China (as elsewhere) in effects ranging from traditional local despotism and vigorously self-censored folk-religious associations or "secret societies" to some contemporary civil society organizations and abused or wholly ineffective village elections. At another layer of analysis, as shown in the high-minded circles of communist puritanism, self-management by disciplined men and women could also be a form of "collective self-repression" (Walzer 1980, 213–14). Moreover, self-managing local communities may well coexist with centralized authoritarianism at the national level and count on the center's aloof approval if not direct buttress.

Revolution and Bureaucracy

Chinese communism had not only produced a people's democracy but also a "socialist bureaucracy"; and the latter was an organic part of the former, creating a stark contradiction within the post-revolutionary state power. Here bureaucracy should be distinguished from bureaucrats—whether or not conceptualized into a "class." Because the state managed the economy and social life, the so-called bureaucrats had included, in formal status and statistics, those who might not be so identified in other societies, such as managers, service officers, shopkeepers, teachers, and doctors, most of whom were administratively ranked. The state was the largest employer, given the lack of alternative job providers. The collective sector, urban and rural, was less bureaucratic, but even there an army of cadres was needed. This observation is essential for any analysis of bureaucratic expansion in China, which is not simply a duplication of modern bureaucratization. Such expansion was immediately evident in the wake of the revolution—in the 1950s "there came a massive process of bureaucratic centralization, a phenomenon that was both the producer and the product of national unification and the drive for rapid economic development" (Meisner 1986, 257). According to one account, by 1958 there were about eight million state functionaries in the PRC, including economic managerial staff. Ten years ago the GMD, which neither assumed national control nor planned the economy, employed some two million. The Qing empire in the nineteenth century had around forty thousand official posts. "Presumably for good and sufficient reasons, the Chinese Communists after a long and bloody struggle replaced the bureaucratic apparatus of pre-modern China with their own version, some two hundred times larger" (Moore 1987, 79).

Communist Bureaucratization

This result was clearly unintended but not surprising. In the first days of Bolshevik power, Lenin had already acknowledged bureaucratization as an inescapable by-product of industrialization and a fatal defect of backward socialism. The contingency of "socialism and backwardness" meant that the bureaucracy had to have a near monopoly over goods and services and rewards and penalties in the conditions of scarcity.[22] That is, state socialism stratified society not only between workers and planners but also between producers and distributors. As such, there emerged enormous "problems of controlling a government, of guarding against the guardians" (Moore 1986, 86; Stavis 1983, 175–76). Capitalist welfare states experienced similar problems only to a much lesser degree in the entirely different circumstances of material wealth and political democracy (cf. Szelenyi and Mannchin 1987). Postcolonial, late-developmental, and socialist states all must mobilize resources to maintain an orderly process of nation-building and modernization; they shared accumulation drives and hence some of the internal dynamism of bureaucratic competition. But in China there were also compelling pressures external to the bureaucracy, from domestic societal pressures (stability, justice, jobs, security, etc.) to international pressures (especially self-defense). Worse still, there were residuals of ancient officialdom and hierarchy, as well as of a peculiar "mountain-stronghold sectarianism" (*shantou zhuyi*) of distinctive loyalties and personal attachment formed in the war years by the command divisions within the party and army. A centralized but also "fragmented, segmented and stratified" bureaucratic power encompassing competing commissions, departments, and government offices continued before and after the reform (Lieberthal and Oksenberg 1988, 3–5, 12, 22–30).

This situation was not challenged by the official ideology of democracy, except briefly during the radically antibureaucratic Cultural Revolution. One possible consolation for the complacency was that compared with the corruption and inefficiency of the GMD regime, according to Richard Kraus, "socialist China's bureaucrats have provided a quality of leadership in both revolution and economic development which, at its best, has been aggressively efficient and honest" (1983, 133). The modern socialist paternalism of a public good regime was also in line with the traditional idea of moral ruling, and a "big state" necessitated by national development did not contradict popular expectations. As Kraus further notes, "Insofar as socialist institutions have improved the lot of China's worker and peasant majority, there is a coincidence of interests on this fundamental point" (146). Although "patrimonial bureaucracy" (patronage and clientalist connections, favoritism, and bribes) was present here and there, the party used disciplinary actions and rectification campaigns and it publicized criminal charges against affected cadres. Since the "Leninist states" were "legitimated and organized according to claims of a very high standard of virtue," as they decayed they found "their own ideological heritage to be a source of trenchant criticism" (McCormick 1990, 196). In popular memory today, Mao's government was clean and close to the people, in sharp contrast with today's "officials" being another word for "corruption" and *guanxi* the engine of governance.

Beyond the Weberian conception of the bureaucratization and rationalization of modern society, bureaucratic proliferation in the PRC exemplified the structural and moral paradox of a socialist bureaucracy. The need to manage capital by the state almost justified the bureaucratic penetration of society, a situation where the revolution was betrayed without obvious alternatives. What makes the Chinese case so intriguing, however, was the attempt it made after all to surmount that paradox. If rational bureaucracy is a virtuous marker of modernity in Western sociological thought, "it is seen in Marxist theory as a principal historical vice in any form and wholly incongruous with socialism, particularly in the Maoist variant of Marxism" (Meisner 1986, 258). The claim, which for a moment or two enjoyed excitement in the West (as much as inside China), that China at one point cleared a path to modernize without bureaucratization is, unfortunately, unwarranted. Yet there was a time when both the Soviets and Americans believed that an outstanding feature of Chinese socialism was its "stubborn, irrational, and ultimately doomed resistance to the bureaucratic, elitist, technocratic urban life of advanced society." And it was precisely such resistance, though unsuccessful, that gave "China's modernization both its unique and its universal character" (Andors 1977, 23).[23] The Chinese experiments, as discussed above, at the very least demonstrated the possibility of searching while informing future struggles. The search cannot be abandoned, if only because professionalization and technocratization more than democratization in administrative reforms failed to achieve honesty, efficiency, and transparency. These reforms falsely made the alternative visions more than ever the utopian fantasies of the past.

As "bureaucratic collectivism"[24] had been partly replaced by a hybrid formation of "bureaucratic capitalism," the trend of market invasion in public institutions progressively undermined them rather than acting to cure their deficiencies. Indeed, it was not until the capitalist turn, so to speak, of China's bureaucracy in the 1990s that the Maoist insight into the danger of an "inner-party bourgeoisie" emerging from within the party's own ranks came to the fore. To the extent that the CCP was instrumental for a newer "new class" of public power-holders to acquire private capital, Mao was ahead of his time in warning against "a bourgeoisie born anew."[25] If the ideology of the Cultural Revolution were mistaken in bolstering arbitrary purges of "capitalist roaders" without private capital, it nevertheless anticipated the conflation of public and private offices some three decades later, thereby to haunt popular anger and social criticism.

"Dictatorship over Needs"

As I discuss in chapter 2, one of the greatest tragedies of the communist revolutions was their degeneration through the revolutionary parties coming to power and hence their reversion from fighting for democracy into ruling with monopoly, from socialism into statism. Even the PRC, which was ambitious in holding on to popular sovereignty and participation, eventually betrayed the mass line for tyranny. After all, it was no accident that in the Chinese political vocabulary "people's democracy" was terminologically interchangeable with the "people's democratic dictatorship" (which was further confused with the "dictatorship of the proletariat" after disputed interpretations of Marxism between Beijing and Moscow). To work to "strengthen the people's democratic state apparatus" in order to guard socialism against subversion, alas, led to a "dictatorship *over* the proletariat" and thus over the people themselves (cf. Sartori 1962, 428). This, again, had an origin in the communist state being built bit by bit from wartime regional governments run by party and army cadres during the revolution. A fully fledged party-state after 1949, growing "out of a barrel of a gun" and in "symbiosis" with the PLA (Shambaugh 1991), was institutionalized under the immense pressure of national defense and development (MacFarquhar and Fairbank, 1987). As a result, top-down, military-style organizational works and networks left a mark everywhere in the PRCs sociopolitical structure. Refashioning itself into the compass and engine of growth where command overrode checks and balances, such a state in a country of China's size was capable of destruction as much as construction, and the scale of both could be enormous.

When resources had to be centrally mobilized and allocated—food rationed and the movement of population restricted—could any regime afford free criticisms? It may be as simple as the "law" that Trotsky once described: scarcity is not only prone to inequality without forced redistribution, but also requires authoritarian policing to maintain orderly queues for basic goods (unless a passive "queue mentality" can be internalized via socialization). Or, as neatly put by the philosophical Budapest school, desperation results in a "dictatorship over needs" (Feher, Heller, and Markus 1983). The odds of socialist islands surviving in the capitalist high seas were such that they would perpetuate and intensify internal adversities, as though the socialist project could not be carried out except by means in violation of socialist beliefs themselves.[26] Limited by the historical possibility, the question of democracy could be raised but not solved (Luxemburg 1961, 80).

Mao was seriously tempted by his "two hundred policy" but then found himself reversing it as soon as the specter of Hungary and Poland 1956 loomed large. Intending to "let a hundred flowers blossom and a hundred schools of thought contend," constructive criticisms and suggestions concerning party and government performance were initially encouraged. It was the unexpected demands on power sharing that led to the abrupt policy change; anti-rightism was the largest campaign of purges in the PRC history prior to the more spontaneous and anarchic Cultural Revolution. Many studies of the campaign underestimate the fear on the part of Mao and party leadership over an escalating atmosphere of anticommunism within the communist world in the aftermath of the East European uprisings. Empirical research, archival and oral historical alike, disputes the widely held conspiracy theory that the "hundred flowers" was a calculated plot to trap critics (e.g., Zhu 1995).[27] Often overlooked is also the profound moral dilemma faced by the country and its leaders in a specific historical situation beyond different personal experiences or evaluations. An inner-party debate over the Great Leap, for example, was repressed not merely by authoritarianism. Edward Friedman observes that those who disagreed with Mao, highly placed officials as well as rank-and-file members, nevertheless "kept silent because of a felt patriotic need for unity in a world where China was isolated." It was especially painful as "a matter of both nationalistic pride and socialistic dedication" (1982, 204–5). From another political perspective, Lucian Pye detects a Chinese "inability" to engage in real politics by missing a distinction between national and partisan interests while upholding the ethical code of conformity (1968, 229–31). Without this dimension of moral dilemma, the tenacity of communist regime, despite grave policy disasters before the reform and also, to a lesser extent, after it, would not be explainable.

The "dictatorship over needs" was surely rooted in its international environment as much as within the general conditions of a socialist political economy determined to overcome backwardness even without a revolutionary transformation of the capitalist heartland. Before the desperate adventure of the Soviet Union, the Marxists were convinced that "socialism in one country" was a contradiction in terms and thus doomed to defeat. This remains a reason for many of those who refuse to apply the term "socialist" to the former USSR or the PRC. But the international constraints still hold true even in a postcommunist era, in which defense modernization for the remaining communist regimes continues to be imperative. Adam Przeworski along with his collaborators contemplate that the arms race and militarization of the economies in the former Soviet bloc was the cause of their decline (1995, 2). The defense factor certainly also contributes to explaining excessive state power in the communist world, of which the Chinese case was nevertheless an envy of many underdeveloped countries lacking state capacity. The urgency of defying negative externalities postponed, if not altogether canceled, the pledged correction of the moral failure of bureaucratic collectivism. The predicament of socialism and backwardness in one country cemented the mindset of the communist elite. Its power monopoly over production and the surplus, as much as political and cultural affairs, was then rationalized in terms of "historical necessity" at the cost of socialist belief in freedom and liberation.

Rare among democratic socialists (in ironic contrast with conservative modernization theorists) who frequently fail to recognize the indispensability and dilemma of the post-revolutionary state, Ralph Miliband writes that "where power has been seized, revolutionaries have to create a strong state in place of the old if their revolution is to survive and begin to redeem its promise and purpose." This is bound to be an arduous task, "particularly because the material circumstances in which it has to be undertaken are likely to be unfavorable and further aggravated by the hostility and opposition of the new regime's internal and external enemies." In particular, the new regime must retain the support of popular involvement or it will go under (1977, 181). All things considered, the model of Chinese socialism proceeded to the detriment of its own goals when civil liberties were sacrificed for security and growth and when resources had to be directed to the military more than to goods for consumption. Yet, "for all its brutality, intolerance, and violence," the Chinese communist regime had once possessed moral authority as a "powerful, effective and honest dictatorship" (Jenner 1992, 156, 160).

Mobilization and Participation

The established narrative of the history of the PRC uses as milestones the following years: 1957 (the anti-rightist campaign preceded by the 1955 suppression of intellectual "counterrevolutionaries" and leading to the Great Leap Forward in 1958); 1966 (the launching of the Cultural Revolution); and

1976 (Mao's death and the beginning of the post-Mao power succession). The "good days" of 1949–1956 came before "ultra adventurism"; followed by the 1961–1965 period of recovery from famine; and, finally, the restoration of sanity and order after the "ten chaotic years" and the pursuit of prosperity since 1977–1978. This effort at periodization takes into account nothing about the (potential) justice and gains of a people's democracy, such as the centrality of the people and popular political participation. There was, no doubt, a huge gap between rhetoric and reality, yet ideological power over public thinking and communicating would also intensely shape reality. Thus viewed, the periods of the Great Leap and Cultural Revolution may both come out in a different light from, and more accurately than, how they are now told as history. Side by side with massive destruction and human tragedies, and despite a personality cult and other forms of manipulation, there were explosions of individual freedom in a "grand democracy." Big-character posters and self-organization were only among the most notorious expressions of the unprecedented energy of society. The fact that they became notorious speaks volumes about China's changing political climate, which allowed some leeway for market integration by ignoring popular discontent over the deterioration of welfare public policies. The trade-off thesis explicit in the official propaganda between material benefits and political participation is mistaken, because the degradation of labor in social status was responsible for its decline in working and living conditions. Within the framework of a one-party rule, apparently the system with a mass line would be far better than the one without.

Further into the problematic narrative of contemporary China, the Cultural Revolution officially lasted ten years, from 1966 to 1976. Historians seeking to be more precise prefer to use the period 1966–1969 in recognition of the end of revolutionary upheaval and the resumption of normality after the ninth party congress (1969). The phrase "Cultural Revolution" (or the "Great Proletarian Cultural Revolution") is of course misleading if "culture" is limited to its narrower, commonsense signification. In the Maoist perspective, however, what is cultural is not only political, but also social and straightforwardly personal in terms of the personal being political. "Culture," taken politically, leads and revolutionizes society. The notion of "politics in command" thus turns the orthodox Marxist base-superstructure edifice upside down. In China's actual trajectory, egalitarianism, populism,

and totalitarianism each peaked in a supposedly self-liberating mass movement, finding inspirations in "justice of rebellion," "equality of poverty,"
and "permanent revolution." Meanwhile, education, literature, the arts, and
the media were assaulted to the degree of such impoverishment that the
Chinese later reversed the term "cultural revolution" (*wenhua da geming*)
into "destroying culture" (*da ge wenhua ming*).

Yet, equally important were the egalitarian and populist drives to reduce
the gaps between urban and rural lives and between cadres and ordinary
people, and to curtail the rigid sectoral and gender divisions of labor. Even
in the sphere of cultural production, one-sided stories would not do justice
to history. The fact that Mao publicly criticized the "city-lord Ministry of
Sanitation" had a much wider appeal beyond medicine. Like the ministry
that responded by sending skilled medical professionals to work in the
countryside on a fixed-term shift, many other government organs also took
a "rural turn." Village schools and communal "cultural stations" thrived
even in some poorest areas; movies and local operas were shown in the
remotest places for free. Many scientists and technicians volunteered with
pride to work at the grassroots level, contributing to a measured agricultural modernization and rural industrialization (Hinton 1983; Gao 1999).
The universities were shut down for a few years, but as soon as they re-
opened their students were drawn from the ranks of workers, peasants, and
soldiers. Inevitably, college entrance exams were resumed in 1977 to ensure
normal standards of higher education; but was it not an honorable idea that
science and social sciences, like everything else for the people, should "walk
on two legs"?[28]

These and related events had a tremendous impact overseas on the
generation of "1968" in the West and on the liberation movements in the
third world (and on splits of such movements along with the Sino-Soviet
divide). The extent of the destruction of the Cultural Revolution revealed
itself only slowly, and it brought the country to exhaustion and reorientation after Mao. John King Fairbank remarks that what happened in China's
1960s "was as full of surprises as the 1790s in France. In terms of scale,
impact, and complexity, however, the Cultural Revolution was of course a
much bigger event than the French Revolution."[29] If it was still "too early" to
make a fair judgment on the French Revolution nearly two hundred years
later, as Zhou Enlai famously stated in the early 1970s, then it would surely

be premature to seek a conclusive verdict on the Chinese Cultural Revolution. Its total condemnation by the reform regimes may turn out to stand poorly in the more-nuanced test of future historiography once the legacies of people's democracy can be soberly appropriated.

The launching of the Cultural Revolution was justified by Mao's "line struggle" within the party between the proletarian and bourgeois lines extending from class struggle acting as the "key link" of politics in the transition from capitalism to socialism. The future of socialism, and hence the plight of the Chinese people, as the ideology goes, depended on the outcome of this struggle in the realm of superstructure. Although the thought of Mao did not appear to be more systematic and coherent than a wealth of reflective ideas, to "sinify Marxism" he reordered historical materialism in the Chinese context: ideology and politics came before production relations, and production relations came before productive forces. This is an idealist intervention, perhaps, but Maoism was nevertheless borne of splendid historical experiences of a collective endeavor. The communists in China were, after all, "part of the great Chinese nation, flesh of its flesh and blood of its blood" (1991 [1938], 208), and any talk about Marxism in China must refer to concrete Chinese characteristics.[30] Of course China was far from the only site where Marxism was radically and pragmatically localized to take a fresh national style; Marxism outside nineteenth-century Germany and Europe existed only in manifold local voices. The Cultural Revolution, by prioritizing the superstructure and its transformative power, was just another invention of a sinified Marxism after the 1949 revolution of surrounding the cities by the countryside. Toward the end of his life, however, Mao expressed doubt as to whether he succeeded in the second undertaking.

The elitist and factionalist schools in China studies too often, and too easily, dismiss the argument that the Cultural Revolution was primarily motivated to prevent decay in communism, as negatively exposed in the Soviet Union. But this motivation was clearly detectable not only in what was publicly stated (of which the importance lay in the foundation of legitimation), but also in the passionate and concrete strife against domination, privilege, bureaucracy, alienation, and the "three great distinctions." Mere power struggle at the top cannot explain how and why calls for defending the revolution could have attracted tens of millions of followers.

The Chinese case may not be exceptional in the familiar pattern of revolutions. Again and again, as Engels summarizes it, victorious revolutionaries split between those who are satisfied and those who know that they must go still further if only to safeguard what the revolution has initially achieved (1895, 51). Slavoj Žižek (2002) repeats the motto in his essay title "Revolution Must Strike Twice"; the old state apparatus cannot be dismantled by the first strike alone (e.g., the unfinished Russian February revolution and the Chinese 1911 revolution). The core lesson of "revolutionary materialism" is that without a second step of painstaking social reconstruction, the revolution is incomplete and could be aborted. Hence Jefferson's constitutional thinking that the tree of liberty needs periodic rejuvenation "with the blood of patriots and tyrants"; and Mao's proclamation that a socialist system needs to be baptized every seven to eight years. The dialectic of "continuing revolution" has it all in which the state is the ultimate obstacle but its eventual removal depends on the strength of a "proletarian state" itself. In practice, what Žižek says about Lenin is probably more accurate for Mao; "[He] succeeded because his appeal, while bypassing the party nomenklatura, was understood at the level of revolutionary micropolitics."[31]

As in Soviet Russia, citizens' communes and revolutionary committees were set up throughout China, shunning a great deal of the existing governmental authorities. They were not developed institutions of self-management but intended to become a democratic alternative to bureaucratic administration. An outright dismissal of the short-lived Chinese adventure would be too cynical, as well as a misreading of the events, but it remains to be answered as to what there is in the awkward historical parallels to be learned. With Meisner, we ask: "If the Paris Commune of 1871 was a tragedy, was the Shanghai People's Commune merely a farce? Did Red Guards and 'revolutionary rebels' who imitated the Parisian Communards make history or merely act out a historical parody?" (1982, 135).

Popular participation in the Cultural Revolution was organized in self-groupings known as the "red guards" or "rebels" along with more formal channels of communes and committees. Social life as a whole, urban and rural, was also in a mood of "self-liberation," featuring both individual and collective actions. The old mass line infrastructure was largely ignored, but the idea of people's democracy was energized in the new push for anti-bureaucracy by extensive inputs in decisionmaking from below. This was possible initially due to the "four big freedoms" of speech, dissent, public criticism, and debate that were highlighted in Mao's appeal to a "grand democracy": "speaking out freely, airing views fully, holding great debates and writing big-character posters." These instigated freedoms, disregarding any corresponding legal and procedural order, were hallmarks of cultural revolutionary populism, which quickly plunged into the lawlessness and fanaticism of the miniregimes of a "mass dictatorship." Mao's successors, determined to bury once and for all what must be the largest mass movement in world history, condemned that these freedoms "never played a positive role in safeguarding the people's democratic rights" but rather only caused harm and instability (the 1980 party plenum). They subsequently gained sufficient consensus to remove in 1982 the relevant items (Article 45) from the constitution (along with the "freedom to strike"). Here the difference between removing a constitutional right and constitutionally denying it should be obvious; yet indiscriminately denouncing "grand democracy" permitted (illegally) the criminalization of critics. To be sure, the four freedoms were by no means universally exercised even at the peak of the Cultural Revolution. Even for the "revolutionary masses" there were strict limits on free conscience and speech. Still the ideological insistence on such freedoms made a difference for political participation. Perhaps only by their extraction can we critically appreciate the Maoist breakthrough, for all its blunders, in an otherwise closed authoritarian system.

The three most striking problems with political participation in the Mao years were the manipulation by the personality cult of Mao, the lack of legality to protect individuals, and the exclusion of certain people as non-participants. Mao demanded that history writing and the theater stage be occupied by commoners and rebels rather than rulers and heroes ("only the people themselves are heroes in creating history"), but he failed to envision a society without a "supreme helmsman." In the end the author of a people-centered ideology did not distinguish himself more definitely from other modern popular dictators.[32] Mao was also responsible for political and social exclusion in a polity defined by class hatred, and for the anarchy and violence supposed to be redeemed by confidence in "great order under heaven achieved through great chaos." As now a nightmare in the Chinese collective memory, factional fights among the "revolutionary masses" suffered impulsive incivility and cruelty. If the earlier suppression of counterrevolutionaries during hot and cold wars by a young regime could be seen as a perpetuation of the civil war, purges heightened in the Cultural Revolution were barely justifiable.[33] To the extent that a large number of citizens were victimized through public denouncement, personal deprivation, and labor camps, the word "people" in "people's democracy" or "people's dictatorship" was not only thoroughly abused but also reduced to an utmost abstraction.

Another problem, which also poses theoretical difficulties, was the conflation between mobilization for state purposes ("instrumental") and voluntary participation ("ontological"). The two concepts may well coincide—as seen, for example, in the state-led mass campaigns for sanitation, disease control, and literacy in the early 1950s.[34] Commentators recognize communist China, because of a mass-line democracy with its own institutional infrastructure, as one of the most participatory societies in history. For decades the regime relied on activating people and localities, furnishing "a government by campaigns" (Moore 1987, 83–84) and a country of "permanent mobilization" (Dittmer 1987, 141). Popular revolutions always show inertia in "the rapid expansion of political consciousness and the rapid mobilization of new groups into politics," as Samuel Huntington recognizes it, and "Revolution is the extreme case of the explosion of political participation" (1968, 266). But puzzling still is whether the communist success in mobilizing the population should be counted as democratic. For Theda Skocpol, "whether we in the liberal-democratic West like to acknowledge it or not, the authoritarian regimes brought to power through revolutionary transformation . . . have been democratizing in the mass-mobilizing sense" (1994, 281). Or, as Bernard Crick argues more bluntly, as long as the power enjoys a popular basis, the communists "do not pretend to be democratic"— "they are democratic" as a matter of factual judgment when the party was voluntarily followed by the majority of the people (1962, 56). The "nonliberal systems" in the Soviet states and in many nationalist countries of Asia and Africa, according to C. B. Macpherson, "have a genuine historical claim to the title democracy" (1966, 3). If these generalizations of a "participatory democracy" are disputable (Linz 2000, 193), then the term "mobilizational democracy" in the Chinese lexicon does make sense in characterizing a fermenting societal experience of revolutionary penetration in some of the country's most memorable episodes of political history.[35]

The term "democracy," however, is no less ambiguous than "mobilization" as far as participation is concerned. Mobilization explicitly implies (but participation may also implicitly) a large dose of manipulation as well as moral and peer pressure on duty or solidarity, producing "subject-participants" (Townsend 1967), "licensed participation" (Strand 1990), and "mobilization without emancipation" (Molyneux 1985). Opposing demobilization, the organizers of society may also (to borrow from Albert Hirschman 1970) opt for "voice" in unison while blocking an "exit."[36] Participation could be hijacked by elite exploitation as much as mobilization could be institutionalized into a democratic process. On the other hand, even truly autonomous and participatory politics may be far from unproblematic, as amply demonstrated by left-wing and right-wing "tyrannies of the majority." Communist populism was reminiscent of certain trends in fascist agitation (Walder 1991, 47), though their morals and programs could not be more opposed. The power of totalitarian politics stems precisely from its ability to draw popular participation, and totalitarian leaders obtain loyalty and support by appealing not only to reason (however construed), but also to emotion. Soviet communism was arguably an ideological project of "participatory totalitarianism," in which every life involved "internalizing and integrating oneself into the practices of the dominating discourse of the time" (Hedin 2004, 174).

Without tracing an intellectual lineage against "mobocracy" in Western political thought, or incurring the truism of "civic culture" about legality and civility,[37] the point (in which Marxism agrees with liberal elitism) is that people are capable of prejudice, cruelty, and (self-)destruction as much as rational self-management. Leninism, in particular, has no illusion about the spontaneity of even industrial workers (e.g., "syndicalism"), let alone any "petty bourgeois spontaneous tendency." This distrust is not concerned with passivity but rather with correct class-consciousness acquired only through outside injection. A major difference between the Leninist and Maoist outlooks and methods is in how the populist impulse is disciplined in the former and celebrated in the latter, though both Leninism and Maoism adhere to the role of a vanguard party. In contemplating the puzzle we are compelled to clarify under what circumstances participation might be unqualified or even adverse to a democratic order. Giovanni Sartori has a reason to complain that the concept of participation "is by now so ill-defined that it might even lead to the finding that (on a participation measure) the fullest democracy ever to exist was China at the time of its so-called cultural revolution" (1987, 183–84).

But then, what is so right about democracy and so wrong about the Chinese Cultural Revolution? Were they actually linked, and is it not exactly because of that unacceptable linkage that democracy theories are threatened? For all its faults and horrors, the Cultural Revolution in its ideological originality and historicity was as much a democratic revolt against privilege, bureaucracy, and perversions of revolution as it was a mass mobilization opportunistically used for power struggle. In this connection, it is worth noting a telling contrast between a high-energy participatory politics of Maoist socialism and a "low-intensity" one brought about by liberalization and deradicalization.[38] If political indifference is typical of many electoral democracies around the world, is this not a problem for democracy, and a no less serious problem than overparticipation? What, then, should be the criterion for evaluation without prejudice? Where does participation fit in, if it is understood as a matter of institutionally guaranteed popular input on decisions? If by consensus "the most defensible and attractive form of democracy is one in which citizens can participate in decision-making in a wide array of spheres" (Held 1987, 8), how should the Cultural Revolution be viewed in the comparative light of political apathy?

Some of these questions may never be answerable because "people's democracy," even at its sanest and most developed moments, endured sheer ideological, structural, and operational contradictions; for example, among the most visible, between voluntary participation and imposed mobilization, populism and vanguardism, grassroots activism and state instruction, and liberation and dependency. The theory of line struggle might represent, in Lowell Dittmer's words, "an attempt to absorb some of the advantages of political opposition and meaningful mass participation within a still basically authoritarian order" (1977, 711). But under a single party rule, even a participatory politics was, as Gordon White states, "not allowed to develop into autonomous political forces capable of checking or supervising the institutions of state power" (1983, 29). Such forces were openly promoted at the beginning of the Cultural Revolution, but then were shattered into total disarray because they could not be really independent and they lacked appropriate institutions. In the end, what was kept in place was more like a "people's democratic modernizing autocracy," as Stuart Schram calls it, in which an active citizenship was instrumental for state tasks (1989, 90). What a paradox that democracy could have been enhanced through a public conviction in people's sovereignty and popular involvement in politics while simultaneously crippled by systemic flaws of power—from party monopoly to unprotected liberties. Revolutionary turmoil notwithstanding, it is notable that the issue of decentralized governance was addressed "for the first time in the annals of Marxism" by the Maoist movement (and surely also in Tito's Yugoslavia). Yet Mao's analysis of the bureaucratic sclerosis of the USSR was correct, as Meghnad Desai points out, "but his solution remained a Bonapartist rather than a democratic one" (2002, 242). Writing in 1968, Ralph Miliband suspected if political debates in China were meaningful. Yet he also recognized that the Chinese "are the only ones to have really tried to respond in practice, and in theorizing their practice, to the 'challenge' of elitism." Weak in theorization, they nevertheless did "raise, and try to resolve, well or badly or both, the problems which are at the vital core of the whole socialist project." Increasingly repulsed by the absurdity of the events in China, later Miliband predicted that "in 3, 5 or 7 years we will witness a large-scale 'demaoization' " (quoted in Newman 2002, 230–31).

His prediction was remarkably accurate. The political logic behind it was the idea of Cultural Revolution being utopian at its time in the sense that regular government was not yet replaceable, and that when antibureaucratism amounted to a socialist antimodernism the paradox became unsolvable. It is clear with hindsight that if the Cultural Revolution was to revive China's revolutionary identity, the reform was a conscious countermovement to make a final break with revolutionary politics. And if the Chinese communists had "created one of the most bureaucratized social systems known to man" (Whyte 1973, 252), even a storm as devastating as the Cultural Revolution could not have it rectified. Mao's populist alternative to bureaucracy was banished as monstrously futile in the post-Mao atmosphere of law and order. Deng's "recentralization" thus stood for a return to sanity, as disgraced cadres were brought back with ever greater power and privileges (Shue 1988). But is it not precisely because of its failure that the Cultural Revolution must be seen as one of the first attempts to take a step forward to self-management and self-realization, of which the forms are yet to be freely, willingly, and competently invented by the people themselves?

Until then, Alec Nove among others might have a point in dismissing the Chinese venture when he asserts, in economic terms, that between free commodity production and hierarchical central planning, there is "no third way" (1983, 44).[39] The iron rule of the modern so far remains intact.

Using as an analogy the French Revolution's obsession with the condemnation of the past, François Furet (1998) sees the "communist utopia" as similarly fictional in making its own relationship with the past hidden. That is, communism shared with the system that it was determined to overthrow a "polity of absolutism." As the new regime turned out to be even more despotic in its zest to bury the old one, it overlooked the fact that such a passion for separation was itself a legacy of that past. Furet's critique is cogent, yet it neglects the necessity of utopian desires for—and hence collective social engineering of—higher types of modernity and civilization. Such desires were particularly noteworthy in the Chinese model of transcending not only capitalism but also Stalinist socialism. To arrive at a sound balance sheet in debating people's democracy is thus to confront every aspect of its contradictions, taking into consideration both its emancipatory potentials and its mixed record of attainments and catastrophe. It has to be seen as an uncompleted project to be continued through reformist transformation rather than yet another cycle of revolutionary absolutism.

"Total Politics" and "Totalitarian Democracy"

The magnitude of a successful communist revolution was manifested in China's social-national-developmental objectives after 1949, along with the expansion of a mass party as the ruling party and the consolidation of its power. It would not be an overstatement to say that the PRC was initially legitimated by the revolution and the revolutionary aspiration of people's sovereignty, and hence embodied distinctively democratic qualities. Counting not only forms of political participation other than periodic voting exercises but also relevant socioeconomic indicators of human development, the Chinese advance might even be viewed as ahead of some formal democracies. A. K. Bagchi, distinguishing between "democratic society" and "democratic polity," observed that China "may be more democratic than a society governed under a procedural democracy, such as Brazil or India" (1995, xvii).

Yet, returning to the background of Cultural Revolution, bureaucracy, and the "dictatorship over needs," the notion of people's democracy in its various forms fell short of a socialist democracy as normatively prescribed (e.g., by the Marxist critics of both capitalist democracy and "socialist" dictatorship), even when functioning at its closest to the ideal model of mass line and democratic centralism. It did not facilitate a free and open society in which the government is transparent and accountable, decisions are influenced by popular preference, dissenting views are respected, and the minorities protected. The regime was subject to no external checks by any organized opposition, and it met few institutionalized limits on its power. Citizens found themselves lacking certain constitutionally granted freedoms, some of which were as minimal as freedom of speech, faith, association, and movement. Although social control "rested much more on psychological pressures of indoctrination and persuasion and on close personal supervision by cadres than on police terror" (Townsend 1974, 15–16), the system was stifling, and "even a Michel Foucault would have had difficulty imagining" its effectiveness (Wakeman 1991, 88). The Gramscian ideological hegemony in effect made force or forced submission unnecessary. By the same token, hunted by enemies and hostile external circumstances, the party was able to persuade the population as a whole to endure periodic purges of dissidents in the absence of a strong notion of due process and minority protection.

In bypassing negative freedoms, then, was not people's democracy illiberal? Was it not actually totalitarian as succinctly captured in Jacob Talmon's (1952) caption of "totalitarian democracy"? Born of popular liberation struggles, the communist victory in China was subsequently caught in its own institutionalization. It was marred, once again, by structural and ideological contradictions intrinsic to the historical predicament of all that was attributable to "socialism and backwardness." While the CCP's monopoly of power always coexisted with inner party divisions and also with "multiparty consultation," the system displayed an overall "totalizing" character that was different from but also traceable to China's tradition of imperial despotism.[40] This character may also explain something in the persistent tendency toward extremism in Chinese politics: that is, a total power tending to preclude negotiated piecemeal changes must be either tolerated (hence obedience and conformity), or, once it becomes intolerable, destroyed (hence rebellion and revolution). Following Robert Lifton's

1961 study of "psychological totalism," Tsou Tang depicts a "total politics" in which political games often resolved into "one side winning all and/or the other side losing all" (1995, 97). In an essay in 1991 he offers Tiananmen in 1989 as a telling example.[41] But Tsou's "totalism" conceptually differs from Lifton's or Furet's polity of absolutism through its emphasis on the legitimating constraint on communism as a moral as much as a physical authority. In this model, the moral constraint is perceived by and dependent on the leaders themselves who may decide on reforms "unilaterally" from above. By subjecting state-society relations and regime types to separate levels of analysis, "totalism" concerning such relations is disentangled from "totalitarianism" concerning the nature of the regime (Tsou 1983; 2000). These terms remain interchangeable for Tsou, however, when he ponders if it is theoretically possible to have a "democratic totalitarian" polity in which political power is decentralized and persuasion substituted for coercion. The people "participate actively in the selection of their governors and express a preference for the state to penetrate all spheres of society or at least exhibit a spontaneous willingness to allow the state to do so" (Tsou 1988, xxv).

The most obscure issue, however, is the place of political opposition. If both reforms from above and rebellions from below had not been unusual to either dynastic or modern rulers in Chinese history, legitimate oppositional politics remained alien to China's political thinking and development until democratization in Taiwan gathered momentum in the late 1980s. It is quite logical that there could not be any space for oppositions in a zero-sum situation sustained by a moral preoccupation with the power of and for the people. The CCP led the country out of national humiliation and traditional social injustice, so it was able to act as the true and sole representative of the nation and the people, leaving no room for contenders for leadership. As Robert Dahl explains the rationale, if socialism has eliminated fundamental conflicts of interest, what is the need of political antagonism except as a dying residue of old society? And why should any opposition be permitted, if by its very nature such a force must be in opposition to society's fundamental interests? "On what ground could anyone in a socialist society claim to possess a *right* to oppose a government that was ruled by and governed in the interests of the working classes?" (1986, 14–15). Other lines of argument include consociational democracy that relies on consensus or on corporatist approaches more than competition, such as the "corporate-bargaining state" of Nordic countries against "distributional coalitions" (Olson 1982, 43–47). When Arend Lijphart is tempted to see nonadversarial cultures allegedly found in non-Western societies, he hints as though democracy without opposition parties would be more desirable (1999).[42] Critics of "illiberal democracy" spot the merit of "polycentric corporatism" among a string of potential credibilities of a somehow generalizable Asian politics (e.g., Bell et al. 1995).

As socialism was incompatible with a passive society and the party was in need of "supervision" by the masses, Chinese communism normatively allowed constructive criticisms (but not opposition, even loyal) through the use of mass line methods, consultation within the united front, and many forms of bargaining. This pattern echoed the Confucian tactics of dissolving, containing, and dispelling discontent. Mao was especially aware of the importance of minority protection and warned against "one voice" (*yiyantang*). "Insisting on the truth" at the expense of challenging the authority should not only be permitted but also regarded as a communist duty. But in contrast with the federalist founders of American democracy, Mao overlooked the institutional side of the matter. Even in his most rebellious mood "against the tide," he merely praised the "minority who mastered the truth" without thinking through a means of institutional provision for their legitimacy. Democratic centralism precluded any organizational expression of dissent.[43] In due course, predictably, the knowledge and interpretation of the creeds of the system became religion-like and unquestionable, thereby suffocating independent reasoning and critical judgment. A monolingual propaganda machine, as mentioned, translated ideology into everyday language and communication to reinforce socialization and thought reform. If "people's sovereignty" was all too abstract by itself, in a twist of persuasion, it attained a tangible meaning via state performance. As communism in China first exploited its popularity to perpetuate a one-party rule, and later, along the way of forcing market reforms, abandoned a mass line democracy altogether, the Chinese ambition of being a democratic alternative to the Soviet model was plainly unfulfilled.

Is there, then, a need for understanding China in the concept of totalitarianism that dominated Soviet studies until the revisionist turn promoting pluralist approaches in the 1970s? With a cold war overtone, the totalitarian model betokens a will of rulers to impose a code of thinking and conduct in every corner of life, thereby controlling society in its totality—a modern order postdating "Asiatic despotism." The degree of structural differentiation, infrastructural autonomy (political parties, interest groups, the mass media, etc.), and secularization of political culture are its principal variables (Almond and Powell 1966). Yet totalitarianism does not work descriptively; nowhere had total control ever succeeded. Heuristically it is not a matter of outcome but of purpose. Radical or revolutionary totalitarian regimes (as opposed to conservative and reactionary ones), in particular, ruthlessly pursued uniformity necessitated by rapid and fundamental socioeconomic changes (Townsend 1974, 22–24).

Temptation notwithstanding, the totalitarian model offers both too much and too little for the Chinese case. If it may account for a monopoly of power and ideology in a highly organized society, it still does not explain the dynamics of the internal workings of the system. Also, contrary to its prediction, communist states had nowhere ever been monolithic and had everywhere proven capable of transformation from within. Most commentators agree that ruling Chinese communism was much closer to the characterizations of "bureaucratic authoritarianism" or "developmental state" than those symbolized by the Gulag or Holocaust. The factionalist and informal politics schools in China studies thus could focus on cleavages in the official class without underestimating the autonomy of a unitary state from particularistic social interests; as Lucien Pye notes, "Any failure to disaggregate the components of the 'state' would be to close one's eyes to precisely the tensions and conflicts which make up so much of Chinese politics" (1992, 1167). The reform had certainly pluralized the country and its power structure in an unprecedented scale, when "the character of the state alters so as to facilitate the introduction of foreign and domestic capital" (Howell 1993, 6). It then became even harder for anyone to miss "the multifaceted character of state power and the simultaneously centralized and decentred nature of state politics" (Rofel 1999, 36). So much so that more reserved labels displaced totalitarianism; for example, "fragmented authoritarianism," so as to stress the erosion of either the willingness or capacity of control (Lieberthal 1992); and "consultative authoritarianism," so as to accommodate the decline of personal command in a "complex bureaucracy" (Harding 1986).

The totalitarianist perspective also explains too little, essentially because it precludes democracy as both an ideological inspiration and a pragmatic device in the intensity and extensity of the contradictory Chinese experiences. In this connection, it is worth revisiting "totalitarian democracy," of which the obvious terminological and conceptual contradiction is where Maoist populism could be captured. Jacob Talmon might not have done Rousseau justice and did not have the new state of PRC in mind while writing. To invoke his analysis is to admit a degree of emulation by the Chinese of Jacobin democracy on the one hand and Soviet pretention on the other.[44] Another hybrid category, deployed in Alexis de Tocqueville's 1856 comparative study of France and America, is "democratic despotism" (which has nothing to do with "popular tyranny"). Tocqueville imagines "a people composed of individuals nearly alike and entirely equal," a "confused mass" "recognized as the only legitimate sovereign, but carefully deprived of all the faculties which could enable it either to direct or even to superintend its own government" (quoted in Sartori 1962, 461). In similarly blending seemingly incompatible components, it is "totalitarian democracy" rather than "democratic despotism" that specifically targets modern left-wing dictatorships with an intrinsic democratic dimension.[45] Totalitarian democracy emphasizes elite idealism and popular enthusiasm mediated by ideological messianism. It is premised on each individual's reason being recognizable and desire being achievable, though only through social transformations. Such transformations in turn involve all as participants who thereby attain freedom by transforming themselves at the same time. This confirms the Rousseauean-Marxian insight of seeing "free individuals" as both the condition of, and preconditioned by, their "free associations."[46] For Talmon, the difference between liberal and totalitarian democracy is thus not between freedom and its denial; both models affirm the supreme value of reason and liberty. What distinguishes the latter instead is its assumption of an absolute and single truth in politics, its exclusive understanding of human freedom that incorporates popular sovereignty into one party leadership, and its nearly divine self-knowledge as an ideological instrument of unity.[47]

Thinking along the line of Talmon's "socialist messianism" (1960, part 1), utopian or scientific, Jacques Derrida recognizes in the Marxist secular messianic movements "a certain experience of the emancipatory promise" as "an idea of justice, and an idea of democracy" (1994, 59). Those ideas go beyond philistine liberal reasoning confined to legal rights, and they cannot be denied validity in their specific context. Noting ideological intolerance inherent in the seductive power of "messianic charm," Furet (1998) acknowledges how the sublime revolutionary utopia is guarded against its own failure. Trying to understand "why so many well-intended schemes to improve the human condition have gone so tragically awry" in Soviet and third world socialism (e.g., Tanzania), James Scott explains how the ambition of "authoritarian high modernism" had been materialized: The "legibility of a society provides the capacity for large-scale social engineering, high-modernist ideology provides the desire, the authoritarian state provides the determination to act on that desire, and an incapacitated civil society provides the leveled social terrain on which to build." Without appreciating the paradoxical totality of state autonomy being just another word for societal integration, he has no quarrel with utopian aspirations per se; they go wrong only when the ruling elites disregard the knowledge and "art of locality" (1998, 4–5, 89, 316).

Yet like any theoretical models, "totalitarian democracy" cannot "fit" perfectly. For all its stimulation beyond the paradigms of totalitarianism and pluralism alike, it is still too monolithic for China where, even at communism's triumphant moments or, in fact, especially during those moments, the system was far more flexible. The evolution of PRC politics would not otherwise be explainable, concerning especially reform ideologies and policies that were possible above all because of a critical space gained within the system for self-reflective adjustment. Saying farewell to the tormented years of revolutionary turmoil while seeking incremental changes, the regime slowly came to terms with the redistribution of power resources. Political liberalization and administrative decentralization entailed a redefinition of participation, even a legitimization of organized oppositions. This gradual political opening without shunning the party and the morality of a socialist democracy did not follow the paths of transition elsewhere.[48]

The Moral and the Institutional

By looking deeper into the ruins of the Great Leap Forward and the Cultural Revolution before a people's democracy could have ever reached its promised land, three intertwined sets of comparisons can be made. The first is between the idea and institutions of people's sovereignty to which Maoist socialism committed itself, highlighting institutional weakness. The second is between the fading centrality of the people and the heightened focus on legalization, which featured post-Mao reforms. The "neo-authoritarian" style rationalization positioned itself as a preparative stage for future democratization, without ordinary citizens being empowered as the agents ever to carry it out. These historically successive developments are then compared to show how reconstructing democracy in China would require the morality of the power of the people to be reasserted in the institutionalization of political reform. The moral ontology and procedural prerequisite by no means automatically support each other.

Procedures and Substance

Politics for the most part is an ethical matter in the Chinese tradition of political culture. Although Confucianism was only one part of a rich bundle of traditional thought, over many centuries it came to dominate the elite quest for an ideal polity.[49] The moralistic constraint was so forceful that, as Lucien Pye notes, "the Chinese cannot talk straightforwardly about power in their politics, but must turn politics into an ideological question" (1985, 188). Here the assumption, unlike many other cultures in which moral and political powers are supposed to coincide as well, is that government does not rest so much on formal rules as on its assumed moral authority, and officials are self-disciplined without needing external watchdogs. As the Confucian teaching clarifies it, "He who is right is followed without giving a command. He who is not right commands without being followed" (The Analects Book 8, 1992, 123). This optimism about an all-embracing reign of virtue is also fortified by the belief in attainable harmony between rulers and the ruled. Cultural particularity cannot be pushed too far, however, for morality and politics are hardly separable and the question of legitimacy is a universal one. Surely the Kantian categorical imperative presumes higher ethics to feed into the rights and law? And the primacy of civic participation lies in the Rousseauean maxim that "politics itself is the solution to the moral problem"? (cf. Colletti 1972, 144–48).

In other words, institutional and moral dimensions, like means and end, are not readily divisible; and even an instrumental reading of democracy, pure and simple, cannot be free of value judgment. The binary is not quite the same as between formal procedures and substantive outcomes. In the familiar framing of "process versus substance,"[50] it is frequently asked if democratic institutions should be expected to serve any normative goals. Should they "be imbued with a moral content or should they be just a system of laws regulating conflicts" (i.e., "ballots against bullets")? (Przeworski et al. 1995, 40–42).[51] The standard argument in favor of the procedural option goes by the observation that competing political forces find it necessary, in their own interests, to compete by democratic regulation. No other system provides a compatible degree of security and fairness, though some enlightened autocracies did achieve peace through effective conflict management. Hence Joseph Schumpeter's well-known statement about democracy being "a political *method*" of choosing and changing offices through free elections; that is, "governments should emerge from competitive struggles for votes" (1947, 411, 242). Further, democracy must not be conflated with content-wide outcomes, insists Brian Barry, among others, except for "those required by democracy itself as a procedure"—or formal political equality and freedoms of deliberation and organization for the formation, expression, and aggregation of public preferences (1989, 25).[52] It is reasonable to argue that socioeconomic concerns be kept conceptually separate from political issues, and economic democracy kept separate from political democracy. But even within the realm of politics, can any "method" exist without its own "substance" of moral (un)desirability? If democracy is defined (e.g., in the Aristotelian tradition) as a mode of collective decisionmaking in which citizens exert control (Aristotle 1981, 362; cf. Beetham 1993, 54; Held 1987, chapter 1), is it a matter of procedure or outcome, form or content? Distinctions made between the moral and institutional therefore have to be concrete, as here in the specific Chinese context.

Electoral politics, central to formal democracies, had been marginal in Chinese communism where elections were not for party contentions and election campaigns did not exist. The impact of local elections on central policies, if any, had been trivial. The PRC's first election law was proclaimed in 1953 (when the new democracy project was still alive) and was revised three times after 1979. The current text (adopted in 1995) reads like a fantastic call for participation, which guarantees the right of "everyone over 18 years of age, regardless of ethnicity, race, sex, profession, family background, religious belief, education level or financial statues" to elect and be elected. All that is needed by a candidate wishing to run for local legislature is a petition signed by a minimum of ten supporters. The gap between the law and practices was, unsurprisingly, huge, mainly due to political obstacles.[53] A citywide referendum in Nanjing, the capital of Jiangsu province, identified and removed dozens of corrupt officials in 2002, but similar exercise elsewhere were rare. The pledge for self-government in the state-instructed movement for village elections raised expectations (Jacobs 1991), but many of the awaited benefits were impeded by economic disparity, kinship exclusion, corruption, and other electoral irregularities. The 1983 stipulation on direct votes for deputies to the people's congresses at the county level had not been widely implemented.[54] By 2002 over a million villages and about 85,000 neighborhood committees in 660 cities cast ballots;[55] a positive development that was nevertheless celebrated much less inside China than among well-intentioned Western observers and advisers (cf. Kelliher 1997). The Carter Center in Atlanta and the European Union were among those international organizations that regularly dispatched workers to the sites, often in collaboration with the Chinese Ministry of Civil Affairs, which was responsible for overseeing elections on the ground.

In light of these background factors, three critical reflections stand out. First, contrary to a common myth, local elections were by no means new to communist politics in China, which took for granted the modern norm of universal suffrage. The election law of the Shan-Gan-Ning region (May 1937) asserted the "universal direct equal suffrage by secret ballot . . . regardless of sex, religion, race, financial situation or culture." The CCP's news agency, *Xinhua*, was a forum for promoting democracy in Yan'an. One of its editorials stated that the "election right is among the very minimum political rights to which the people in a democratic country are entitled. The people are the masters, officials their servants" (2 February 1944). Another editorial statement criticized the "excuse to delay the implementation of democracy," namely the low literacy rate of the villagers (24 January 1946). Attacking the GMD regime, the paper asked, "How is democracy possible without ending one-party rule, without popular suffrage? Return the people's rights to the people!" (27 September 1945).[56] Local and community elections were indeed held in the base areas and continued to be relatively routine after 1949 in work units, service institutions, party and government offices, and mass organizations. The peasants invented various voting methods to counter illiteracy and other wartime difficulties; and in so doing they demonstrated the feasibility of a popular electoral democracy (like modern India) that defied the contemporary orthodoxy about democracy's economic prerequisites of a middle class and an educated population resulted from modernization. Dong Biwu, then chairman of the Regional People's Government, proudly claimed that the revolutionary peasantry made "the poorest part of China the most democratic." Mark Selden thus compares favorably "the seeds of democracy sown in the resistance" with mobilizations in the PRC. He contends that such seeds were crushed before having a chance to germinate by the ruling CCP.[57]

The second reflection is that village elections had thus far failed to visibly impact on central and local government; and neither did they logically pave the way for provincial and national elections. Any breakthrough in more general elections requires a different conception and strategy of political development. Accumulated pressures in recent years on agricultural policy reforms came from leadership change (in 2003) and mounting rural riots— anywhere but from village elections. The structural ambivalence of grass-roots administration in rural China was itself a problem: the commune-turned-township level lost many of its old functions, yet it kept absorbing resources; and the artificial "village" covering several natural villages blended "state" and "locality" in a supposedly self-governing community.[58] Administrative mergers were underway but until a rational structure could stabilize without cadres (elected or not) living on peasant taxes, the elections would not even be a token showcase of any democratic significance. Indian democracy, often used to rebuke modernization theory but still utterly unattractive to the Chinese in social terms, might have shared with China a discrepancy between laws and regulations on the one hand, and their imple-mentation on the other. Village democracy (*panchayati raj*) in India, how-ever, had a legal quota for women (40 percent), which was not even a concern in the relevant institutional design in China where women were deemed liberated. Both cases largely confirmed that "a national framework of democracy does not guarantee real democracy at the local level and an authoritarian national framework does not completely block democratic elements at the local level" (Sovensen 1993, 23). Experiments in the former Yugoslavia similarly posed the question as to how forms of "self-governing socialism" might flourish locally under a formally undemocratic central power. Local elections in China have yet to chart a way to reconcile direct (community and workplace) and representational democracy nationally.

This leads to the third reflection on the ineffectiveness of village voting: in terms of benefiting the electorate, most such exercises made no real difference in rural lives.[59] The village committees, even if not in the hands of clan oligarchs or manipulated by the wealthy, were still mostly powerless. They did not have the means, for example, to retain local land and other resources when developers and (extra-tax) fee collectors were backed by the county and township governments. Typically, decollectivization first reduced tensions between top-down command and bottom-up demands, but then created new tensions among polarized groups and between farmers and local officials. Lacking funds that previously would have been generated through governmental and collective channels, little could be done, even by democratically elected leaders, about the deteriorations in welfare maintenance. The withdrawal of the center had taken with it the socialist moral and financial commitment to rural public service, of which a deepening health crisis was one consequence, and a jump in the school dropout rate another. The rural population, whether or not participating in elections, possessed no power to alter these conditions. Until they could form their own representative organizations, "grassroots democracy" would be irrelevant; and anyone with any historical knowledge about modern China knew only too well that nothing could be more powerful than the peasant associations in waging a revolution from the countryside.

Morality and Legality

The tensions between substance and procedures are mirrored in those between morality and legality. The initial making of a people's democracy— even when expressly democratic as judged by the principles or experiments of popular sovereignty, the mass line, and self-management—was missing a legal dimension. The socialist state was highly capable of mobilizing human and natural resources, and hugely successful in organizing mass campaigns to eliminate prostitution (through medical aid and employment), combat endemic diseases, and reduce illiteracy. But the successes almost solely relied on the popularity of such campaigns and of the new regime itself. The lack of institutionalized legal means subsequently prevented the constitutional power and rights of the people from being materialized. A massive victimization under a popular dictatorship was reflected during a collective soul-searching at the onset of reform. The lessons drawn, as represented in a one-sided reform discourse, were exclusively about "negative freedoms," which indeed were necessary, but not sufficient, conditions for a democratic citizenship.

China's traditional political culture of morality over legality (hence Confucianism over the Legalist school or revolutionary over normal politics) might have played a role in the prevalence of ideology and personal rule in Chinese socialism. But the Maoist neglect of legal procedures and judicial independence was deliberate. Mao himself showed contempt for all forms of "law," from any "scientific law" of historical development to the legality of modern society. Following Lenin, he declared that by definition the revolution was to disdain the existing law and order, human or divine (*wufa wutian*). It was the impossible situation of total anarchy and lawlessness of the Cultural Revolution that led to the "decent burial" of Maoism.[60]

Post-Mao political reforms were marked by the steady empowerment of the NPC and, through that body, a deformed "parliamentary democracy" of progressive lawmaking. Institutionally speaking, the people's congresses, national and local, are part and parcel of a people's democracy. By virtue of being so designated and thereby combining executive, legislative, and judicial power, the NPC is antithetical to the "bourgeois" theory of checks and balance between the three separate powers. There is a mere division of labor among them. Neither bicameral nor unicameral, the NPC and its standing committee appoint the government and enjoy "supervisory supremacy" over the State Council, the Supreme People's Court, and the Supreme People's Procuratorate. There was some speculation that the Political Consultative Conference might become a second chamber in a Chinese-style bicameralism, but the existing structural negation of liberal democracy's institutional prerequisite remained intact. By an alternative principle of socialist democratic centralism, all power belongs to the people and all of the state organs are produced by and answerable to the NPC. In theory, then, what could justify inefficiency and wrangles in the formal democratic processes?[61]

Even for those who reject such a principle and believe there to be no democracy to talk about without free competition for offices, the people's congresses had gained greater autonomy from the party and hence independent prominence and authority (O'Brien 1994; Dowdle 1997). The deputies had increasingly engaged themselves in serious debates, at times clashing with party leaders. The best-known examples include the lasting controversy over the Three Gorges Project and, more recently, the issue of the fair treatment of migrant workers. As the prestige and importance of the NPC rose (ironically also due to the transfer to its standing committee of power holders retired from key party and government positions), its annual conventions were no longer mere rehearsals of political rituals. It had even begun to move toward safeguarding the constitutional mandate against the concentration and abuses of power (Christiansen 1994, 166–68). In the same vein, political liberalization saw a contraction of crackdowns on dissidents; the professionalization of law-enforcement and court procedures; enforced measures against arbitrary detention and torture; and open discussions of reforming the judiciary (Keith 1994; Tanner 1999; Lubman 1999). Other indications of "socialist legality" include promoting legal aid to the poor, encouraging litigation by citizens against government wrongdoing, and the legislative provision for local self-government.

Democracy and legality are not the same, however, and whether or not a legal order is democratic depends on the nature of the law rather than its mere existence. Further, democratization cannot remotely be identical with bureaucratic fragmentation and decentralization (in confusion with privatization), as is assumed implicitly or explicitly in the reform thinking. Technical, quantitative leaps in formal rules and laws may not forestall tyranny, corruption, or government breakdown.[62] Legality alone is no solution to the problem of the powerlessness of citizens. In fact, legal reform will be misleading when taken to be equivalent with democratization without the people being brought back to the center. To be sure, rulers, ancient and modern, always need some legal tools in order to rule. Such tools by themselves are no guarantee of rational legality or civil rights (with or without the language of right), let alone democratic power. Legalization is one thing, building democracy in which the fundamental law is crafted by the people according to their own will is another; likewise compiling laws needed by a market transition is not the same thing as democratization of the economic structure. The two sides—legal institutionalization and democratic construction—should be closely connected but may not in reality, depending not only on the purpose of the state and its lawmakers but also social consciousness as a whole. The distinction between "rule by law" and "rule of law" is useful, with the latter aiming at equality of citizens before the law and transparency of legal codes.[63] Even the "rule of law," however, is a liberal rather than a democratic parameter without confronting the issue of whose law. For democracy is predicated on the nature, the justice, or "ontology" of law (Supiot 2002)—a higher law that must be the foundation of legality and of legitimacy. In other words, the moral core of people's democracy is yet to be rediscovered to substantiate China's legal reforms so that they do not repeat an authoritarian path to repression.

The reform had embarked on a dual course of degrading an abstract notion of the sovereign people and institutionalizing "socialist legality and political civilization." The conflation of democratization and legalization in effect legitimated neoauthoritarianism among bureaucratic technocrats.[64] The farther China traveled on this path the more impossible it seemed it could ever obtain a system "representing the interests of the greatest majority of the people" as stated in the "three represents" theory. The reluctance to even touch on the notion of people's sovereignty was a symptom of weakness and fear, of a crisis in regime legitimacy precisely because of the absence of democracy needed at a time of diversity and change. Democracy could be a threat to the state power exposed to both external pressures and internal conflicts. It is also quite straightforward that if popular articulation of interests no longer featured Chinese politics, it was because the current reform project had a vested interest in gratifying domestic and international capital. China's political and intellectual elites had thus taken a static, black-and-white approach in their "great escape" from the contradictions of Chinese socialism. Despising a flawed people's democracy without rescuing its moral fundamentals was both a part and a cause of the country's departure from reform socialism in the early 1990s.

In the end, the question of institutions is not separable from that of morality. The Chinese communists were "assigned" by the revolutionary victory, so to speak, the job of representing the people, but eventually found themselves caught in a chain of political predicaments. Their inherited legitimacy had had its day: "natural" representation just could not last, and the relationship between the leaders and the led eroded, draining sources of support in the regime's historical constituency. Robert Tucker sees de-radicalization as the fate of Marxist movements that might survive and flourish "*without* remaking the world" (1967, 347–48). Even the Maoist world, thought to have been so solidly made, vanished in a time span of merely a generation, leaving little trace apart from nostalgic feelings among "losers" in the marketplace. The conquest of capital was such that, as Fredric Jameson notes (without religious sustenance of some sort), "all appeals to moral incentives (as in Che) or to the primacy of the political (as in Maoism) must fatally exhaust themselves in a brief time" under siege (1988, 355). Yet it is no less true that even a "normal" politics in a post-revolutionary society like China required legitimation on some of the same grounds that initially legitimized the revolution itself. Although transcendental ideologies could be defeated by nontranscendental decays and injustice, the possibilities of life ("not our modern world, but something far nobler, something yet to be achieved")[65] and the substance of procedures, morality of law, and democracy beyond formalities must be resurrected.

Ideology and Institutions

Looking further at the moral-institutional complexities, what stands out is the mutual embeddedness of state and society in the Chinese political tradition. The case of state penetration in society is largely uncontroversial in the China studies, which, however, conceals the other side of the story about societal influence on the state, insofar as the two spheres remain more or less distinguishable. The following fourfold elaboration may bring this latter perspective to light in terms not of "civil society" (see chapter 4) but of democracy. First, as noted, a mass movement can be destructive or constructive in terms of perceived social benefits, contingent on the specific origins, objectives, contexts and circumstances, and organization and leadership. The potential democratic value of collective action lies in broad participation, and hence opportunities of self-realization, especially for hitherto marginalized groups, disregarding whether elections are held and which electoral systems might be in place. Formalists and proceduralists may well stick with the idea of indispensability of voting, but normative justifications for participation in multiple forms not confined to a ballot would be hard to overturn. Extensive public engagements by a highly enthralled population in the Mao years, whether spontaneous and voluntary or simultaneously also directed and even coerced, were paradoxical in the sense of "totalitarian democracy," mass line style.

Yet a mass movement could also be turned into a nightmare for democracy, as demonstrated by the bulk of cultural revolutionary experience of direct participation without civil and legal regulations. The inability to ensure individual security and minority protection, and the exclusion and discrimination against people on the "wrong" side darkened the day. This is my second point made against a background collective violence. Majority tyranny is, of course, always a danger and misfortune for democracy. This inherent ambivalence compels theorists in the Platonic tradition to repulse democracy in relation to unwanted clashes between the rulers and the ruled, educated and ignorant, propertied and poor; it is certain to be a deviation from the republic or commonwealth, like despotism from kingship or oligarchy from aristocracy. Immanuel Kant, deeply distrusting majority rule, contrasts it with aristocratic rather than autocratic rulership and holds that republican government based on universal rights is impossible in a democracy (cf. 1991, 29). The repulsion of popular culture by the first generation of thinkers of the Frankfurt school is attributable to the fact that fascist parties enjoyed a wide margin of faith and loyalty—no less vindicated by elections. Communist populism, laid bare above all in the CCP's ambiguity of preserving the revolution while ruling, is only a latest explosion in a long line of "built-in contradictions" and "intrinsic and extrinsic dilemmas" of democracy (Diamond 1996; Schmitter 1996).

Third, as noted earlier, mass line democracy did gain a degree of integrity between ideology and institutional procedures. If an underlying assumption of Chinese socialism was harmony of interests between state, society, and individuals, and if public welfare thereby set an ultimate test for government performance, the articulation of interests through a continuing spiral of "from the masses (inputs) and to the masses (outputs)" was a rational choice. However, such an active, participatory process of interest formation and aggregation, presumably under a communist dictatorship (which enjoyed measured popularity), was lost in an allegedly less repressive, liberalized reform era. But Tocqueville must be right to see political apathy and material greed as "despotism's safeguard because they divert men's attention from public affairs."[66] Since political institutions cannot be value neutral, and political ethics requires institutional instruments, critiques of Maoist bias against (bureaucratic and legal) institutions need qualification. The inventive methods for mass mobilization—not to mention the organizational triumph of the party itself in terms of leadership, discipline, and ideology—displayed rather a sophisticated and powerful web of state (and indeed also societal and ideological) apparatus. This web of apparatus was no doubt based on high-minded "ethical" values that defined society's self-identity and public consciousness. So much so that the exhaustion of Maoism was triggered by itself being pushed to extremes of absurdity. The truth is that Mao's uninterrupted revolution against law and order did not defy but rather revived a political culture of "rule by virtue" that did not only cherish a future ideal polity but also claimed to possess its own mandate. By overlooking the sublime of revolutionary yearning for liberation, the pragmatist frameworks of analysis in the critical literature in communist studies are of little use.

A core issue, and this is the fourth layer of the argument, is the problematic claim of the people being collectively sovereign, and hence the fundamental morality of people's democracy as such, even though an abstract totality of the "people" is by no means unique to the PRC. The commoners in the Confucian idea of a people-rooted politics emerged around the same time as Athenian democracy, but they were both more inclusive than and, without the status of political citizenship, completely different from the demos in the classical polis. Visibly connected with the ancient Chinese concept of the mandate of heaven, rather than with the Western traditions of democratic government, democracy since the Chinese revolution had implied party-mass courtship and popular participation more than individual rights or pluralistic interests. As a result, the concept of the "people" was torn between being the unified and supreme power-bearer and an internally divided category ("contradictions among the people"). Mao's axiom that "of all things in the world, people are the most precious" did not prevent him from launching fierce campaigns against "bourgeois humanism." The constitutional declaration of "all power to the people" legitimized at once an excessively powerful moral state and unending attacks on bureaucracy. Mao was keenly aware of the implications of the party's ruling position and warned that even a communist regime would be capable of errors and corruption and, consequently, challenged by the people in whose name it ruled. He told the party that the masses were fully entitled to resist any privileged "new lords" sitting on their backs. The gist of people's democracy was the continuation of revolution in the sense that democratic rebellions from below were justified.

Also pertinent is the Confucian doctrine on remonstrance or moral duty—in the absence of the modern language of right—to dissent or revolution (Nathan 1985, 24–25). Although Maoist reasoning needed no blessing from a "feudal" legacy, if there is anything remotely "democratic" in Confucianism as compared with the *realpolitik* of Legalism, it would be the moral (as oppose to legal) "right" of popular revolt: any government that has lost the mandate should be replaced.[67] Over two millennia before Jean-Jacques Rousseau, Mencius coined the enduring concept of the will of the people (*minyi*; literally, people's will), calling it the mandate of heaven. Mainstream social sciences are yet to look into the fact that popular rebellions were officially justifiable in certain non-Western and nondemocratic cultures. Throughout Chinese history, as Elizabeth Perry notes, "mass protests have played a special role in bestowing political legitimacy . . . whether framed in terms of the Mencian Mandate of Heaven or in terms of Mao's Mass Line." This, in admitting a causal linkage, "argues for acknowledging a larger, more pro-active role for the state" (2002, xxi). The centrality of ordinary working people, ideologically and socioeconomically, however, was a distinctively socialist project. Only its contradictions kept replicating old discrepancies rooted in tradition.

Collective Will and Representation

Revolutionary democracy found a retrospective echo, even some revealing explanations, in Rousseau, who appeared to be a natural ally of the Chinese attempt at an alternative democracy, not only because of the affinities between the French and Chinese revolutions but also because he was a socialist of his time.[68] Unlike John Locke, who also talks about "one people, one body politic under one supreme government" while defending the "natural rights" of private property (in the Second Treaties on Civil Government), Rousseau refuses property in his conditions of social contract.[69] The long-entrenched controversy, ever since Edmund Burke's *Reflections on the Revolution in France* (1790), over whether Rousseau's political legacy is liberal democratic or totalitarian is heuristic for debating PRC politics. In particular, the idea of "general will" has redrawn the landscape of political thinking, inspiring numerous attempts to reinterpret Rousseau. If that name among others and the grand narratives of modernity and universalism sound dated, so should be democracy—yet remarkably the latter has triumphed in "postmodern" cultures. However alarming to contemporary commentators in the shadows of twentieth-century totalitarian horrors, the idea is worth investigating as, in particular, a fine elucidation of the ideal-type mass line democracy and democratic centralism. Rousseau's assertion that one retains freedom while obeying the law because "the people that is subject to the law must be its author" (1993, 191)[70] speaks surprisingly well to the Chinese, then (the aspiration of people's sovereignty) and now (the problem of legality without democracy). Both the eighteenth-century revolutionary imagination and twentieth-century Chinese socialism hold a distinction between freedom within and freedom relative to social constraints in terms of the nature of the governing law (Rousseau 1968, chapter 6). Both take nothing for granted in morality and moral socialization, which come into existence only through intense education. And for both to make sense there must be the "mechanisms by which individual decisions are aggregated and combined into collective decisions" (Dahl 1961, 770).

The general will, as the "one and indivisible" will of a people, must be distinguished from the "will of all" as a summation of private and particular preferences (Rousseau 1968, 72–75; 1988, 100).[71] The Maoist parallel of the "will of all" would be the aggregation of scattered views from the masses; the outcome of their systematic processing would be the "general will." The difference between "will of all" and "general will" is between inputs and output of a democratic production of decisions, which cannot be a numerical question but rather a qualitative one about deliberation and consensus. The theoretical possibility of a general will or fundamental consensus being attainable is what in principle enables members of a free society to be simultaneously free individuals and rule-binding citizens collectively exercising power. The assumption of "common good" in the oldest utilitarian sense of the greatest good for the greatest number of people, however questionable for radical liberal pluralism,[72] is central to any coherent politics (cf. Dahl 1989, 282–98). Democracy is not only about difference, recognition, and competition but also, inevitably, about negotiation, cooperation, prudence, and solidarity. And socialism would not even be accessible without a public commitment to common or collective good. If free-born individuals "are everywhere in chains," it is not only because of inequalities but also because civilization must rise from the law of jungles. For Kant's union of republics or Hegel's "ethical State," as for Rousseau's human community after the State of Nature, the universal reason or general will is also the marker of enlightenment.[73]

In the Rousseauean model of direct democracy, the sovereignty cannot be transferred from the citizenry to the state via so-called representatives: "sovereignty cannot be represented." While elected individuals "rule" in a representative democracy, they are merely agents without the decisionmaking power, which resides only in the people who "ratify" rules and laws. Citizens as individuals are the only foundation of sovereignty in a democracy; they need not and cannot be represented. He thus treats as "gravely mistaken" the belief that people are free because they vote.[74] He sets a standard critique of formal democracies in his discussion of the fallacy of confining democracy to periodic elections that alienate the electorate from politics in the long intervals. In contemporary advanced democracies civic and political associations and social movements do engage politics between and during elections. But does not "social capital" (Putnam 1993) only confirm the validity, even in large modern societies, of the Rousseauean opposition to representation overtaking participation and to democracy limited to elite politics?

It is interesting to note that China's NPC and its local assemblies happen to be formally in line with Rousseau in their institutional concept that the deputies, in contrast to professional politicians, do not occupy parliamentary seats when the congresses are not in session. They return to normal works and roles after congress meetings while the state power is retained as embodied in the body politic of the NPC. The deputies are "delegates" not merely of their constituents but of the entirety of a sovereign people, even though the Chinese terminology does not tell the difference—the word *daibiao*, meaning "representation" or "representative," is in daily use within and outside legislative procedures. The notion of the communist state fundamentally representing the Chinese people is perhaps only a remote replication of the general will, but the latter plays into the former to preclude competitive politics. In practice the deputies were more likely to play out "functional constituencies." Elections were held but they would not take place until the completion of carefully arranged recommendation, consultation, and selection processes to ensure not only desirable candidates but also a desirable balance of social groups by gender, age, profession, sectoral occupation, region, religion, nationality, party affiliations and so on. The quotas were often insufficiently proportional—the peasants, for example, had been vastly "underdelegated"—but meant to achieve fair representation for interest articulation and resource allocation. Here distinction between representation and delegation collapsed. These groups were structurally—rather than individually by the delegates—represented in the people's congresses intended to be all-inclusive, a contrast with interest groups in liberal democracies. Their specific interests would be conveyed by the deputies who formally shouldered a national duty but were also expected to transmit specific entreaties and deliberate policies. Simultaneously, the NPC was positioned at the top of the power structure while its deputies mediated mostly in an upward flow of information to the government.

China was not the only country that had sought meaning, measurements, and institutions for democracy alternative to the regular two-party or multiparty systems.[75] After all, political parties in modern nation-states are relatively recent creations (where direct democracy at the national level is thought to be impracticable), and they neither possess inherent virtue of eternity nor provide a guarantee for democracy. Numerous authoritarian electoral regimes have allowed standard party competition and opposition. This said, it is worth repeating that the Chinese experiment did not achieve a democratically attractive alternative model. The point remains, though, that the political organization necessary for a participatory citizenry can take forms other than competitive political parties. Nationally and locally instituted public forums backed up by legislation may coordinate autonomous associations and political participation. It is not inconceivable that many offices can be run, as they have here and there in history, by citizens in rotation or selected by votes or lot, rather than by professional politicians and bureaucrats. This could be part of a depoliticization of politics toward the withering away of the state. The institutional question is widely open even before the age arrives, if ever, of the post–nation-state.

The essence of Rousseau's proposition is such that it does not matter whether his absorption of the individual into the collective, and individual freedom into a general will, amounts to totalitarianism (through socialization as brainwashing). The two categories—individual and collective—in his account can perfectly coincide in terms of freedom (retained by the individuals while obeying the law) and direct democracy (attainable in small and large republics). This relies on a conceptual and functional distinction preserved between the legislature (citizens) and the executive (government), with the former mandating the latter. For Rousseau, as for a people's democracy, at issue is not the democratic institution per se but the distribution of power in which a sovereign people have the command over, more than just the "influence" on, public decisions. Popular input in political processes (the infrastructure and techniques of the mass line) is therefore necessary but secondary to the moral authority of the people (the foundation of the mass line). As it turned out, the communist systems, in the words of David Beetham, "required much more political participation than liberal democracies, yet they were very short on popular control of major collective decisions" (1993, 61). A true failure for sure; but we also wonder if liberal democracy itself has ever lived up to such high expectations. The focus on "influence" in the early pluralist theories of democracy (Robert Dahl and his followers) grossly underestimates asymmetrical power relations among interest groups in a "polyarchy."

Critics of the "general will" as a concept find it "fictitious, fallible, and seducible" (Offe 1996, 90), even religious, and neither verifiable nor falsifiable; and the "will of the people" in the PRC is cited as an intangible "myth" and a "fantasy of collective spontaneity" (Womack 1991, 70), if not a horrendous joke. A major problem, as time and again is brought up to attention, is concerned with individual disagreement and minority rights to representation and protection, which are conceptually excluded from a "general" (as opposed to "majority") will. The voluntarist construction and universalist impulse of social contract theory seem to be overtly optimistic about normal human conditions, failing to see their "non-modularity" (Gellner 1995, 40–41).

The "people," in singularity, leaves a loophole allowing dissenting views and stakes to be repressed or neglected, and hence parts, however small, of the population are sacrificed for the sake or in the name of the whole. In so doing the totality of the people asks for more than a convergence of what is "freely and willingly" willed in affirmation of the law for mutual benefits, despite the recognition of difference between diversities in the "will of all" and the unified "general will." Consequently, freedom becomes either conditional on conformity or hierarchical in accordance with collective priorities, which involves education or "moral liberty." While civil liberties only bend to a possible congruence of duties and inclinations, moral liberty is a self-imposed Kantian rule of reason over emotion, which can easily be translated into the universal over personal (Rousseau 1968, 365; 1988, 95). A socialist project, likewise, would require "for its redemption not just the peaceful aggregation of the will of the many, but a rational cognitive process which determines what must rationally be willed by all" (Offe and Preuss 1991, 155). Much more than consent, it entails ideological belief, selfless devotion, puritanical zeal, and (self-)repression of "incorrect" thoughts (cf. Offe 1996, chapter 5; Walzer 1998, 134–38). This is where a degree of popular power in China's revolutionary democracy came to be vulnerable to both elite hijacking and destructive tendencies in mass mobilization. In other words, moral bankruptcy could happen even prior to institutional deficiencies, and the moral and institutional intertwine to sustain each other. Typically, this was the case of identity labels imposed on individuals and groups in communist China by the ostensibly collective power of a singular, sovereign people identified with the socialist state.

The question, ultimately, is who makes the judgment on what is subjective, the personal and emotional, and what is objective, the rational and universal; assuming the former to give way to the latter? That is, how might the will of the people be constructed and known? Intersubjectivity is too easy an answer, but a general will, if plausible at all, is not predetermined and does not politically exist until it is contested and embodied in formal and informal institutions. In a critique of Rousseau's "democracy of non-public opinion" or "consensus of hearts rather than of arguments," Jürgen Habermas locates democratic deliberation in the Arendtian tradition of the "rise of the social," the "public realm" and a "discursive path to reconciliation" (1989, sec. 12; cf. Benhabib 1996; Villa 1997). Communicative reason in "the interactions among legally institutionalized will-formation and culturally mobilized publics" (1996, 301) is a political culture that serves the common denominator and "simultaneously sharpens an awareness of the multiplicity and integrity" of forms of life (1992, 7).[76]

Although wholly unintended for a distant context, the model of "discursive formation of will" based on information sharing and intersubjective communication resonates in the Chinese conceptualization. Not far from solicitation and aggregation of preferences back and forth between the party and the masses in the public arena and dialects of a popular-language, Habermas's "post-bourgeois" structural transformation of society focuses on the institutionalization of public thinking by private individuals, and hence secretly resembles the mass line, though without any room for a communist party to play an organizational and educational role. Such a role, of course, makes all the difference, especially for the concern with "inner colonization of the lifeworld" (Habermas 1987, 365). Yet it is not the denounced experiment in China but rather the highly acclaimed theory of the public sphere that bears the weakness of losing sight of the Hegelian rationality of the state as the locus of any attainable general will or common good (before it would ever wither away). Michel Foucault's skepticism toward a neutral "ideal speech situation," in which (symbolic) power and power relations disappear, is shared by many. Missing in the Habermasian dialogical process are the elements of suppression and manipulation analogous with carnival mirror distortions: "The extent to which the speech characteristic of one realm of power is, in part, a product of the speech that is blocked or suppressed in another realm of power" (Scott 1990, 176). Without taking into full account the importance of state and of struggles over persuasion, Habermas's democracy is "underpowered" (Anderson 1992, 330–31; cf. Forbath 1996; Fraser 1997). In contrast, the extensive and decentralized deliberation that once engaged Chinese politics did not idealize deliberative and argumentative situations. Seeing state power as not only physical but also ideological and discursive, and seeking forms of participation alternative to polling and election campaigns permitted to be "bought" by the rich, China's instead was deliberately a Gramscian undertaking for "a new hegemony" (Blecher 1989).

On the other hand, radical pluralist objections to Rousseau's singular people and general will—not to mention cultural relativism or the feminist dismissal of a "general male will"—insist that the faith in the potential coincidence of individual and collective preference is misplaced. No society would ever obtain rational aggregation of diverse (and irrational) desires and interests without hurting freedoms at one level/sphere or another, and in that sense democracy is either impossible (as a universal good) or unacceptable (as a majority rule). Right or wrong, these objections are supported by a history of sheer failures of totalitarian attempts or, more accurately, by a historiography in which different trajectories become indistinguishable in the narratives of totalitarianism. Yet the conflation or compression of freedoms, identities, particular and general will, local and central interests, and so on inevitably privilege the totality. There is almost a perfectionist impulse intrinsic to the Rousseauean polity of complete integration.

The influential Foucauldian antidote is dispersed power (and the material, technical, and localized operators of domination) that deconstructs state-centered perspectives of power, including the oneness of people as the subjective sovereign. For Foucault, models of democracy conceived in such perspectives are too "objective" to be self-reflective or too rational and invasive to be resisted (1980). Rousseau would not have an answer to, or indeed an interest in, these challenges. A democratic reading of his view, however, is not implausible. Precisely because of the multiplicity of values and diffusion of power, there is a compelling need to seek a reconcilable common ground. Democracy is likely, or at least more likely than in non-democracies, to lead to socially desirable and beneficial policies in the long run. In the end, the fundamental integrity of humanity is perhaps a given that binds individuals into "the indissoluble and unanalyzable organic whole," which Rousseau identifies with the people, Burke with society, Hegel with the state, and nationalists with the nation (and for a long while the Chinese with socialism) (Berlin 1998, 591). China's modern path has had no escape from that organic whole overwhelmingly with honorable public reasons, above all national liberation and socialist development.

Whose Democracy?

People's democracy does not need theoretical legitimation or delegitimation by conceptual connections with far-away thinkers from Rousseau to Habermas. But the fact that such connections exist shows the intellectual relevance of the Chinese case to critical theory. The ready verdict that as long as its national government is not chosen through free, fair, and competitive elections the PRC cannot be a democracy is obvious but beside the point. It would be more appropriate to not ignore any genuinely democratic components of Chinese socialism and historicize them in such a way that the country is seen as yet to accomplish its own unfinished democratic project (e.g., White 1983; Womack 1989; Shaw 1996; Nathan 1997). After settling the communist headquarters in Yan'an right after the daring Long March of 1934–1935, Mao explained to the British journalist James Bertram, who found democratic centralism a contradiction in terms, that what mattered were not terms but reality, and without an impassable gulf between the two: "The government we want must be truly representative of the popular will; it must have the support of the broad masses throughout the country and the people must be free to support it and have every opportunity of influencing its policies. This is the meaning of democracy" (1991 [1937], 354). Remarkably, democracy was already being envisioned in terms of national power.

A timeline of events is important here to enable the rise and fall of a people's democracy to be examined and understood by comparing the experiences before and after 1949; before and after 1976; and, finally, before and after 1989. Visible and hidden differences between each comparison, and especially between Maoist and post-Mao politics, still unfolded in the new century. What had been constant, however, was the persistence of "socialist democracy" in the official rhetoric, sometimes with more prominence than others, despite Deng's effort of de-ideologization. "No democracy, no socialism" remained a standard slogan that was restated, by President Hu Jintao, for example, with references to democratic elections, decisions, and management and supervision. This ideological preoccupation had rendered democracy and democratization in the PRC an inherent source of legitimacy, by which the regime itself had to be legitimized or was otherwise delegitimized. Mounting pressure from public discontent and labor protests can be seen as an indication of the bearing of people's democracy as well as a reformation—the crisis of the PRC state was caused by its shift away from the party's traditional constituency. What follows, then, is that democracy as a normative idea of the Chinese revolution and socialism had enjoyed splendid indigenous backing; it was to rectify and develop itself but it did not require the overturn of a system that still in certain ways embraced socialism.

The logic, then, as Brantly Womack acknowledges, would be that "to understand China's self-understanding of its search for democracy has the potential to be far more fruitful for a cosmopolitan political science than would a search for Western democratic traits in Chinese politics" (1991, 55). This is a plea especially worthwhile in the high tide of globalization using democracy as its ideological banner (or mask) in which worsening global inequalities and injustices only damage democratic credentials. When parochial values and institutions deemed global are transplanted at the expense of local needs, struggles over meaning and hence legitimation will intensify.

To be sure, hard and soft criteria for democracy must be retained—diverse national and cultural settings have something fundamental to share insofar as the concept makes common sense. However plural democracies may be, they cannot deny "a certain sort of universalism," such as self-determination and public control over decisionmaking in state and social affairs that are congenial to difference but also constrain it. For "there are the makings of a thin and universalist morality inside every thick and particularist morality" adopted to local contexts (Walzer 1994b, 2, xi, 63ff). What compels the social sciences to take people's democracy seriously is not its evident departure from, but rather where it is fundamentally in line with, established conceptual and empirical cases of democracy. Perhaps Mao's sober recognition of "the good points of capitalism" (quoted in Winnington 1986, 98) deserves reciprocal appreciation of socialist strengths in search of democracy.

The Chinese self-understanding of democracy, however, is but itself contested as a process of searching and learning. Four sources of inspiration might be accentuated here. The first remains the model of the Paris Commune and the democratic Marxist tradition as defended by Rosa Luxemburg and many others. Claiming a debt to that tradition are Maoist populism on the one hand, and arguments for inner-party and socialist democracy advanced by China's dissident Marxists on the other. A major example of the latter is the debate provoked by what came to be known as the (pseudonymous) Li Yizhe manifesto, "On Socialist Democracy and the Legal System" (1974, translated and annotated in Chan et al. 1985; cf. Chen 1986; Rapp 1987; Goldman 1994). The second influence, especially strong on the intellectuals, is liberalism, ranging from the Hayekian condemnation of social engineering as a "road to serfdom" to the Rawlsian elaborations, earlier of justice and later of the "law of peoples." Postcommunist transitions to a liberal market democracy in the former Soviet bloc are frequently referred to in a negative light more than a positive one. The third influence—democratization in East Asia, mostly of an authoritarian developmental state—appeals mostly to the policy elites immersed in a Chinese version of modernization theory. It is also known as neoauthoritarianism, promoting economic growth, social stability, and a middle class as the preconditions for, or at least positively correlated with, democracy. The final source is Confucian modernism, which with some ambiguous official endorsement has sought accommodation with Western democratic ideas.

Reinventing an ancient mode of thinking, which was resolutely rejected by modern Chinese revolutions precisely for its anti-democratic characters, is part of an unfolding revisionist movement for a reevaluation of the May 4th legacy, and hence all revolutionary legacies. Yet Confucian revivalism, just like the other sources, may not necessarily serve democratic development.

Whichever individual (or blend) of these intellectual and political trends may work, the truism is that the historical constraint in China, whether a drag or catalyst, is inescapable. In contrast to those colonies where a formal democracy was directly adapted from a metropolitan center, revolutionary modernity naturally resisted what was prized in a naked imperialist order of hypocrisy. There is not only a contingent, path-dependent effect but also a general factor of a plurality of values entailing institutional diversity. In addition, and in the same vein, any "Whig history" expectations in China, such as an imitation of any of the prevalent party and electoral systems, could be wishful thinking. Neither Taiwan, which is culturally compatible with the Chinese mainland, nor Russia, with which Chinese communism has historically shared some political affinities, can be posed as a proof for predestined global convergence. In the end, the Chinese distinctiveness, cultural and political, is a matter of national choice, though the space for choosing has been increasingly and ruthlessly squeezed by the dominant forces of globalization. Leaving aside for the moment China's multiplicity and internal divisions over the country's political future, it is reasonable to minimally assume that the power of the people resides only in a sovereign polity whose members solely decide what to say or do about their government. Democracy, then, is ultimately "an endogenous question, of this people's power" (Womack 1991, 54).

The fact that communism came to power in China through a violent path of an armed struggle, and later encountered international blockages, predicated both the initial regime legitimacy and the crises of that legitimacy in subsequent historical tests. Even an adventure as bold as a people's democracy did not succeed in training the revolution's massive supporters into an independent citizenry. Nor did it redress traditional asymmetries of duties over rights or collectivity over individuality. As such, and in view of the sea changes in the country's internal and external conditions in the past two to three decades, politics in the PRC may well have arrived at an unaccustomed terrain where power can no longer be safely held without measurable public contests for popular approval. Democracy of whatever style does universally exclude unchecked power and require government to be accountable to and changeable by citizens. What then, if any, is the "privilege of backwardness" to be actualized in China's "late democratization," morally and institutionally, beyond the populist phase of Chinese socialism? What will be its local and regional variations? A touch of cultural sensitivity and political optimism is needed to link democratic and socialist goals for reform. Yet the trials and errors of modern political development suggest no certainty but "democratic experimentalism" (Unger 1998). Between familiar patterns of revolutionary politics versus routine politics, as Roberto Unger points out, a third type of politics is in the horizon: "A transformative politics combining negotiation among the organized interests with the mobilization of the disorganized majority" (2003, 6). Given the magnitude of both Chinese socialism and its transformation, China's own third type of politics, an unparalleled democracy, is yet to be born.

▬▬

The modern concept of democracy is modeled primarily on the Euro-American and capitalist experiences, with a liberal consensus on its definition and application. Like modernity, it has achieved certain monumental and universally recognizable propositions and norms. Its limited empirical bases and narrowness of self-image and projection, however, are yet to be corrected in the political discourse and imagination of the day. The ideological nature of the paradigm of liberal democracy is nowhere more revealing in its conceptual closeness, discounting any actual or potential competitors. Giovanni Sartori is far from alone in believing that "to say 'democracy' is the same thing as to say 'Western-style democracy'" (1962, 416; cf. 1987, chapter 7). This monopoly over democracy's meaning and signification has deceived even the sharpest critics of conventional models, stifled innovations, and imposed a ready-made package for every society to imitate, sometimes by force. But just like globalization having no chance to homogenize the globe, democratization too is bound to proceed unevenly in accordance with local yearnings while redrawing boundaries, rediscovering resources, and redefining its own movement in concrete localities.

If the "general will" is not altogether unfeasible and not doomed to totalitarian degeneration; and if a participatory citizenship is a democratically normative value, then an attempt at a socialist democracy in China must be a very large and powerful case of democratic experiment for political science scrutiny. Chinese socialism's self-identification with democracy was of crucial importance for the system to be understood. Also to be counted is the institutionalization of that moral identity, however flawed: Socialist democracy took the form in the NPC and its local branches, in the "transmission belt" organizations, in the other infrastructural support for popular participation and self-management, in administrative decentralization, and in the "united front" of limited political pluralism to mitigate one-party domination. The moral and institutional complexities implicated such tensions as between ideological fundamentalism and opportunist pragmatism, revolutionary radicalism and ruling conservatism, voluntarism and realist normality, a people-centered social consciousness and subordination of the people to the party. High-minded and full of rituals, the system nevertheless lacked formal procedures. Its tenet appeared to prioritize substantial justice over procedural justice and positive liberty over negative liberty. This enabled the regime to speak and act on the people's behalf with extraordinary confidence, contrasting sharply with "postsocialist" alienation and confrontation. As that earlier historical endorsement of the communist power faded, the rules of normal politics began to apply.

That is, there would no longer be any unlimited sovereignty of the (abstract) people as the state. Constitutionalism would develop to define institutional norms and to constrain power holders and political actors. Legally and civilly conducted selections of officials would take place, extending upward from the grassroots to integrate provincial and national levels. The reform had been preoccupied with legal construction, but in due course it would have to clarify the moral issues from the centrality of citizenship to national purpose and social justice, hence the means and ends of public deliberation. If the underdevelopment of alternative institutions and institutional thinking was a barrier to the democratic promise of Chinese socialism, then only a just, institutionalized redistribution of power by the "will of the people" could rescue that promise. Insofar as democracy retains its philological meaning of people's rule, the will of the people must arise from a seductive myth or utopia to something real and tangible. Positive moves had been those made toward a constitutional framework, a powerful people's congress, a functional consultative process outside the communist party, the professionalization of civil service, and the rule of law. By taking the postcommunist world order as an inescapable battleground, the Chinese could now explore theories and tools advanced in liberal and social democracies for political change. But their rich and diverse local knowledges about democracy accumulated from the country's indigenous pasts, traditional as well as socialist, would be an especially precious asset.

The vicissitudes of people's democracy, once brought to light, demonstrate innovations and achievements but, just as daunting, they also reveal the tragic, indeed criminal, side of a horrendously abusive "proletarian dictatorship." Doubts deepened, culminating with the April 1976 protest movement that took the form of spontaneous mourning in Tiananmen of Zhou Enlai who died in January. Although the movement was crushed, it catalyzed the demise of the Maoist cultural revolutionaries and brought into office Deng's reformers who, in turn, radicalized themselves in the market transition. It was soon discovered, however, that there was no necessary correlation between market and democracy; the power of capital, rather, came to undermine that of the people. The coming of age in the 1990s of a neoliberal fever was a far cry from either civil-political or social rights. The withdrawal of a socialist public good regime (and arguably the emergence of a procapitalist order) was a deprivation of labor. It remains to be answered as if a democratic citizenship could ever find the marketplace fertile, where instead greed, fear, inequalities, and political indifference might prevail.[77] History had come full circle when the nostalgia for an effective, popular, and publicly committed state became a shared feeling beyond the Chinese peripheries. "We the people," lost in the transformation of socialism, are yet to recover their rightful place; and should they rise not through another revolution but through a democratic reordering of the reform, their supreme moral authority would necessitate a renewal of its institutional basis.

The rights and wrongs, pride and sorrows, of a people's democracy cannot be irrelevant to discussions today of the democratic prospect for China with its great local varieties. As democracy ought to signify "this people's power," a Chinese democracy has to be interpreted and judged in the Chinese language and contexts. The point is not about each society following its own path to flourish (or perish), although that may well be the case even in an era of global communication and interdependence. Nor is the point to give in to any sinocentric insistence on democracy being culturally specific and confined to the West. "Concrete universal" makes sense to a dialectical mind and invalidates essentialist dichotomies in either a romanticized or a patronizing manner in regard to the particular or the other. For the choice is not exactly between generalization and its rejection; "the alternative is not intractable" and universals and particulars intertwine (Sartori 1994, 25–26). The argument here, rather, is *political* about democratizing socialism more than it is cultural about a democracy with national characteristics. The essence of democratic rationality, again political, is that there is no single solution, sole truth, or one super model; and imposing democracy is antithetical to the democratic idea of self-determination. It is true that the liberal versions of democracy have far from exhausted their potentials. But to say this is also to recognize that visions of an alternative democracy that cherish rather than deny liberties are still underdeveloped both historically and theoretically.

Chapter 4

Liberty and Liberation

THE CHINESE REVOLUTION SET ITSELF LOFTY GOALS. AS STATED IN THE "Resolution of the 7th National Congress of the CCP" from 11 June 1945, these goals included the effort "to free the Chinese nation from the aggression of foreign imperialism, to eliminate the oppression of the Chinese masses by domestic feudalism, to establish an independent, free, democratic, united, prosperous and strong alliance of all revolutionary classes [as well as] a New Democracy federal republic based on the free union of all nationalities, and to strive for the realization of peace and progress throughout the world." One of the great riddles of China's revolutionary and socialist struggle was the dissonance between civil liberties and national-social liberation, as that between personal and collective freedoms, and between prohibiting organized opposition and promoting political participation. The CCP, once personalized in Mao, was the "great savior," the liberator of the liberated. "We the people," the "historical subject" in ideology and constitution, were instrumental of the state, albeit a "people's own state" (as perceived in everyday language after 1949). The absolute power of this state left little room for free individuality. The chilling line in *Doctor Zhivago*—"personal life is dead in Russia"—was just as apt for China, which, instead of arousing anticommunist sentiment, profoundly moved those who "grew up under the red flag" because they understood the nobility and sacrifice of the revolution, as well as its tragedy.

The conscience of scholarship in the field—if only to be fair to the revolutionary participants, of whom tens of millions perished—tries to make a difficult separation between the inevitable and the avoidable in terms of cost. Lost battles and other unsuccessful efforts do not automatically invalidate the ideas and ideals of a cause; indeed, the cause may revive and achieve better in yet another round of struggles if the right lessons can be learned. This pattern of political education pertains to the current global transition in which it becomes all too evident that civil liberties by themselves cannot substitute for liberation; and liberal societies are not the same as liberated ones. The dilemmas and local complexities in China around liberty and democracy, liberalism and socialism, and the rival models of legitimation involving state, society, and the individual are addressed in the following pages.

At stake are not the paradoxes of liberalism itself (such as the hidden dangers of self-destructive liberal neutrality and the obvious tension between group and universal rights) or of the "plebiscitary legitimacy" of a constitutional democracy vulnerable to radicalism (Schmitt 2004). The issue is, rather, the uses and abuses of liberal doctrines in China's national and international politics. In this chapter I start by focusing on the contemporary Chinese versions of liberalism so as to clarify its key problems and conceptions as locally deployed. Liberalism's defeat in twentieth-century China cannot confirm the view that Chinese political culture is inherently illiberal and hostile to modern values (which assumed equations between Christianity and liberalism; liberalism and modernity). An explanation should be found instead in the nineteenth-century historical conjunction of liberalism and colonialism, symbolized by the opium and cannons (misnamed "trade") that represented the modern West to the East. The lasting effects of this appalling association still resound today in the background of Chinese popular rhetoric against "Western bias," "foreign intervention," and downright "imperialism." Oversimplified binaries, such as those of liberal individualism versus socialist collectivism, civil society opposing the state, and democracy fighting the other civilizations, do not work. They leave uncounted a range of reasons and movements in between and beyond, thereby confusing concepts along the way. The socialist opposition to either past "liberal" imperialism or present neoliberal capitalism (which is essentially anti-liberal as contrasted with traditions of classical liberalism) transcends such binaries. The first section therefore examines different kinds of democracy and civil society, diverse pathways of the recognition and protection of rights, and multiple sources of legitimacy. These questions are then further probed, in their epochal conditions of globalization, in the second section.

Liberalism and Its Chinese Fate

The communist dreamland of liberated individuals and universal solidarity cracked in the People's Republic when the regime alienated itself from the population by allowing bureaucratic privileges on the one hand and excessive persecution of opponents on the other. But it was not until the revolution's emancipatory promises were broken in a "feudal tyranny" toward the end of the Cultural Revolution that many believed that much of the original communist strength had been destroyed. The exhaustion was so evident that the power transition after Mao died in September 1976 would be initiated by a "coup" to remove his widow, Jiang Qing, and her allies, an event that had been waited for and was celebrated in the streets. The breakthrough, no doubt a case of political secrecy and Byzantine politics, nevertheless brought to the fore a broad consensus on the need of the country to open up, liberalize, and democratize.

Both hopeful and dismissive commentators often ask if liberal democracy is normatively favorable and in practice feasible in China. Apart from confusion over the terms and concepts involved, the question is not even necessarily appropriate without addressing the burning concerns of society. As argued earlier, post-Mao reforms carried out radical economic and political liberalization rather than democratization, thereby effectively separating the two. So as not to undermine the established moral foundation of the state and thus endanger political and social stability, the reform regime was yet to harness new class and other disparities. In diverting liberal from democratic changes, the reform was simultaneously depriving the Chinese people as a whole of its supreme constitutional status and bringing the country toward the institutionalization of normal politics. On the one hand, revolutionary democracy had been discredited, and the party had suffered devastating corruption scandals and policy errors since the 1990s. It had thus come to fear the masses and made the "fish-and-water" metaphor a lost tradition of the past. On the other hand, the end of campaign-style mobilization and victimization, and the beginning of legal construction to achieve the rule of law had widened the scope of civil liberties. The expanding market economy also created spheres of freedoms and independent undertakings, while eroding nonprofitable public services. These mixed developments require a renewed political argument for democracy that can redress fundamental yet hitherto neglected issues. Conceptually, it argues that democracy must be rehabilitated from the preoccupation with legalization without citizens being part of lawmaking, and from personal liberties without the collective power of citizenship. Practically, it insists on rebuilding the channels for political participation and public debates, so preferences can be aggregated into policy decisions.

Liberalism without Democracy

Beginning with what actually happened rather than what "should" happen as projected in a dogmatic liberal democratic perspective, it is worth noting that the phrase "democracy movement," popular in the scholarly and media discourse on China, is obscure. It is often used to exclusively refer to the demands and activism of an urban, educated group of people seeking liberal more than democratic values. The university turbulence from 1986 to 1989 prior to Tiananmen, for example, had a specific trigger each time, ranging from anger with "too soft" a position taken by the Chinese government on Sino-Japanese relations to rage over poor management of student welfare.[1] A free press and free speech and association, rather than popular political participation or direct national elections, were demanded. There was, however, an earlier historical moment of democratic agitation. The civic rebellion across China's urban centers in the form of mourning Premier Zhou in 1976 was later described in the *People's Daily* in 1978 as the "April 5th people's uprising." Between 1978 and 1980 an unprecedented movement for a socialist democracy overtook party and government conferences, documents, and editorials, as well as classrooms and work places. The newspapers and open discussions were filled with honest self-criticisms of past damages and serious proposals for building a "highly civilized and highly democratic" China. This goal, officially framed as such, was formally adopted in the party's seminal plenary session of 1978.

Largely overlooked in the literature was the remarkable fact that this initiative from within the party was welcomed by and echoed in the popular mood for political change. The "Democracy Wall" was not, as standard accounts have it, a lonely happening only to be crushed by Deng who could no longer tolerate the tone of posters. For a brief but crucial period the voices from the offices and from the streets actually joined force, "as if two groups were calling to each other across an alpine valley" (Garside 1981, 324; cf. Goodman 1981 for texts in the unofficial publications at the time). The

Democracy Wall was banned and the party line shifted in 1980; and like Mao's retreat from a "hundred flowers" in 1957, the fear of turmoil prevailed. A lost opportunity in hindsight, this episode followed the only rationale of reform communism: the party must seek self-transformation rather than falling through by outside challenges. Wars, disintegration, and economic hardship in the aftermath of the velvet and violent revolutions around 1989 and the dissolution of the USSR in 1991 thoroughly demeaned postcommunist transitions in the Chinese view. These situations amounted to a vindication of the rational choice by the ruling CCP (cf. Lieberthal 1992b). As its ambition for a political renovation receded, the party curtailed its promotion of democracy and, instead, embarked on a conservative campaign for patriotism and "spiritual civilization." The "neoauthoritarian turn" was perfectly logical for a hegemonic strategy of repair from above.

It is quite wrong to take for granted the "democratic" identity of China's liberal intellectuals in their bid to distance themselves from the system. Such an identity ignores two important factors: persisting democratic reformism within the party; and daily striving for democracy in relation to social justice. Democratic forces in China's transition were identifiable less in either Martin Lipset's middle class or Barrington Moore's bourgeoisie than among workers, urban and rural, and common citizens at large. These forces had gathered momentum wherever social crisis mounted and socioeconomic rights were pressed along with civil-political rights. As such, unengaged liberals cannot be the key agents of democratization as depicted in the conventional conception of political development, in which liberal democracy is customarily read into mere liberalism or (mostly negative) liberties. Moreover, China's liberal elites did not agree among themselves on the basics. Some self-claimed "neo-authoritarians" were attracted by the typical paths in East Asia that are anticipated in modernization theories, and they believed that China was "immature" for democracy until it could attain a sufficient level of economic growth and literacy. Others advocated a free market and a stable society with or without democracy. Still others promoted democracy while differing in their interpretations, which ranged from representational elitism to romanticist traditionalism, and from open elections to contained pluralism. These positions were a part of the transforming political landscape in China, in which what remained missing, remarkably, was the old question of the power of the people, the possible formation of their collective will, and corresponding institutional carriers.

In this connection, it is also erroneous to confine the movements for democracy in China to dissident politics. Not to be forgotten in the general historical context is a crucial difference, thanks to the Chinese revolution, between the excommunist societies in Eastern and Central Europe and China: in the former the voices of "the moral majority" were in opposition,[2] while in China such a voice alternated between being supportive, disapproving, or resistant according to state performance. Writing in the early 1980s, Andrew Nathan noticed that "uniquely among democratic movements in socialist countries, the Chinese activists almost all saw themselves not as challenging the regime but as enlisting on the side of a faction within it." And many "angrily rejected the label of 'dissidents' as implying antagonism to the state" (1985, 24). The greatly altered political scenes after 1989 and in the new millennium still did not make it less superficial to take nonofficial intellectual discourses (and popular culture) as by and large anti-state (Wang 2001). That is, even if normalized and organized oppositions could exist, they would hardly find a popular following on any neoliberal platforms and, in fact, such a platform would disqualify their position as in opposition. The specific circumstances in China were such that dissident politics was not necessarily democratically oriented and democratic development was possible without dissident politics.

The "democracy movements" of university students and liberal intellectuals were born out of an "individualist turn" in post-1978 Chinese political culture to conclude three decades of high collectivism. In contrast to the critics of liberal market societies who saw a deformed democracy resting on atomized individuals, the idealist liberals inside and outside of China tended to romanticize such societies and hold them up to the country for imitation. At issue were not the intrinsic good of individualism and pluralism and their fundamental importance for democracy—an unprecedented scope of freedom for personal pursuits along with flourishing public forums, a "shadow media" of critical journalism, feminist, human rights, and environmentalist NGOs, and so on. But as long as the liberals—or neoliberals in this context—turned a blind eye to the social consequences of laissez-faire, not exactly by denying them but by seeing further market liberalization and privatization as the solution, they were opposite to popular preference.[3] Committed democrats would have to confront the reality that China's laboring masses, individually and collectively, had been downgraded and marginalized in all spheres of life as money and capital took their place. The loosening of the grip of the party was by no means the same thing as the empowerment of the people.

It was this degradation in the official regard of the people and in the corresponding public policies that fueled the protests in spring 1989, which were signified, almost accidentally (the trigger of the death of former party secretary Hu Yaobang), by the student occupation of Tiananmen Square in Beijing. And it is for this reason that the Tiananmen events must be seen as a spontaneous social movement for democracy understood essentially in social, rather than liberal, terms. Resembling the April 5th Movement of 1976, the mobilization in 1989 was inspired by a popular leader. But unlike the earlier revolt against political repression under a fanatic clique in Mao's name, in the background in 1989 were issues of social insecurity and inequalities exacerbated by a market transition, from inflation following attempts at price liberalization to corruption in the form of *guandao* ("officials engaging profitable trade") involving a *taizidang* (the princely party) (cf. Davis and Vogel 1990). The frustration was caused by increasing discord between expectations from a socialist reform and seemingly capitalist threats, and by the absence of democratic means to bring the changes under popular control. Tiananmen was an act of self-empowerment of demonstrators across Chinese cities, which included not only students but also workers and ordinary residents, as well as state functionaries. There was no notable rural participation at a time when the daunting problems of agriculture were yet to emerge. The movement demanded recognition of itself as a "patriotic" one—by the students' choice—and above all a clean and socially responsible government.

A variety of interests were directly expressed among participants as diverse as students, intellectual professionals, workers, and private entrepreneurs, who also differed over strategies and tactics. While students first focused on media presentation and civil liberties, workers were more concerned with inflation and welfare erosion, and *getihu* (petty private entrepreneurs) policies toward small business. What united these groups was the demand for ending corruption, adjusting polarizing economic policies, and protecting social security. Democracy thus appealed the most in terms of government accountability.[4] The weakness of the movement was not primarily its internal disunity but, as later admitted by one of the student leaders, Wang Chaohua, the missed opportunity of seizing the ideological high ground to formulate a program along the line of democratic socialism. Consequently, the movement was unable to transform spontaneity into a long-term, institutionally sustainable method of political protest (which would be achievable, however, only with some political shake-up from above).[5] Missing in China in 1989, as compared with democratization in many other countries, was a negotiated pact between government and opposition. Yet this was not because independent students' and workers' unions were still illegitimate, but because of a unique conception of democracy owing a socialist commitment from the past, and because the movement was after all not oppositional in the sense that it did not aim at regime change (as delineated in chapter 3).

The liberal elements were evident in the calls around the Square for the freedom of the press and of expression and association, and for wider political reforms. Wang Chaohua observes that prevailingly negative liberties fed into self-centred student elitism.[6] Judging from the broadness of its participation from all walks of (urban) life and its dominant concerns, however, the movement was neither particularly elitist nor "liberal democratic" relative to anticommunism in Eastern Europe. For Marie-Claire Bergere, Tiananmen's "democratic prestige was, to a large extent, conferred on it by foreign observers and media, misled by the vocabulary used by the intellectual vanguard." As "freedom" and "democracy" were taken "as 'fetish words'; the young demonstrators were unable to give them any meaning other than their own immolation" (1992, 247). Perceptive as this critique goes, Bergere did not recognize the true democratic potential of a truly "people's movement" that might have a chance to develop into a Chinese chartism for popular political participation in a democratic norm after a people's democracy.

Tiananmen 1989 was "an egalitarian reaction against bureaucratic corruption and privilege, a liberating cultural radicalism, and a demand for political democracy" (Meisner 1996, 467). It was a miracle in its autonomy, idealism, and discipline in terms of organization and principle of nonviolence. The June 4th crackdown had lasting repercussions despite a relative quick turnover of internal shock and international sanction. The country certainly had not recovered from the tanks and machine guns, and an official reversal of the verdict that the incident was a "counterrevolutionary turmoil" (though the adjective had been quietly dropped out of public reference) is yet to arrive. Nor had the government even remotely resolved the social problems that had just then loomed to give rise to the crisis. The unwillingness (pressures of capital) and inability (loosening central command) here were precisely what prevented a re-evaluation of Tiananmen, which would require the confidence that the present regime lacked. This was a stark contrast with the Mao leadership, which with its loyal multitude of revolutionary cadres and masses had no difficulty admitting severe mistakes committed by the party itself. Controversies over the movement went on, mirroring not only a post-Tiananmen political and intellectual realignment but also how "democracy" had accommodated different positions and interpretations. Unanticipated even by the most radical in 1989 was the post-1989 policy shift toward greater deregulation, faster privatization, and farther global integration. It looked as though popular appeals to social protection and justice only led to worsening conditions of income disparities, unemployment, and corruption. Paradoxically, the failure of a protest movement that did not want to overthrow the government must be a failure of the state itself, which was still to answer those who rose to seek a democratic solution. Wang Hui, in a penetrating essay on "China's neoliberalism" sees the social mobilization in 1989 as a popular resistance against the impending tide of market extremism eventually coerced onto the Chinese population by state violence (2003, 65). In that sense, the year served as a temporary suspension of state-led market expansion and globalization (116–19), which was resumed with full speed after Deng's southern tour in 1992 to boost special economic zones.

Debating "Civil Society"

The year 1989 was, of course, a watershed in the entire former communist world and in global politics. Tiananmen stood alone in the chain of events to be reformist, not revolutionary, in its outlook and agenda. Even in front of the cameras of an intensely manipulative international media (whose numbers jumped when Gorbachev visited China in May), students in a political theater of "acting out democracy" did not produce a single antisocialist slogan (cf. Esherick and Wasserstrom 1990). The fact that the students made a categorical distinction, by reason or instinct, between particular leaders and policies on the one hand and the PRC system on the other, speaks for itself about the peculiarity of the Chinese in comparison with communism and postcommunism in Europe and Central Asia. The exiles in the West radicalized only after various personal transformations through reflection on the crackdown and subsequent repression. Their comments after the fact had no way to retrospectively "prove" either a Chinese "counterrevolutionary" or a foreign "anticommunist" assessment.

What evoked a civil society debate in a burst of scholarship on 1989 in the 1990s is the assumption in received theory about the demarcation of and opposition between state and society. But despite its popularity, the notion of "civil society" is an inappropriate model for the Tiananmen protest, if only because it cannot account for the actual call of the protesters for better (in kind) state intervention in the marketplace. The conflation of the East European and Chinese directions of proposed change is unfounded. Also remarkable were the officials from central and municipal party and government units who, side by side with ordinary citizens in Beijing, marched with eye-catching banners from various ministries including the Xinhua News Agency, the *People's Daily*, and the district police departments. Further still, there was no fundamental ideological conflict between those on the streets and those in Zhong Nanhai (the party headquarters) concerning public welfare and social justice. The extent of how much these commitments were lingering at the top could be measured by how far-reaching the mobilization scale was of mass protests from below, because the social responses to government behavior in China did not assume separation and competition between state and society. Any conceptualization dependent on their antagonism would therefore be dubious.

The confusion between liberalization and democratization is quite pronounced in the replication of the concept in China studies of "civil society" (frequently in conjunction with the "public sphere") as a fluttering flag (cf. Gu 1993–94; Perry 1994). The trends toward liberalizing the country naturally nurture society-centered approaches as opposed to state-centered models. Political outcomes are now seen as relying more than ever on voluntary forces of pressure groups, issue-defined networks, and functional associations (cf. Brook and Frolis 1997; Lindau and Cheek 1998). Instead of viewing the institutional core of civil society as outside the realms of state

and economy (Habermas 1996, 453–54), "civil society" and "market society" are often treated as indistinguishable in research. This identification
is old (as with a "bourgeois society" in Hegel or Marx) but misleading when
civil society becomes a normative requirement for democracy. It deprives
society, in theory and reality, of a critical space for self-reflective adjustment
through mobilizing social defense wherever market functions are socially
undesirable. The problem is not about the notion being invented in the
early modern European estates and mercantilism, and evolved in a Christian culture and consociational tradition, which were all absent in China.
For there has been no shortage of conceptual transplantation in the Chinese
soil. Rather sensible would be caution against the ideological baggage of
dominant social science concepts traveling eastward. Uncritically applied,
"civil society" could be, as Fleming Christiansen notes, "an ideological
preoccupation imposing irrelevant norms and dogmatic judgements" as
well as analytically "wasteful" (1998, 980; cf. Howell 1995, 81; Calhoun 1994,
197).

   More specifically, the enduring difficulty with starting with state-society
relations in understanding recent Chinese politics lies in the direct involvement of the state in social organization and civic activism. The embeddedness of the state in society, and indeed of society in the state, to the degree of
a symbiotic identity, forestalls the clarity of their mutual exclusion needed
in a civil society perspective. Gordon White's (1981) empirical observation
on state and society politically "engaging" each other in China (as in the
case of education) and Peter Evans's (1995) theoretical formulation of "embedded autonomy" of the state come close to tackling this difficulty. But
even their conceptions inevitably permit two entities in which at most the
state is speaking in the voice of society and vice versa. This mutual embeddedness seems to have marked, in very different forms, both traditional and
modern China. The idea that the interests of rulers and the ruled must be
harmonious (as in the Confucian "mandate of heaven" or the *dao* in Taoism), or that the party has no separate interests from those of the people (in
Chinese socialism), are incompatible with dichotomized liberal conceptions. Similarly, the priority of collective good over personal desires or
executive authority without judicial contradiction differs from the political
cultures and institutional arrangements of the liberal state. So much so that
Andrew Nathan concedes that the way China works is full of paradoxes

"constitutive of a system in which power is so all-encompassing yet decentralized that the trinity of state, society, and economy have become one" (1997, 230). The shrinking state in the economic and social spheres since the reform may have gradually redistributed and devolved power, thus rendering "society" a more distinctive scope for independence. Tiananmen, nevertheless, remained a strong case of a state split rather than a state-society confrontation.

In line with the postcommunist habit of thinking, some new works on China's late-imperial and post-imperial civil and local societies suggest that the Chinese revolution, to the detriment of "the rise of the social" (and of modernity in Western Europe), wiped out significant liberal reforms and civic developments. More accurately, however, scholars have long noticed how certain traditional methods and ties of organizing social relations never died away but were incorporated in state control since 1949. Moreover, the myth about a virtuous civil society should already be shattered by the rampant spread of vices: contrary to wishful projections, a market-facilitating state had not produced a democratically inclined middle class to lead a civil society (Brown and Jones 1995). Civil organizations of private entrepreneurs were tied to the bureaucracy, on the one hand, and followed the market logic to enhance profit seeking on the other. The renewed All China Federation of Industry and Commerce affiliated to the CPPCC and with a membership of a million was a "new *de facto* officially-sanctioned federation of capitalists" (Chan 1993, 47). As labor was marginal, the reborn bourgeoisie was dependent, the middle class was weak and small, and the intellectuals tended to be elitist (if not blatantly neoauthoritarian or market fundamentalist), we might wonder who the agents of democratization could be (cf. Rowe 1994; Howell 1998; Pearson 1997). Where might the social forces that are capable of mitigating cleavages and investing "social capital" be located? It is also far from clear as to whether, given power asymmetry, the coming of age of competitive interest-group politics would really be a sign of "democratic normalization," and whether civil society would not be the indisputable—let alone the sole—basis of democracy.

There is further cause for skepticism when it is revealed that civil society does not possess any inherent mechanism to curb uncivil and undemocratic tendencies. Astonishingly unconcerned, the more-conservative models of civil society (which may amont to "abuses of civil society" [Wood

1990; Foley and Edwards 1996]) hold up unchecked private power as unequivocally positive in its resistance against the regulatory and redistributive roles of the state. Yet in China, given the continuing practice of private accumulation of both political and economic capital through rent seeking, connections, and irregular privatization, the question is where to draw the line between civil and uncivil, or good and bad, civil societies. By the same token, as unemployed workers, sweatshop laborers, and poor farmers struggled to get by with few chances to make themselves heard, what was a civil society that depended on their labor, yet excluded them from many supposed benefits? As Rousseau sees it, along with the predominance of private property, civil society gives rise "to a horrible state of war," in which each individual must make the others his or her "tools" and the rich dominate to the disadvantage of the poor (as discussed in Colletti 1972, 163–71). Although the "freedom of property" may no longer necessarily be a defining component of today's civil society, the "associative action," as opposed to the political process of universal participation, cultivates "civic privatism" (Offe and Press 1991, 152). In China as elsewhere, a civil society brought into existence by market transition could not be innocent of exploitative and anti-democratic propensities. A democratic public stand for social defense, supported by public forums, networks, and social movements, would be obliged to check not only state power, but also the private concentration of power, wealth, and resources. It is here that the critical edge of the notion of "public sphere" can be utilized to counter the superficiality of the self-congratulating usages of civil society. For example, Frederic Wakeman (1998) finds China's first "modern" public sphere in the sixteenth and seventeenth century, in which modern-minded intellectual and political works were developed to push for public reforms in both society and state.

Idealistic neo-Confucian humanists regard the view of government being a necessary evil (along with private property, social contracts, and so on) as "alien to the value system" of the sinic tradition (Tu 1991, 116). In the Chinese socialist vocabulary, the words "state," "public," and "social" are customarily interchangeable. Absent in these perceptions is the confrontation between an intruding state and a dissenting society as depicted in classical liberalism in general and in liberal critiques of state socialism in particular. In tracing the rise of modern thought in China, Wang Hui historicizes the recent tradition of statism as found in the late Qing reform-ist thinkers as a response to the "racial" crisis of the Chinese perceived at a time of a weak government in the face of imperialist incursion. Their dual conception of the individual versus the state as the public/collective (*gong/qun*, for Zhang Taiyan and Liang Qichao) is missing an intermediate domain of society that is core to social explanations in the West (2004, 1047–78). This intellectual tradition was only buttressed during the battling years of an isolated socialism, of which the survival depended on an ex-traordinary state power. Even in the wake of market reform and an expand-ing private sector, it has been argued that corporatist frameworks still fit better than those of state-society antagonism (Pearson 1994). Such accom-modating labels as "state-led," "managed," or "guided" "civil society" and "semi-civil society" are therefore not only of limited use but essentially insufficient insofar as they are complacent with that term's normal concep-tual expectations. These expectations, imposed on different historical situa-tions, render a negative connotation of anything "less" than a fully-fledged civil society. But after all, many so-called NGOs enjoyed government spon-sorship in China. If this connection disqualifies their nongovernmental status, then there is the puzzle that it must also discredit their socially beneficial work, which was immensely influential in, for example, women's studies and environmental protection. Government involvement had been vital in enabling China's new social movements. Would it really be "demo-cratic" to denounce it merely for the sake of an imported theory?

Among alternative conceptualizations, Philip Huang's (1993) "trinary conception" allows a "third realm" of a collective, intermediate layer be-tween state and society. This layer is mainly constituted of a localized and institutionalized sector of cooperative and voluntary activities and is seen as more resourceful and reliable than any standard civil society actors for democratization. This structural differentiation resembles the notion of a "third space" to bring to light hitherto unnoticed dynamism and initiatives (Bhabha 1990). It entirely differs from specifying the familiar middle do-main of power brokers and policy mediators in Chinese politics. These are parallel perspectives on a complicated milieu between, as much as encom-passing and mingling, state and society. The "third realm" can also be related to the reconceptualization of the "local state" as both a political and economic-market actor in its relationship with the TVEs (Oi 1995). An important observation of both conceptions is the blurred public and private boundaries in Chinese social relations (in part an inheritance from the tradition), not only in institutional terms of management or ownership but also in moral-cultural terms of the customs of the commons and communities.[7] After all, the rise of the social in China was not brought about by a burgeoning bourgeoisie, as in Europe, but rather by a peasant revolution led by communist intellectuals. As the revolution came to state power, it brought with it, so to speak, a society to both sustain and benefit from that power, and hence the historical contingency of social-state symbiosis in the PRC.

A Gramscian deconstruction of "civil society," by way of refining corporatist models, may facilitate an interpretation of the Chinese structural and cultural peculiarities referred to here. By replaying the Hegelian insight on "political society," Antonio Gramsci sees society as part of the state in the duality of political and civil society in a "class state" (1971, 12, 52, 245; cf. Eley and Nield 2000, 12–13).[8] As the apparatus of the state encompasses broad social institutions determining the nature of civil society, the latter in effect belongs to the "superstructure" or "state life" while carrying out ideological, cultural, intellectual, and spiritual functions more than economic relations. As such, using Hegel and Croce, Gramsci's "ethico-political sphere" is a civil hegemony or the image of a state without a state (1971, 261, 268; also Bobbio 1988, 83, 263). Making no distinction between class power and state power and between the dominant class and the ruling class, the inclusion in the "ideological state apparatuses" (as later in Louis Althusser 1972, 143) of churches, schools, the media, and so on is ambiguous and debatable (cf. Miliband 1977, 48–56). So is the thesis's deliberate disregard of the juridical lines between public and private status. But this is useful for us to think through the case precisely because of the factual obscurity of such distinctions and lines in China and, consequently, because of the situation in which struggles for hegemony are bound to generate from within the state. Consider how apt Gramsci's following observation is: "Since in actual reality civil society and state are one and the same, it must be made clear that laissez-faire too is a form of state 'regulation,' introduced and maintained by legislative and coercive means. It is a deliberate policy . . . and not the spontaneous, automatic expression of economic facts" (1971, 160). The Gramscian insight is as fresh as ever: "Laissez-faire liberalism is a political program, desiged to change . . . the economic program of the state itself" (160).

The CCP could thus be recognized as a socially penetrating organization, with a compelling ideology and a massive power base across social cleavages. The reach of its rank-and-file was far and wide to such an extent that it became conceivable, as Timothy Cheek bluntly puts it, that "the party *is* civil society," while its propaganda department operated in a "directed public sphere" (1998, 237; cf. Fewsmith 1991). In this light, it is not particularly convincing to describe the PRC as a "capstone" state that sought to block horizontal linkages between groups (Hall 1986, 51–54). More accurately, it was the party state itself that formed (though also monopolized) such linkages. A possible inference, which a Gramscian reading of Chinese politics would logically draw (whether willingly or not), is that democracy in China is a matter of recapturing the state from within the state and party through a hegemonic "war of position." This would then most likely not be a war to fight a socialist state in order to win a capitalist democracy, as is often imagined from abroad, but rather a war to democratize socialism as a self-initiated movement. Causing a general societal crisis in the process would, as already in sight, be the dislocation of a communist party losing hegemony over the "ethico-political sphere" of a political-civil society, while the party is not yet subject to electoral contentions of power as elsewhere in formal democracies.

This said, it would be wrong to treat hegemonic penetration in any way as monolithic. The wealth of diversities in the forms and resources of China's social organization has ensured colossal spaces of complex experiences hardly accounted for by the available terms from state and society to "third" (and fourth) or intermediate or grey realms. Still, attempts to separate state and society in China could be infertile. Whether such a separation is viable is not the issue—liberals would think it essential; traditionalist variants for different reasons might be reluctant to see it happen; and democrats, those holding out for the modern forms of direct democracy in particular, should find it a false question. What really matters is the admission that state retreat may not, as it did not, imply societal advance in China. This was so not so much because state and society were intermingled, as because political and economic capital in an "autonomous sphere" in confusion with the marketplace only left that sphere unequal and open to abuses—managers rocketing their income by privatizing state firms was an outstanding example. Individuals and associations divided in a polarizing society would not chant in unison in the name of civil society. The retreat of the state from public welfare hindered social gains and, without social security and solidarity being adequately rebuilt, Chinese society was getting weaker, not stronger. The public health and education crises occurring since the 1990s, as mentioned, hurt human development in positive correlation with poverty alleviation, and the failure there was a straight state failure despite the possibility and importance of nonstate provisions. The relevant question therefore could not be how independent a society must become, but rather how socially committed and publicly serving the state must be or be made so through democratic struggle. Assuming consonance between a powerful state and a powerful society, at stake is not how much the state "intervenes" (amount) but what the state does (performance), aims to do (nature), and can accomplish (capacity). An ideology of civil society paying little attention to this consonance is powerless and misleading. Further, a "global civil society" of transnational social movements cannot be innocent as well and would do a disservice to its own objectives by neglecting the social responsibilities of national states in global integration. This brings us back to the argument on rethinking and renovating democracy.

Liberal and Republican Democracy

The problems related to models of civil society are symptomatic of those theories of liberal democracy that take for granted the idealization of civil society and its global application. Those critical of a liberal democratic framework may want it to be more institutionally legitimate, efficient, flexible (e.g., debates over the electoral systems or forms of executive power); or more socially beneficial, participatory, and inclusive (e.g., arguments for equality or multiculturalism). There is no fundamental disagreement among critics on the conventional and minimal requirements for liberal democracy, such as free elections, fair play, checks and balances, and rational conflict resolution. It is seldom about the power of the people beyond these technical instruments. Having taken a revolutionary and socialist path, China's unrealized ambition, however, points to something different from a polyarchic liberal state preoccupied with voting. The Chinese design of its own future democracy may have a great deal to learn, selectively, from the methods and institutions of various democratic systems. Yet the Western precedence, or even that of Asia and especially Taiwan, were distant. By contrast, the legacies of a people's democracy, for all its catastrophic experiments, were just too intensely educational, in either a positive or a negative light, to be discarded.

Critiques by social democrats of liberal democracy in its own terms are pertinent to the Chinese as an antidote to the prevalence of a "false necessity" or "institutional fetishism" (Unger 1987) toward a "democracy without citizenship" characteristic of Latin America after import substitution (Cammack 1994). Even in advanced Western democracies, asymmetrical life-chances injure personal autonomy and impede political participation, to be corrected only by democratic justice (see Held 1995, 171–72, on "nautonomy"; and Barry 1989 on "liberal egalitarian principles"). Similar notions of "social citizenship" (Marshall 1973) or "equaliberty" (Balibar 1994, 46–47) are read into the French Declaration of the Rights of Man, even if tensions between liberty and equality in political theory are not solvable. A necessary dimension of liberal democracy is thus brought to life: if "the most fundamental challenge to liberal democracy derives from inequality," the power of money and multinationals must be countered by democratically managed workplaces. Democracy, political and economic, implies "a rich bundle of substantive goods" (Dahl 1985, 175). What is theoretically controversial is not the desirability of democracy's socioeconomic substance but whether that substance is intrinsic to the workings of a democracy. In fact there is the long-held liberal consensus on basic social welfare as a precondition for political development, sometimes with a condescending flavor concerning an undesirable "underclass" that threatens a democratic breakdown. Even the modest middle class thesis is egalitarian in the sense that it considers reducing polarization to be a social requisite for democratic negotiations and stability. For Martin Lipset, typically, a "society divided between a large impoverished mass and a small favored elite results either in oligarchy . . . or in tyranny" (1963, 31).

In these circumstances the error is all too obvious in treating "liberal," "market," and "capitalist" as equivalent adjectives for democracy. Free choice in a "free market" (as in the case of those among China's rural poor who choose to dig in private mines that are barely equipped with safety facilities) cannot be the same as economic freedom; economic freedom cannot be the same as political equality and liberty; and political liberty cannot be the same as political participation. Elections may not have much to do with democratic decisionmaking; and the low voter turnout that has persisted in some mature democracies amounts to "a property franchise"; for example, in the United States where half the population, the least well-off, never vote (Anderson 2001, 8). Human freedom aspires to be far greater than what the "free world" has managed to offer, despite fundamental obstacles such as those of ecology that will punish future generations and for which the present global system has no cure. Democracy may be a natural, though unstable, political form of bourgeois society, "the best political shell for capitalism" (while a sham for workers, as Lenin puts it).[9] But capitalism also needs to be self-limited in order to be at least formally democratic.[10] The wishful connections in the received theories between private property and the dispersion of economic power, between market competition and a competitive politics, and between such a politics and democracy, are insufficiently tested or have indeed been falsified. Tatu Vanhanen, for example, is naive to assume that in China "privatization and the adoption of mechanisms of [a] market economy will disperse economic power resources and create a favorable social environment for the emergence of competitive politics" (1997, 149). The transformation of Chinese socialism is yet to strike a balance between market dynamics and private incentives on the one hand, and social cohesion and justice on the other. The truth is not only that people may not become sovereign and free even after the revolution, but also that they could be so deprived after a superficial democratization.

If a liberal component is tautologically prerequisite for liberal democracy, liberalism and democracy remain two distinct concepts.[11] Their paradoxical conjunction is "both one of mutual necessity and a source of tension or antagonism" (Beetham 1999, 34). The former is about constitutionalism and the rule of law, which recognize certain individual rights and plurality of values, whereas the latter is about power distribution, mainly majority rule and minority protection. Historically, as Bhikhu Parekh clarifies it, democracy preceded liberalism in the Western political systems; in the modern age, however, liberalism preceded democracy, thereby creating a condition in which democracy finds itself structurally and culturally constrained by liberalism. Having lost a populist connotation, liberal democracy "rightly fears unrestrained popular sovereignty but goes to the other extreme and disempowers the people." For a polity to be democratically liberal, democracy then should not be made the subordinate partner; it instead "cherishes and respects individuals, but defines them and their rights in social terms" (1993, 166–67). Similarly, David Miller in his comparison between "freedom" in republican and in liberal politics suggests that the former is more closely linked to democracy via an interpretation of personal autonomy in terms of political dialogue and a common understanding of a self-determining citizenship. In contrast to the "libertarian alternative" of fragmentation, the "republican solution" involves the "search for a higher level of agreement between individuals and social groups" (2000, 58–60; 82–85).

A liberated life as an integrated attainment, at once liberal-individual and republican-collective, is not given; it has to be instituted. And for Rousseau, only within certain stages of social development can the construction of freedom be possible. His analogy is socialization: as future citizens, children must learn to connect themselves with the "greater whole" of society, so humans in general need to be trained ("forced to be free") in time before the rise of "all our vices." He is not, unlike contemporary thinkers, concerned with the boundaries of a political unit, or the legitimacy of communal claims, or the plight of individuals and groups as minorities within a given community. Instead, politics (with or without Kantian cosmopolitanism) is for him what resolves moral problems, primarily through education. By the time of the writing of *Social Contract* (1762), Rousseau is almost fatalistic in regarding most European nations as having already missed the opportunity to obtain freedom, yet he nevertheless seeks a remedy in potential revolutions to transform state and citizens, as he describes in *The Geneva Manuscript and Discourse on the Origins of Human Inequality* (cf. Mason 1989, 91–98). In this perspective, it looks as though it is individualistic capitalism, rather than revolutionary collectivism, that fell off course in the order of history. For instance, children in China were taught to honor their intimate collectives—a class, team, or school—and by extension society and the nation at large. They were encouraged to "be always prepared" (the vow of the Young Pioneers) for voluntary works en route to their future shouldering of social responsibility. Had not China enjoyed an advantage in having first established a relational collectivist culture?

Surely ingredients of liberal individualism were not alien to the Chinese soul, as those referring to traditions from Confucianism, Taoism, Buddhism, and folk cultures. Furthermore, individualism and collectivism can be made compatible. Classical Neo-Confucian scholars in particular argue for self-conscience and moral autonomy, as well as equal potential for individual perfection and the coincidence of the personal, family, state, and cosmos (Twiss 1998; more critically, Kwok 1998). Although the notion of individually based rights "had to be 'imported' into Chinese from the west," some similar ideas existed early in China (Lo 1947, 186). Without the language of rights, there was both the vocabulary and concept of "freedom" (*ziyou*) (Zheng 1995; cf. Rosemont 1991, 57–78; Kelly and Reid 1998, chapters 4–5). The realm of freedom in the Confucian desire is the highest human attainment as complete harmony between *xin* (heart/intellect or subjectivity) and *wu* (things or objectivity), and between *rendao* (social rules) and *tiandao* (divine rules). By the age of seventy, "a gentleman does whatever he pleases without violating the rules." Perhaps Rousseau had read Confucius when he wrote that the "virtuous man is always free, for in doing his duty he never does anything except what he wants" (1987, 32). We may see such a conception of freedom as "totalitarian," but there is no contradiction between that conception and the ethical being of individuals (cf. de Bary 1983). Likewise, "loyal opposition" or "civil disobedience," terms not familiar to the Chinese political discourse, nevertheless did not contradict the basic moral code of either traditional or communist cultures in which the "right to remonstrance" has "strong theoretical affinities with Western liberalism" (Moore 1987, 73). Only in a black-and-white manner catalyzed in a polarized world between "liberal" and "totalitarian" regimes could there appear an "utter difference between the whole moral atmosphere under collectivism and the essentially individualist Western civilization" (Hayek 1946, 139–40).

Still, it was undeniable that liberalism had never fully developed in China, not even with the controversial intellectual movement known as the "new enlightenment" in the 1980s. The traditional subordination of individuals was transformed into collectivism, which was taken as another word for socialism. Negotiations between the common good and self-interests were part of a life mediated by official as well as many nonofficial and informal channels. Unlike liberal societies where individualism competes with public interests and demands trade-offs, in communist China the societal "will" naturally outweighed personal desires. But this was less a result of coercive measures than of a shared norm of coherence between private and public good nurtured by socialization and manipulation. Freedom meant collective belonging more than civil liberties; and it required security in terms of subsistence more than autonomy against state intrusion. The popular wisdom in the Mao years was that "Small streams are full only when big rivers flow." Even consumerism in a market era after Mao could not destroy altogether the cultural root of collectivist values. Worth noting is the paradoxical role of education, which is no doubt universal, as both enabling critical faculties and disabling them with brainwashing. "Totalitarian freedom" only adds to it a utopian perfectionist touch. Yet Mao's answer to the riddle as to who educates the educators is a democratic one: that is, "self-education" and the principle that "the educator must be educated" (by the masses). This conviction in mutual learning refuses arrogance as much as ignorance and appreciates the limitations as much as the importance of spontaneous local knowledge.

Could both liberal individualist and social collectivist trajectories be (further) democratized, each making its own big next step? The liberal individualist mode is to transcend atomized individuals and formal procedures to achieve more in the social and substantial, and the social collectivist is to reconstitute a democracy in which individuality is cherished and citizenship thriving (cf. Claude 1976, 41–46). Critical to such possibilities is whether what has been positively gained in each social setting can be treasured and developed. As T. H. Marshall optimistically propounds, the chronological stages followed by the Western welfare states from civil-political to socioeconomic rights might be reversed in the developing countries (1981, 157–75; cf. Kent 1993, chapter 1). If welfare democracies had already pioneered the projected step in liberal societies, it would be China's turn to exalt freedoms and rights while retaining the socialist commitment to public welfare in a Chinese brand of liberal-social democracy. There must be even comparative advantages for the country to explore, such as the strength of organizational networks and the deep-seated notions of redistributive justice, which could be turned into a vehicle for political reform. Reflecting on the Gramscian interpretation of Machiavelli, Louis Althusser rejects the alleged contradictions between the absolute power advocated in *The Prince* and the republican ideal elaborated in *Discourses on Livy*, because he sees the two as successive moments of a new polity (cf. McClelland 1996, 151). As J. G. A. Pocock ponders on the self-doubt of American durability in fulfilling these "Machiavellian moments" (1975), Cui Zhiyuan asserts that "China's revolution has yet to reach its 'second Machiavelli moment'" (2000, 199–200).

The temporal sense of "late development" is only relative; and the progress that respectively is expected in the two journeys cannot be a one-way business of catching up but a process of mutual appropriation. Social policies in welfare democracies had matured under the pressure of domestic labor movements but also external competition from their socialist counterparts. Major social reforms achieved in the capitalist world were at least in part impelled by its communist competitors (Carr 1946).[12] Even some conservative liberals agree on not dismissing the Bolshevik and Chinese revolutions on the ground that their "lasting effect would be to spread the already established principles of liberty and equality to formerly backward and oppressed peoples" (Fukuyama 1999, 66). And such an effect would also press developed democracies formally bound by these principles to actualize them. Axel Honneth's social theory of an ethical life centered in recognition spells out the intellectual and structural compatibility between law-binding collective virtues and personal freedom. Without any reference to the Chinese experiences, his "moral grammar," like Quentin Skinner's (1998) "republican liberty," which is neither positive (communitarian) nor negative (contractarian) but both, echoes at a distance the ethos of Chinese socialism.[13] The Chinese, of course, had bypassed a great deal of the relevant philosophical debates in the West, but in the process they had ventured a great deal further from them as well (cf. Fraser and Honneth 2003). Their ongoing search, in defiance of setbacks and confusions, was for an equitable social power that accommodates popular and individual sovereignty, and public and private choice.

For those who subscribe to a republican conception of democracy, individual self-realization is possible only through social empowerment; and the paths to human freedom can be taken only alongside collective solidarity. The famine of 1959–1961 in China, as mentioned, illustrated the indispensability of basic liberties for the very "right to life and develop-ment" to which the PRC committed itself. Conversely, political and eco-nomic liberalization could not imply democratization as unruly market forces eroded liberty while hindering democracy. Disparities and inequali-ties simply jeopardized both personal and collective capabilities. For this to be redressed, democratic mobilization would be inevitable so public affairs could be publicly deliberated to compel government policies to accord the preference of the population. As the Maoist bias against individualism has in reformist critiques been misconstrued as an opposition between liberty and equality, the best arguments in both liberalism and socialism are yet to be revisited, which present no inherent obstacle to their mutual reinforce-ment. The two modes of thought are one in the idea of people exerting rational control over their lives and surroundings. To that end, the reduc-tion of inequalities and alienation is a condition for, and an indicator of, the development of freedom. Liberalism and socialism thereby converge, mak-ing their differences secondary;[14] and such a synthesis is exactly what is to mark China's "second Machiavelli moment."

Constitutionalism and the Individual

With reforms evolving, the real barrier to liberty and democracy was no longer (or was it ever?) the collectivist bias of socialism but rather post-socialist construction and destruction. The constitution was amended to legitimize a private sector (in 1992 and 1999) and "nonwork income" in-cluding "lawful profits" from exploitation (in 2002). The more radical de-mand on adding to the existing clauses a new one that declares the property rights of private capital "sacred and inviolable" was put off by obvious ideo-logical difficulty and popularly backed opponents. In the highly charged debates around constitutional amendments, a focus was how not to legiti-mize illegitimate flows of public assets into private pockets and, for that matter, how to prevent public power from being in effect privatized.[15] Also contested was the issue of land rights in the context of the formal public ownership of the land (by the state and village collectives) with a limited scope of trading and leasing. Any move toward privatizing land would threaten the loss of one of the revolution's most fundamental achievements as well as the last reserve for security provision in the countryside to avoid the re-creation of a landless peasantry. The new "Farm Land Contract Law" adopted in March 2003 was to be implemented for the stable and guaranteed rights of farmers to land use. The problem, however, remained unsolved as to how the grossly deprived rural population—from infringements as serious as land seizure through unregulated deals between local governments and private developers without proper consultation and compensation—might be best protected by constitutional means.[16]

It would be too elementary a mistake to forget that a modern polity is measured, above all, by its abandonment of social status determined by heredity. Any legal privilege or disadvantage derived from an individual's economic background is a violation of citizenship. The Chinese, like their European, American, and Soviet predecessors, underwent bloody revolutions for the ideals of justice, equality, and freedom ensuring, as a first move toward democracy, the franchise independent of property. What a regression that a virtual equation between individual and property rights was even considered in the Chinese debates! Especially awkward is the fact that nothing of the sort, the sacredness and inviolability of private property, is stated anywhere in the capitalist constitutions. In the Declaration of Independence, Jefferson famously rewrote Locke's "right to life, liberty and private property" into "right to life, liberty and the pursuit of happiness," though he was not a socialist in denouncing private property. A comparison between the Jeffersonian and Madisonian conceptions of property rights (as republican versus liberal) illustrates this point (Cui 2003, 19–20). In particular is the question of why private property should require special treatment if the rights of citizens—including the rights to possessions, income, and indeed property—were generally protected; and, further, whether it was the issue of labor rights, far more than the right of capital, that had been neglected. The new institutional economics doctrine of clarity of property rights had a dogmatic following in the Chinese reform circles; it did not win in 2004 when constitutional amendments confirmed equal protection of public and legally acquired private properties.

A quick sketch of the origin and evolution of the PRC constitution reveals that the Chinese political elites had been informed by constitutional thinking since the late Qing period; they even staged multiparty elections and attempted federalist provincial assemblies in the wake of the republican revolution.[17] If the Constitutional Outline by the Imperial Order (1908) was irrelevant, neither did the republican Provisional Constitution (1911) have much impact. A vital difference between these early developments and those after 1949 lay in the communist ideology about the supremacy of the people. The 1954 constitution, based on the Common Program (1949), took a year and half to be drafted with more than a dozen drafts being nationally scrutinized. The process involved more than eight thousand experts and concerned individuals in the CCP's consultative system, who posed over five thousand solicitations from which more than one hundred were adopted. The provisional draft was then published in the *People's Daily* and provoked a nationwide discussion that lasted three months and drew over 150 million participants at the grassroots level as well as 1.18 million suggested motions (Central Documentary Research Office 1996). The 1982 constitutional amendment was also widely deliberated, but the popular spirit and scale displayed in 1954 has yet to be repeated.[18]

Two generic arguments are relevant here, both of which were introduced in previous chapters and sections. One concerns the nature of constitutionalism in the context of Chinese socialism; and the other is about the constitution's intrinsic yet insufficiently elaborated foundation in individual citizens. The two arguments are interdependent, and only in their integration can light be shed on China's next round of constitutional and political reforms. It is important to first realize that, in relation to the moral and institutional strengths and weaknesses of a people's democracy, the PRC constitution was a watershed in Chinese history in the sense that it formally encoded the revolution's unprecedented recognition of the people as citizens and "masters of society." Whatever the relationship between constitution and democracy in political theories, this revolutionary origin of the constitution in the People's Republic would make any constitutional amendment fundamentally illegitimate without seeking to secure and enhance the supremacy of the people and the popular mandate. The trend in the market reforms that steadily downgraded the collective subject of the common people could thus be seen as unconstitutional.

To institutionalize the moral core of the PRC constitution, there certainly could be experiences to learn from the existing constitutional democracies. The government had indeed sponsored targeted research in its think tanks and university centers, including, conspicuously, the central party school. The Madisonian model of constraining majority rule in order to protect the minority was studied, for example, and so were comparative parliamentary and presidential power and federal and consociational structures. Also instructive might be the Spanish transition to democracy through creating a Law of Political Reform within the old statecraft to furnish a packed regime change (Linz and Stepan 1996, 87–105). The benefit of independent judicial review for safeguarding the constitutionality of legislation and the justice of laws and lawmaking was being considered, in light of the fact that the NPC and its standing committee had not played, and could not play, the role of a constitutional court as suggested on paper. In moving upward from current local elections, the NPC may well be on its way to becoming a directly elected legislative body, and China should seize this progress as an opportunity for institutional democratization. It is perhaps no accident that developed nations have all adopted electoral democracy as a method for aggregating interests when traditional religions and morality are no longer capable of social cohesion. However different the Chinese political, cultural, and spatial conditions might be from such democracies, the CCP may find a chance to reestablish itself as a national mass party only by taking the initiative to institute elections. As Gan Yang notes, by "exploiting the advantages of being a ruling party, it could then use the electoral lever to expand its social bases" (2003b, 268–69). Wang Lixiong further contemplates a novel structure that combines direct and indirect, participatory and representative, systems in self-governing committees as "layered blocs" (*cengkuai*) constituted of the elected as well as the electorate for the next upper layer (2004, 100–112). As substituting decentralization (let alone privatization) for democracy is not only mistaken but also politically dangerous, a function of national elections is precisely to strengthen the right kind of central authority while curbing centrifugal regional powers. Examples at hand are wildly abused standards for pay, safety, taxation and fees, land management, the environment—abuses and violations that are often permitted by local governments in contradiction to the center's policy objectives.

The second argument stems from the first and from the notion of combining liberal individualism and republican collectivism. The basic building block of a modern political community has to be the individual as the citizen; and the central power of the community, directly authorized by citizens, has to be rooted in popular sovereignty. The "principle of a constitutional democracy is that the individual citizen should be the foundation, and a unitary constitution should be the framework, of the nation" (Gan 2003b, 262). That Chinese political tradition did not escape a perpetual pendulum swing between centrally concentrated and locally oligarchic power structures was because of the absence of individual citizens constituting the basis of sovereignty. Once democratic steps can be taken to overcome this tradition, China's unitary preoccupation could be a great asset for the liberal concept of citizenship presupposing the idea of state (Gan 2003b, 262–64). Liberalism, however, possesses no monopoly over theories and practices of individual freedom or constitutional democracy. Republicanism, like socialism, is also premised on individualism. Departing from this very premise, an essential weakness of the communist systems was the fact that "constitutions played a marginal role" and China in that respect looked "the least constitutional" (Lindblom 1977, 128). The highly advanced PRC constitution since half a century ago, however, has scarcely existed beyond its glorious wording. "A state can be liberal and not democratic; equally, a state may have a constitution without being constitutionalist" (Finer 1999, 3:1568).

This lack of constitutionalism was symbolized by one of the most unforgettable scenes in recent Chinese history—when in 1966 Liu Shaoqi, the chairman of the PRC, held up a copy of the 1954 constitution in desperate self-defense while confronted by cultural revolutionary rebels. Clearly it is not the right to private property but every person's right to life that must be "sacred and inviolable," no matter if he or she is the head of the state or a cleaner of public toilets (Liu famously told such a worker, Shi Chuanxiang, that "our jobs are different but we both are the servants of the people"). Without unimpaired constitutional mandating, even a conscious emancipation movement can be blind and destructive; and even a well-intended regime may slip into mismanagement and repression. Time and again, it has been shown that an assertive and participatory population may not acquire civic consciousness but can be prejudicial and fanatic, sustaining autocracy rather than democracy. Communist populism in China failed— in its own terms of political education—to lift up the masses and arm them with weapons of criticism. "Scientific" progress and voluntarist impulse were both incorporated into idealistic devotion as much as fundamentalism. Members of a cultural revolutionary generation growing up full of the "mentality of struggle" against "bourgeois humanism," alas, turned themselves into inhumane attackers of their fellow citizens, with their own teachers among the people considered "class enemies."[19]

The more orderly political world of Chinese socialism did not fare better in this regard. The norms of morality over utility, ideology over materiality, and cooperation over competition took a heavy toll on individuality. "Thought remoulding," peculiar to China's class politics, featured the "thought reform" of "bourgeois" and "petty bourgeois" elements such as the intellectuals, peasants and the urban youth to be "re-educated" in the countryside (ironically, by the peasantry). The label "bourgeois" in the "bourgeois theory of human nature," "bourgeois humanism," and "bourgeois liberalism," as noted, was least defined in the Chinese vocabularies of identities. As a political act of naming, it served the purpose of waging class wars at base and superstructure, home and abroad. Participation was instrumentalized by internalized dependency, in the form of the submission of the personal to the political and transcendental—the socialist universe, the motherland, the people. The romantic perpetuation of the revolution, a totalitarian sublime of sorts, in many ways devastated the personalities that should be the "most beautiful flowers" on earth in Marx's words. The violent denial of the right to dissent was "justified" and reinforced by the severity of China's international environment. The accused and persecuted were often also among the most conscientious and courageous supporters of communism—the logic of a revolution devouring its own children. In vowing to prevent the "mass dictatorships" from ever recurring, the reformers succeeded in a de-radicalization of Chinese politics. What they had left out in envisioning a substantial political reform was the idea of democracy encompassing but not substituted by legality, in which the constitutional architecture would be built on the foundation of individual citizens and their collective power. Liberalization in China has yet to go beyond market freedoms and legalization, preparing for the morality and institutions of a democracy.

It is classical liberalism, not the neoliberal variants prevailing today, that is a compelling source for the Chinese reform imaginary (assuming the indispensability of a state responsibility to protect free citizens). Kant insists on the necessity of people thinking freely (and acting within the hard shell of laws), for, in the long run, governments "can themselves profit by treating man, who is *more than a machine,* in a manner appropriate to his dignity" (1991, 60). In truth, John Stuart Mill remarks, "a state which dwarfs its men, in order that they may be more docile instruments in its hands even for beneficial purposes—will find that with small men no great thing can really be accomplished" (1956, 141). Indeed, communist China had accomplished some great things when it cherished its people; since a dwarfed state (by colonialism or civil strife or the archaic rulers) would not prize its men and women. But when the regime repressed individuality and allowed itself to destroy its honest critics, it was destined to crumble in crises of trust, confidence, and legitimacy.

The importance of individual freedom, of each person being an end and not a means, cannot be stressed more for political culture in China to be reformed, in which individual rights had traditionally been subordinated to the state or collective good. But individualism, along with the notion of freedom as earlier mentioned, is not an entirely foreign concept. Chinese socialism, in particular, owes a debt both to Marxist humanism and to indigenous wisdom about personal cultivation and moral authority. Marxism, of course, is typically criticized for its inadequate understanding of "autonomy and unity," which "are claimed not on behalf of the individual but of the 'generic being' (Gattungswesen) of man" (Taylor 1979, 71). A Chinese response would be to ask if the individual does not exist only in the species-being (without presuming ontological priority of either the individual or the species). Like Rousseau, Marx believes in the simultaneity that human destiny can be self-controlled by each only when controlled by all. The individual must be seen as an ensemble of social relations, and individual freedom a matter of class (and of national, gender, and so on) emancipation. For Marx, "true liberalism" means striving for "a completely new form of state corresponding to a more profound, more thoroughly educated and freer popular consciousness" (quoted in Stedman Jones 2002, 102). Yet he also warns against what a stream of liberal commentators call "democratic tyranny," not excluding a proletarian one: "One must above all avoid setting 'the society' up again as an abstraction opposed to the individual" (1844, 117). That is, liberation is only exemplified (however utopian it may sound without specifics) by free members freely associated in a free association; and it cannot be an association standing above, or developing at the expense of, its members. For Marx, "the individual is the end and society the means, while the common good is not the good of some entity separate from and above individuals" (quoted in Lewis 1961, 15). Socialism and liberalism, in their true forms, share the commitment to individual freedom against alienation and oppression. Discussions of socialist aliena- tion earlier in the Soviet bloc and later in China demonstrated that the problem could be addressed within the Marxist tradition (e.g., Markovic 1975, 418ff; Brugger and Kelly 1990, chapter 6).

Following Hegel, for whom "the principle of the modern world is free- dom of subjectivity," Habermas confirms that "the *moral concepts* of mod- ern times follow from the recognition of the subjective freedom of individ- uals" (2000, 16–17). To invoke this line of argument for modernity (which has been adopted by the standard discourse) is to highlight a particular failure of people's democracy as a modern enterprise. No doubt the sheer limitations of the individual as the knowing subject or political actor must be taken into account in any self-reflective critiques of a self-congratulating modernity. A more important point, however, is contemporary. Let us admit that state socialism failed in that the attempts at a total politicization and control tore down the "core of unalienated social life" (Graham 1992, 200)—not disputing the assumption that such life had ever existed in more "natural" systems. However, had not market transitions just done the same in an even more devastating manner? If the individual was instrumental to state goals (of which many should be recognized as socially beneficial), had not the market, too, enslaved its participants? Can individuals, divided into "winners" and "losers" in the first place, thrive in the marketplace of choices and opportunities as well as greed and fear? Would a polarized citizenry sustain a healthy democracy? Turning people into machines may take different forms, including those of the market, that today's neoliberals, who are no match for the giant liberal thinkers of previous eras, are unable to comprehend. When profit making becomes the only goal, supported by laws without the people being themselves lawmakers, it mentally and phys- ically injures the people as individuals and as citizens. China's "comparative advantage" in cheap labor in the international market is but a great disad- vantage for low-paid or jobless "lumpens," of whom tens of millions lived in poverty and worked in dire conditions. The well-known Tang verse (by Du Fu)—"While the wine and meat rot inside the grand gates, bones of the dead from cold and hunger lay by the road"—now occasionally is featured in media commentary. One does not need to be a Marxist to see the injustice and irrationality of those transitions which not only made a sham of democracy but also of individualism.

This brings us back to the nature of a socialist constitution and the project of constitutional reform in China. Ideally, syntheses must be sought between the moral basis of law and legal procedures, between limited state power and strengthened state capacities, and between individuality and social harmony. Constitutionalism entails no obsession with either state or market, it endorses neither collectivist nor individualist fetishism, and it diffuses both populist and elitist-formalist extremes. By no means an easy task, cautious optimism points to the facts that not only does the PRC already have a superb written constitution, it has also entered into a new stage of political development with a much stronger sense of constitutionalism among its citizens and leaders. Democracy in China, at long last, is to emerge to be thoroughly socialist modern and definitely Chinese.

Ideology and Legitimacy

The puzzle as to why the Chinese revolution as a far-reaching liberation movement would have despised "Western liberties" has to be deconstructed against its political background, rather than the traditional one of culture. To be highlighted is the origin of this discord in the nonaccidental coincidence of China's first encounter with liberalism and imperialism, or, more precisely, liberalism through imperialism, which caused the country its deepest-ever survival crisis. "Modernity" was for the Middle Kingdom an abrupt and catastrophic catalyst of compressed social changes. The introduction of liberalism not only was contemporaneous with, but also a part of, violent foreign invasion and humiliation. In other words, for the Chinese, with their territory bombed open to (opium) trade and divided by colonial "spheres of power," liberalism was from the outset linked to an imperialism to be condemned. Elite intellectuals, although busy translating and debating the liberal ideas of Herbert Spencer, James Mill, John Stuart Mill, John Dewey, Bertrand Russell, and others, were appalled, and many were radicalized (Schwartz 1964; Liu 1997).[20] It is a shame that most scholars both inside and outside of China have not seriously confronted themselves with the truth that "liberalism thus has a foreign taint" of international injustice (Lindau and Cheek 1998, 10). Moreover, the supposedly "liberal" imposition by foreign powers stifled liberal ideas themselves and blocked the way, if any, of liberal democratic development in China at its modern threshold. As Marie-Claire Bergère puts it, to say that liberalism was powerless to heal the ills of a country beset by wars and disfigured sovereignty is an understatement: "the very magnitude of those ills made it impossible for liberalism to gain a footing" (1989, 226).

The Liberal Solution?

Two immediate conclusions can be drawn here: it was the defeat of an obsolete empire that deprived the Chinese of even a viable state to constitute a liberal solution;[21] and, while an anti-liberal defect in the making of nationalism and populism in China might be detected, a mighty historical fact is also that the Chinese revolution was a rebellion with a cause of freeing a people. After all, why should the freedom that the men and women fought for in rural and urban China throughout the twentieth century, with extraordinary persistence and heroism, be written off from what liberalism aspired to achieve? As national and individual emancipation came together for those who escaped the sufferings of exploitation, repression, forced marriage, and so on by joining the revolution, was not their participation a manifestation of revolutionary liberty? What a paradox that an epic liberation struggle would have arisen against a liberalism poisoned by imperialism, colonialism, and hypocritical double standards. Moreover, the "semicolonial" condition also signified collaboration between modern imperialists and their puppets among the premodern local tyrants, a condition that clarified the dual task of the Chinese revolution. Fighting on two fronts to remove both a native ancien régime and foreign domination, communism in China was firmly a modern and democratic force. The habitual dichotomy between tradition and modernity, between Chinese backwardness and Western progress, and between communism and democracy, is false. This also explains why Marxism rather than other Enlightenment ideologies eventually prevailed in a Chinese "new culture" in opposition to xenophobia as much as traditionalism. Marxism was in demand for an oppressed people to break with the past, and thereby to be modern; and to repel imperialism in which liberalism was implicated, and thereby to be free.

Yet there was no way for the revolution to be "liberal" when countered by white terror and military encirclement, hence the imperative of loyalty and discipline. Even in power the new regime was not relieved from the continuing predicament of tight external and internal constraints. The types and degree of control and repression it then allowed were not only unacceptable in liberal societies but also in striking contrast with the fact that the communists themselves had been liberal as political and cultural rebels.[22] In becoming a ruling party, and to retain that position, their priority changed. China's ordeal of hardship and struggle certainly contributed to a political culture of contempt for liberal individualism and pluralism (as "liberal lightness" or *ziyou sanman*), a political culture that in turn undermined and drained the sources and resources of socialism itself. The contradictions between the ideas of liberation and self-fulfillment on the one hand and the demand for unity and stability (and thus intolerance of dissent) on the other were "resolved" by labeling anything independently individualistic as "bourgeois" or "bourgeois liberal." In so doing, the project of Chinese socialism turned conservative and was forced by threats and the party's own making to let its opponents take away the lofty banner of liberty.

In the "ideological vacuum" of deradicalization, intellectual liberalism began to flourish with "new enlightenment" writings in the 1980s. For the cumulative effect of anti-liberalism to wane in the political circles, however, a more favorable international environment would be required. As long as the global liberal ideology with an open or unspoken anticommunist (and racist) inference continued to be (perceived as) destabilizing, with the collapse of the Soviet Union in the background, official fear and public caution readily joined forces in China. If historically the weak and vaguely proposed liberal solution fell through in revolutionary China because of the liberal-colonial alliance, the constant economic and political "China bashing" at the present had a similar impact. The cold war survived in hot globalization to keep the concept of imperialism alive.[23] Further on the negative side was the neoliberal hijacking of the Chinese socioeconomic thinking and public policies, which had resulted in widespread discontent. It looked as though personal freedoms and civil-political rights (China's "second Machiavellian moment") had not been pushed forward but rather held back by the confusions of laissez-faire libertarianism with liberalism, subtracted liberalization with liberties, and consumerism with freedom.

Furthermore, the inability of elitist liberals to take up the question of democracy was self-damaging. The liberal critiques of "radicalism" or populism (e.g., of a "lumpen culture") and the lack of the rule of law were thorough. But the liberal project did not appeal to the common people without a willingness to see their empowerment, including in lawmaking for social justice, as key to political reform. The voices of workers in and out of work, and farmers with or without land, were seldom heard in the liberal discourse of democracy focused on ending the one-party rule. And even there it was completely obscure in terms of a viable alternative and the pathway to a future system enabling broad participation in decision making. Attributing this impotence to the ban on opposition is not wrong but beside the point; at issue, rather, is democratic legitimacy weakened by the current global interpretation that desubstantiated democracy. That is, democracy retaining its fundamental, people-centered connotation was not only off the official agenda but also missing from liberal rationalization. By insisting on an erroneous discontinuity between liberalism and socialism, liberal critics in China cut themselves off from the general public as the source of support.

In the same vein, the ambiguity about a democratic concept of the state in Chinese liberalism led to awkward positions ranging from postponing, if not abandoning, democratization ("neoauthoritarianism") to dismissing central governing and macro planning altogether. Every problem was blamed on the "incompleteness" of market transition, as though a mature market economy would automatically resolve all the problems consequential to the reform. The reality, however, suggested that nothing less than democratizing the state could provide the country with the means needed to tackle the challenges it faced. By disregarding voices from below, liberal advocates became indistinguishable from neoliberals. As noted by Wang Hui, the "hegemonic status of Chinese neoliberalism," in turn, "took shape as part of the process by which the state used economic liberalization to overcome its crisis of legitimacy" (2003, 44). Failing China again, deformed liberalism bypassed the democratic solution. However, there would be no liberal solution without democracy in a country where the rightful claims must be coded with *minyi* or popular mandate. By the same token, democratic changes in China would be different from what had been aggressively promoted on the global stage by the world's postcommunist ideological powerhouse backed by the international trading and lending institutions.

Ideological Globalization

A global ideology of democracy would be a good thing if it were not packaged with neoliberal doctrines used to dismantle socially desirable state capacities, not defined with particular interests and bias in a unipolar world order, not opportunistically imposed on countries and regions, and not blocking democratic imaginations in transitional societies. Yet that ideology, discursively popularized since Samuel Huntington's "wave theory," is precisely guilty of these errors. It is also grossly confusing concerning the difference between "free trade" (never mind protective trade barriers maintained by rich countries) and free society, democracy and human rights, or the "international community" and imperial domination. Worse still, it has a distinctive Western-centric religious aura around Christian virtue that goes far beyond the secular Weberian thesis about the spirit of capitalism. And, further, its total disrespect for the democratic principle of self-determination is fundamentally self-delegitimating. The totalitarian justification for imposition—in the best interest of the people, which they themselves cannot see—is unapologetically replicated, again and again, without a sense of irony. Betraying a favorite liberal doctrine of the "natural order" of development, the "democratic globalizers" have turned anti-Hayekian in their obsession with social engineering across borders.

A consequence of this, inevitably, is that democracy is discredited or trivialized. Obviously, an electoral system by itself does not guarantee political participation and the delivery of policies in accordance with public preference. As it happened, democracy today does not even have to meet its own procedural prerequisites of ensuring equity among citizens in access to resources and information, in rich and poor nations alike. While a general election makes for "instant" democracy, abuses of power and violations of rights are routinely committed in both consolidated and "young" democracies. The notorious role of money in campaign politics (especially in advanced democracies) or in law enforcement (especially in third world democracies) reduces democratic fairness and justice to exclusion, backdoor deals, and mere euphemism. Does democracy deserve the prestige it enjoys when it is so elusive or banal and compliant?[24] Given its globally hegemonic and even "theological" status, democracy could actually also legitimize unpopular and locally destructive measures such as those related to "structural adjustment" in the name of good governance.

Just like postmodern critiques being a possible antidote to the modern predicament of instrumentalism, poststructural theories are persuasive in illuminating how discourse organizes knowledge. As noted by Joan Scott, from the Foucauldian perspective, it "identifies objects for study and explanation, it establishes concepts and facts, and it designates structures and identities" (2000, 71). The global discourse of democracy organizes normative conceptions, and dictates relevant theorization, in which it is assured that alternative articulations of democracy do not emerge. This is how an ideology exerts power, and where ideological struggle takes place. That is, caught in a global ideology, democracy does not exactly become empty; rather, it acquires new content by which the world is interpreted and changed in the way preferred by those who exert power over interpretation and direction of change. Struggles for democracy in China are therefore also a struggle of reinterpretation and reorientation in line with the Chinese and socialist understanding, which is much closer than the global ideology to the idea of government for, of, and by the people.

Given its search for an alternative modernity within, not outside or cut off from, modern civilization, Chinese socialism should therefore be prepared, with abundant intellectual, cultural, and political resources, and definitely in a manner better than that of the nonsocialist developing countries, for the work in transforming the flawed project of globalizing democracy. Marx and Engels foresaw that potential more broadly at the dawn of China's awakening to modern challenge: "It may well be that Chinese socialism is related to European socialism just as Chinese philosophy is related to Hegelian philosophy" (1969, 49–50). At the very least, it must be repeated here that modern trajectories, including that of China, cannot be traced without reference to international capitalism; and they interact while reshaping the very epochal conditions in which they evolve under competitive pressures. Like modernity itself, which is still unfolding (into "late" or "post" or alternative types or phases), democracy also unfolds and renovates in local settings, and it is bound to take manifold forms as "a hundred flowers to blossom."

There is a question as to whether nations and cultures have been brought to convergence by waves of capitalist democratization, and if countries like China that have sought socialist alternatives would eventually comply. The responses were understandably hesitant. Particularly notable was that after a century of revolutions, nation building and state building, and socioeconomic transformation, much intellectual energy and public culture in China continued to muse on modernization versus Westernization. Globalization did not solve the old tensions, and *jiegui* had been everywhere contested. The information technology, from televisions and fax machines to cell phones and cybernetics, did not just aid a one-way drift toward the rules and standards set by the global powers. Messages and ideas for urban mobilization, through the Internet and email, in addition to telephone, fax, and post, could travel far and fast translocally and transnationally. Accessible online materials and open debates ranged from WTO negotiations and constitutional amendments to the rights of labor and public health, as well as Taiwan, Iraq, and other international issues.[25] On the one hand, the process of "going global" began to erase the country's Chinese and socialist distinctiveness; on the other hand, the most intimate national characters and local varieties were not actually erasable. As Rousseau warns, while commenting on the design of the Polish constitution, one "must know thoroughly the nation for which one is building" so to avoid errors or impracticality; and "the more certainly if the nation be already formed, with its tastes, customs, prejudices, and failings too deeply rooted to be stifled by new plantings" (quoted in Przeworski 1991, 36). In Charles Tilly's words, as lessons from history, "the fact that European states formed in a certain way, then imposed their power on the rest of the world, guarantees that non-European experience will be different" (1992, 16).

It is a truism to say that globalization contains in itself localization and that it is a double-edged process. But it makes perfect sense for efforts in China to harness a measured and selective process of transition. These efforts could also contribute to the creation of an international conversation about "taming" globalization to benefit the greatest possible majority of the world's population, and to nurture the social movements for labor, women, the environment, peace, and poverty eradication. The flourishing intellectual campaigns for "global civil society," "global justice," "global governance," "cosmopolitan democracy," and "human rights" are cheering signs. However, unless they can critically distance themselves from the ideological globalization led by unilateral ideologues in Washington, they are only deceitful and incapable of positively impacting on political changes locally or globally.

Human Rights and Public Welfare

Many of the expectations raised by a global ideology, amounting to what critics called "democracy fetishism" to promote human rights and social development, are proven to have been misplaced. Some of the world's most powerful democracies, as a matter of current history, either themselves abused rights in domestic or international situations or were allied with dictatorships in foreign countries for political and strategic purposes. Their fluctuating policies on both democracy and human rights were indeed highly opportunistic. Coupled with "human rights diplomacy" and humanitarian interventions, democracy had frequently been self-contradictory while violating national sovereignty as the necessary and normative basis for any democratic state. Although disregarding this norm might be morally justifiable, doing so violates international law: acts that could be imperative and ethical but neither legal nor democratic. By the touchstone of the moral justification for law, this shows that democracy cannot be regarded as the only or the highest criterion for judgment in international relations. "Democracy" is thus a wrong term for intervention or imposition on whatever moral grounds; whether or not the intervening state is democratic is simply irrelevant. Such a clarification does not dispute the view that a democratic regime is more likely than an authoritarian one to support human rights, if only because a government that performs poorly in terms of human rights could be replaced in a democracy. Nor does the argument question the unquestionable universality of human rights and thereby the universal responsibility for their protection, though the word "human" makes "universal" redundant, and any human right may yet be appropriated only within concrete cultures and localities (Lin 2001). The conceptual conflation between democracy and human rights is just another symptom of ideological monopoly.

Democratic legitimacy notwithstanding, democracy still cannot monopolize sources of legitimation. Subsistence needs and redistributive equity are examples of essential public good that may be assisted by, but do not require, formal democratic procedures. The "public good regime" of the PRC, founded on needs-oriented production, pursued welfare and social justice in the world's largest poor country in defiance of waste, mismanagement, and external blockades. Socialist citizens in China as elsewhere in the formal communist world were granted the right to work (in legally protected labor conditions and "equal pay for equal work" schemes in the state sector), to education and health care, and to equality—gender and otherwise. Gaps between coded rights and their actualization or between urban and rural provisions could be huge, but not logically unbridgeable. Constraints on civil liberties did not countervail the fundamental betterment of life. Since 1981 the PRC had been a member of the United Nations Human Rights Commission and subsequently had signed and ratified most international covenants. Although far from fulfilling its obligations, there was nevertheless nothing in the official position that prevented the communists from championing human rights. In fact the CCP "came to power partly as an advocate of human rights against the dictatorship of the Kuomintang" (Nathan 1994, 623). The emphasis on collective, more than individual, "rights to life and development" reflected a deep-seated egalitarian commitment; and China's human development record generally contrasted favorably with that of scores of developing and transitional societies.[26]

More broadly, welfarism in peace times (excluding periods of war, terror, or famine) was an outstanding feature of the communist states comparable with welfare democracies.[27] Political freedoms were strictly limited and elections nominal, but universal franchise activated in other forms of participation must be recognized. Free and quality health service was (and still is!) sustained in Cuba; gender parity had spread in Vietnam; and workers' well-being was legislated in Eastern Europe and the USSR.[28] The Chinese government committed itself to schemes of alleviating poverty. The former socialist countries, including those in the third world, typically demonstrated a high level of literacy, a low rate of infant mortality, and a decent index of life expectancy. These achievements must not be nullified by the extraordinary events leading to the human (and ecological, etc.) disasters under communism. By the same token, there were postcommunist catastrophes to be noted: examples include a drastic decline of male longevity in Russia; hardship and demographic tangles in parts of Eastern Europe; atrocities and ethnic conflicts in the Balkans and other places. Many such catastrophes were caused by misguided transitions in the name of democracy as much as by collapse of the communist empires.

For all their differences, welfare capitalism and state socialism resembled each other in the welfarist allegiance to state provision. As Charles Lindblom acknowledges, certain nondemocratic governments could be more strongly motivated to guard the material safety of their population than could democratic governments. Both were dedicated to organizing society to benefit its members; liberal and communist regimes shared some "humanitarian" ideologies and social policies. "In some important ways," communism was even "more humane than most market-oriented systems, showing a greater concern for income equality, for job security, and for minimum standards of health and other necessities" (1977, 6). It helps neither democracy nor human rights to deny this tendency in forms of welfare authoritarianism. As far as legitimacy is concerned, John Gray recognizes the evidence and feasibility "of regimes that clearly meet the test of the minimum universal content of morality, and do as well *or better* than liberal states on other criteria relevant to human flourishing" without adopting Western norms of democracy (1995, 83).[29] It may be argued that basic needs as "natural rights" are inherent in human worth and dignity and need no democratic consent to approve. In the contemporary language of rights, food, clothing, shelter and medical care, side by side with negative freedom from intrusive harm, constitute the right to life.[30]

Superseding, if not in the place of, personal liberties, the Chinese installed the notion of the "people's livelihood" (*minsheng*), one of the three people's principles. This moral conviction, cultural or otherwise, stretched into developmentalism, socialist and consumerist alike.[31] As the concept of "human rights" found its way to China's successive modern legislatures, it had been spoken in Chinese with local characteristics. *Minsheng* or "human capital," of course, also relies on and must be completed by personal integrity against murder, torture, arbitrary imprisonment, or any other form of bodily harm. Only those governments, as Henry Shue (1980) argues, that protect human life in both positive (subsistence) and negative (immunity) terms (of which the distinction is itself problematic) can be regarded as legitimate; there cannot be a trade-off between these two aspects of life and life's autonomy and dignity. Freedom of speech, conscience, and dissent are of primary importance, and so must be subsistence. Human rights diplomacy, however, had been one-sided, concentrating on the intimidation and persecution of political dissidents. Is poverty also a violation of human rights? What about neglected safety regulations in the workplace?[32] The democrat, not being cynical, knows only too well that a healthy, educated, and socially cohesive citizenry free from hunger, war, and other injuries is not only good in itself but also prerequisite for political democracy. Civil-political rights have no meaning without being exercisable, though they might not be exercised (in the choice of nonparticipation). Socioeconomic well-being is a fundamental freedom. Extended liberties alone may not improve human conditions in other spheres where some hard-won gains could even be lost.

Democracy and Legitimacy

In the context of decoupling democracy and human rights, and democracy and liberty, "human capital" (in post-slavery usage) in a political economy—that is, knowledge, skills, and other inborn and acquired abilities as initially elaborated by Adam Smith—is an outstanding example of legitimate pursuits that are good for, yet independent of, democracy. Human capital is also echoed in such formulations as "human development" (measured in HDI) and "human capabilities" as analyzed in social philosophy (Sen and Nussbaum, discussed in Nussbaum 2000, 70–86). It is typical of the Asian developmental states, democratic and authoritarian, that they invested hugely in public education and medical care, and were dedicated to relative equity along with growth. Despite depressed wages and unions, the build-up of human capital had enabled such countries not only to revive from economic downturns but also to develop politically. The welfare authoritarian regimes, of which some had undergone democratization, socioeconomically outperformed most electoral democracies in the third world. The concept of "social capital," narrowly defined to refer to civic communities and associational engagements, offers an interesting comparison: although any causal relation here may be dubious, social capital apparently depends on the material existence of a viable citizenship and therewith takes human capital for granted (even in the poorer parts of the industrialized West; e.g., Putnam's southern Italy). Conversely, human capital in late development seems conditional, and also likely conducive, to social capital. "Trust," as a component of a broader application of social capital and entailing interpersonal reliance, informal networks, and cooperative relations, is certainly feasible and can be especially strong in some "traditional," agrarian communities, hence positively affecting human capital. In either case, a logical correlation between human capital and democracy is yet to be established.

Overlooked in much of the literature are the salient links between state capacity and both human and social capital. If social capital improves government responsiveness and quality of governance (e.g., the cases of affluent democracies in Putnam 2002), and if trust is an essential, enabling factor of prosperity (for both East and West; e.g., Fukuyama 1995), then purposeful public policies to enhance human capital have been evident also in socialist and other state-led developments. The state, whether or not formally democratic, may also play a role in creating and shoring up social capital so as to reduce transaction costs in organizing society. The CCP, as mentioned above, sponsored a nonconfrontational or, indeed, dependent "civil society" in a corporate manner. A severe handicap in the Chinese case of developing human and social capital is not the state but rather the relinquishing of state's public duties.

Not without its ambiguities, the "European social model" had entered into the Chinese rethinking of the reform paths. Tempting, above all, was that European social democracies seemed to have sustained a high level of both human capital and social capital and both political representation and economic provision, and they did so by willing to go beyond the polling stations. In contrast, a socially "polarizing democracy" would be unattractive and, in the end, the opposite of the people's yearning (Friedman 1999, 70). Samuel Huntington is right to see democracy, normally defined as open, fair, and free elections, as only "one public virtue, not the only one" (1991, 10). Beneficial results are not guaranteed—elected governments may turn out to be inefficient, corrupt, and divorced from public preferences. And, as Huntington further notes, "these qualities make such governments undesirable but they do not make them undemocratic" (quoted in Zakaria 1997, 21). There is nothing to worship in the voting machines, even when they are finely tuned and functional. Joseph Schumpeter's instinct is that when a democratic procedure produces criminal or foolish outcomes, "it seems much more natural . . . to speak of the rabble instead of the people and to fight its criminality or stupidity by all the means at one's command" (1947, 242). This dilemma is real, even though presumably the fight must continue to take place within a democratic framework until a better outcome is reached, which democracy does promise in the long run. The point here is simply that democracy cannot pretend to be able to solve all the difficulties of society, but when it is reduced to formal elections it resolves even fewer problems. Nor, for that matter, does electoral democracy necessarily forward civil liberties, and it is no wonder why many liberals still see democracy as a threat (cf. Zakaria 1998, chapter 3). The conceptual distinction between liberty and democracy will not disappear until republican and liberal conceptions of freedom can converge.

The Chinese leadership had more or less deserted the party's ideological tradition of democracy, which enjoyed a brief renaissance in the late 1970s. Instead the party resorted to a "civilizational" boosting to patriotism at a time when nationalism's socialist content was ebbing, which in turn made national solidarity itself linger. The reinvention of "Chinese civilization," however, could backfire not only because it was insensitive to the legacies of the empire but also because political nationalism had been a marker of Chinese modernity. That is, China's present crisis was one of political authority, not cultural identity (cf. Townsend 1992, 113). Officially sanctioned propaganda on Confucian values was thus incoherent and ineffective. And when it came to be resonant with so-called Asian values as a strategic construct by defenders of authoritarianism in the capitalist NICS, the discourse lost much of its appeal. In fact, the notion of "Asian values" became so absurdly tautological that only those elements in whatever schools of thought deemed authoritarian or illiberal were treated as belonging to such values. Association with the label hence only jeopardized China's cultural identity. "Values," of course, never just existed but depended on the specific systems of meaning production.

Many other problems with a politics of cultural nationalism might be identified, not least for its ethnocentric and essentialist fallacies. Critics have also been divided between those who reject a Western-Asian dichotomy (e.g., Sen 1997) and those who call for a recognition of certain positive promises in certain Asian alternatives to Western norms (e.g., Bell 2000a). Regardless of such divisions, at stake is whether the priorities given to economic growth, political stability, and social cohesion in China were justifiable as "public reasons." In a country where foreign invasion, warlordism, lawlessness, and outbreaks of violence were by no means remote memories, did not the obsession with unity, stability, and territorial integrity maintain some validity? The temptation here to answer in the affirmative would be similar to the seduction of antidemocratic "guardianship" that coincides with the elitist "shadow theory" of democracy, and that reads state or public "paternalism" (*jiazhangzhi*) in Chinese. For Robert Dahl, the notion of guardianship "not only was espoused by Plato in democratic Athens but has appeared throughout the world in a variety of disparate forms, of which Confucianism and Leninism, different as they are, have influenced by far the greatest number of people" (1989, 4). Paradoxical as it may be, the only plausible argument would have to be along the lines of democratic stability; that is, for stability to sustain, nothing is sufficient but sound public policies arrived at through extensive participation and rational deliberation. Counting on economic growth alone for regime legitimacy had proven to be an illusion. The democratic solution in China, again, will defy the ideological misconceptions and build the strengths of both the state and its citizens for the collective and individual goods of utmost importance, such as freedom, security, and equality as fairness. The peoples of the periphery have the choice of "a national popular democratic advance" over "a backward-looking culturalist impasse," as Samir Amin contends. In order not to reduce democratic development to mere periodic elections, Amin asserts that "democracy must be linked to gigantic social transformations or perish" (1989, 148–49).

An argument I make in chapters 3 and 4 is that the ultimate desirability of democracy in China is about a morally grounded and institutionalized power of the people. None of the critical reflections in the preceding pages should be read as discordant with this proposition. Thus, taking issue with global ideology or democratic fetishism is an attempt for, not against, a democratic answer to China's problems and it is to defend it at its roots. Meanwhile, to question the monopoly of democratic legitimacy is not only to accept what a formal democracy cannot do, cannot be expected to do, or even damages as a result of its displacement of other normative objectives. It is also to appreciate nondemocratic rationalities of legitimation, such as the "primary goods" historically achieved in some authoritarian systems— paternalistic, corporatist, populist, nationalist, and even imperialistic (in periods of successful empires). Democracy is normatively good in itself, but it cannot prevail without being congruent and conducive to other constituents of the common good. Without engaging certain important insights in postmodern (and postliberal, etc.) critiques of the Enlightenment tradition of rational humanism, it is within that tradition that we must treat political democracy as something subordinated to the imperatives of human needs and human rights, public welfare and social justice, peace and ecology. Chinese socialism and its transformation have been breathtaking in testing these suppositions where political and ideological struggle was waged, legitimacy disputed, and hegemony contested.

By transcending traditional liberal-individualist and republican-collectivist versions and visions, democracy has been re-created in different national, transnational, and local conditions. In China, the popular pressure for democratic change would necessitate deliberative, associational, and electoral participation from an inclusive and vibrant citizenry. A people's power that prizes liberties, legality, and civility as much as social justice and public welfare will encompass the creed of liberalism and socialism. To attain and safeguard such a power are the functions of constitutionalism. The PRC constitution is yet to be consolidated as a foundation made on the individual citizen and in limiting the state while enhancing its public-serving capacities. The existing institutions, such as the people's congresses and local elections, are important preparation for creating what the Chinese describe as a "highly civilized society" (compared to "civil society" as conceived elsewhere). Institutional reforms and design, however, remain an acute challenge largely because of the inescapable and complicated legacies of the ruling Communist Party as well as the ethnic-regional makeup of the PRC.[33]

Rethinking the Chinese Model

WITNESSES TO THE DEVELOPMENTS IN CHINA SINCE THE 1990S DO NOT
have to be Marxist to be reminded of the arresting descriptions in the
Communist Manifesto about money dissolving the commune through the
globalization of markets and commodification and exploitation of labor, or
the subordination of country to city and East to West. Such processes have
been intensified globally since the late twentieth century by the ever-greater
(post)industrial-technological-military powers, ever-larger and weightier
multinational companies and financial institutions, and ever-faster "creative
destruction."[1] The globalizing forces that have realigned around international capital continue to revolutionize the world and destroy not only
precapitalist societies in the capitalist peripheries but also elements and
variants of socialism North and South. Such forces have certainly helped to
derail the Chinese reforms from socialist self-adjustment. Contrary to some
utopian free market assumptions, what then emerged in China was a mixture of nineteenth-century "conditions of the English working class," Latin
American patterns of rent seeking and dependency, and a Russian-style
privatization blended with the native Chinese traces of bureaucratic capitalism. It thus appears questionable as to whether socialism is relevant any
more in the forward march of capitalist global integration.

My aim in this concluding chapter is to provide a critical affirmation of
the persistent relevance of socialism, in particular possible revitalization of
Chinese socialism. The unprecedented challenge that China has confronted
is the "iron market logic" that any socialist or socially oriented system
would strive to bend or mutate while utilizing the markets and market
mechanisms. It is no easy task "to join the market in order to beat it" via
relinking, borrowing, and embracing; indeed, such an effort is almost a
gamble in a supposedly postsocialist era in which socialism is by definition

obsolete. Might "private" capital be simultaneously "social" in a socialized market to serve public interests? What would define and constitute a socialist market? Could such a market survive and eventually overcome the capitalist world market, and on what historical and institutional basis? In posing these questions we can recognize the truism that even a socialist society cannot avoid being "structurally dependent on capital" (as in the capitalist welfare democracies).[2] On the other hand, however, the preserved demarcation between capital and capitalism indicates the feasibility of preventing the logic of profit from colonizing the political, social, and cultural spheres—that is, if the right agency and institutions can be put in place.[3] For what is necessary is not capital, or profitability, as such, but rather its specific operation and allocation. In the end, structures are historically configured and modified by human actors through reforms and revolutions, and they must continuously be changeable—though not without constraints. Such restructuring might be directed to support socially beneficial functions of capital. This point brings us back to the need for a powerful and democratic socialist state, which, rather than any external or ideological pressure, is the fundamental reason for promoting democratization in China. Here the political-institutional aspect of socialism, forgotten in reform thinking, is yet to be rehabilitated in the self-consciousness of the Chinese nation seeking to advance "a higher form of modern civilization" by surpassing modern capitalism.

I begin here by explaining how "capitalist roaders," infamously anticipated by Mao in launching the Cultural Revolution, came to be real only after that "surreal" episode, in China's bitter "honeymoon" between national communism and international capitalism. The broker was the state itself in a daring attempt to reconcile socialism and market in a "socialist market economy." Both the amalgamation and the competition between the two forces were best illustrated by various bureaucratic transmutations in the marketplace. Following this discussion I make some tentative reflections on the compatibility and incompatibility between socialism and the market in the Chinese practice. As quasi-capitalist groups and interests had been allowed to (re)emerge or were created directly by the (nominally) socialist state, the next moves made by that state would be decisive for China's future. As I show in this study, the orientation and capacity of the state are chief variables of the analysis. And, incidentally, it should be noted that unlike related debates in socialist Eastern Europe and the West (Roemer and Bardhan 1993; Ollman 1998), "market socialism" has not been a common phrase in the Chinese discourse.

Later in this chapter I evaluate the making, unmaking, and remaking of the reform model in China. The predicament of reform's second phase was also manifested in a mounting ecological crisis coupled with grave social and demographic problems. Together they began to compel the country to revise its developmental path through a collective soul-searching of repudiating developmentalism. It is recognized, however, that development per se cannot be forsaken but must be reconfirmed as "development as freedom" (Sen 2000). In order to do so, not only circulation and redistribution have to be reorganized but, more fundamentally, the mode of production and the management of society must be transformed.

In particular, I look into the readjustment of reform since the leadership succession in 2003, and I note the opportunities to seize or lose along this third phase of reform. I interpret the idea of *xiaokang* independently of the official version by focusing on some urgent policy implications on small business, unemployment, land management, and the natural environment. In the long run, *xiaokang* also indicates the concrete prospect of integrating life and work according to the undistorted needs as well as the aesthetic desires of individuals and communities against alienated labor and consumerism. This prospect would also be in line with economic and political democracy. My discussion of these themes can be delivered in full only in a separate volume.

Against the background of the Chinese alternative, a question that is immediately relevant is whether there has been a paradigmatic shift from modernization to globalization that is cognitive as well as historical. The two paradigms to a large extent overlapped in actual global movements, especially after the cold war; neither would make sense unless they involved dependent and independent variables of capitalist expansion. That is, these movements in their unevenness and compression continue to substantiate a conception of history alternative to those that are capitalist-centric (rather than Western-centric). Such a conception is faithful to modern norms but is receptive to potentially plural, noncapitalist modernities. As such it is an antidote to a political refusal or an intellectual inability to discern hitherto unknown developments. The last section (again only a sketch), aided by the insight of historical institutionalism, puts the transformation of Chinese socialism in a nutshell. Imagining and constructing a healthier and happier society might be path-dependent on old and new traditions but such a society cannot be "brought back" from any idealized past. The sources of political willingness and creative politics for a path-breaking development can be drawn only from a people empowered in a sovereign nation and by a democratic state. In the final pages, my arguments are summarized in a replay of the context of tensions between integration and autonomy, high-lighting China's effort to carve out a space outside global capitalism, from which a tortuous quest for socialist modernity can be critically appreciated.

Socialism and the Market

As I note in chapter 2 in an account of the national bourgeoisie, within the last hundred years China's business circles had born separate class identities. Further, as industrial capitalism had never fully developed in the country, the native classes of capitalists and workers alike were formed "with Chinese characteristics" and did not resemble the earlier European bourgeoisie and proletariat. This situation is even truer in the market reforms that have revived or created an array of social groups and strata that did not exist or were eliminated in the Maoist universe of socialism. It is this re-sounding development that makes such a puzzle out of determining the nature of the reform under a communist regime.

Bureaucracy and Capitalism

There is surely nothing new about capitalism being sponsored by the state. In deconstructing the laissez-faire, Karl Polanyi (1957, 66) shows how the early capitalist economies were embedded in their political institutions and vice versa: that is, free trade owed much to state intervention to first be freed from the confines of privileged towns and, thereafter, to identify the state itself with the market in Europe. Nor is "state capitalism" at issue as in the cases of new economic policy in Soviet Russia ("capitalism without cap-italists") or East Asian developmental states ("capitalism with capital-ists").[4] The Chinese novelty lay in the phenomenon where the Communist Party enabled private profit seekers to grow from within its own ranks and apparatus. This unorthodox "legitimation" was nowhere anticipated, neither in Leon Trotsky's notion of "privileged bureaucrats" nor in Milovan Djilas's "new class"—not even in Mao's warning against "capitalist roaders."

The new "bureaucratic-compradore bourgeoisie" was only a part, albeit a mighty part, of China's transitional economy. This label was deemed old but readily transferable from its original reference to the monopoly over economy by the well-connected families under the GMD regime. Other actors included industrial and commercial "quasi-capitalists" who looked to be no more than remotely distant successors of the early national bourgeoisie. Easily identifiable are the classes and subclasses categorized by size, ownership, function, and "class-consciousness": small business people; entrepreneurs in the private sector; managers in the public sector; and (former) officials-turned-private-owners of sold SOEs. Among the latter three groups foreign links were common, yet these linkages were made without uniting them into the strongly nationalist, generic transnational capitalist class found in some other developing countries. The first category (*geti*, or the "petit bourgeoisie" in the Marxist terminology) was the least protected, yet it survived in a poorly regulated and also unequally competitive market environment. The second type (*minying*) was the most hopeful one for the advocates of the "middle-class thesis" of the civic and political virtue of free enterprises. The third group (*guoying* and *dajiti*), assumed to be the backbone of China's socialist market, had been steadily encroached upon, and its future depended on the next moves of reform to hold privatization at bay. The power holders of public offices in the fourth category (*guanying* or *guanshang*) along with their families and clienteles had posed the biggest threat to any conception of a socialist economy.

These groups coexisted and interacted uneasily both with each other and with the government. Indeed, they all were in one way or another dependent on the state. Compared with China's first national bourgeoisie in its unfavorable conditions, which, however, gained significant economic autonomy and initially displayed a degree of political leadership, present-day business classes obtained neither, despite the fact that their activities were now often beyond state control. In particular, bureaucratic capitalists, contributing to the transformation of the state itself, further blurred the public-private demarcation. In one of the ironies of contemporary Chinese development, the market transition designed to break down a bureaucratic command system had instead strengthened the place of bureaucrats and their crown princes and protégés (Meisner 1996, chapter 11). Quite a few of these bureaucrats held huge shares through abusing their government positions or taking over state firms and assets at a time when laws and rules were obscure with large loopholes. As money was sent to the private accounts in Swiss or U.S. banks, China's capital flight reached a level of a countercurrent to FDI, of which the loss through illegal means was estimated to be as much as 8 percent of China's annual GDP since the late 1990s.[5]

By enriching themselves through stealing public wealth, from outright corruption to more subtle forms of exploitation such as stock options, such cadre-managers combined in their hands political and economic power, as well as public and private power. Many also had foreign ties. This superclass embodying a pathological fusion between communism and capitalism is clearly distinguishable from the familiar agents of either state capitalism or a developmental state. One variant of state capitalism aside from that of the NEP and the NICs is defined in the postcommunist context as the subordination of firms to bureaucracy and the appropriation of market profits by state functionaries (Resnick and Wolff 2002). This definition stops working when such state functionaries cease to function on behalf of the state as in the case of management buyout Chinese style (which seems more of a "management buy-in," as pointed out by critics). As to the late development model, public and private societies/properties would be legally and normally separated despite cronyism, bribes, and the involvement of money in politics. The Korean *chabols,* for example, were strongly nationalist actors but also distinctly private in their collaboration with the state. The Japanese bureaucrats, likewise, engaged themselves in economic planning and organizing by "guiding" private corporations via various "deliberative councils" without mixing up the businesses of office with market transactions. The peculiar nature of the Chinese collusion between officials and businessmen was reminiscent of China's own semicolonial situations before 1949, of "dependent development" in part of the third world, and of "cadre capitalism" in postcommunist transitions.[6]

If the Chinese approach could initially be favorably compared with the Russian "loans for shares" scheme that resulted in an economic breakdown and the rise of oligarchs acquiring privatized national assets (Unger and Cui 1994), the comparison became problematic as authorized and unauthorized privatization proceeded into the late 1990s in China. The policy of "grasping the large, releasing the small" was abandoned to allow firms to be sold (even large and profitable ones), sometimes at giveaway prices. Qin Hui uses more recent evidence to show that China went further in privatizing its soes than did Russia, the Czech Republic, Hungary, and Poland. In some places (e.g., Zhucheng in Shandong), local state enterprises at the county level were all "sold out" through "insider deals" among managers and their personal networks. In Changsha, the capital of Hunan province, the property rights of three large, well-managed, and cost-efficient soes were swiftly "transferred" to their managers as private owners in 1999 to 2000 (Qin 2003).[7] This trend of "bureaucratic privatization" (Walder 1994) was rightly seen as sheer robbery by both the workers affected and the population at large. The Ministry of Finance called to suspend the trend in April 2003, and the State Council issued in January 2004 a circular on regulating ownership shifts and corporate mergers and acquisitions, which required law-abiding, public supervision as well as disclosure. However, things did not begin to change until Larry Lang, a Hong Kong based economist, investigated and revealed how a few giant model soes changed hands through irregular means (cf. Cui 2004). A heated public debate then followed, involving massive media reports and Internet protest, which by the end of the year forced the State Assets Supervision and Administration Commission to decide to halt the process. Approximately twenty million workers were already laid off and many were left without even a meager package of compensation. As a result of frequent violations of policy principles and directives, public funds accumulated through decades of hard labor was drained away, causing widespread protest. At issue was not the expansion of the private sector but the private embezzlement of public resources and the infusion of political and economic capital. As Maurice Meisner bluntly states, the "communist state breeds a bourgeoisie" to permit a market to function, which "ironically, could be performed only by the 'socialist' state itself" (1996, 336–37). Some other developing countries also had to create from scratch a class of capitalist entrepreneurs. China did so only more deliberately and effectively and, by logic if not intention, produced a virtual sector of bureaucratic capitalism betraying the state itself.

In light of this development, the Communist Party, a mass party that continued to recruit among young people, had to be repositioned because its own organization and ideology could not bypass the period's profound social changes. In a controversial speech on 1 July 2001, the party's eightieth birthday, General Secretary Jiang Zemin indicated that the ccp was ready to receive "private entrepreneurs." Numerous such quasi-capitalists had of course already been in the party as a result of the waves of those "going into the business sea" (*xiahai*) among former government functionaries and state-sector employees, many of whom had previously joined the party. Hu Jintao, then the PRC vice president, refined Jiang's proposal in terms of "absorbing excellent elements from the new social strata" while upholding strict admission standards. Quoting Jiang, he also restated that the party must regard its "members from the working class, the peasantry, intellectuals, soldiers, and cadres" as "the most basic components and backbone forces of the contingents of the party."[8] Jiang's proposal, as ideologically and politically inconsistent as the reform course itself, provoked angry opposition from the old guards who called for safeguarding the "proletarian" nature of the CCP. The party's liberal wing, on the other hand, argued that new social strata should be allowed to set up their own parties alongside the CCP. It was argued that the time had come for the communists to embrace more political pluralism beyond their archaic ruling structure.

To modernize the CCP, the doctrine of "three represents" had been propagated since 1998 and written in the party constitution of 2003, which states that the party represents "the demand of advanced productive forces, the direction of advanced culture, and the fundamental interests of the overwhelming majority of the Chinese people." Nothing was politically incorrect in this banal statement; rather it simply signaled that the party no longer even pretended to be the vanguard of the working class.[9] Predictably, Jiang was criticized throughout his tenure from all sides, and his "theory" was internally debated.[10] The intensity of ideological and political battles reflected problems as well as the intrinsic difficulty of the Chinese reform project in the context of capitalist globalization and communist demise in the former Soviet bloc. Jiang's younger successors were now under increasing pressures to regain the legitimacy of the reform. Although the work of reorienting social policies while surmounting bureaucratic pathologies is ongoing, still to be addressed is the need to repair rather than desert the weakened yet abiding social-national-developmental consensus.

State and Market

The institutionalization of reforms had been the main task of the market-facilitating state in China, of which industrial restructuring, despite local plunges, was on the whole moving forward cautiously by trial and error.[11] The fundamental change of China's political economy was an accumulative effect, starting with tax breaks and other incentives for foreign and private investors in the special economic zones as well as the "economic-technological developmental zones." These experimental links with the world market began to open up China economically and, to a lesser degree, politically (cf. Shirk 1994).[12] Local autonomy in foreign contacts and contracts was monitored by government agencies, though gradually foreign investment, trade, and joint ventures augmented their own autonomy, not just that of the SEZs. China's membership in the International Monetary Fund and the World Bank brought in large volumes of grants and loans to improve infrastructure without, notably, the "conditionality" attached in most other recipient countries. In shifting from a peculiar form of import substitution, export promotion was adopted to obtain, as optimistically intended, technological upgrading, quality control, and international competitiveness (cf. Chang and Nolan 1995).[13] Since 2001, China had been the fourth-largest trading economy in the world, with an export wing contributing to more than a quarter of the national GDP (as compared to 11.8 percent in 1989). By 2004, it became the third-largest trading economy, behind only the United States and Germany. In 2004 it grew sevenfold and reached a GDP per capita of $1,000; a remarkable feat given China's population size, which had in the past kept the country in the low-income category. The World Bank statistics for the late 1990s showed that China had moved into the second ranking destination for FDI (after the United States), and its foreign exchange reserve was so large (over $500 billion in 2004) that it violated the cost-benefit calculation of rational economics.[14]

The Corporation Law adopted in 1993 by the NPC was a landmark; according to the law, the state in state firms is no more than an investor and controller of its assets and stocks. Private and foreign investment may be accepted by the SOEs within a proportional limit (i.e., below 49 percent) and, in the case of failure, they will be permitted to declare bankruptcy. Going further, the constitutional amendments in 1992 and 1999 formally legitimized the private sector. The "individual business" (*geti jingji*) by "town and country laborers" and the private companies (*siying qiye*)—both preferably called a "people-operated" economy (*minying*)—are recognized as "important components of the socialist market economy" in the 1999 constitution. At the primary stage of socialism, the government protects their "legal rights and interests." The capitalists, who in the 1954 constitution were to be "used, restricted, and educated," were upgraded in 1999 to be "guided, supervised, and regulated" (as already had been stated in the 1988 amendment). This recognition, further, had been duly coded in various civil and criminal laws. "The inviolability of citizen's private property," which refers to lawful income, savings, houses, and other personal possessions, is postulated in Article 13. The sixteenth party congress in 2002 confirmed the protection of "legitimate work and non-work income" from labor, management (as "managerial labor"), technology (e.g., patents), and capital, including profits, shares, dividends, interests, and stock options.[15] The redefinition of "exploitation" to exclude "socialized entrepreneurship" and small business, derived from the "Wenzhou debate," had been reconfirmed. These legal, ideological, and policy moves continuously enabled a private sector to prosper.[16]

By 2001, many of the price control measures had been removed and only thirteen essential goods in public consumption remained under subsidies or monopoly. The degree of "marketification" was measured as 69 percent in 2003, which, as the Chinese government argued, was adequate to qualify China as a market economy.[17] Rapid expansion occurred in the nonstate sector (including also collective, cooperative, and shareholding firms), which held a growing portion of capital in stocks and contributed substantially to the economy.[18] The private sector—including big and small enterprises hiring workers; self-employment; partnerships; and family business without wage labor—made up a third of the national economy with more than two million firms in 2002, nearly thirty times that of 1989. Between 1990 and 2002, private entrepreneurs increased at an annual rate of 17.7 percent (Lu 2004, 241–45). A bolder estimation puts the figures as high as 60 percent for private contributions to fixed domestic capital investment by 2004. Seventy-five million jobs had been created in a quasi-private shadow economy. In fact, it is difficult to pin down accurately the size of public and private sectors alike. As the *Economist* noted on 20 March 2004, "some state businesses are, in effect, run on private lines by their management. Conversely, many firms labeled private by the official statistics . . . are in truth controlled by local government" such as TVES and employee-owned collectives. The confusion here is exemplified by the same observer's label for Pearl River

Piano, the world's second-largest piano maker, and Legend, China's major personal computer manufacturer, as "private" while for Haier, the nation's leading producer of household durables, as "collective." Yet, at the center of the restructuring debate they were all officially seen as model SOEs.

Meanwhile, powerful multinationals had made headway into the Chinese market and were obtaining access to China's commanding and high-tech industries, pushing state restrictions and controls steadily to the sideline. The rocky negotiations between the PRC government and the giant European and American developers over the management of the telecommunications industry, for example, were in actuality efforts to strike a balance between economic security and market benefits on the part of Chinese policymaking. Similarly, as intense trade liberalization had allowed foreign (and private) companies to enjoy tax and trading privileges to the extent of seriously disadvantaging the SOEs and domestic producers, policy measures to level the ground of competition were admitted to be in an urgent need. The restructuring package included 196 quasi-monopoly SOEs to be turned into market-oriented conglomerates that would be sufficiently competitive in a WTO-dominated environment. Except for the two thousand state enterprises to remain under state protection, eight million firms (of which one hundred thousand were SOEs) would be subject to a unified bankruptcy law.[19]

The astonishing speed of an economic autarky being transformed into an export-oriented and trade-dependent economy also brought about China's acute security concerns in a volatile global financial market.[20] The PRC had been portrayed in the media as a gigantic manufacturer of cheap consuming goods by low-paid labor. To comply with the WTO rules, it had to radically lower its tariffs (e.g., to zero on certain information technology products from the United States in a five-year period from 2001) and open its vitally important markets such as that for agriculture and personal computers. As many earlier demands on transferring technologies were no longer in place for foreign investment, and because over 80 percent of China's technology-intensive exports were produced or handled through foreign firms, "tech-nationalism" became a pressing issue (Chen and Yue 2003).[21] Foreign banks, already operating in China and in Chinese currency within a quota system, would be allowed to freely compete with domestic banks. The threat of fiscal instability was all too real in light of the recent

Asian financial crisis. Although China was the least hit in the region due to its macro and capital controls, the crisis still caused bankruptcy of a few large state investment companies and crashes in the inexperienced, poorly regulated stock market (cf. Nolan 2004, 49–59). Moreover, the "Chinese miracle" turned into disillusionment in the face of mounting social problems as a consequence of market integration. As the protective policies of labor—urban, rural, and "floating"—diminished at the same time that inequalities, injustice, and corruption grew pervasive, the notion of a worker and peasant state became a mockery.

A trigger in this process was the unintended twist of a decentralizing measure to "devolve political and economic power" (*fangquan rangli*): privatization (aided by globalization) corroded decentralization and effectively weakened central state capacity as well as central control over local government. The state treasury received 35 percent of GDP in revenue in 1978 but less than 12 percent in 2000, and roughly 20 percent in 2003.[22] The symptoms of a "weak state" logically hurt state-led development and threatened insecurity and disability. A compliant center vis-à-vis assertions and frauds at local levels in particular led to ineffective policy implementation detrimental to long-term national and social goals. Remarkably, China had so far preserved a nationally integral developmental project and retained its party-centered organizational integrity. Yet, like Maoist socialism, sheer contradictions also marked China's "socialist market economy," making its nature confusing and its future uncertain. Did the symbolic significance of the phrase—which replaced "socialist commodity economy" at the fourteenth party congress in 1992—reside in the word "market" rather than "socialist"? And did this adjective mean anything outside of the CCP rule? More concretely, did not the initial confidence among early reformers (as distinguished from later "revolutionary" globalizers) in the idea that China could "make use" of foreign capital and market mechanisms for its own socialist objectives prove to be wishful thinking?

There is no simple answer to these questions given the different aspects and tendencies in different perspectives and locations of China's development. The country's participation in the world economy was a multifaceted and open-ended undertaking. Stressing the contradictions, Carl Riskin, in disagreement with Maurice Meisner's pessimist portrait, notes that "[comparatively] early, capitalism did not have to deal with a healthy, long-lived and literate population steeped in powerfully egalitarian values" as was the case in China. Capitalist industrialization was not accompanied by an immediate general rise in living standards; nor did it expand in an age of global communication (1997, 14). Riskin's own research, meanwhile, shows a surge of household income disparity in the 1990s as China speeded its integration into the global web (Riskin and Khan, 2000). Theoretical debates of (in)compatibility between socialist principles and market logic will continue to engage thinkers and policymakers, particularly regarding the strong thesis that market socialism is not only superior to capitalism but also the sole form of socialism (Schweickart 1998). The question, however, is ultimately a practical one. Worth noting here is the historical factor that borrowing tools (money, knowledge, technology, expertise, etc.) had a traditional attraction and legitimacy in the modern Chinese consciousness since the failed "Westernization movement" featured a "*ti-yong*" doctrine. The "Chinese essence" (*ti*), now transformed into socialism, is hoped to absorb "foreign instruments" (*yong*) into an organic constituent of itself for its own purposes, a pattern that is inherent in late, uneven, and compressed development.

Globalization, in contrast to its passive reception or active rejection elsewhere in much of the third world (which can further be compared with the Eurasian "second world" of the former socialist countries), has from the outset of the Chinese reform been considered to be affordable as a calculated political decision. Surely the ideology of communist internationalism is no less "global" in its call for human emancipation and for workers to unite than that of the "bourgeois globalism" of market conquest. But real battles on the world stage have long been waged between internationalist capitalism and nationalist systems, socialist or otherwise, including welfare social democracies resisting "Americanization." Once borders could no longer be sealed, the only realistic option for an economy to be both open and secure seems to be "shallow integration" measured by state autonomy and a local ability to maneuver. An obvious advantage of China is its size, and hence it has a huge domestic market to support a middle path between the traditional approaches of import substitution and export reliance. The perpetuation of an export-dependent growth model is not only antithetical to China's real comparative advantages other than "cheap labor," but also costly to Chinese development in social terms as much as to the regional and world labor market (Lin 2005; Hart-Landsberg and Burkett 2004, 81–101). Only by altering this model could the existing global order, at stake in China, also be redressed.

The seemingly capitalist development was seen by some in China as a sensible return to the "new democracy" of a mixed economy (if not yet Mao's coalition government as proposed in 1945) that was overtaken by an "adventurist" socialist transition in the 1950s (Yan 1991). Others took Lenin's state capitalism after war communism as an analogy. Still others believed that, by political and economic logic, a full-scale "capitalist restoration" (assuming, problematically, a capitalist past in China) had been in operation (cf. Sun 1995; Dirlik 1998).[23] From a normative reform-socialist point of view, however, the new democracy argument does not offer a convincing explanation for the current globalizing conditions in which the aborted project of new democracy cannot be replicated. Likewise, the NEP in a surrounded, war- and poverty-ridden Soviet Russia was not so much a choice as a tactical and temporary retreat (though the Bukharin faction argued for its prolonged validity). In contrast, a market transition was articulated in China as a strategic advance; and, in this view, it was for China a magnificent victory rather than a defeat to have finally broken down the cold war blockade and surmounted the alleged "isolationism" that had carried on a closed political system ending in a deadlock in the mid-1970s. In other words, the reform initiative was a fundamental breakthrough, internally and externally, in the PRC history, aspiring to defy capitalist global homogenization and play a part in changing the rules of the game. The ambition was that financial capitalism would be countered so as to prevent a market meltdown caused by bubbles and speculation, as well as to permanently change the situation whereby core countries extract values generated in the peripheries. China could endorse institutional initiatives in creating an international regulating regime on capital movements as well as any other means of crisis prevention to reduce speculative transactions and short-term portfolio investment. An Asian Monetary Fund, for instance, might not be inconceivable, given the region's abundant financial resources yielded from high savings rates and accumulated foreign reserves. Already, a regional free trade zone had been contemplated as a counterbalance to WTO domination. Challenging the hegemonic "Washington consensus," a "Beijing consensus" featuring national autonomy, state capacity, human capital, and local innovation has been debated both inside and outside China.

Is this not utopian thinking, or even a mere pretension, on the part of the regime to avoid ideological rupture? Fredric Jameson (1996) is not alone in his opinion that the collapse of the Soviet Union was a result of the rush to "relink" with the world market.[24] The Chinese attempt was instead a partial delinking or a selective relinking in the faith that national and societal participants in world capitalism—itself in mutation—must strive not to subordinate to that order but to reconfigure it. If capitalism as the epochal context and condition is everywhere, it has also been to a great extent constantly shaped and reshaped both locally and globally depending on politics played out on the spot. Political determination, wisdom, and leadership of the contending forces at specific localities make a big difference. In this connection, we are reminded of the decisive role of the state in the rise of capitalism itself. As John Gray puts it, laissez-faire as an "Anglo-American singularity," a mere historical aberration, was never a natural happening but a political project to be centrally engineered, even coerced, as in Victorian England or the postwar United States (1998, 13, 17). After all, the Chinese knew only too well that commercial societies existed long before capitalist forces came into being—the market acquired its specific social forms somewhere in history. Even capitalism per se has no lawlike configurations. It could be, and has been, organized in different ways with different social consequences.

At issue, then, is how might "global linkages" be kept in check for national and local benefits as a matter of moral realism in search of an optimal balance between profits and needs, competition and cooperation, growth and sustainability, and prudence and innovation. To pursue such a balance, what could be more vital and effective than a socialist state supervised, supported, and enabled by a democratically organized citizenry? It is on this ground, on the demand for government responsibility, accountability, and efficiency that democracy makes concrete sense for the Chinese. This dimension is meanwhile a deliberate and crucial addition to Deng's incomplete definition of socialism in lofty terms of liberating the productive forces, eliminating exploitation, and attaining common prosperity. The idea that a market economy could rationally function within the parameters of socialism and that private and foreign businesses would be contained within China's political and legal framework does to some degree resemble Lenin's state capitalism or, for that matter, state socialism. The significance of the Chinese navigation, however, lies not in a compromise between the two conflicting systems but in the possibility of a market economy being molded to satisfy needs as the end, via profits as the means. In opposition to conventional wage labor as a commodity that is subject to exploitative pricing and other abuses in a free-wheeling labor market, the market should be reorganized in favor of direct producers. Public ownership and control can take multiple forms (e.g., universalized shareholding), and even private capital may be socially utilizable within an open system of dispersed and tradable property rights. Such are the concepts of a social or socialized market based on the socialization of capital, labor, technology, and information.[25] The Chinese approach is thereby also fundamentally distinguishable from that of the capitalist developmental states.

Curiously, policymakers in search of a socialist market in China have not looked into the price system as a decisive issue other than accepting the neoliberal doctrine of "getting the prices right," albeit gradually through a dual-track system. Or, more precisely, they regarded market prices as a threshold of the reform and were willing to cross it at all costs. What was confronted by the economists engaged in the "socialist calculation debate" in the 1930s and 1940s (Blackburn 1991), however, completely passed them by. In his famous polemic against Ludwig von Mises's objection that a socialist economy cannot rationally allocate its resources "based on a confusion concerning the nature of prices," Oskar Lange proposes two measures that he believes to be essential for a socialist economy to be practical. The first is to set up "accounting prices" that imitate market prices for the sole purpose of cost-benefit calculation. This "technical" point has not been picked up in contemporary debates situated in a different and far more complicated web of national and international economies. Lange's second proposal is concerned with wages in relation to profits, which retains its logical force for any market socialist contemplation today. Along with distribution of incomes, he considers another feature to distinguish a socialist economy from a capitalist one to be "the comprehensiveness of the items entering into the price system." That is, private producers do not usually include in the production cost the "social overhead" of the workers' welfare such as medical care and compensation for vacation, injury, or unemployment. In contrast, a public producer must evaluate all such services required for the workers' well-being to be taken into the cost accounts (Lange and Taylor 1938, 59–65, 99–106). Entirely new notions of value and surplus, inputs and outputs, wages and profits, and the like would then follow. In the years to come, serious attempts at a socialist market in China will have to revisit this pivotal issue of surplus retention (concerning workers in a national economy as much as that concerning nations in international production and trade). As various local experiments have been quietly underway, the ideas of "profit sharing," "labor hiring capital," "labor's property right" and democratic co-management are beginning to gain attention in policy research (cf. Wong 1995; Lu 2004).

Returning to the theme of alternative modernity, the rationality behind it was the conviction that capitalism as a ruthless and wasteful mode of accumulation would devastate the social and natural environment of human societies. Socialism built in backward countries was premised on anti-capitalism in the belief that it would be "more humane, more efficient and in some cases plausibly more resonant with national traditions" (Bunce 1996, 87). This desire had resurged among those who had experienced a transition in which a free market society could be so "free" that its members were left unprotected with minimal security. The human cost in such transitions is hardly justifiable. The point about market socialism yet to find its Chinese expression, then, is that the blind pursuit and supremacy of profits are a drag on as much as an engine of the market, and that a market economy cannot be healthy without being brought to rational human control. As Fernand Braudel (1977) has pointed out, capitalism's intrinsic tendency to monopolize is fundamentally antagonistic to free competition, and for that matter the free market cannot be the marker of capitalism. For Joseph Schumpeter, industrial expansion, entrepreneurship, and technological innovation are market rather than capitalist virtues (or vices); and he too sees no stable equation between the two systems.[26] It is not surprising then that the U-turn from "plan ideological" to "market ideological" (as opposed to "plan-rational" and "market-rational" as discussed in Johnson 1982, 19) did not bring about a "perfect market," which, of course, never existed (Appelbaum and Henderson 1992, 21). Instead, the turn, or the "market as salvation" assumption now as a "shared societal understanding" (Steinfeld 2004), destroyed much of the social commitment and its welfare foundation in the former socialist countries as well as in the PRC. However, if the battle is over elsewhere, it is not finished in China where the problems are so alarming and challenges so great that a reorientation is forcing itself

on the agenda. A historical opportunity for the Chinese rethinking of development is within reach and should be seized so as not to be lost again.

Toward *Xiaokang* Socialism

It was a time of high hope and optimism for the future of Chinese socialism
when the post-Mao leaders embarked on a course of reform socialism with a
popular (though not electoral) mandate. The confidence among friendly
foreign specialists was expressed in a booming literature produced after research access was gained as a result of the generally receptive and self-
reflexive postcultural revolutionary atmosphere. At this time, Edward Friedman remarks, in addition to power the CCP was "fighting over *how* to
develop a nation that could avoid the exploitation, dependence, and inhu-
manity of capitalism and imperialism"; and in this effort its "dedication to
seeking an answer through socialism" was "total" (1983, 148). Other writers
also considered the slogan "socialism with Chinese characteristics" to be "an
extremely important political symbol," even though it could be a symbol of
nationalism more than socialism (Townsend and Womark 1986, 394). As late
as in the early 1990s, a sympathetic observer could still identify the trends
toward a "social market" in which private profit-making would be limited
for public welfare (White 1993, chapter 8).

The actual reform trajectory nevertheless followed its own logic, and
given the tremendous pressures of ideological and institutional globalization, it was not "allowed" to adjust until it would meet the "standards" of
postsocialist transition set up within the framework of global capitalism. As
increasingly radicalized, the reform in effect legitimized much of what
socialism stood against in terms of values and practices. Workers, while losing state protection, found no space to organize themselves outside of official trade unions; and farmers remained in a situation of "taxation without
representation" (Bernstein and Lu 2003). Thus polarization, money fetishism, greed, and corruption poisoned social cohesion. As soon as the state of
hypergrowth began to take a heavy toll in the perceived common good of
society, the Chinese model slipped into its own destruction. It became at
the same time vulnerable to foreign dependency, private domination, rent
seeking, and short-term behaviors largely due to state failures. Unbiased
commentators would find that wherever the reform failed, the failure was
conceived in comparison not only with its earlier phase but also with cer-

tain pre-reform developments. It is extremely disturbing and ironic that a public good regime would have dismantled itself when the country is many times richer. The contrast between basic needs being minimally yet grossly met in a period of general scarcity on the one hand, and their neglect for a sizable portion of the population in the midst of accumulated wealth on the other, is daunting.[27] To be sure, it is no trivial matter that 1.3 billion people had been largely better off in their standard of living. Such gains, however, were stained and also held back by the negative social consequences of reform—above all the loss in human capital amassed over decades of hard work and arduous struggle. As what was intended to be a renewal of socialism turned out to be like a conversion to capitalist exploitation and polarization, a deepening crisis of political legitimacy following the Tiananmen event was ensured.

The Crisis of Reform

As I detail in the previous chapters, sheer contradictions were a feature of China's reform model. If the open policy enabled the PRC to break free from a cold war blockade, it also permitted the relinquishing of the country's autonomy and self-protection. The economic restructuring ended the overaccumulation achieved through the repression of wages and consumption, but it did not correctly tame the market, including the labor market and the financial and equity markets. A basic security maintenance system broke down in many areas without credible replacement. The market brought about immense opportunities and incentives in economic and innovative dynamism, but it eroded public control as well as services. The reform facilitated a mixed economy without reducing bureaucratic privileges, which, on the contrary, proliferated to be "normalized" in the marketplace. Having rejected misguided mass campaigns, the political reforms did not conceive of the need to restore the centrality of the people, let alone to establish a schedule to democratize the country's power structure. Instead the regime's unfulfilled social obligation worked to alienate it from the commons. The government had generally withdrawn from intervening in personal pursuits and privacy, and even tolerated an expanding public sphere and a voluntary sector. Yet it was ineffective in either implementing laws against crimes in the private sphere (e.g., human trafficking and domestic violence) or encouraging public participation in policy deliberation.

Indeed, the "new society" that took a bloody revolution to found looked pathological, explosive, and "old" as multinationals marched in; sweatshops mushroomed; insecurity for the jobless, old, sick and disabled increased; and the rich and poor became socially segmented.

There is, however, nothing inevitable in how China came to be where it is; and in a state-led transition, market failures are mostly the fault of the state. That is, disoriented reforms must be open to reorientation through political actions, whether by the authorities voluntarily or pushed by public opinion and social movements. It was already evident that the farther the policies moved away from the popular values of Chinese socialism, the stronger those values were popularly felt and reclaimed.[28] Nostalgia went deep to reconstruct a People's Republic that at one time was proudly independent of superpowers, its government was clean, its army was the model of "serving the people," its working men and women were dignified, and its life was meaningful without commodification and consumerism. After all, Chinese socialism as an alternative to capitalist modernization was a logical development of the Chinese revolution; and it developed within, as much as in defiance of, the epochal parameters of global capitalism. The achievements, failures, and limitations of the Chinese endeavor can to an important extent be explained by the catalysts and constraints in these fundamental historical conditions. The fact that a native or "sinified" socialist tradition has survived a postcommunist world speaks volumes to the revolution's lasting impact because of its indigenous origin, nationalist roots, and socialist outcomes. By the same token, the crisis of the current transformation is also considerably attributable to the transformative power of international capital fully armed economically, militarily, and ideologically with a penetrating network of global communications.

In 1978, when the pragmatist leaders replaced the Maoist faction, they vowed to renovate an ailing system that suffered ideological fanaticism, political repression, and scarcity of consumer goods, if not economic stagnation. The very term "reform" (*gaige*) indicated the objectives of correcting, improving, revitalizing—hence realizing rather than reversing—the socialist cause. As the market forces began to grow, a political shakeup was in the offing, calling to redefine the role of the party and to redesign state, economic, and legal institutions. The first ten years saw many successes, although the protest movement of 1989 already revealed that problems were brewing, mainly inflation and corruption. With the Tiananmen event as the demarcation (which coincided with the upheavals in Central and Eastern Europe), many of the earlier gains of the reform were lost in the next decade. It was the boost of further economic liberalization in 1992 that, by the second half of the 1990s, led to an urban reform accomplished by massive layoffs and rampant privatization. These developments departed from socialist self-adjustment and amounted to a near-"revolutionary" transformation aimed at repealing the Chinese revolution and socialist alternative. Intentionally or not, this was a work of China's own "rational agents" of capitalist globalization.

The reform had thus taken two successive but opposite steps—reformist socialism initially, and compliance with capitalist impositions afterward—before a third turn after a "long decade" from 1989 to 2003. The third step, if taken in all likelihood given the magnitude of China's present crisis, would be nothing less than a redefinition of the reform and development. Such a step, with broad national consensus, could forge yet even a newer social contract (after the Maoist and Dengist allocation of freedom and security, respectively) while rebuilding the country's national and social strength.[29] The concrete meaning of the third phase, however, would be worked out only by a collective search through open, informed, and widely acted out deliberation and experimentation. Neither yielding to the wto nor changing the composition of the party could be a responsible response to the crisis.

But why the mid-course turn of the reform? The pressure of globalization was no doubt intense; and for latecomers, the deeper the degree of integration of a country, the more it would be coerced to comply even at the expense of domestic benefits ("increasing returns" as a self-reinforcing process). It was not until the approach of the end of the cold war—with Gorbachev's fatal gait toward the disintegration of the Soviet Union, and hence the consolidation of U.S. hegemony—that the Chinese project of building a market-geared socialism fell apart. Meanwhile, there was the wild illusion among China's political and economic elites that all "global linkages" to the rules made in Washington would be positively correlated with their vested interests. Further still, Tiananmen in 1989 was a watershed not only because of its unparalleled shocks but also because of their unintended consequences, including the push for overall economic liberalization as a strategy to break off the post-1989 international trade sanctions against China. As other sources of regime legitimacy receded, development became the single "iron principle" (*yingdaoli*), as declared by Deng on his tour to Shenzhen in 1992. Even though this new form of developmentalism was tied with nationalism, the latter was necessarily compromised in one way or another in trade dependency, and together they sidelined socialism. In suppressing ideological controversy, Deng managed to contain inner-party political debate and dissent and thus pave the way for single-minded economic growth, which is considered by some China scholars as one of his "greatest accomplishments" (Naughton 1993, 501).

In the end, difficulties with reforming the core institutional establishment were so great that they seemed either unattainable or unaffordable. Urban reforms, in particular, entailed genuine threats of bankruptcy, unemployment, and financial turmoil. The students in Tiananmen Square reflected and anticipated these external and internal forces as they performed under the gaze of an encouraging global audience. As much as they were for patriotism and reform, they did not challenge the ideologies of globalization. The trick, however, was that the crackdown on the movement helped the government to gain price liberalization and had little to do with defending socialism. The damage to the CCP in this round was even greater than that of the Great Leap Forward or the Cultural Revolution. In the shadow of 1989 and the derailing of reform in the 1990s, the one sure thing was that debating where China was headed could no longer be avoided.

The Dystopia of Development

After two and a half decades of spectacular growth, China awakened to its horrendous cost and its ultimate social and natural limits (cf. Smil 1993; Wu 1999; Edmonds 2000).[30] While some of the predicaments were traditional (e.g., overpopulation relative to the arable land and oversupply of labor) and some were modern (e.g., industrial pollution and the ecological hazard of urbanization), all had been intensified by the market transition. At the heart of the problem, as succinctly noted by Wen Tiejun, was "a peasant society seeking industrialization in a labor-abundance and resource-scarce economy" (1999, 3).[31] The shortage of most mineral deposits, oil fields, and other mining resources no doubt contributed to China's increasing dependence on foreign energy supplies, which indeed also generated the fear of future conflict between China and its competitors over raw materials.

According to official statistics widely circulated in government documents, publications, and the mass media, China's per capita land by 2003 was less than one third of the world's average. Its cultivated land—measured at a scant 0.085 hectares per capita, and ranked at a low of 126 out of 140 countries—still was in constant diminution. A total of 2.54 million hectares of farmland were lost in 2003 alone. The country's forested land had been so depleted that at a per capita 0.11 hectares, it was considered to be one of the worlds sparsest (ranking 107 out of 140). Desertification too was at a pace of more than 10,000 square hectares yearly, with desert covering nearly 28 percent of the PRC territory. The level of serious air pollution was also rising, in part due to coal combustion, which remained a primary energy source in China. Water pollution was such that the drinking water supplies for 600 million people were substandard, and two thirds of the total number of Chinese cities were short of water. Many rivers dried up, and phrases such as "the mother river Yellow is crying" or "the river runs black" made newspaper headlines. According to the 2002 China human development report, air and water pollution has caused increased incidences of respiratory deaths and chronic illness such as cancer. The nation's capacity to protect the environment has lagged behind the speed of destruction (UNDP 2003). Finally, China's contribution to greenhouse gases, especially from carbon emissions, was at a level considered appalling (Nolan 2004, 27–30).

Meanwhile, the demographic situation was no less disturbing. The country was aging at a rate faster than that of any other major nation, as its median age, thirty-two years in 2004, was projected to soar to forty-four in 2040. "China will get old before it gets rich," the *New York Times* noted on 30 May 2004. Chinese sociologists had warned that the magnificent achievement in rising longevity (a life expectancy of over seventy-two years) and falling fertility had also produced a population time bomb in the context of the 1979 one-child policy and the terrifying male-to-female sex ratio of 118 to 100 (census 2000).[32] Labor Minister Zhang Zuoji reported to the NPC in 2003 that about thirteen million people had entered the labor market annually in recent years and the number was expected to escalate to a peak in the tenth five-year-plan period. Some twenty-two or twenty-three million urban jobs would thus have to be created each year, yet even in the currently overheated economy there had been a deficit of at least fourteen million. Indeed, an intrinsic obstacle to slowing down growth (the "soft landing") was the imperative of job creation in an economy with surplus labor, urban and rural combined, estimated at no less than three hundred million people. Further, to continue to increase growth by counting on the huge expansion of service industries could not solve the problem of structural unemployment, which instead followed an even sharper upward curve.

In rethinking development, a growing consensus in China's post-2003 mood of reforming the reform was the need to adjust the social and ecological costs of the developmental pattern. By implementing the Environmental Impact Report Law (2002) that required expert ecological assessment and public approval for all development projects, the State Environmental Protection Administration (SEPA) had adopted more resolute measures and a stream of new concepts ranging from animal rights to ecosocialism. The scattered green NGOs started to work together to form a united pressure group for policy change. Most remarkably, the two levels, governmental and nongovernmental, sometimes coordinated with each other. In early 2004, the Beijing-based organization called the Green Earth Volunteers was informed by SEPA officials about the plan to dam the Nu River in Yunnan province—a project that was believed to be harmful to a pristine area and local ways of life, mostly those of ethnic minorities. In response, organized efforts resulted in the State Council's halting of the project in order to submit it to SEPA for further scientific and public scrutiny. This incident was seen as a milestone for China's green social movement as well as its green policies.[33]

"Developmentalism" in its existing signification was thus criticized for its single-mindedness and nonsustainabilility, which differed from the developmental imperative (discussed in chapter 2) of the three-pillar foundation of Chinese modernization. The term "developmentalism" might have earned its prominence first with Raul Prebisch and his UN Economic Commission for Latin America, which opted for import substitution without expected success (and its failures were misjudged in textbooks as miserable and inevitable). Late development in Japan and the Asian NICs revived the debate around export promotion and the model of a developmental state. In China, as in twentieth-century socialist experiences on the whole, development logic is rooted in the unexpected historical condition of socialism and backwardness, and the mission of socialism overcoming backwardness. This mode would continue as long as the Chinese alternative is held up to refuse conformity with the world's hegemonic political economy and culture. In other words, rethinking development in China cannot imply renouncing development as such on either ethical or environmental grounds. The grand social need of economic development remains very real and justifiable.

In Search of a Vision

For China's development trajectory a likely turning point, as noted above, is embarking on the third stage of reform. To be sure, Hu Jintao and Wen Jiabao did not come to power through a popular electoral mandate and had thus far made no clear break with certain previously misguided methods and policies. Political repression continued, as did privatization and deregulation. But these leaders also began to address mass discontent while reevaluating the reform path. Also promised were what had been specified as "democratic" elections, decision making, management, and supervision. The prospect of "pushing forward first inner party democracy and then people's democracy" and "broadening citizens' rights and participation" filled both the official and semi-official media since the NPC convention in 2003. The Hu-Wen team also vowed to correct growth excesses and follow a people- and nature-friendly development model. To do so, party and state cadres were called to regain humility and prudence in a straightforward and upright working style, which was insisted on by Mao at the threshold of the communists turning themselves from the revolutionary to the ruling position.[34] Some promising changes had taken place: apart from introducing the notion of a "green GDP," legal and policy revisions were sought so as to improve workplace safety, retrieve unpaid wages, cancel agricultural tax, protect migrants, expand social security (especially provisions in rural public health), and cultivate the domestic market.

Compiling a system of computing a "green GDP" is a long-waited response to the predicament of a high-cost, resource-hungry, and export-dependent approach to development. The SEPA and the State Statistics Bureau are preparing for socioeconomically and environmentally integrated indicators—such as pollution levels, water and other resource consumption, and job loss—to go along with those of growth. Further, a few provincial/municipal governments (Beijing, Shanghai, Guangdong, and Zhejiang) have been selected to apply experimental calculations of growth, which will also be used to evaluate the performance of local officials. This proposal is part of a new, "scientific" conception of "people-oriented, comprehensive, coordinated and sustainable development," which aims at "all-round human development, . . . high productivity, affluent life and [a] sound eco-system by properly balancing urban and rural development, development among regions, economic and social development, development of man and nature, and domestic development and [the] opening to the outside world."[35] Although such efforts are still short of being a grand vision of socialism for a missing dimension of democracy, redefining development is nevertheless an honorable and ambitious goal in a country of China's size and in the face of its formidable obstacles.

The official statements about readjusting development deserve serious treatment here because they are both imperative and practicable with a public backing, and because they have opened a fresh terrain for a social imaginary and creative politics, notably the politics of nature, nurture, and leisure. The new possibilities could be captured in the still-to-be-drawn blueprint of *xiaokang* socialism.[36] The idea of *xiaokang* is as ancient as that of *datong*, or great harmony, cherished in the Book of Rites; they complement each other in a utopian agrarian communism.[37] What potentially makes *xiaokang* a futurist "big idea" to be adapted to modern Chinese ideals is the space it instantly provides for envisioning a market socialist society in a postcommunist world. Within a market economy of large-scale socialized production and service, there must also be nonmarket, nonprofit, and decommodified sectors at local-regional and community levels. This line of thinking comes quite naturally to the Chinese, given the host of their traditions of local autonomy, self-reliance, cooperation, and diverse productive and caring methods. Yet it suggests no simple restoration of past practices. *Xiaokang* socialism is rather a matter of creative politics of the present, premised on a pragmatic approach toward valuable human experiences, ancient or recent, native or foreign, once celebrated or abandoned. Politics, as Ashis Nandy insists, is nothing less than a means of identifying a society's selfhood by renegotiating the distribution and legitimacy of power in different spheres of life, in which the "moral choices" of people at the grassroots take precedence (2003, ix).

Here, *xiaokang* socialism might be outlined in four intertwining components: community, security, integrity, and democracy. Community is a core idea not only in various premodern traditions in China but also in Maoist socialism, which blends traditional, modern, and "postmodern" (e.g., de-specialized, antibureaucratic) ways of living. After all, the Chinese revolution was part of a modernization project with a strong sinified meaning of antiformalism. That project was not merely, or even mainly, about industrialism, central planning, and legal-rational bureaucratization. Unlike both the Weberian instrumental reason of democratic modernism and the Soviet "authoritarian high modernism" (Scott 1998, chapter 3), Chinese socialism was more rural based, decentralized, and even deliberately patrimonial in its ethos of disregarding a Western-clocked "world time." It did not destroy the communities other than the most repressive clan patriarchalism, but rather revitalized them in the communes and work units. Even post-Mao industrialization heavily and unconventionally featured the TVEs, small towns, and mini cities. Treating "earthbound China," as the sociologist Fei Xiaotong describes it, as a developing as much as a communist country is therefore a methodologically sensible choice (Riskin 1991). Whether China should also follow the usual path to urbanization is debatable; the point is that modernization processes have profoundly transformed, yet did not totally disintegrate, its urban and rural community-based patterns of work, life, and nurture. These communities retained their basic strengths in the Chinese political economy.

This is a general, empirically testable background against which *xiaokang* after state socialism can be contemplated (Lin 2004). As an idea, xiaokang socialism will prize direct producers as participants in socialized production as well as locally organized activities both within and outside of the market, including voluntary sectors and nonmoney exchange.[38] In line with self-management beyond the ability of central planners, the adjective "direct" is important in characterizing producers, providers, and consumers intimately engaged in socially useful productive, circulating, distributive, and service sectors. The notion of direct producer, not the same as self-employment, is also an alternative to wage labor defined in the capitalist market of alienation and exploitation. Without redeeming a closed society, the physical and spiritual health of human society and human flourishing may better rely on rationally managed local resources for locally stimulated needs, even in a market age of global interdependence. One instant implication here would be the absurdity of the notion of "cheap labor" in the framework of the FDI production for foreign export and Fordist assembly lines. Another such implication is the necessity of policies to stimulate and protect small businesses in the domestic markets. Also implied would be democratically reached decisions in accordance with undistorted needs (or in any case less distorted than commercial "demands") and local knowledge over market dictation. Direct producers can therefore control the surplus of their own labor through various institutional arrangements to minimize alienation and exploitation. They may well consume part of their own products (goods and services), a mode of consumption that reduces cost, pollution, and waste inevitably generated in long-distance transportation and multimediated trading distortions. This would also be a critical contrast with statism in its worst-ever form of abusing power. Meanwhile, mutual help networked in the neighborhood and communal settings, with or without market values, could become ever more widespread as a substantive component of a reciprocal "caring economy" or a "solidarity economy." Ecological gains in the "organic" and nature-friendly ways of production and consumption could be duly expected.

Universal material security would form a material foundation of a *xiaokang* society, of which the institutional form is yet to be invented. Such a security base might progress from the current "three-line" scheme of ensuring pension, unemployment benefits, and a basic living allowance for urban residents and land use rights in the countryside. A visible merit of *xiaokang* is that alongside governmental obligations, a "welfare society," in contrast to a welfare state, neither presupposes abundance nor requires expensively and bureaucratically administered provisions. Having amply reached a developmental stage in which it makes both economic and moral sense to overcome insecurity and poverty, the main barriers in the Chinese path to prosperity are no longer the constraints of underdevelopment but rather political adversaries. Such adversaries, given China's path-dependent development, should not be insurmountable. The distant debates in Europe over a guaranteed basic income might one day find themselves learning from the Chinese, who would fashion a form of such income as an answer to structural unemployment and demographic and land pressures. It is certainly also a rightful socialist response to the "lumpenproletarianization" typical of "*capitalism* and backwardness." Only with social security for all can a society enable full activity without full employment, disregarding the differences between the formal workforce and an informal sector, paid and unpaid labor, and regular and flexible job contracts. The notion of "social wage" is the key that separates conceptually and institutionally the income from the price of labor sold in the market.

These steps will then help individuals develop multiple skills and wide-ranging intellectual, cultural, and artistic interests by gradually liberating them from the drudgery and routine of uncreative, repetitive, or tedious jobs. An entire terrain for experiments could thus be opened in which life may not yet be without toil, but will be more humane (as opposed to mechanical), free, and ability-enhancing with increasingly fewer narrow and rigid tasks. In the same process, also transformed will be the perceptions, attitudes, desires, career patterns, and lifestyles of working men and women who, meanwhile, gain time for social capital and political participation. The reduction in hours of the legal workweek from forty-eight to forty-four in 1996, and forty since 1998, has already made a profound impact on Chinese society. The "future of work" and the "politics of time" as debated in the West and the quests for alternative developmental paths in the global South are both pertinent to the Chinese condition, in which pre- and post-industrial maladies intertwine.

There is a wealth of indigenous sources of *xiaokang* socialism that await exploration. China's once iconoclastic political and intellectual classes are yet to take pride in their country's cultural treasures buried indiscriminately in revolutions, industrialization, and commodification.[39] And they may do so not abstractly (e.g., without appreciating valuable elements in the preserved traditions at the grassroots) or opportunistically (e.g., short-sighted "patriotic propaganda" campaign). To rebuild the Chinese subjective self in all its diversities and wisdoms requires honesty, confidence, and sophistication. As such we must also carefully look into the socialist legacies, especially the Maoist ambiguity of "anti-modernism" (or "critical modernism") against statism and capitalism. That is, the Chinese project of alternative modernity would contain not only a revolutionary break with the past but also a reinvention of the modern by removing its statist and capitalist prerequisite. Its utter self-contradictions notwithstanding, there are cogent traces to be critically identified in the Maoist tradition of decentralism, populism, multidimensional development, and multifunctional community. These traces are in opposition to the rigid division of labor, and are anti-bureaucracy and anti-alienation, as expressed in Mao's rejection of the "three great distinctions." But Mao is only one in a line of thinkers in utopian, anarchic, "petty bourgeois," or moral economy socialism. However flawed and defeated Maoism had been, even failed struggles have had a cause and reason, and may leave invaluable legacies and lessons for the next round.

Path-Dependence and Path-Breaking

As argued above, the initial model of China's transition was premised on the possibility that a socialist market could employ foreign capital and import managerial skills and technologies without sacrificing the sovereign interest of the Chinese nation and people. The desired strategy also aimed at revising those global parameters that hurt disadvantaged nations in the developing world. However, the actual course of the reform led to a state retreat in public management and services, the fusion of private profits and bureaucracy, and the fragmentation of both the authorities and the society. As significant market transactions often evaded the regulation by laws and rules that themselves were insufficient, decentralization in many areas became indistinguishable from privatization, thereby impairing the original objects of reform. Predictably, as Charles Tilly warns, "to the extent that it undermines the capacity of states to deliver on their commitments to citizens, the globalization of the world economy and polity will weaken both citizenship and democracy" (1996, 236). If the reform was designed to be a negation of, while also based on rather than superseding, Maoist socialism (thus a "negation of negation," taking socialism as the first negation of a pre-1949 "old society"), in actuality it slid into a sidetrack no longer exemplifying the Hegelian dialectic of progress. As the reform began to radicalize to the extent of allowing elements of a (counter)revolution, its own turn to be negated came along. The pledge of returning to the fundamentals of a socialist reform while correcting developmentalist wrongs marked the beginning of the next "negation of negation." This other attempt to remake socialism once again in China, would then be path-dependent on traditional and revolutionary as well as reform socialist experiences.

"Path-dependence" or institutional inertia is a useful insight of historical institutionalism. Apart from the truism that "history matters," path-dependence is also explained by "increasing returns": the farther a path is taken, the more difficult it might be changed, due to transaction costs and limited chances of timing. The institutional matrix, formal and informal, limits the "free choice" of actors (cf. North 1990, 44, 115–16; Arthur 1994; Peters 1999, 68–70).[40] What makes these commonsense expositions more interesting is the borrowing from non-Darwinian macroevolutionary theories. The ideas, for example, of contingent pathways in "punctuated equilibrium" and "multiple equilibria" explains hybrid-turned-stable beings (species and social phenomena alike) after the interruption of (ecologically or socially) accumulative trivia by sudden and rapid changes (Gould 2002; cf. Krasner 1984, 223–46). Such revolutionary episodes stand in the way of reductionist notions of one-dimensional and steady progress. In thinking about continuity, contingency, revolution, and agency, China's path must be open to "hybrid" formations (as described in the available cognitive frameworks and language), which may contain unprecedented potentialities. Alternative paths that are not yet taken might be "seen" in counterfactual and imaginative possibilities, especially in our times of great radical transformations and uncertainties.[41] Indeed, as Charles Taylor writes, "it may easily be that the road taken has excluded other roads [which] would also have conferred great benefit," assuming a positive yet in many ways also questionable modern development. "This is what all those suspect who sense that modernity has come at great cost—be it proponents of an ethic of heroism (Tocqueville, Nietzsche), of a fuller and more intense community (Rousseau, Marx), of a greater communion with nature (the Wordsworthian tradition), of a sense of transcendence (Hopkins, Chateaubriand). Each of these lines of criticism may be right, as well as others" (1999, 163).

By applying historical institutionalism in "transitology," a study of European postcommunist politics identifies its "triple past" of communism, precommunism, and "exit" (i.e., regime changes to various degrees), which exercised causal influence in the region. The study (Elster et al. 1998) argues that the past can shape the faiths and norms, constrain choices and behaviors, provide comparative examples for institutional rethinking, and serve as a repertoire of arguments in political discourse (35, 60–62). Although similar mechanisms are also at work in China, the Chinese path differs markedly from those of its exsocialist counterparts. Compared with many East and Central Europeans, for whom communism was an outside imposition, most Chinese do not perceive any precommunist "golden era" to which they would want to return. Another conspicuous difference is, of course, the persistent eccentric position of the ruling CCP, which has not found itself in competition with any opposition parties. Chinese communism has displayed far more resilience than the former Soviet satellites. The fact that the Chinese revolution was indigenous and China's postrevolutionary regime had not depended on Moscow is important. But it cannot ever fully explain why Chinese nationalism could still mobilize in a way distinct both from the nationalist movements on the ruins of the Soviet empire and from "subaltern nationalism" in parts of the postcolonial world (cf. Hardt and Negri 2000, 105ff). There apparently are other explanatory variables around an unbroken "Chinese wall" of institutional legacies and social rules (Bowles and Dong 1999).

By allowing for convenience an oversimplification in a schematic categorization of the past, we can clarify from where the country moved as well as where it might be moving. In a broad picture of the active impact of history, we may identify the following paths: prerevolutionary traditions; revolutionary legacies, including those of the republican revolution; the Maoist model of socialist transformation; and market reforms in conjunction with capitalist global integration. Concerning the first path, the premise that the PRC was founded on a revolutionary break with the past is no doubt only a relative judgment. Traditional spaces and boundaries—cultural, political, and territorial—as a burden or asset, as sources of resistance or renovation, are a given, however mutable and situational they might be. The second path, the revolution, is linked to the notion of a "post-revolutionary regime" that is the antithesis of what has been rejected in the old society. Memories can fade and recollections be reordered, and even the revolution's participants may falter as the pride wears off. But monumental history, rewritten time and again, may still not be erasable, especially at a time of nostalgia when some unacceptable prerevolutionary conditions have been restored. Likewise, the third path, that of socialism, seemingly vanished in the twenty-first century, traverses the reform path itself. The continuities and discontinuities between the two eras have been discussed in previous chapters. A classical case of an unaffordable transaction cost—that is, where there would be too much to lose for too many people—has so far guarded the reform agenda against wholesale integration or subordination. Since global capitalism is now considerably embedded in the Chinese political economy with local, private, and foreign dealings frequently bypassing central government regulations, the fourth path, that of reform, is still unfolding and is the least definable. The concurrence of these four paths—uneven, compressed, and subject to contingent disruptions—restrains as much as stimulates China's future development.

Concerning the reform path, only a "selective globalist" approach may permit China to actively ride on, rather than be swept by, the tide of globalization. Socialism, after being made and unmade, could still be remade. This point is not so obvious in the *jiegui* fever when, for example, progressive Chinese intellectuals were busily reading John Rawls while failing to note their splendid indigenous heritage of egalitarian justice. Similarly, a bizarre tendency in women's studies depicted a need to "localize Western feminism" as though women's liberation never existed in China and gender equality was a new importation from the West. There is nothing to romanticize about the pasts—their importance is no more than the force of their residues in the present. An outstanding case with such force of China's paths, on which its development depends with "increasing returns," is the role of the state as a market facilitator as well as a national planner. Charles Lindblom is certainly right: "That as of today the world has never seen a democratic central planning state does not at all deny that it too may be possible" (2001, 226–27). As I argue in chapters 3 and 4, it is necessary to form on the one hand a government politically and financially capable of managing the market transition, and on the other hand a democratic public equipped to hold the government accountable and the market socially beneficial. The state and its regulatory and law-enforcing institutions are both responsible and instrumental for the success of reform.

In speaking of a modern alternative to capitalism, China's greatest comparative advantage (other than market competition), in line with its latent privilege of backwardness, is its ability inherited from the communist revolution of a developmental strategy alternative to the disastrous capitalist mechanism of competing for cheap labor and the world's limited energy resources. Path-breaking that takes place in the midst of a path-dependent development would not only be desirable as a Chinese choice but also the country's only way out of poverty, dependency, and impending conflicts with other importers of bottleneck materials. This defiant openness cuts into Roberto Unger's notions of "false necessity" and "deep structure" of institutional fetishism. He may have overstated the "plasticity" of established systems and institutions, but a determined "transformative politics" indeed transforms existing models and their predicted destinies (1997, chapter 8).[42] The outcomes of globalization are contingent on what is being globalized in whose interest, and how it is transmitted globally and appropriated locally.[43] In this sense, it is no exaggeration to say that for its sheer scope, complexity, and importance, the ongoing transformation in the PRC "represents something akin to a laboratory for social science" (Little 1989, 3). In particular, the Chinese case holds "the promise of making a significant impact on theory-building in political science" concerning the transition debate over state socialism (Harding 1994, 701).

Path-breaking does not happen automatically (as in natural evolution) without political will and complex politics. One cannot cross a river by touching the stones without seeing or knowing the bank on the other side. The compatibility between a socialism worthy of its name and a market in healthy function is nowhere proven but is a formidable task to accomplish, if ever possible. Worth stressing again is "China" being never a unitary entity without boundless local particularities. Rural China remains a world away from urban China, as does the inland from the coast, the minority regions from the rest of the country, and so on. As "space becomes a central category of explanation" no less than time (Harvey 2000, 83), any conceptual compass will have to be sufficiently inclusive. Carl Riskin concludes his monograph on China's political economy with a remark (in the late 1980s) that the PRC is not the first country to pursue a historical compromise between backwardness and socialism: "But with vastly more people than its predecessors, a still more backward starting point, and a new world of technology to contend with, China must find its own path." Its future will be unprecedented. Yet, as Riskin also observes, "where Mao kept alive Utopian principles to light the distant goals but failed to chart the way there consistently, his successors focus on the immediate footsteps ahead but neglect the goals" (1987, 310–11). The missing clarity in the post-Mao development, however, reflects a more fundamental inability, a more historically sanctioned limitation, than mere "losing sight." After all, a socialist market system is still unparalleled in the human journey, only to be discovered after the "end of history."

Socialism the Specter

Socialism is presently so out of fashion that even socialists themselves now tend to consider the term anachronistic. Eric Hobsbawm, depressed by the catastrophes of the "age of extremes," predicts that "the debate which confronted capitalism and socialism as mutually exclusive and polar opposites will be seen by future generations as a relic of the twentieth-century ideological Cold Wars of Religion" (1994, 564). The language of socialism is also virtually lost in the functional equivalence between socialist and capitalist systems in their modern productive and technological transformation. As the global forces are ever more penetrating in spite of the resurgence of nationalism, communalism, or forms of "civilizationalism," communism in its failures is seen as either a shortcut or a long detour to capitalism. But a crude social science confined to a superhistorical "timeless present," in which market capitalism and liberal democracy must go together to qualify and signify modernity, is implausible (cf. Toynbee 1954, 420–21). At issue is not defining "socialism" and "capitalism" with their many varieties respectively, but rather the conflation of capitalism and the modern standards. The fact that capitalism has historically been linked to imperialism toward poor countries, and toward native peoples and cultures, remains testimony to the fallacy and hypocrisy of equating capitalism with modernity, globalization with national development. Both sides of these mistaken equations are meanwhile impoverished by a missing space for internationalism in its nineteenth-century communist commitment to workers of the world to be united.

In China's social-national-developmental triad, the attempted alternative was, in its historical sequence (and despite a lingering second phase of reform), to colonial modernity, Stalinism, and the neoliberal package of transition. Each of the models being resisted—foreign domination (colonial modernity), bureaucratic statism (Stalinism), and market fundamentalism (neoliberal globalization)—must be seen as the antithesis of development as well as democracy. For all its grave failings, Chinese socialism did not conform to the "master" course and discourse of modernity; it was doubly alternative to both historical communism and peripheral capitalism. In other words, modern Chinese paths had long defied the orthodox in which non-capitalist developments are deemed pathological deviations. For the Chinese people, rather, being modern implied development as overcoming capitalist injustice, domination, and underdevelopment, a choice made during a century of liberation struggle. It is their determination, pressuring the government, that may rationally bend the market logic of capitalism and the state logic of communism. The search, successful or not, will continue with an open conception of history.

With a sense of tragedy, we can see in Chinese development, how growth becomes more costly when many old obstacles to it, external and internal, have actually receded. It is under this condition that socialism retains its immediate relevance. "Cheap labor," as noted, could be a potential comparative advantage only in an exploitative global market. Likewise, polarization or "internal colonization" might be tolerated elsewhere but must not be in a socialist market. Socialism will be there to stay if human lives and life's capabilities must be safeguarded and cherished, and their destruction opposed and prevented. The classical distinction between socialism and capitalism, as that between production for profits and for needs, is crystal clear; but the Chinese people will activate this distinction with practical clarity. That capitalism does not have an answer to China's and the world's fundamental problems is what sustains the quest for alternatives.

China's unique "postsocialist" path is conditioned on the prevention of another revolutionary rupture. The term "postsocialism," like other "post" prefixes (or "the third way," and so on), is a negative signifier—more descriptive than prescriptive—of where the process has departed from but not where, properly named, it is moving toward. Yet in its linguistic and conceptual inference, it simultaneously indicates a continuation and a disruption of conventional socialism, thereby having also a positive connotation, even a causal connection with its predecessor.[44] Postsocialism must therefore also imply postcapitalism, as even at a "primary stage" socialism by definition is already postcapitalist, no matter whether or not in a given locality there was any actual capitalist development before the socialist. If socialism is no longer a coherent metatheory of politics, "its articulation still premises a non-return to capitalism" (Dirlik 1989, 364).[45] The nature of the ongoing transformation in China is yet to be determined. The reform movement, however, cannot go very far without specifying an aspiring vision. To ask whether China has a future in socialism, or whether socialism has a future in China, is thus to press for a vision in an open-ended transformation of Chinese society.

Intellectual reflections on the Chinese trajectory need to go beyond denouncing the dark side of the revolutionary and socialist past, a past that also was stamped by a long march for liberation. E. H. Carr wraps up his thinking of Soviet Russia by reminding us that "the danger is not that we shall draw a veil over the enormous blots on the record of the Revolution, over its cost in human suffering, over the crimes committed in its name. The danger is that we shall be tempted to forget altogether, and to pass over in silence, its immense achievements" (1978, 25). The same can be said about the Chinese revolution and socialism.[46] Even though nationalism and developmentalism at times prevailed at the expense of socialism with all that followed, repression of freedom included, socialism has remained the flagship throughout China's modern journey. Heroic struggles on that journey are haunting in the Chinese collective consciousness at a time of confusion when it seems as though the (socialist) revolution must strike the third time. The past thus cannot pass and only becomes a specter in the present.

NOTES

Introduction: The Making and Remaking of the Chinese Model

1. An easy objection is that the nationalist party, the Guomindang (GMD), the rival of the communist party, did better in Taiwan in terms of both economic and political developments. Any balance sheet of comparative evaluation here, however, will have to take into full account the vital role of cold war geopolitics. A huge amount of American aid was transferred to its Asian allies and the U.S. market was also open only to such allies, in stark contrast with military threats and economic blockade against the communist regimes in the region.

2. Orville Schell, for example, sees China's path as experimental and ambiguous, guided by a "stealth strategy" that was "a curiously leaderless form of reform" without knowing where it was headed (*Straits Times*, 13 December 2003).

3. It is significant that the CCP had sustained some support from the younger, more-educated generation. From 1990 to 2003, 125,000 students and young teachers at the university campus in Beijing joined the party, and about 7 percent of undergraduates and 30 percent of graduates were party members. The Communist Youth League had a membership of 71.07 million in 2003, which was in 230,000 general branches and 2.55 million grassroots groups (Xinhua News Agency: http://xinhuanet.com.cn). In 2002, 17.5 percent of party members were female, 6.2 percent were minorities, and 22.3 percent were under thirty-five years old. In the same period, 124,000 members had been expelled mainly for corruption charges (*People's Daily*, 2 September 2002).

4. I feel intensely uneasy writing these words, not because communism has become anachronistic, but because the CCP is ever farther away from any communist commitment. In this sense, "the CCP has turned China into its hostage—the death of the party would imply the death of the country." (L. Wang 2004, 19). However, I see no evidence that the situation cannot be reversed.

5. This concept was revived to serve post-Mao critiques of "ultra-leftist" adventurism and the argument for making up the missed opportunity of a "new democracy." See Su Shaozhi and Feng Lanrui discussed in Misra 1998, 91–103.

6. Deng Xiaoping warned against inequalities: "If we go for capitalism, it's possible that some will become rich but the majority would stay in poverty. China would then face the problem of revolution" (1994, 229). "Common prosperity is the greatest superiority and manifests the nature of socialism. Polarization, on the other hand, will cause serious conflicts between nationalities, regions, classes and the centre and localities" (364). It is worth noting that Deng believed that market reforms would not lead to polarization and that "millionaires would be very hard to be produced in our socialist system" (quoted in *People's Daily*, 15 September 1986). This sentence was later removed from his *Selected Writings*.

7. See Joshua Cooper Ramo's report on recent innovation in China of "a development approach driven not by a desire to make bankers happy, but by the more fundamental urge for equitable, high-quality growth—because no other formula can keep China from exploding." Privatization and free trade, for instance, would "be approached with incredible caution" (*Financial Times*, 6 May 2004). What he calls the "security

doctrine" along with the factor of human capital strongly echo what has been widely claimed inside China's reform process (Ramo 2004).

8. See Fred Halliday, who notes that China in the late 1990s was "a managed variant of capitalism" without an option of any "middle road" (1999, 285).

9. For example, China's stock of FDI to GDP was 36 percent compared to 1.5 percent for Japan and 5 percent for India (year not specified; Harris 2005, 10). China also depended on foreign supply for energy and other strategic goods. It was second only to the United States as an oil importer, and it purchased 100 percent of its needs in fibre optics and integrated circuits and 57 percent of its mechanical products (*People's Daily*, 3 September 2002). In 2003, China accounted for 7 percent of global oil consumption, 27 percent of steel, 31 percent of coal, and 40 percent of cement (*South China Morning Post*, 7 May 2004). As such, the power of foreign capital over economic life seemed to be "assuming dimensions far greater than when China was a semi-colony of the major capitalist powers in late 19th and early 20th centuries" (John Chan, "Chinese Capitalism: Industrial Powerhouse or Sweatshop of the World?" World Socialist Web site, 31 January 2003, http://www.wsws.org).

10. In 2003, the Chinese benchmark was the annual income per capita of 627 yuan (or US$77), which, adjusted in purchasing power parity, was less than U.S.$0.78 a day (*China Daily*, 21 May 2003; 2 May 2004). By the end of 2004, 22 million urban residents living on a monthly income below the official bottom line of 159 yuan (US$19.4) were, on average, entitled to receive a minimum living allowance from the Ministry of Civil Affairs (Xinhua News, 9 February 2005, http://www.xinhuanet.com.cn). The official media reported that the Ministry of Civil Affairs was preparing to expand the existing rural minimum-living subsidy program, which was initiated in Shanghai in 1994 and covered 4.1 million people nationwide by 2003.

11. In Shanghai in May 2004 the World Bank sponsored the Global Conference on Scaling-Up Poverty Reduction. Hui Liangyu, China's vice premier, vowed after the conference to eliminate rural poverty before 2010 (*Xinhua Daily*, 3 June 2004).

12. The Labor Ministry recorded about 120,000 cases of labor disputes in 1999, a 29 percent increase from 1998; and an annual average of 10,000 demonstrations since 1998. Another internal publication indicated 30,000 protests of significant size in 2000 (*Washington Post*, 21 January 2002, www.washingtonpost.com). In 2003, "more than 58,000 major incidents of social unrest" occurred in China, an increase of 15 percent over 2002 and nearly seven times the figure reported by the government a decade ago (*Washington Post*, 4 November 2004, www.washingtonpost.com). For a collection of case analyses, see Perry and Selden 2000. See also A. Chan 2001.

13. See CASS 2002, 135; Qin 2002. Khan and Riskin (1998, 247) arrived at a similar figure of 0.452, which was "higher than those for India, Pakistan, and Indonesia, and perhaps the same as that for the Philippines. It has been repeatedly reported in the state media that 20 percent of the population possessed 80 percent of total national savings and that this new "upper stratum" made up only about 10 percent of urban residents. According to Zhao Renwei, the ratio between high-income and low-income groups rose to 5.4:1 in 2002 and could be as high as 8:1 in some poorer areas (*Xinhua News Agency*, 19 December 2003, http://www.xinhuanet.com.cn). The official figures for the rural-urban income ratio increased from 1:2.47 in 1997 to 1:3.24 in 2003 (*People's Daily*, 10 February 2004). "If non-currency factors were taken into consideration, China's urban-rural income gap is the widest in the world" (*Finance and Economy* (Beijing), 23 February 2004).

14. The burden of taxes and fees added by arbitrary surcharges triggered daily incidences of riot and conflict, sometimes violent. In 1993, "according to a top-level government report the countryside witnessed some 1.7 million cases of resistance . . . The confrontations that year exacted a staggering toll of deaths and injuries on some 8,200 township and county officials" (United States Foreign Broadcast Information Service, 8 August 1994). An informed local party worker described rural China as "really in a revolutionary situation" in the 1990s (quoted in Perry, 2002, xiii). A national survey showed that in a medium-sized county with 5,000 officials, 10 percent of them collected their salary through fining farmers directly; at the township level the figure was 35 percent (Saich 2004, 158). See also, in particular, C. Li 2002.

15. The first detailed analysis of the experiment is given in Chang 2004.

16. See Isabel Hilton, in the *Guardian*, 22 May 2003. The statistics from the Public Health Ministry show that from 1990 to 2000 medical costs grew at a rate about six times that of the average income increase. Only 42 percent of urban residents had some insurance in 1999 as compared to nearly full coverage before 1978. Infant mortality, moreover, rose to 60 per 1,000 by 2001 in poor regions as compared to 30 per 1,000 for the national average—a reversal of the steady decrease since 1949 (Wang Yanzhong, "On Rural Medical Security in the New Century," *Hong Kong Dispatch*, Beijing, 20 February 2002). The economist Zhu Ling remarked that, as things stood, "China is not achieving its own basic health criterion" (quoted by Elisabeth Rosenthal in the *New York Times*, 14 March 2001). Indeed, the government had been slow in responding effectively to the rapid spread of AIDS. In Henan province, local governments involved themselves in a "free market" of human blood without minimally adequate equipment and procedures. As many as 25,000 donors among the 200,000 people who sold blood in the early 1990s, mostly poor peasants, have been confirmed as HIV carriers and AIDS patients. Nationally in 2003 there were 80,000 AIDS patients, along with 840,000 people tested HIV-positive, giving China the second-largest number in Asia after India. Yet the crisis of public health was not officially addressed until the attack of SARS in 2003. (See Hu Angang and Hu Linlin, "Health Care as a Basic Right of All," *China Daily*, 24 April 2003; and S. Wang 2003).

17. *People's Daily*, 14 May 2003; 6 September 2003.

18. Joseph Kahn, *New York Times*, 25 January 2004. In a survey conducted by the Communist Youth League in Guangdong, half of the migrant workers made only 400 to 800 yuan (US$50 to US$100) a month in 2001, which was similar to their earnings in the 1980s despite two decades of growth and accumulated inflation. More than 70 percent of the migrant workers received no welfare benefits and were not offered to sign a labor contract with their employers, as required by law. In addition, many knew little about their legal labor rights (*South China Morning Post*, 17 January 2002).

19. A total of 4,150 people were killed in mine accidents in the first eight months of 2003 (*People's Daily*, 19 September 2003). The State Administration of Work Safety vowed to change the mine-safety situation, but it had not made any significant progress.

20. The AFL-CIO filed a document in March 2004 with the Congress in seeking sanction against China. See Mark Barenberg, "The Condition of the Working Class in China" *Dissent* (summer 2004): 12.

21. China since the 1990s had witnessed probably the greatest human migration in world history, creating a "floating population." One report states that "China had 113.9 million migrant workers from rural areas in 2003, who accounted for 23.2 percent of the total rural laborers" (Xinhua News Agency, 14 May 2004, http://xinhuanet.com.cn).

22. Such a crisis was frankly acknowledged in the official documents. An example is "Correctly Understanding and Handling Contradictions among the People under New Conditions" by the CCP Central Committee's Organizational Department (2001). To curb corruption, the party punished more than 846,000 members between October 1997 and September 2002, including 98 ministerial ranking officials. Disciplinary actions were taken against 175,000 party members on corruption charges in 2001 (a 30 percent increase from 2000); and 164,831 members in 2004 (Xinhua News Agency, 15 February 2005, www.chinaview.cn).

23. Right after WTO accession, even with the initial protection of double tariffs that limited extra imports, China suffered from importing soybeans from the United States in summer 2002, which compelled the government to rush to work out new restrictions on agricultural imports such as genetically modified goods. Kerstin Leitner (UNDP's China representative) estimated that China's membership would cost the nation 40 million domestic jobs in the short run (*Guardian Weekly*, 31 January to 6 February 2002).

24. According to published official reports, China had an exceedingly large collection of nonperforming loans, which reached $205 billion in 2003 (*People's Daily*, 12 March 2004). Its total national debt including foreign loans stood at 176 percent of GDP (Morgan Stanley's estimation, reported in *Business Week*, 12 January 2004). Capital flight amounted to $52 billion between 1997 and 1999, and in recent years amounted to another tens of billions in US dollars (*Stratfor's Global Intelligent Report*, 16 January 2004). According to Standard Chartered, "There is continued upward pressure on government spending. The debt to GDP level is around 30 percent. But contingent liabilities, in terms of pensions and non-performing loans, could push this up to around 150 percent of GDP" ("China: Avoiding Banana Skins in the Year of the Monkey," *Special Report* 3, 2 February 2004, 8). See also Lardy 1998 on China's vulnerabilities such as "too much debt."

25. Nicolas Lardy has in many reports identified these unnecessary concessions and unique provisions to the PRC's disadvantage in China's WTO accession package; see, for example, his "Problems on the Road to Liberalization" (*Financial Times*, 15 March 2001) and his speech to the Credit Lyonnais Securities Asia Investors' Forum in Hong Kong on 23 May 2002. See also Robert Wade: "The US would retain extraordinary provisions for tariffs to defend its domestic market against . . . Chinese imports, whereas China would concede to a brutally swift dismantling of protection for local farmers and manufacturers and vastly increased freedoms for foreign firms and financial services" (2004, 151). China had also given up a crucial set of previously held requirements on technological sharing and transfers with regard to foreign companies. The economist Zuo Dapei wrote to the Standing Committee of the National People's Congress in February 2002 and again in 2003 in protest against China's negotiation team. The letters were posted online on several large Web sites, such as http://www.1911.cn.

26. The use of quotation marks here indicates the actual counterrevolutionary nature of those postcommunist developments in the sense that they partly restored a pre-revolutionary order.

27. "Deep" and "shallow" global integration are compared in Haggart 1995. We might ask further if the party, trying to be more "realistic" in facing the gaps between its rhetoric and the reality, has not "downgraded" its blueprint from "socialism with Chinese

characteristics" (1978) to "a moderately well-off society" (2002) by quietly dropping the word "socialism"?

28. There were 86 million registered e-mail users at the end of 2003 and the number is predicted to exceed 100 million in 2004. Laid-off workers in Liaoyang and Daqing, for example, drew widespread support through the Internet. (See, for example, Jim Yardley's report "Chinese Go Online in Search of Justice against Elite Class," *New York Times*, 16 January 2004.

29. See Hu's keynote address at the party's national organizational working conference on 17 December 2002 (*People's Daily* 18 December 2002) and his speech at the French National Assembly on 27 January 2004 (Taiwan Affairs Office of the State Council, http://www.gwytb.gov.cn).

30. These themes are detailed in Lin Chun, *Xiaokang Socialism*. Limited by space, also omitted is the cultural and intellectual scene of the Chinese transformation. The determinant of international relations is also beyond the scope of this work but crucial to be kept in the milieu and horizon of the analysis.

31. Obtaining accurate statistics is a tricky business, not only because of the problems in China's own accounting and reporting systems (both "under" and "over"), but also because of some fundamental flaws in economic growth itself. Statistics on GDP, for example, have been contributed by a huge number of costly but unproductive projects (e.g., empty airports) as well as underconsumed projects (e.g., luxury housing). Different international institutions at different times and for different purposes also adopted different computational methods. China's growth rates since 1978, in particular, have been under fierce dispute among foreign experts (see Thomas Rawski's Web site, http://www.pitt.edu/7Erawski). Generally speaking, numbers, official or otherwise, cannot be merely neutral analytical tools but rather "enter constitutively into the social universe from which they are taken or counted up" (Giddens 1990, 42–43).

Chapter 1. China and Alternative Modernity

1. By "continental" Weber refers to a cluster of characters rather than geography and size.

2. The paradox, as described by Partha Chatterjee (1986), is that the state nationalist discourse (in India) is simultaneously resistant to colonial legitimacy and subordinated to that legitimacy's ideological foundation of modernity.

3. For an overview of the literature, see Amin et al. 1982, 1990. (Note the important disagreements among the authors summarized in 1990, 181–87.)

4. Bhabha (1990), among others, regards theories of development as a form of colonial knowledge produced to justify conquest and domination. Escobar (1995) offers a Foucauldian deconstruction of the "colonization of reality" by the development discourse as a regime of representation.

5. See Evans et al. 1985, especially chapter 11, where the authors evaluate the role of the state within such parameters in their "world historical context."

6. "Globalization pulls and pushes societies in opposing directions, it fragments as it integrates, engenders cooperation as well as conflict, and universalizes while it particularizes" (Held 1999, 14).

7. For a brilliant poetic replication of this idea, see Charles Olson, *The Kingfishers*, annotated in P. Anderson 1998, 9–11.

8. Even John Gray, claimed to be a postliberal iconoclast, considers "universal goods," as opposed to "universal evils," to be the bottom line for value pluralism (2000, 9).

9. Habermas traces the "epochal concept" of modernity in Hegel: "The discovery of the 'new world,' the Renaissance, and the Reformation—these three monumental events around the year 1500 constituted the epochal threshold between modern times and the middle ages" (2000, 5). Pocock (1999) explores plural enlightenments in barbarism and religion. I use the single noun enlightenment here to exclude, for the sake of clarity, any non-European enlightenments that may not endorse distinctly Western ideas of reason and progress.

10. Also gaining influence is an anti-anthropocentric literature in which the relationship between humans and other animals (and their natural surroundings) is entirely rewritten. See, most thoroughly and pessimistically, Gray, 2002; see also Latour 1993.

11. As Hodgson remarks, Arabic and Asian civilizations once looked "intimately . . . the Occident": without their contribution through an Afro-Eurasian commercial network the "western transmutation would be almost unthinkable" (1993, 86); see also Northrop 1946. The distinguished literature on the subject also includes Needham's work on scientific-technological diffusion from China as well as McNeill's work from Europe. "Indeed, Europe would have been a lot poorer—economically, culturally, and scientifically—had it resisted the globalization of mathematics, science, and technology" in the pre- and early-modern times (Sen 2002, 2).

12. For Wallerstein, the fact that "China, India, the Arab world and other regions did not go forward to capitalism" enables them to be "better immunized against the toxin" (1999, 181).

13. David Landes, for example, remarks that Wittfogel's thesis of oriental despotism "has been roundly criticized by a generation of western sinologists zealous in their political correctness" (1998, 27).

14. "To the Young Generation," the 1861 populist manifesto, quoted in Walicki 1969, 117. N. A. Dobroliubov, Alexander Herzen, and N. G. Chernyshevsky were among those who saw collectivist and egalitarian virtues in traditional peasant life in Russian-Slavic communes—in contrast with capitalist decadence in the West (cf. Herzen 1956 [1851]).

15. See the famous correspondence between Marx and the editorial board of *Otechestvenniye Zapisky* (Homeland Notes) in 1877 and between Marx and Vera Zasulich, the Russian translator of the communist manifesto after Barkunin, in 1881, annotated in Shanin 1983, 97–126, 134–37. Pressed by Zasulich for a clarification, Marx at one point even suggested the possibility of such a leap without a proletarian revolution in the capitalist West (cf. Stedman Jones's introduction to the communist manifesto [2002, 261]). Engels later abandoned Marx's speculation and supported the position of Russian Marxists who argued that the peasant communes had decayed by the turn of the twentieth century due to capitalist development in Russia.

16. Amin (1980) explains these cases. Trotsky uses Germany and the United States to illustrate the same point in his seminal history of the Russian revolution. The Prussians themselves found the idea of privilege of backwardness appealing (Veblen 1990, 253).

17. This might be achieved by the politics of pricing, for example. Cf. Wallerstein, who finds that "one obvious way would be to seek to increase the price of labor or the price of sale by the direct producers. These prices, like most prices, are controlled by market considerations, but market considerations *within parameters established by political struggle*" (1991, 121).

18. In purely economic, even narrowly technological, terms of assimilation, Marx famously stated that "the country that is more developed industrially only shows, to the less developed, the image of its own future" (1967, 8–9). He went on to note that Germany along with continental Europe, as contrasted with England, suffered not only from capitalist development but also from the incompleteness of that development.

19. For the "reflexivity of modernity," see Giddens 1990, 36–45. Even in "the heart of the world of hard science, modernity floats free" (39).

20. Cf. Latour 1993 on the representation and critique of such ideology. On the "spatial turn" of globalization, see Jameson 1994, 156.

21. Schram views China's early-twentieth-century cultural radicalism as "iconoclasm from within" (1973, 6). On "moving beyond tradition and modernity," see Cohen 1984; see also Dreyer 1993.

22. See Cui (1998) for a discussion of the pattern of interplays between power blocs in China. In a "three-layer analysis," he frames the upper layers (the center), the middle layers (local bureaucracy and business), and the lower layers (labor and commoners) in a "mixed constitution" as a modern version of Aristotle's "one, few, and many" in a mixed polity of monarchy, aristocracy, and democracy. The vested interests of the intermediary strata should be controllable by law and regulations from above and by norms and pressures from below.

23. Cf. E. P. Thompson 1971, 50. Reading Scott's *The Moral Economy of the Peasant* (1976) or *Weapons of the Weak: Everyday Forms of Peasant Resistance* (1985) makes one wonder what he would have to say about China. He does mention that when informal economies that could in a thousand ways supply what the formal economy failed to supply, the cost has been economic ruin and starvation, as in the Great Leap (1998, 261). But a great deal of what the Chinese peasants, hundreds of millions in number, went through cannot be fully explained by the existing scholarship: e.g., their participation in a social revolution that partially destroyed their own traditional foundations of life.

24. For "new collectivism" as a counter ideology, cf. Y. Wang 1994. For various explanations for the privatization of TVEs, cf. Whiting (2001) on the national fiscal reform of 1994 that removed the incentives and constraints by local governments behind more collectively oriented rural enterprises in Jiangsu province. Wang Xin 2003 traces the economic history of the region and considers the change "natural."

25. Walzer also depicts the irony of the self-congratulating American social scientists who became defenders of social change in the third world: "If only modernization offered some solution to the problems of the modern! And if only these writers were revolutionaries at home!" (1980, 190).

26. It is notable, for example, that political culture and political development in various treatments by the leading modernization theorists such as Samuel Huntington, Martin Lipset, Lucien Pye, Gabriel Almond, and Sidney Verba all fall in the Marxist base-superstructure perspective. In fact, "historical materialism in its very structure presupposed Eurocentrism" (Dirlik 1994, 24).

27. The term here is borrowed from European historiography, cf. Brook 1999, 131–40. "Feudalism" was manufactured in the Chinese national political vocabulary to refer to the peasants being exploited by, and subordinated to, the landlords, even though class relations in China, at least in the period after Qin unification (221BC) and before 1949, were markedly different from typical feudal systems elsewhere. The term was also

applied to the warlordism of the 1920s and has since then "acquired its present-day connotation of backwardness, patriarchy, and superstition" (Fitzgerald 1996, 159). As long as the term does not presume capitalist development as the next stage of a telo-history, it poses no major conceptual problem (cf. Moore 1966, 162–64).

28. Mao, among the May 4th generation of modernists, argues that "we should cherish soviet experience . . . But we should cherish even more China's experience in revolutionary war"; and, more generally, he states that the history of China "has its specific characteristics and is full of treasures" (1967, 165). See also his 1936 interview with Edgar Snow, in Schram 1989).

29. He even imagines that as China will be industrialized, it should become "an approximation of modern western society" (1970, 8).

30. On cultural adaptation and assimilation in China, major examples include the long episodes of the conquest by the Mongols and the Manchus, who subsequently transformed themselves into Chinese. Comparisons might be made between the Islamic expansion in interactions and conflicts with the European and Indian civilizations on the one hand, and the resilience of the Chinese empire and civilization through assimilation on the other. Also notable is how the Chinese social revolution must be distinguished from, for instance, the religious Iranian cultural revolution, though both are nationalist to their core. On the Maoist effort to "make Marxism Chinese," see Dirlik et al. 1997, part 2. For an early debate over whether the Chinese revolution was original and indigenous or a Russian creation, and, for that matter, whether Maoism was independent of Leninism, see the Karl Wittfogel vs. Benjamin Schwartz debate published in *China Quarterly* 1–2, 1960. Meisner (1982, chapters 3 and 4) clarifies the matter in a lucid comparison between Leninism and Maoism.

31. A well-known example is Nanjie in Henan (see Deng, Cui, and Miao 1994). In the Western media, see, for example, Ching-Ching Ni, "Between Mao and Capitalism, a Village Finds the Good Life," *Los Angeles Times*, 30 January 2005.

32. Levenson is perceptive to also note that "'the people,' located first at their most particular in the local earth of the provinces, then move into the abstract as the transnational, trans-cultural, universal ground of a more-than-Chinese vision of the world" (1967, 286).

33. For the differences between the two, see Smith 1998. Commenting on Eric Hobsbawm, he notes that analytically "we can usefully distinguish between 'ethnic,' 'civic' and 'plural' types of nation and nationalism" (126) yet "these types frequently overlap" in actual history (212).

34. See also Dittmer and Kim, who write "this proud country has had enormous trouble finding a comfortable niche as a nation-state in the modern international system" (1993, xi).

35. On this point see Unger, who notes that a Chinese political and cultural entity may have stretched back two millenniums—an entity that "comprised a civilization and empire but was not truly a 'nation' whose people were imbued with an abiding sense of 'nationalism' in the full modern sense of those terms" (1996, xii). In contrast, Olson does not hesitate to say that "China was among the earliest, if not the earliest, of the nation-states" (1982, 152).

36. Contemporary commentators frequently overlook the condemnation of capitalist expansion in this passage. Gellner, for example, is mistaken in holding that for Marx and Engels, "the East can only be liberated by courtesy of the West" (1994, 163). Cf.

the summary balance sheet of "moral evaluation of colonialism" in Abernethy, 2000, 403–7.

37. Japan, perhaps alone in Asia, was willing to join a celebration of "shared heritages" with its Euro-American trading partners at the four hundredth anniversary (2000) of the arrival of the first Dutch ship in Deshima. A research initiative in the Netherlands, called "Towards a New Age of Partnership," is said to be part of an effort of "legitimization for Dutch colonial presence in 19th-century Asia" (Leonard Blusse, quoted in the *Dutch Institute for Asian Studies Newsletter*, 18 February 1999).

38. The CCP line was heavily influenced by the Comintern (guided by Lenin's theses on the national and colonial question), which conditionally supported the national bourgeois revolutions in Asia in the hope that it would lead to the downfall of metropolitan capitalism in Europe.

39. Gellner is Marxist when he writes that "only when a nation became a class . . . did it become politically conscious and activist . . . a nation-for-itself" (1983, 121).

40. This, in the classical Marxist interpretation of the "national question" in Europe, is because a unified national state was required for the national bourgeoisie to build its industrial foundation and commercial networks. Toynbee (1954) and Gellner (1983), among others, follow this line in discussing the coincidence of the formation of capitalist industrial society and national identity. The case made by Anderson (1991) for modern nationalism arising from a "print capitalism" is a different argument, yet it confirms the capitalist basis for modern nations.

41. "New democracy" is best outlined in Mao, "On New Democracy" 1991 [1940], and in "On Coalition Government" 1991 [1945a]. See also Liu Shaoqi, 1993.

42. Skocpol (1979, 303) treats the "Chinese revolution" as one continuous process encompassing 1911 and 1949.

43. Chinese Academy of Social Sciences (CASS), "China's Social Situation, Analysis and Prediction, 2004–5," *People's Daily*, 24 January 2005.

44. Yu Ying-shih's comments on radicalism and conservatism in modern Chinese thought have since 1988 provoked a lasting "radicalism debate" in the Hong Kong–based journal *The Twenty-first Century*. See also Li and Liu 1995.

45. The mostly Marxist body of work on the near impossibility of capitalist development in the economically dependent peripheries (led by, for example, Baran 1960) was largely offset later by the countercases of the "tiger" economies. The successes of the latter, however, were to a very considerable extent attributable to cold war geopolitics, especially the U.S. aid and the U.S. market. Regarding state capitalism as understood in China, Liu Shaoqi writes: "What is state capitalism? It is a system in which the state is ruled by the proletariat and the capitalists are supervised and serve the state in certain adequate conditions" (1993, 52–3).

46. Skocpol (1979, 154) is representative in advocating a structuralist approach at the expense of rational "agency" and microexplanation. She is, however, cautious in not using the revolution of 1949 as a typical case for her approach.

47. Cf. Amin 1998, 50–54; and Naughton 1991, 228–29. Selden and Lippit (1982, 19–20) put the figure at 4 percent to 6 percent in real terms (11.2 percent for industry and 3.2 percent for agriculture), and 2 percent to 4 percent per capita, while taking into account average annual population growth of about 2 percent.

48. Tani Barlow explains the category "colonial modernity" as a "useful innovation": it is a frame "for investigating the infinitely pervasive discursive powers that increasingly

connect at key points to the globalizing impulses of capitalism" (1997, 3, 6). Her concern is with semicoloniality rather than revolution in the Chinese case, but both should be complementary. Meanwhile, if modernity is plural, it would surely entail many possible adjectives (such as Islamic, Confucian, and so on).

49. Sen (2000) most forcefully argues that India has avoided major famine since independence, due in particular to a guaranteed free press as a primary feature of democracy. This point, however, is debatable. Sovensen, for example, points out that in view of malnutrition and starvation, the "lack of progress on the welfare dimension in India has led to human suffering and loss of life, not through spectacular disasters like in China but through the quiet, continuous suffering of the 40 percent of the population who are in absolute poverty" (1993, 76).

50. As reported by the United Nations Development Program, "Over a long period of time, China has invested liberally in human development. So, despite its low per capita income, it falls in the medium HDI category" and thus "has the largest positive gap (+49) between its HDI rank and its GNP per capita rank, showing that it has made judicious use of its national income" (UNDP 1994, 100). The human development indices (HDI) have made "human development" cross-nationally comparable since 1990. In terms of life expectancy, China had improved from less than 40 years in the early 1950s to 65 years in 1978 and then to 71.8 years for men and 73 for women in 2003, as compared with, for example, 64 years in India in 2002. China had by 1997 completed the demographic transition "from a high fertility and high mortality society" to a low one as well as effectively reduced poverty (UNDP 1998). Adult literacy rate in China was 91% and 75% for male and female population respectively in the end of the 1990s, which were also markedly higher than most developing countries. Cf. fDeborah Davis, "China's 'Human Software' Will Keep Economy Humming" (Straits Times Interactive, http://straitstimes.asial.com.sg, 19 September 2003). For a systematic comparison, see Bhalla 1995; and Nolan and Sender 1992.

51. The Indian state of Kerala, for example, with a record of social development much more advanced than the Indian (and Chinese) average under a democratic communist local government, persuaded a foremost third-world revolutionary thinker, Samir Amin, to admit that "it is incorrect to think that nothing can be done without a revolution. On the contrary, Kerala shows there is room for progressive reforms" (see Parayil 2000, blurb). Other apparent examples in Asia may include Malaysia, Thailand, and South Korea. Louis (2002) claims that British Malaysia has accomplished a "social revolution" through colonial restructuring of rural relations.

52. Dirlik, however, makes no distinction between colonial and revolutionary modernity: China, like others, was "compelled into modernity not as its subject but as its object" (1997, 68).

53. Cf. Halliday 1991, chapter 2. The situations in 1989 in East and Central Europe, then, cannot be treated as revolutionary events conceptualized in terms of alternative modernity.

54. Despite a prolonged recession, Japan today continues to be at the top on HDI indices in terms of the world's highest "healthy life expectancy" (89 years). For the nonstate model of welfare provision, see Goodman, White, and Kwan 1998.

55. Hegel quoted in Wright 1960, 245. Hegel saw China—a cultural sphere marked by strong continuities, in European eyes, anyway—as the land of a hydraulic "recurrent principle" of waterworks (Wolf 1982, 51). The Euro-Asian dichotomies are generally

made between the old, backward and stagnant on the one side, and the modern, advanced and progressive on the other; and further between the pre-nation civilizational and despotic on the one side, and national and liberal on the other. Wolf breaks them down into three components: first is the polarity between smallness and bigness (e.g., dynamic city-states versus changeless uniformity); second is maritime versus continental; and third is freedom versus slavery. Condorcet, for example, contrasts laws in Greece (the West) as "the conditions of a common pact between man and man" with them among "Eastern races" as "a yoke under which people were bound into slavery" (1982, 20–21). Marx's "Asiatic mode of production" is a most elaborated conceptualization of this thesis.

56. For the concept of "world time," see Eberhard 1973, 25–28. The concept has been used in various senses, of which a more common one is to "measure" the transnational contexts of revolutions that are seen as being at once shaped by and affecting "epochal modernizing dynamics" (Skocpol 1979, 23–24).

Chapter 2: Chinese Socialism

1. As John Gittings put it decades ago, "the western attitude towards China today may be as decisive in the long run as it was in the past" (1967, 214). Isaiah Berlin observed in 1981 that "if the Russians . . . had not been treated as a barbarous mass by the West in the nineteenth century, or the Chinese had not been humiliated by opium wars or general exploitation, neither would have fallen so easily to a doctrine which promised they would inherit the earth after they had . . . crushed all the capitalist unbelievers" (quoted in the *New York Review of Books*, 18 October 2001).

2. Gittings 1967 documents how Mao would have preferred an open-door policy to a closed-door policy were it not for cold war coercion. In an interview with American diplomat John Service before the communists won the civil war, Mao's message was that the United States would be invited to help with China's postwar construction (quoted in Winnington 1986, 72). Mao also admired certain aspects of the American system, including federalism (see Shambaugh, 1991); the United States, however, did not respond to that call. Without a choice, Mao then made it clear on the eve of the founding of the PRC that in learning from the history of Chinese struggle, "we are firmly convinced that in order to win victory and consolidate it we must lean to one side . . . either to the side of imperialism or to the side of socialism. Sitting on the fence will not do, nor is there a third road" (1991 [1949], 415). As Edward Friedman writes, "If China's war-torn economy, hungry people, and unfulfilled great dreams were to come alive in a world where the United States was threatening to blockade and embargo Mao's China, and if Western Europe and Japan were dependent on the United States, what alternative was there to turning to Stalin" who "imposed harsh terms hoping to make China dependent and subservient?" (1982, 163). China and the United States, after all, were war allies and the Americans were supposed to mediate the CCP-GMD peace talks in 1946–1947. Moreover, Stalin did not fully trust the Chinese communists—neither in their ability to win the war nor their loyalty to Moscow. The factors surrounding the initial Sino-Soviet friendship and subsequent conflict are discussed in Gittings 1974.

3. The CCP produced nine long polemics (published in the form of "open letters" to the Soviet Communist Party) to elaborate its position. Relevant to the dispute were the

Sino-Indian border war of 1962, the Sino-Soviet border clashes of 1968–1969, and the Chinese invasion of Vietnam in 1979. For a collection of discussions on these and related events based on new archival materials, see Westad 1999.

4. Bruce Cumings notes that China's attempt was "extraordinarily courageous, if not foolhardy," and that "it led to palpable threats by both superpowers to launch preemptive nuclear strikes on China. This can only be explained . . . by Mao's judgement that the Soviet Union had joined in a condominium with the United States at China's expense" (1983, 7).

5. And, as Bramall further notes, China's strategy of defense industrialization "was confirmed by American imperialism in Vietnam" (1993, 336).

6. See, representatively, Ralph Miliband's comment quoted in Newman 2002, 231–32. See Van Ness 1993 for a critical examination of the case. On the other hand, Meghnad Desai observes that "for the first time in two hundred years the powerful white races (that is how the Chinese and many other Asians saw it) came to see a Chinese leader on a basis of equality. . . . This time China had beaten the USA to a standstill" (2002, 248).

7. American aid made up 40 percent of gross investment in Taiwan or 6 percent of its GDP throughout the 1950s. See Wade 1990, 82–84, 357. Commenting on the Asian NICs, Philip Golub notes that "as part of the cold war compact, they traded their political sovereignty for unrestricted access to the US market. Until the mid 1980s the US accounted for more than one-third of Japan's exports, 40% of Korea's, and 44% of Taiwan's. This structural dependency gave the US powerful political leverage over its East Asian allies" (2003). Wallerstein also points out that "Japan was a very great economic beneficiary of the Korean War as well as of direct U.S. assistance. Both South Korea and Taiwan were supported (and indulged) economically, politically and militarily for cold war reasons" (1999, 37).

8. Following Marx's Critique of the Gotha Program (1875), and in an oversimplified fashion, socialism in the conventional Chinese interpretation is a transitional period between capitalism and communism. The difference between socialist and communist stages is summarized in the Marxian motto that for both it is "from each according to his ability," but for the former it is "to each according to his labor," and the latter "according to his needs." For related debates in China, see Yu Guangyuan 1984.

9. The lasting debate over the role of colonialism and the slave trade in European capitalist development remains inconclusive. Patrick O'Brien, for example, holds that colonial trade was much less important than the industrial-technological revolutions for capitalist primitive accumulation. "For the economic growth of the core, the periphery was peripheral" (1982, 18). Kenneth Pomeranz, in contrast, argues that "until well into the nineteenth century, the fruits of overseas exploitation were probably roughly as important to at least Britain's economic transformation as its epochal turn to fossil fuels." His controversial thesis of "ecological relief," if plausible, would be especially pertinent in a comparison between early industrialization in England and the communist effort to industrialize China. In England, one third of the population immigrated to America and the land-intensive products were obtained from the New World, relieving the country's demographic and ecological pressures. In China, the population doubled between 1949 and 1976 (2000, 6–7, 23, 187–88).

10. Bukharin compared socialist and capitalist accumulation in *The Economics of Transition* and was positive about the former before abandoning the phrase "socialist primi-

tive accumulation" in 1922 when the Trotskyists were purged. Evgenii Preobrazhensky's *New Economics* was a rare treatise on this topic. See Lewin, 1975. See also Nolan 1988 (12–28) for a discussion of the implications for China of Bukharinist versus Stalinist strategies.

11. On the first industrial revolution as a state project, see O'Brien 1993. Moreover, that revolution was also accompanied by "state-sponsored and subsidized imperialism" (O'Brien 1999, 54). Later, in Russia, the Bolshevik revolution "destroyed the old ruling classes . . . to make way for the communist version of an industrial revolution from above" (Moore 1966, 160).

12. For example, China and Mexico, and to a lesser extent Brazil, share "structure of feelings" from their respective national revolutions and shifts in developmental strategy from import substitution. See Lindau and Cheek 1998.

13. Goran Therborn sees shared elements of social Darwinism in "scientific socialist" and Nazi ideologies, but treats European fascism "as a modern project to rival the liberal and socialist project" (2000, 152).

14. Meghnad Desai succinctly points out that the fundamental difference between Stalin and Hitler hinged on their attitude toward capitalism. Stalin's challenge to the liberal order was that high-level development could be achieved without resorting to private property and profit making: "It was to declare the profit motive redundant to accumulation and economic growth." Hitler's challenge was, on the other hand, "to declare the free market wasteful and unnecessary for economic growth under capitalism" (1990, 166).

15. Did workers support Nazism in Germany? According to Michael Mann, the answer lies in social sector, not class, as "the principal economic explanatory variable" along with the ideological determinants in the cross-class mass movements (1995, 40). The issue continues to be debated. James Gregor, for example, insists that fascism— through syndicalism especially in Italy—was a "variant of revolutionary Marxism designed to address the reality of lesser developed nations" (2000b, 133).

16. For Lindblom, especially in view of the Maoist practice, the "preceptoral emphasis on decentralization, initiative, resourcefulness, and generalized competences has a counterpart in market-oriented systems" (1977, 61). See Wolf 1999 for a discussion of the formation of Nazi ideology and collective violence mediated by manipulating emotions.

17. The model is described by Robert Wade as "those states whose internal politics and external relations have served to concentrate sufficient power, authority, autonomy, competence and capacity at the center to shape, pursue and encourage the achievement of explicit developmental objectives" (1990, 284).

18. For criticisms of "crony capitalism" and other vulnerabilities of the state in the NICS from neoliberal points of view, see Richter 2000. For the concept of "surplus retention" in dependency theory, see Amin 1977.

19. The developmentalist notion universalizes paradigms of economic growth without paying appropriate attention to social development and environmental protection, thereby concealing global and local inequalities and destruction behind such paradigms and also cutting off ties between development and freedom. See Huang 2000.

20. According to the traditional consensus in China, "scarcity is not a worry but inequality" (*bu huan gua er huan bujun*). In a major study of China's class structure conducted by the Chinese Academy of Social Sciences, Li Peilin, the chief author, writes

that by 1995 "Chinese society has not suffered serious income disparity"; and that the situation looks alarming only "because the reform was launched against the background of extreme equalitarianism" (1995, 7).

21. An influential article is Wang Xiaoqiang 1980. The Chinese conception of agrarian socialism is independent of the usage of the phrase elsewhere, such as in Martin Lipset (1950), written about a Canadian local government. The Chinese critiques of the "feudal tyranny" of the Jiang Qing group and the "feudal remnants" in the party culture and general social relations were extensive. Friedman 1983 reflects on the friction of these critiques. See also Tsou 1983.

22. Cf. Mao, quoted in "On the Questions of Party History" (CCP 1985), adopted by the Party's sixth plenary session of the eleventh central committee on 27 June 1981, p. 593.

23. The administrative aspect here included such matters as assessing variations in entitlement to provision (Kraus 1981, 77).

24. For example, Myron Cohen in an overstated argument shows that through making "farmers" into "peasants," "tradition" into "feudalism," and "religious customs" into "superstition," the communists "invented" an "old society" to be uprooted (1993, 154–55). See Blecher 1996 for a more affirmative discussion. See also Potter and Potter 1990.

25. Mao describes the cooperative movements in China as waves of a "socialist high tide." For the details of the process, see Selden 1979.

26. For comparisons, see Lewin 1975; and Mayer 2000, chapter 10.

27. Defending collectivism throughout the Great Leap and the Cultural Revolution, Hinton argues against the view that agriculture is by nature not suitable for collective management. See also Hinton 1990 for a critique of post-Mao decollectivization.

28. For Naughton, "The crucial point is not that the burden of saving and financing government services falls on rural people, but rather that agriculture becomes nonlucrative relative to other types of productive activity." Moreover, the policy of urban bias was accompanied by the rising living standards across the country (1991, 231–32).

29. See the series of research reports by Wang Mei and collaborators from the Ministry of Public Health, 1998–1999. In "The Implications of Redistribution on the Health of the Population," they proved the hypothesis that "the lower the per capita GDP of a country is, the larger the impact of equitable redistribution of the population's healthy level would be" (1997, 2, 6). See also Hu 1980.

30. The official assessment of the famine admits state responsibility but also attributes it to externally imposed difficulties, i.e., "the errors of the great leap forward and of the struggle against 'right opportunism' [go] together with a succession of natural calamities and the perfidious scrapping of contracts by the Soviet government" (CCP 1985, 596). In the urban areas the effects of famine were minimized through a tight ration system. The total number of deaths, mostly rural and estimated between 15 to 30 million, remains seriously disputed. See Riskin 1998. Werthheim 1995 shows that the unexamined yet widely accepted figures mostly relied on the unreliable 1953 census that put the total population at the 600 million mark; this number seems improbable given that the population in 1949 was 450 million.

31. By 1995, "the modification of China's industrial structure has provided an opportunity for over 100 million agricultural farmers to become industrial workers" (CASS 2001, 7). The TVES contributed up to 43 percent of China's industrial GDP (*China Statistics Year Book* 1996, 375).

32. Even the disastrous Great Leap "was not without its beneficial aspects" in that it enhanced rural participation in industrialization, despite such extreme experiences as massive backyard blast furnaces. See Rawski 1980, 197.

33. This institutional design, confirmed in the party's landmark "No. 1 Document" in 1982, is elaborated in Lin Zili 1982–84. In addition, Nolan 1988, 1–2, pairs double-management with the "Japanese path" that combines family farming and service cooperatives along with technological and informational aid from the government.

34. Oi 1989 examines collective bargaining strategies at local and village levels in the early reform period. Wong 1997, chapters 9 and 10, compares the Chinese and European experiences of local protests in the forms of grain seizure, food riots, and tax resistance.

35. See *Xinhua Digest* (Beijing), 10 July 2001. Neil Hughes notes that because workers have everything to lose if they lose jobs, "they will not go quietly" (1998, 77). As Callum Henderson observes, "China is a potential powder keg" when "the proletariat for whom the Communist Revolution was officially dedicated—take to the streets to demand jobs, housing, and even food" (1999, 44).

36. The draft Trade Union Law (2001) reaffirms the right to strike along with unionization. Focusing on the nonpublic sector, the law requires any firm employing twenty-five workers or more to set up a union that is to conduct its work "independently according to the charter of the Trade Unions" (New China News Agency, FBIS-CHI-2001–0827).

37. *People's Daily*, 9 March 2004 (online at http://english.peopledaily.com.cn).

38. See A. Chan 1993 for an earlier account of union reform "from above." Demands from below have sharply increased since the mid-1990s due to the intensified process of privatizing SOEs. For actual proposals in reforming the official unions, see Sun, An, and Feng 1997.

39. Xinhua Domestic Service, 23 June 2002.

40. Xinhuanet (http://www.xinhuanet.com.cn), 19 November 2003; *People's Daily*, 14 March 2002 and 7 September 2004. The boundary of the "public sector" that includes collectively owned firms is inevitably vague.

41. For example, Japan's three sacred treasures—lifelong employment, seniority-based wage system, and enterprise unionism—helped to enable the Japanese economy to grow rapidly and in a healthy manner in the postwar period. See Johnson 1982.

42. Hu, reported in Xinhuanet (http://www.xinhuanet.com.cn), 28 September 2003. Zeng Qinghong, vice-chairman of the PRC, states that "the historical status and role of the working class has not changed, and should not change" in the reform conditions (*Xinhua* Domestic Service 30 April 2003, FBIS).

43. Labor disputes were rapidly rising. According to the Ministry of Labor and Social Welfare, there were 207,605 cases of dispute in 2000, an increase of 12.5 percent from 1999 and equal to the number during the entire decade of the 1950s (*South China Morning Post*, 3 March 2001).

44. See Wakeman and Edmonds 1999. For China's modern economic history in which the bourgeois class is treated as an important player, see Perkins 1975; and Myers 1980.

45. For the general and controversial models of "bourgeois revolution," "revolutionary bourgeoisie," and "capitalist regime transition," see, for example, Comninel 1987; and Keddie 1995. A discussion of the CCP's policy toward the bourgeoisie is in Mao 1991 [1948].

46. In 1979, the government returned to the former capitalists the fixed dividend withheld during the Cultural Revolution, which amounted to a total sum of over $600 billion. See *Beijing Weekly* quoted in the *New York Times Magazine*, 17 March 1980.

47. See, for example, Jason Leow, "China's Entrepreneurs Giving More to Charity," *Straits Times*, 10 May 2004.

48. The annual growth rate of agriculture in 1979–1984 was 7.8 percent, which contrasts sharply with 2.1 percent as in 1955–1979. As peasant household income grew at 13.4 percent annually, the urban/rural income ratio dropped from 2.4:1 in 1978 to 1.7:1 in 1984, or, in terms of the disparity rate, from 3.09 in 1980 to 2.26 in 1984 (*China Statistics Year Book* 1985).

49. "Between 1988 and 1995, China experienced the most rapid increase in income inequality of any country ever tracked by the World Bank. In 1990, per capita urban incomes were 2.2 times those of rural households. By 1999, the ratio had risen to 2.6, and just one year later, to 2.8." Moreover, when these ratios are adjusted for higher tax burdens and lower subsidies in rural areas, "average urban incomes are actually more than four times as high as average rural incomes" (Deborah Davis, "China's 'Human Software' Will Keep Economy Humming," *Straits Times*, 19 September 2003).

50. A distinction is made between "national state" and "nation-state" by Charles Tilly who recognizes China's "nearly three thousand years' experience of successive national states," but not one year as a nation-state "given its multiple languages and nationalities" (1992, 3). Anthony Smith's "historical ethno-symbolism," on the other hand, allows dominant "ethnic cores" through incorporating outlying "ethnies" over time to form a nation and hence nation-state (2000, 12–13).

51. Marx was addressing the Irish question when he warned that "the English working class will never accomplish anything until it has got rid of Ireland" (quoted in Chauhan 1976, 101–12).

52. The 1949 Common Programme, the predecessor of the PRC constitution, advocated the flourishing of nations: "All national minorities shall have freedom to develop their spoken and written languages, to preserve or reform their traditions, customs, and religious beliefs." It also promised government assistance "in their political, economic, cultural, and educational development" (Article 53). Policies in accordance with this commitment followed. For example, "great efforts were made to bring education to all the minority areas, and in some cases this meant first of all creating a written language which could serve as the basis for education." Not until later was learning Chinese stressed at the expense of minority languages (Ferdinand 1991, 241–42). As another example, the "one child policy," rigorously implemented in the Han areas since 1979, had not been applied to the national minorities (Goldstein and Beall 1991). For a summary of China's policy line, see Dreyer 1976, 262–63.

53. "Why Terrorism Bypasses China's Far West." *Asia Times* (Hong Kong), 22 April 2004.

54. See the report by Dawa Toinzhub, deputy director of the regional statistics bureau of the TAR, in *China Daily*, 6 May 2003. According to the State Council "White Paper on Human Rights in China 2000," absolute poverty in the Tibet Autonomous Region further decreased from 0.48 million in 1994 to 70,000 in 2000. The *People's Daily* (28 January 2004) reports that the net per capita income of farmers and herders in the region surged 11 percent annually to reach a record 1,690 yuan (about $204) in 2003, thanks to the anti-poverty projects mainly financed by the central government (more than $42 million in funds in 2003 alone). Such statistics, as those gathered elsewhere in

China, are sometimes disputed by different international agencies (which use different measurements). For a balanced assessment on social development in Tibet, see Grunfeld 1999.

55. This was confirmed by official sources in China. For example, in 1986–1999, the per capita income ratio between east and west regions increased from 1.15:1 to 1.4:1. By 1995, the gap in terms of GDP per capita had been 31 times larger than that in 1978 (L. Yang 2003).

56. Guangdong, once the richest province in capital and trade surplus because of its SEZs, is losing out to Shanghai and is widely expected to be surpassed in the next decade. See Jacobs 1997. For a discussion of rivalry and trade wars between provinces, see Saich 2004, 148ff.

57. In Goodman and Segal 1994, see the essays on transnational zones in Guangdong and "greater Hong Kong" (by David Goodman and Feng Chongyi), in north China and Russia (by Michael Yuhuda), in Xinjing and Central Asia (by Peter Ferdinand), and in Yunnan, Thailand, and Vietnam (by Ingrid d'Hooghe).

58. In the Chinese press, it is taken for granted that imported consumerism in minority regions is a gain for the locals. On the Tibetan responses, see Goldstein 1990. The State Council's effort in March 2003 to attend to "ecological work and environmental protection in Tibet" is a positive move but it remains silent on the issues of culture and migration. The nuclear tests conducted in Xinjiang, which caused widespread discontent in the region, cannot even be freely discussed. A grand proposal for "creating another China" by redirecting waters from the Tibetan Plateau to the dry northwestern provinces typically pays no attention to such a project's impact on ethnic relations. See Deng, Wang, and Cui 2001.

59. Taiwan's critical intellectuals have voiced dissenting views, including one view that holds that a unified China would be an indication of, and required for, the eventual defeat of U.S. imperialism in East Asia. They also criticize Taiwanese economic "sub-imperialism" on the mainland and in other neighboring countries. See, for example, the 1996–1997 issues of the influential journal *Taiwan: A Radical Quarterly in Social Studies* (Taipei).

60. These resolutions of the CCP's sixth congress 1928 and the first All-China Congress of the Chinese Soviet Republic (1931) are quoted in Connor 1984, 68; and Mayall 2000, 192. Connor, in noting that the phrase "the toiling masses of the national minorities" is taken from Stalin's call to halt separatist movement after the 1917 revolution, complains that the CCP statement did not address the minorities as such (74).

61. In 1922, the party called for the unification of China without mentioning Taiwan. In 1934, Mao acknowledged the independent status of Taiwan, Korea, and Annam to their communist delegates to the Jiangxi Soviet Republic, and he kept the promise for a distinct Taiwanese nation until 1943. In 1935, he encouraged Inner Mongolia to obtain independence until the party changed its position in 1947. In 1936, he likened Taiwan to Korea, saying that both territories should become independent states following the defeat of Japan. He told Edgar Snow that Tibet, Mongolia, Burma, Indo-China, and Korea should be autonomous republics attached to a Chinese (con)federation. Korea and Taiwan remained on the list of possible future independent entities in the 1945 party constitution. See Connor 1984, 82–83; Harding 1993, 679; and Yahuda 2000, 27–30. The early documents of the Chinese Soviets are collected in Brandt, Schwartz, and Fairbank 1967.

62. Political imagination is more likely to flourish without both internal censorship and international intervention. It appears, for example, that the concept of "territorial sovereignty" should be rethought. Perhaps even sovereignty can be shared, as done in Malta by the United Kingdom and Spain. See the daring Chinese proposal by Yan Jiaqi translated in Bachman and Yang, 1991.

63. According to the 2001 government white paper on human rights, wage employment by females in all sectors accounted for 330 million or 46.7 percent of the total figure in 2000 (State Council 2001). Sociologists see a large portion of China's urban population as "career women": engineers, scientists, teachers, managers, and civil servants and officials.

64. An example is Lisa Rofel's study of three cohorts of women workers in the construction of post-Mao gender identities. The case might have been overstretched, however, when she dismisses any shared meaning of equality and argues against any "ontological status" of women's liberation as misconceived "homogeneity of modernity" (1999, 47–48, 256).

65. Other notions recently transplanted into Chinese included "domestic violence," "sexual harrassment," and "queerism." For a systematic discussion of conceptual and terminological issues in the Chinese feminist discourse, see Barlow 2004.

66. Wang Xiaolu and Fan Gang in *People's Daily*, 20 May 2004.

67. Whether women should "return home" was debated in the academic journals and media, but the idea was strongly resisted in wider society and had not found its way to affect official ideology and policy. See Z. Wang 2000.

68. Women's achievements may or may not be evaluated on the basis of gendered qualities, and may either be similar or different from those of males. They therefore can be appreciated in the ways that are either gender specific or gender blind (Haug 1995).

69. There had, of course, been dissenting voices and many heated debates. But the case of Li Xiaojiang exemplified the point. She traveled a full circle from a feminist Marxism in the early 1980s to a Marxist feminism in 2003. See, most recently, Li 2003.

70. Dorothy Solinger, *Straits Times* (Singapore), 14 February 2005.

Chapter 3: People's Democracy?

1. Geraint Parry and Michael Moran regard "people's democracy" as among the "strange formulations" used by nondemocratic regimes. But they also suggest that liberal democracies are in need of looking at their own deficiencies (1994, 2, 8). Peter Moody typically views "people's democracy" as "a friendly version of the old totalitarian model" (1977, 12).

2. Weber, in commenting on the relationship between ethics and politics, stresses that "with equal honesty from their point of view," one's political opponents in "their ultimate intentions are [equally] noble" (1994 [1958], 216).

3. See the following examples in Saich and van de Ven 1995: the Futian incident against the "AB Corps" of 1930 (Stephen Averill); the execution of Wang Shiwei in 1944 (Timothy Cheek); and the cases of persecution during the Yanan rectification campaign. See also the battles over Trotskyism mostly within the CCP discussed in Benton 1992 and 1997; and see Chen 1994.

4. See Morgan 1988 for an account of the *demos* rising in the English revolution that replaced the "king's two bodies" with the "people's two bodies" and of the popularization of "we the people" in the American revolutions. See also Wallerstein 1991a.

5. In one of the controversies around Soviet history, it is noted that the Bolsheviks did win a majority in the second All-Russian Congress of Soviets. By contrast, "in the only reasonably free elections (they dissolved the Duma weeks after the assault of the Winter Palace), held just after the October Revolution, those for the Constituent Assembly, the bourgeois Liberals scored 5 per cent and the Mensheviks 3 per cent" (Hobsbawm 1997, 246). What later turned the Russian communists away from elections was a paradox in a way similar to that of today where secular democratic forces found themselves facing religious fundamentalism winning an electoral majority.

6. It is interesting to note that the Indian rebels in Chiapas, Mexico, for example, saw the notion of power rising from below as an "Asian" concept. At the same time China seemed to embrace the opposite as well; that is, as Lucien Pye observes, "the myth that legitimate power comes only from above" (1985, 184).

7. Note the following statement by Gao Gang, the chairman of the Shan-Gan-Ning border region: "What is democracy? The first condition is that the peasants have plenty of millet, that is, the people must eat well and be well clothed" (quoted in Selden 1971, 207). He apparently did not distinguish democracy from its necessary conditions.

8. Lucian Pye's remark is tricky but amusing: despite the violent travails that China had gone through, its "culture is devoid of any sense of tragedy. Politically the Chinese are undaunted optimists. . . . No other political culture relies so much on the psychological pleasure of suspending disbelief" (1985, 182–83).

9. When Confucius is asked, "Is there one single maxim that could ruin a country?" He replies, referring to "the pleasure of being prince" to not suffer contradictions, and that "if you are right and no one contradicts you, that's fine; but if you are wrong and no one contradicts you, is this not almost a case of 'one single maxim that could ruin a country?'" (1992, 125).

10. As Meisner notes, "Had it not been for the Populist orientations which drew Mao to the countryside in the first place, and also provided him with that very non-Leninist faith in the spontaneous revolutionary creativity of the peasant masses, it is most unlikely that there would have been a successful Communist revolution in China" (1982, 116, 148).

11. See the standard Marxist criticisms of Maoist idealism and adventurism put forward by Soviet Marxists in Rozman 1985.

12. According to Unger and Chan (1995, 43), the PRC had quietly accepted the International Labor Organization's tripartite corporatist principle: the official union federation is to represent workers, the government's Labor Bureau is to represent the state, and the new Chinese Enterprise Directors' Association is to represent employers. In the major industrial city of Liaoning, for example, more than fifteen thousand state firms staged a "democratic appraisal" of their managers through employee representative assemblies in the first four months of 1998. The result was that about 2,300 managers were demoted or fired after failing to obtain the necessary 60 percent of votes to keep their jobs (*China News Digest*, 1 June 1998).

13. For state corporatism, see Robert Wade, who notes that in corporatist systems, "the state charters or creates a small number of interest groups, giving them a monopoly of representation of occupational interests in return for which it claims the right to monitor them in order to discourage the expression of conflictual demands" (1990, 27). See also A. Chan 1993, 45, 59–60. Chan's only (and unlikely) example of "socialist societal corporatism" is the Jaruzelski regime's recognition of Solidarity in Poland. For studies of Chinese cases, see M. Yang 1989; and Nee 1995.

14. It was a CCP convention to use the label "democratic parties." In 1948, the May Day slogan was formulated to appeal to all "democratic parties, people's organizations and public personages" (quoted in Schram 1966, 249). These parties had been the Revolutionary Committee of the GMD, China Democratic League, China Democratic National Construction Association, Chinese Association for Promoting Democracy, Chinese Peasants' and Workers' Democratic Party, China Zhigong Party, Jiusan Scholarly Society, and Taiwan Democratic Self-Government League.

15. *People's Daily*, 12 September 2003.

16. However, commenting on the controversial evidence of village assemblies around 500 BC, Moore holds that "the general idea of ordinary people coming together to discuss critically the policies of the ruler did exist in ancient China" (1987, 72).

17. For a survey of the existing literature in the Chinese and Japanese languages on traditional self-government in China, see X. Zhao 1999. On the evolution of state-rural society relations under different political regimes in China, see Shue 1988.

18. The model is described in Mao's "May 7th Directive" (1967) with reference to the "cadre schools" set up in the countryside for party and government officials at the beginning of the Cultural Revolution. In Mao's "anti-urbanist" vision, "cities were gradually to be absorbed into a modernized and communized rural milieu as society moved to the ultimate goal of abolishing the distinction between town and countryside" (Meisner 1982, 72). See also Starr 1979, 230; and Meisner 1989.

19. Stephen Andors observes that "in organizing production within the modern industrial sector, the Soviets . . . adopted the same patterns of control, authority, and incentive represented by the latest scientific management theories of Frederick Taylor" (1977, 17). They briefly tried workers' control but retreated when economic reality impinged in 1918.

20. Andrew Walder holds that "the problems characteristic of centralized Soviet-style economies were intensified, not alleviated, by Maoist efforts at reform" (1982, 216). This assessment is premised on the view that only market-oriented reforms can offer an alternative to the Soviet model; and "the only 'Maoist experiment' that ever existed was to be found in the intellectual reconstructions of Western observers" (236). In truth, however, the experiment was not only quite straightforwardly an indigenous Chinese product, but also remembered inside China, in spite of whatever might be said by foreign commentators.

21. The rhetoric remained more or less current. For example, in commenting on the need of information disclosure for workers' interest in terms of "corporate governance," Wang Ruixiang, deputy director of the State Assets Supervision and Administration Commission, emphasized "workers' status as the owners of the enterprises" and "their democratic rights" (*Asia Pulse*, 15 October 2003).

22. He thus, in *State and Revolution* and elsewhere, reluctantly accepted Mikhail Bakunin's critique of the Soviet regime as a "red bureaucracy" operated by "state engineers." See Carr 1950, 249–55.

23. Bruce Cumings writes that "whereas socialist revolutions may or may not have been Marxist, after coming to power they have everywhere been Weberian. Modern states, whether socialist or capitalist, are in this sense alike" (1983, 6). In commenting on Russian politics, John Stuart Mill notes that the Czar himself is powerless against his bureaucrats: he can send any of them to Siberia but cannot govern without them or against their will (1956, 136).

24. The phrase was borrowed from Bruno Rizzi by Umberto Melotti (1977, 141–53) to characterize the PRC in Marx and the third world. The book was given relatively little attention by the Italian and English markets, but its Chinese translation in 1979 was a big hit and was heatedly debated in the political and intellectual circles in China.

25. As Mao told his colleagues in 1965: "You are making the socialist revolution and yet don't know where the bourgeoisie is. It is right in the Communist Party—those in power taking the capitalist road." Mao seemed to have not been informed about the notion of "new class" theorized by Milovan Djilas (1957) in Yugoslavia (see Schram 1989, 164).

26. Hence Friedrich Engels, quoted twice by Lenin: "So long as the proletariat still *needs* the state, it needs it not in the interests of freedom, but in the interests of the repression of its opponents, and when it becomes possible to speak of freedom, the state as such ceases to exist" (1932 [1918], 70–75). E. H. Carr explains that "repressive though the dictatorship of the proletariat was, it was unique in being a dictatorship exercised by a majority over a minority; and this not only gave it its democratic character, but enormously simplified its working" (1950, 248).

27. The larger context of "double hundred policy" and the policy shift afterward are documented in great detail in MacFarquhar 1974.

28. See the vivid report by a group of visiting American scientists as detailed in an anonymous pamphlet, *China: Science Walks on Two Legs* (New York: Avon Books, 1974).

29. Quoted in Song 2002. The materials, thirty million words in total, were edited and compiled by a team of Chinese scholars in the United States and Hong Kong.

30. Mao "sought at once to transform China through the general principles of Marxism, and to transform Marxism to meet the demands of China's specific historical circumstances" (Dirlik 1997, 69).

31. "Indispensable though Lenin's personal intervention was, the story of the October Revolution should not be turned into the myth of a lone genius" (Žižek, "Revolution Must Strike Twice," *London Review of Books*, 25 July 2002). This point again can be made for the case of Mao and the Cultural Revolution.

32. It is worth noting, however, that in terms of historical consciousness Mao and the Chinese communists fundamentally identified themselves with peasant rebellions rather than dynasties and emperors, despite their occasional remarks sounding the opposite. Finer (1999, 473, 527) thus missed the point in portraying an uninterrupted tradition of Chinese government from Qin to the PRC. On third world populism with the "plebiscitarian organizational structures" in which a charismatic leader could bypass intermediaries and appeal directly to the "people," see Mouzelis 1995, 234–40. See also Lipset 1963, chapter 5, on the "left fascism" of Peronism.

33. It was not until 1997 the label "counterrevolutionary" was finally removed from the criminal law. In the second session of the ninth NPC in 1999, Article 28 of the constitution was adopted to replace "counterrevolutionary activities" with "criminal activities undermining state security." The legality of the antisubversion law had been continuously debated within the legal profession.

34. See Charles Lindblom, who states "perhaps no nation in the world can match its energy in controlling schistosomiasis, typhoid, cholera, malaria, and venereal disease" (1977, 124).

35. Three periods were identified in the Chinese communist history: a pre-1949 "wartime democracy," a "mobilizational democracy" in 1949–78, and a post-1978 "law-based

democracy" (Village Self-Government Research Group, 1997, chapter 12). The phrase "mobilizational democracy" has been used in other contexts with different connotations. Roberto Unger (1996), for example, sees it as a normative goal for what he calls "the radicalization of the democratic project" along with "extended social democracy" and "radical polyarchy."

36. For the right to nonparticipation in democracies, see Walzer 1994a.

37. The "right mix" of participation, passivity, and deference is promoted in Almond and Verba 1963.

38. The characterizations are explained in Gills et al. 1993. See the critical discussion of liberal democracy displacing popular democracy in Luckham 1998.

39. Many disagree with this statement. For the desirability and feasibility of workplace democracy as a third way, see, for example, Dahl, 1985. See also the reflections on the Yugoslav experiment with self-management in Markovic and Petrovic 1979, part iv.

40. This tradition may reveal something about Chinese history being "super stable" in terms of civilizational continuity, but also exceedingly violent—a common observation that refers in particular to frequent and large-scale peasant rebellions as well as to the brutality of the country's modern experience.

41. Marie-Claire Bergere, who in referring to the inaction of NPC and the slowness of actors in seeking a solution through the body, states that this "non-institutionalization of the conflict proved to be fatal for the movement, in that there were no political alternatives to the intervention of the army" (1992, 244).

42. Lijphart discovers that in the east and the south, the prevalent political cultures are based on a strong concern for harmony and are "much more consensual than majoritarian." A Nigerian scholar is quoted with admiration in saying that "Africans are past masters in consultation, consensus, and consent. . . . there is no sanctioned and institutionalized opposition in our traditional system of governance. Traditionally, politics for us has never been a zero-sum game" (1999, 307–8).

43. In January 1962 Mao told a party conference that "we must bring democracy into play and encourage others to talk . . . Meanwhile, we forbid the organization of secret cliques. We do not fear open opposition, but object to secret opposition" (quoted in Starr 1979, 211).

44. See Furet, who notes that totalitarianism "refers primarily to the pretension of a party to be its own end, precluding its members from possessing any other goal in their lives except to serve it to the death." As an ideal type, this model "has the advantage of closely following the course of events and the disadvantage of potential oversimplification through linear causality" (1999, 137, 161).

45. This democratic dimension is also a humanist one: "While the starting-point of totalitarianism of the Left has been and ultimately still is man, his reason and salvation, that of the Right's totalitarian schools has been the collective entity, the State, the nation, or the race. The former trend remains essentially individualist, atomistic and rationalist even when it raises the class or party to the level of absolute ends" (Talmon 1952, 6–7).

46. Rousseau is seeking "a form of association which will defend and protect every member belonging to it, and in which the individual, while uniting himself with all the others, will obey only himself and retain free as before" (1993, 191). Similarly and famously, for Marx and Engels, in place of the old bourgeois civil society with its class antagonisms, there shall be "an association, in which the free development of each is the condition for the free development of all" (1969, 127).

47. The citizen of Sparta or Rome, as an analogy, was "proudly free, yet a marvel of discipline. He was an equal member of the sovereign nation, and at the same time had no life or interests outside the collective tissue" (Talmon 1952, 11).

48. In Eastern and Central Europe, according to Sabrina Ramet, the decay took five stages: the defection of intellectuals and revival of free thinking, the emergence of dissident and opposition groups, the construction of a civil society, the decline of official legitimacy, and the collapse of established institutions (1996, 4–5).

49. Daniel A. Bell is only slightly exaggerating in describing "Chinese imperial history as a constant struggle between Han Fei's *realpolitik* and Confucian morality" (2000, 29–30). Han (280–233 BC), the Legalist, is regarded by many sinologists as China's Machiavelli.

50. See Dahl 1989, chapter 12. He also discusses "process versus process" (chapter 13) and the paradox that "even a just process might sometimes produce an unjust outcome" (163).

51. Przeworski, for example, sees democracy as "only a system for processing conflicts without killing one another" and "an act of subjecting all interests to competition, of institutionalizing uncertainty" (1991, 95, 34).

52. Larry Diamond, Juan Linz, and Martin Lipset suggest that the "issues of so-called 'economic and social democracy' be separated from the question of governmental structure. Otherwise the definitional criteria of democracy will be so broadened and the empirical reality narrowed to a degree that makes study of the phenomenon very difficult" (1990, 6).

53. As an example, see the ordeal of the failure of citizen in Shanghai trying to become a candidate due to the blocking of the law by local officials (reported in the *New York Times*, 2 March 2003).

54. The 1982 constitution regards villagers' committees as "mass organizations of self-management at the grassroots level." In 1998, the party's Central Committee and the State Council issued a joint circular on implementing "the open principle of village affairs and democratic management," and the NPC adopted a corresponding organic law. The urban "resident committee organizational law" was adopted in 1989.

55. Xinhuanet (http://www.xinhuanet.com), 22 December 2003.

56. These texts are collected in Xiao 1999.

57. For Selden, these elections "were significant not only for the internal politics of the base area; they had national and international implications," even though the party "remained the ultimate arbiter in policy matters" (1971, 127–28, 135).

58. Vivienne Shue (1988) describes petty officials shifting identities back and forth from governmental delegates to communal representatives. See also Esherick and Rankin 1990.

59. Among more optimistic assessments, see Lawrence 1995. Observing a village election process in Hebei, she found that "institutional reforms in the village have clearly made local cadres more accountable than in the past" (66–67). According to an influential Chinese report, the villagers' committee is in its nature "a modern rural management model by democratic principles" beneficial to social coherence of interests and power. It is democratic based on individual rights and will "provide a solid social foundation and precious technical experience for China's democratization" (J. Yu 2001, 43, 437).

60. The phrase "decent burial" is borrowed from Perry Anderson's discussion of the concept of the "Asiatic mode of production" (1974, 548). The CCP central committee

(1985) issued a resolution on Mao's legacy in 1981 with a so-called 3:7 ratio verdict or 70 percent achievements and 30 percent mistakes.

61. Wang Huning explains this line of argument in terms of five layers of integration: party-state, legislative-executive, political-economic, political-legal, and political-social (1987, 76–82).

62. Since 1979, the NPC had adopted over 440 legislative resolutions, of which more than 220 remained valid. Local people's congresses had made over 8,000 locally applicable laws and legal regulations. The autonomous regions stipulated over 480 self-governing and separate regulations (Wu Bangguo, chairman of the NPC, in the *People's Daily*, 2 February 2004).

63. Robert Benewick (1998) sees the distinction as one between neoauthoritarian and democratic legal reforms. Barrett McCormick identifies a major difference as "whereas Chinese law is primarily a tool of state power, American law protects a margin of relative social autonomy" (1990, 125–26). See also Alford 1993.

64. Francis Fukuyama deems it reasonable to think that "a systematic illiberal and non-democratic alternative combining technocratic economic rationalism with paternalistic authoritarianism may gain ground in the Far East" (1999, 243).

65. Christopher Hill writes about "those marvelous decades" of popular revolt as the second front of the English revolution when the radicals "dreamed of all men being equal economically and politically" in the upside-down world. "We may be too conditioned by the way up the world has been for the last 300 years to be fair to those in the 17th century who saw other possibilities" (1972, 294, 312).

66. It is in the nature of despotism that it should foster single-minded material desires and propagate their havoc, hence lower the collective morale. The passage is quoted in Bell 1998, 25.

67. For Joseph Levenson (1959), "the right to rebel" is a contradiction in terms, for people rose not because they had a legal right to do so but because the existing order left them little room to survive. Barrington Moore, by contrast, recognizes such "a right to resist unjust and arbitrary authority" in the Chinese tradition, even though it is still not "the right of revolution" (1987, 73).

68. This was the case even though he appeared also as a precursor of Romantic sinophobia in his portrayal of the Manchu conquest of China as a major example of how civilization corrupts. See Blue 1999, 75.

69. See Janet Coleman's discussion (2005). Her reading, however, also shows that Locke is an egalitarian in his interpretation of private property.

70. Kant also believes in a "constitution allowing the greatest possible human freedom in accordance with laws which ensure that the freedom of each can coexist with the freedom of all the others" (1991, 29).

71. It is unclear, however, if Rousseau's citizenship is inclusive of "all." "Locke and Rousseau accepted, and Mill defended, the principle that a demos might properly exclude large numbers of adults who are subject to laws made by the demos" (Dahl, 1989, 125).

72. A typical statement by Joseph Schumpeter holds that there is "no such thing as a uniquely determined common good that all people could agree on or be made to agree on by the force of rational argument," due to intrinsically pluralist human values and judgments (1947, 251). But there is also a more positive and stronger tradition in Western political thought. See, for example, Isaiah Berlin (1998, 304–5) on Machiavelli's insistence on common good. Kant seems to strike a balance by stressing the

independence of individual citizens as "the condition" for the "unity of the will of *all*" (selected in Hayden 2001, 117).

73. See, in particular, Kant 1991 [1784]. See Charles Taylor, "the fundamental norms of freedom, equality and mutual benefit have to be captured in the right kind of common political culture, which for Rousseau is that of the General Will. The solitary individual of the State of Nature is now seen to be irrelevant to this issue; he represents if anything the pre-human stage of humanity" (1999, 160).

74. Moreover, the English people are "free only during the election of Members of Parliament; as soon as the Members are elected, the people is enslaved; it is nothing" (quoted in Held 1987, 75). In contrast, John Stuart Mill states that the "substitution of delegation for representation is the one and only danger of democracy" (1962, 197). As representative democracy gained dominance over direct democracy in political thinking in the past century, many of the critiques today are directed to "delegative democracy" as a deformed democracy (e.g., in Latin America). See O'Donnell 1992.

75. Experiments with non-party, extra-party, or even anti-party politics in some African and Latin American countries are discussed in Amin 1991. See Kasfir 1988 on "non-party democracy" in Uganda. A Latin American case of the "civic committee movement" aspired to replace party politics is studied in Conroy 1999. For the idea of "demarchy," see Burnheim 1985, 9. Vertical accountability may or may not require a comprehensive electoral system (see O'Donnell 1998).

76. See B. Manin, who notes that "the source of legitimacy is not the predetermined will of individuals, but rather the process of its formation . . . legitimate law is the result of general deliberation and not the expression of general will" (quoted in Habermas 1996, 446).

77. Market transitions today are yet to discover in practice the original utilitarian synthesis of laissez faire and a public-good maximizing democracy, as elaborated by Adam Smith, Jeremy Bentham, or James Mill. On the model of "protective democracy," see Held, 1987, 67–69; and Macpherson 1977, chapter 2.

Chapter 4: Liberty and Liberation

1. The PRC government was conceived to be weak in its handling of territorial disputes with Japan and in its inability to solicit from the Japanese government a long-awaited apology for war crimes. See Wasserstrom 1999.

2. For example, for Renata Salecl, "The moral majority in [East European] socialism was democratic and antitotalitarian—its voice was an oppositional one . . . It thus articulated the distinction between civil society (in the name of which it spoke) and the totalitarian state as a distinction between morality and corruption" (1997, 83).

3. For an ardent critique of China's "enlightenment intellectuals," see Wang Hui 1998. See also Gan's critique (2003a) of the "political philistine" in relation to the liberal dismissal of mass democracy.

4. Wang Hui sees "a multiplicity of significance" in the event: "It was a farewell to the old era and at the same time a protest against the inherent social contradictions of the new; it was (for students and intellectuals) an appeal for democracy and freedom, even as it was (for the workers and other urban dwellers) a demand for social equality and justice" (2003a, 62).

5. In commemoration of the twelfth anniversary of June 4th, Wang wrote "My Position on Students' Mistakes and Government's Crimes," unpublished manuscript.

6. Wang Chaohua, "Unending 1989," unpublished manuscript.

7. See Rong et al. 1997 for the local government reform proposal on the transition from centralized mobilization to a decentralized "pressure system" and, further, to a "democratic, cooperative government organization."

8. See Quintin Hoare and Geoffrey Nowell-Smith's introduction to "State and Civil Society" in Gramsci's *Selections from the Prison Notebooks*. Gramsci sees that "civil society resists *before* the frontal assault on the State." Elsewhere he decries the state in the West as "an outer ditch, behind which there stands a powerful system of fortresses and earthworks." The state is also defined as "political society + civil society" or a balance between the two. In yet another passage, Gramsci stresses that "in concrete reality, civil society and State are one and the same" (1971, 235, 238, 263).

9. See Slavoj Žižek, who notes that "liberal democracy, in truth, is the political arrangement under which capital thrives best. This is Lenin's ultimate lesson: it is only by throwing off our attachment to liberal democracy, which cannot survive without private property, that we can become effectively anti-capitalist" (2002). This logic is confirmed by the market transition in postcommunism where the first urge under a new political democracy was privatization.

10. According to Ulrich Beck, "Market fundamentalism is a form of democratic illiteracy. What the market precisely does not do is provide its own justification. This form of economy can survive only in conjunction with material security, social rights, and democracy" (1992). See also David Held, who notes that "the necessity to minimize inequality in the ownership and control of the means of production is fundamental to the possibility of an open, unbiased political agenda. Without clear restrictions on private ownership, a necessary condition of democracy cannot be met" (1987, 294).

11. As part of a long tradition, Giovanni Sartori distinguishes the two concepts in terms of demo-protection versus demo-power (1987). For his discussion of "democracy without liberalism," see (1962, 374). Isaiah Berlin sees freedom and democracy as potentially conflicting ideals in his 1958 Oxford lecture (reprinted in [1969]). Among more recent watch phrases are "liberal autocracy" and "illiberal democracy." See, for example, Bell et al. 1995; and Zakaria, 2004.

12. Eric Hobsbawm describes the dynamic in (1994, parts 2 and 3). An example at hand is the land reform carried out by the GMD in Taiwan in the 1950s that paved the way for the island's remarkable economic growth, equitable development, and democratization. The same party's violent opposition to an agrarian revolution decisively contributed to its defeat in the civil war.

13. In Axel Honneth's (1996, 175–78) reading of Hegel and James Mead, "community-generating values" coincide with the moral conditions of modern law on the one hand and individual autonomy on the other. They can be so mutually embedded that in the patterns of their interaction all subjects are recognized as simultaneously equal and individually particular.

14. In reviewing the work of the Italian thinker Noberto Bobbio, Perry Anderson (1992, 87, 90–91) offers a random list of recent authors who have ventured to synthesize liberal and socialist traditions. See also David Beetham's summary of liberal versus socialist propositions in (1999, 45–46).

15. See debates in *Dushu* 4, 2003. Articles circulated in a dozen popular sites on the Internet (January-March 2002) in campaigning for a defense of the (socialist) constitution.

16. For the plight of the rural poor, see the book-length report by Chen Guidi and Chun Tao (2003), which provoked a national cry for redress. See also a roundtable published in *Southern Weekend*, 13 March 2003. Among a group of influential intellectuals, Qin Hui (2003, 97–98) argues for a "conditional privatization" of the land. Among other proposals, there was one for granting farmers permanent land lease without changing formal state and collective ownership.

17. Sun's GMD won the parliamentary election in 1913. Lenin wrote a series of commentaries in praise of China in revolution. In contrast, in the United States "people asked to sign the Bill of Rights regularly brush it away as an alien document" (Friedman 2000, 247).

18. The "four big freedoms" (as mentioned in chapter 3) were removed on an earlier party decision. To question that decision is, of course, not to oppose the effort to draw lessons from the destruction of "campaign politics." But the task yet to be fulfilled is the provision in the place of "big freedoms" for civil rights to free thinking, political criticism, and popular participation.

19. The "theory of blood lineage" (*xietong lun*) prevailed to separate those with a "red" family background from those without, followed by discrimination against the latter groups and individuals by the former. It was striking to note how a precapitalist "feudal" notion of hereditary status could revive in a supposedly postcapitalist society. See White 1989.

20. See also Xu 2000; and Zhang 2000 (the title of Zhang's essay, "The Third Road" refers to "the third line" between the CCP and the GMD).

21. On "the bid of liberalism" 1920–1923 by the politically engaged national bourgeoisie, see Bergere 1989, 217–27. "The sorry history of the Chinese bourgeoisie in the 1920s shows . . . that the State is indispensable to the constitution of a society and that liberalism itself must be a product of the State" (226–27).

22. On communist liberalism around the new culture movement that survived into the Yan'an period but was later crushed, see for example, the case of Ding Ling in Barlow 1989 and the case of Wang Shiwei in Apter and Cheek 1994.

23. The recent debate over the "China threat" was initiated in Bernstein and Munro 1997. See also Johnson 1999 and Cumings 1999.

24. Arundhati Roy, who comes from liberal democratic India, calls democracy "the modern world's holy cow" and "the Free World's whore," and she adds that it is "willing to dress up, dress down, willing to satisfy a whole range of tastes, available to be used and abused at will," and becomes "little more than a hollow word, a pretty shell" (www .commondreams.org/headlines, 18 May 2003). Needless to say, here she is not writing for a political science journal refereed for political correctness and sensitivity.

25. An outstanding example of mobilized protest was that in response to the death by gang beating, and police neglect, of Sun Zhigang, a university graduate among immigrants in Guangzhou. The incident and subsequent online protest led to a change in legal provisions to protect individuals in a "floating population." Influential Internet sites promoting the protest were http://www.qglt.com and http://huazhen.net, among others.

26. Gordon White thus suggests the inclusion of "a broader array of rights and freedoms" and an effort to "supplement the language of rights with the language of welfare" in understanding various regime types (1996, 210).

27. For an introductory analysis of the mixed records of democracy and human rights in the former communist states, see White, Gardner, and Schopflin 1982, chapter 6.

28. See Therborn 1995 (337–41) on the three steering goals of East European socialism: socioeconomic development, workers' rights and women's rights, and national security.

29. Gray also notes that a "regime can be highly legitimate without honoring values that are distinctively liberal"; and "it is a mistake to think that as regimes become more legitimate they become more alike" (2000, 106, 109–10).

30. The following passage from the 1948 UN declaration reminds us how far we still are from these minimal goals so well set over half a century ago: "Everyone has the right to a standard of living adequate for the health and well-being of himself and his family, including food, clothing, housing and medical care and necessary social services, and the right to security in the event of unemployment, sickness, disability, widowhood, old age or other lack of livelihood in circumstances beyond his control" (United Nations 1988 [1948], 13).

31. Jiwei Ci (1994) sees Maoism as a sublimated hedonism logically leading to post-Mao consumerism via a failed utopia.

32. Industrial accidents killed about 50,000 people out of the 385,000 incidents reported nationwide in the first five months of 2003 alone; many of these deaths could have been avoided if the regulations had been observed. See the report from the State Administration of Work Safety in the *People's Daily*, 11 June 2003.

33. For example, the prospect of a democracy in China that combines Western liberty and Eastern community is contemplated in Hall and Ames 1998.

Conclusion: Rethinking the Chinese Model

1. The recent history of the computer industry is a good example of "creative destruction" in the patterns of technological innovation and competition that drive capitalism to enormous waste while expanding. See Schumpeter 1947, chapter 7.

2. For James O'Connor (1973, 6), the contradictory relationship between public welfare and capital profitability is based on two premises, one is that the capitalist state must fulfill two mutually conflicting functions of accumulation and legitimation; the other is the fiscal crisis impeding the state. Adam Przeworski and Michael Wallerstein (1988) are concerned with the structural contradiction of the state in social democracies as a historical compromise needing both profits and votes: profits cannot fall so low as to threaten reproduction and wages cannot fall so low as to make profits appear vested interests. See also Claus Offe on capitalist democracy seeking "the collective interests of all members of a class society dominated by capital" (1996, chapter 8). Further, Meghnad Desai argues that "the enfranchised worker, by being brought into democracy, buys into capitalism" (2002 , 308–9).

3. Istvan Meszaros (1994) explains how capital as a "command system" is a mode of accumulation, and thus accumulation may be secured in different ways for different purposes under different regimes.

4. See Samir Amin (1998) who notes that Lenin's state capitalism was in the end replaced by "a capitalism with capitalists" after the collapse of the Soviet Union. Meanwhile his three models of third world development are socialist ("national autocentric"), statist ("capitalism without capitalists"), and capitalist ("peripheral capitalism") (xii). Compared with Sovietism as "a historical misadventure of the Russian revolution," he sees Maoism as "the first major attempt to move ahead" (xxvi-xxvii). And unlike transi-

tions elsewhere, China's post-Mao undertaking had "a very coherent plan" which he calls "a national and social capitalist project" that might be made into "part of a long-term socialist transition" (134).

5. The outflow amounted to $48 billion in 2000 and $50 billion in 2002, which exceeded FDI ($40.7 billion in 2000) and was a close match to Venezuela, Mexico, and Argentina, the world's largest capital-losing countries. See Dong Furen cited in *Far Eastern Economic Review*, 27 March 2003. This did not include China's new FDIs to other countries.

6. Jadwiga Staniszkis describes "political capitalism" in 1991. For the debate between the continuity and interruption theses in light of elite reproduction in postcommunist transitions, see Szelenyi 1978.

7. Qin Hui's analogy is the Stolpypin road: "This is a period when the specters of Stalin and Pol Pot are still on the loose, even while Suharto and Pinochet are riding the tide of the time. The first can still rob people's private property for the coffers of the state, while the second can rob the coffers of the state for the private fortunes of power-holders. In practice, they share a tacit bottom line: the first can still punish 'Havels' as before, and the second have no difficulty dispatching more 'Allendes' " (2003, 107). See also David Zweig, "The Bureaucrats Who Roused a Dragon," *South China Morning Post*, 23 September 2003.

8. Speech at the Central Party School, 22 September 2001 (FBIS-CHI-2001-0924).

9. The 1992 party constitution begins with the following statement: "The Communist Party of China is the vanguard of the Chinese working class, the faithful representative of the interests of the people of all nationalities in China, and the force at the core leading China's cause of socialism. The party's ultimate goal is the creation of a communist social system" (see Lieberthal, 1995, 383). Jiang did not repudiate traditional rhetoric but justified his proposal in the Marxist terminology of pursuing "advanced productive forces" (see his responses to questions submitted by the *New York Times* prior to the interview text publication on 9 August 2001). The fact that the CCP's general secretary had no problem giving a friendly interview to the leading newspaper of the capitalist world, on invitation, speaks for itself.

10. Typically, four "10,000-character manifestos" were produced by the "leftists" since 1995, one of which was translated in *China Quarterly*, December 1996. It might be tempting to liken Jiang's effort with Tony Blair's modernization project of New Labor, though there was little sign that communism in China was turning social democratic. The party had, however, dispatched several mission delegations in recent years to tour Europe and talk with the officials of the ruling central-leftist parties.

11. For a critique of the neo-liberal doctrine of "soft-budget constraint" being overcome only by "clarified" property rights, see Cui 1998. For the Chinese skepticism toward privatization, see Nolan and Wang 1999.

12. For debates inside China over the benefits, costs, and risks of an open policy and its political legitimacy, see Zhang et al. 1996.

13. According to Peter Nolan (as quoted in the *Economist* on 20 March 2004), China had not built even a single truly competitive global firm, including any listed in the Fortune 500. The failure is attributable to the misguided process of reorganizing large SOEs, fragmentation in central policies and central-provincial contradictions, and a widened technological gap between Chinese and multinational companies. See also Nolan 2001.

14. China used most of the profits gained from export to reinvest in its predominantly dollar-based financial assets. There had been an ongoing debate inside China concerning the cost of holding an enormous amount of foreign reserves and the policy of buying U.S. Treasury bonds, which helped finance a huge American trade deficit. Such buying and holding had cost a fraction of annual national income since the mid-1990s. By November 2003 China possessed $144 billion U.S. Treasury bonds, or 9.6 percent of the total holdings of foreign-currency government securities, to the extent that Morgan Stanley's chief economist had to explain "why we ought to be thanking the Chinese" (*People's Daily*, 17 March 2004). There has been some expert pressure on further diversifying the country's currency holding. Cf. Yue, "An Analysis of the Domestic Systemic Origin of China's Participation in Economic Globalization through Forcefully Attracting Foreign Capital," online at http://xueshu.newyouth .beida-online.com, 30 August 2001.

15. "Illegitimate income" is defined as that gained through illegal means, such as "power-money deals" (*quanqian jiaoyi*), bribery, tax fraud and evasion, smuggling, and production or trade of counterfeit goods (Su Hainan, Ministry of Labour and Social Security, FBIS translated text, *Xinhua* Domestic Service 12 November 2002).

16. For the Wenzhou debate, see Z. Lin 1992.

17. See "A Report on the Development of China's Market Economy," *Xinhua* News Agency 13 April 2003. Being a "market economy" measured by such variables as government behavior, entrepreneurial autonomy, productive factors, trading environment, and monetary management is important for China to counter, for example, the "anti-dumping" laws in the WTO framework.

18. In 2001, there were 1.88 million firms and over 21 million employees in China's private sector (CASS 2002, 233). According to an authoritative report, from 1978 to 2001 the contribution by the nonstate sector increased from 42.2 percent to 67.2 percent in terms of GDP, from 22.4 percent to 76.8 percent in industrial output value, from 21.7 percent to 68.1 percent in job creation, and from 18.1 percent (in 1980) to 52.7 percent in tax revenue ("An Analysis of the Marketification of the Chinese Economy," *Economy Daily*, 25 November 2002).

19. By April 2004, China had shut down 3,377 insolvent SOEs through administrative intervention and resettled their 6.2 million employees. Among the 196 state enterprises were such giants as China Mobile, Shinopec, and China Eastern Airlines. See www.xinhuanet.com, 21 June 2004; straitstimes.asia1.com.sg, 10 November 2003.

20. Ranked by the WTO as the world's ninth (in 1999) and seventh (in 2000) largest exporter and, later, the third largest trading economy in 2004, China's total imports and exports were worth $509 billion in 2001, $851.2 billion in 2003, and $1.15 trillion in 2004, or a third in its foreign trade dependency ratio. Over 300,000 foreign companies operated in China with a capacity that accounted for at least 40 percent of China's trading volume. China had a trade surplus of $103.2 billion with the United States in 2003 but a huge deficit with the rest of the world (e.g., $67.2 billion in 2002). See *China Brief* 3:16, 16 December 2003.

21. Stephanie Hoo reported in the *Washington Post* (23 May 2004) on an example of the homegrown Red Flag Linux struggling over maintaining domestic standards for its EVD technology that would also be compatible with the products in the world market. Meanwhile, Rhett Dawson, president of the IT Industry Council in Washington, complained that the Chinese were "trying to grow their own industry on

the technology we've developed. They have a deliberate policy" (quoted in Harris 2005, 14).

22. See the finance minister Xiang Huaicheng's remark reported in the *Asian Wall Street Journal*, 19 June 2002, and Xu Shanda, deputy chief of the State Taxation Bureau, in the *Hong Kong Dispatch* 17 March 2004. See Saich, who notes that government revenue as a percentage of GDP declined to around 11 percent in 1995 and stabilized at around 12 percent in 1999 (2004, 152). The measurement of "comprehensive national strength" had been adopted by the State Statistics Bureau's annual report since 1999.

23. The political and ideological debates in China over the nature and direction of reform had been intense. Edward Friedman (1983) discusses the struggles between "Marxist idealists" (the Maoists) and "Marxist materialists" (the pragmatists). Carl Riskin's (1991) characterization of Mao's political economy as "neither plan nor market" remains instructive for understanding post-Mao changes.

24. Commenting on the USSR and China, Samir Amin is convinced that "even if they didn't create socialism, they are better off for having delinked." Taking "relinking" as a cause of postsocialist difficulties, he recommends "delinking," which would also be a strategic choice for developing countries to be unchained by the "Washington consensus" and structural adjustment conditionality (Amin et al. 1982, 183–84).

25. The Marxist economist Lin Zili (1996) argues most systematically for the "four great socializations" of market, property rights, labor, and knowledge/information. Part of his argument is translated in Toward the Market, Chinese Economic Studies 1996. David Schweickart (2002) proposed a concrete counterproject to market capitalism by using a "successor-system" theory to describe the rationale and workings of a system of economic democracy. In another reading of Marx—and contemplating the complementarity between labor and capital, public goods and private gains, and needs and profits without invoking major inequalities—Meghnad Desai highlights intercorporation ownership in contemporary Germany and Japan. He argues that profitability of the capitalist order is imperative as the alternative could well be fascism rather than socialism. Moreover, "the advantages of capitalism—its wealth-producing ability, its dynamism and innovativeness—are dialectically connected to its disadvantages," and this is why the debate over market socialism cannot be conclusive. For Desai, China's experiment is one of the most interesting episodes in modern political economy (2002, 309, 268, 295, 272).

26. For Schumpeter (1947, 81–86), revolutionary technologies in constant and ruthless competition amount to a "process of Creative Destruction," which in turn destabilize capitalism. Reluctant to endorse socialism defined in terms of large corporations and autocratic central planning, his answer to the question "can capitalism survive?" is nevertheless a resolute "no" primarily because it threatens liberal civilization (61).

27. The GDP in 2002 was at least sevenfold that of 1978 by comparable currency value, while the economy grew much faster than did the population. As admitted in China's official reports, twenty to twenty-five years ago a higher percentage of girls in the countryside went to schools, more clinics were open to cash-short villagers and the urban poor, and far fewer, if indeed any, homeless people or forced prostitutes or drug addicts were on the streets.

28. The persistent "Mao fever" since the 1990s and the unusual popularity of the plays "Guevara" and "Confucius and Mao Speak" (both by Zhang Guangtian) are outstanding examples.

29. Wenfang Tang and William Parish (2000) discuss "a fundamental redefinition of the social contract the government has with society" in the reform period. The socialist contract confirmed an egalitarian, redistributive order and, in return, "the state demanded sacrifices in current consumption, a leveling of individual aspirations, and obedience to all-knowing party redistributors." With the social contract of the market, in return for abandoning egalitarianism, job security and other welfare benefits, there was free reign given to individualistic aspirations (3–4).

30. In the collection edited by Richard Edmonds (2000), see in particular Michael Palmer on relevant laws and regulations, Robert Ash and Richard Edmonds on land resources, James Nickum and Liu Changming on water, Vaclav Smil on energy, Eduard Vermeer on pollution, and others on population. See also, Jasper Becker, "China Awakens to Its Devastated Environment" in *Asia Times*, 28 August 2003.

31. Wen thus holds that China does not have much choice but to stick with gradualism to avoid the rapid technological modernization of agriculture and the fast expansion of capital-intensive sectors.

32. Yet, without the policy, "China today would have a population of 1.6 billion instead of 1.3 billion" (*New York Times*, 30 May 2004). In 2003, the population's natural growth rate was 6.01 per 1,000 (*People's Daily*, 28 February 2004).

33. See the report in *South China Morning Post*, 17 June 2004.

34. See Hu Jintao cited in note 29 to the introduction. See also Wen Jiabao in *People's Daily* online (http://english.peopledaily.gm.cn), 18 March 2004. Gao Fang, a noted party theorist, believes that expanding democracy "would not threaten the party's grip on power. Instead, the changes would strengthen the party, and eventually give it the confidence to compete in multiparty elections (*Washington Post*, 14 March 2004).

35. http://www.xinhuanet.com, 20 February, 4 March, and 24 April 2004.

36. The official goals were set up to enhance national capabilities through poverty alleviation and human development, including high school enrollment and an adult literacy rate of 95 percent or higher, and a well-established, affordable public medical care system for both urban and rural populations by 2010. See "The Program of Action for Sustainable Development in China in the Early 21st Century," http://www.xinhuanet.com, 26 July and 28 September 2003.

37. Sun Zhongshan identified his Principle of People's Livelihood with "socialism, which is also called communism or *datongism*" (1956 [1924], 765ff). *Datong* would be an equal and crimeless society as described in Confucius, *The Book of Rites*. Kang Youwei, the great reformer of China's last imperial dynasty, called for the elimination of class, state and family in a world of great harmony in *The Book of Datong* (1994 [1902]).

38. A total of 4.2 million registered volunteers were working in anti-poverty, community service, education, disability aid, environment, disaster relief, and other welfare programs in 2002, totaling 450 million hours (*People's Daily*, 21 July 2003).

39. It may be not the case, however, that Chinese traditions were more pro-nature in terms of either cultural attitude or preservationist practices. Mark Elvin's splendid study *The Retreat of the Elephants: An Environmental History of China* (2004) tells a different story (of which the title is indicative).

40. For easy access to these ideas, which obviously echo Marx's famous remark on limited human freedom in creating their own history, see North 1990. For the idea of increasing returns, see Paul Pierson 2000: in such a process, "the probability of further steps

along the same path increases with each move down that path" because the costs of exit rise (252).

41. As Habermas writes, the "horizon open to the future, which is determined by expectations in the present, guides our access to the past. Inasmuch as we appropriate past experiences with an orientation to the future, the authentic present is preserved as the locus of continuing tradition and of innovation at once (2000, 13).

42. For an example of non-"deep structure" thinking, see Simon 2000 on "organizational economy" (751–52). Different polities and politics respond to the same events and injections differently. Arguably, structural adjustment worked for Chile but not much elsewhere; shock therapy revived Poland, perhaps, but not Russia. Local performances can be as different as in the states of Kerala and Uttar Pradesh in India.

43. Sarah Cook notes government efforts at unconventional activities of delivering public goods in China and sees them as a challenge to the "predictions of established theories of transition, in particular that bureaucrats will resist changes that reduce their own power, that they are motivated by rent-seeking opportunities, and that clearly defined property rights are a prerequisite for successful economic development" 1999, 61, 83–84.

44. For a critical usage of "postsocialist condition" without reference to China, see Nancy Fraser (1997, introduction) on the three background factors for social theory: the absence of a credible emancipatory project as an alternative to the present order, a general decoupling of cultural politics from social policies, and a decentering of the struggles for equality in the face of market domination.

45. Hence Samir Amin's optimism: whatever the ups and downs of the postsocialist policies in Russia and China, "their societies will probably impose on the governments the submission of their external relations (even if intensified) to the logic of their specific internal choices. In that sense, they are not prepared to reintegrate into the world-system and return to capitalism. In that sense, 1917 did not inaugurate a mere bracket in history which is now ending, but launched the era of postcapitalism" (1990, 183).

46. See Bruce Cumings's commonsense remark: "The crimes of the cultural Revolution do not make the Maoist vision empty of content, just as the blighted lives of millions of minority people in the United States do not make American democracy nothing more than a cruel and empty promise" (1983, 6).

REFERENCES

Abernethy, David. 2000. *The Dynamics of Global Dominance: European Overseas Empires, 1415–1980*. New Haven, Conn.: Yale University Press.

Alford, William. 1993. "Double-Edged Swords Cut Both Ways: Law and Legitimacy in the PRC." *Daedalus* 122:2 (spring).

Almond, Gabriel, and G. B. Powell. 1966. *Comparative Politics: A Developmental Approach*. Boston: Little, Brown.

Almond, Gabriel, and Sidney Verba. 1963. *The Civic Culture: Political Attitude and Democracy in Five Nations*. Princeton, N.J.: Princeton University Press. Althusser, Louise. 1972. *Lenin and Philosophy, and Other Essays*. London: New Left Books.

Amin, Samir. 1977. *Imperialism and Unequal Development*. New York: Monthly Review Press.

———. 1980. *Class and Nation*. New York: Monthly Review Press.

———. 1991. "The Issue of Democracy in the Contemporary Third World." *Socialism and Democracy* 12 (January).

———. 1998. *The Future of Maoism*. 2nd ed. Delhi: Rainbow.

Amin, Samir, Giovanni Arrighi, Andre Gunder Frank, and Immanuel Wallerstein, 1982. *Dynamics of Global Crisis*. New York: Monthly Review Press.

———. 1990. *Transforming the Revolution: Social Movements and the World-System*. New York: Monthly Review Press.

Amsden, Alice. 1989. *Asia's Next Giant: South Korea and Late Industrialization*. New York: Oxford University Press.

Anderson, Benedict. 1991. *Imagined Communities: Reflections on the Origins and Spread of Nationalism*. London: Verso.

———. 2001. "Western Nationalism and Eastern Nationalism." *New Left Review* 9 (May/June).

Anderson, Perry. 1974. *Lineages of the Absolutist State*. London: New Left Books.

———. 1992. *A Zone of Engagement*. London: Verso.

———. 1998. *The Origins of Postmodernity*. London: Verso.

———. 2001. "Testing Formula Two." *New Left Review* 8 (March/April).

Andors, Stephen. 1977. *China's Industrial Revolution: Politics, Planning and Management, 1949 to the Present*. London: Robertson.

Appelbaum, Richard, and Jeffrey Henderson, eds. 1992. *States and Development in the Asian Pacific Rim*. London: Sage.

Appleby, Joyce, Lynn Hunt, and Margaret Jacob. 1994. *Telling the Truth about History*. New York: Norton.

Apter, David, and Timothy Cheek, eds. 1994. *Wang Shiwei and "Wild Lilies": Rectification and Purges in the CCP, 1942–4*. Armonk, N.Y.: M. E. Sharpe.

Apter, David, and Tony Saich. 1994. *Revolutionary Discourse in Mao's Republic*. Cambridge, Mass.: Harvard University Press.

Arendt, Hannah. 1963. *On Revolution*. New York: Viking.

Aristotle, 1981. *The Politics*. Harmondsworth, U.K.: Penguin.

Arrighi, Giovanni. 2001. "Global Income Inequality and the Future of Socialism." In *The Illusion of Development*, edited by Xu Baoqiang and Wang Hui. Beijing: Central Compilation and Translation Publisher.

Arthur, Brian. 1994. *Increasing Returns and Path Dependence in the Economy*. Ann Arbor: University of Michigan Press.

Bachman, David, and Dali Yang. 1991. *Yan Jiaqi and China's Struggle for Democracy*. Armonk, N.Y.: M. E. Sharpe.

Bagchi, A. K. ed. 1995. *Democracy and Development*. New York: St. Martin's Press.

Balibar, Etienne. 1994. *Masses, Classes, Ideas: Studies on Politics and Philosophy before and after Marx*. London: Routledge.

Baran, Paul. 1960. *The Political Economy of Growth*. New York: Monthly Review Press.

Barlow, Tani. 1989. *I Myself Am a Woman: Ding Ling*. Boston: Beacon.

——, ed. 1993. *Gender Politics in Modern China: Writing and Feminism*. Durham, N.C.: Duke University Press.

——. 1997. "Colonialism's Career in Postwar China Studies." In *Formations of Colonial Modernity in East Asia*, edited by Tani Barlow. Durham, N.C.: Duke University Press.

——. 2004. *The Question of Women in Chinese Feminism*. Durham, N.C.: Duke University Press.

Barry, Brian. 1989. *Democracy, Power and Justice: Essays in Political Theory*. Oxford: Oxford University Press.

Beck, Ulrich. 1992. *Risk Society: Toward a New Modernity*. London: Sage.

Beetham, David. 1993. "Liberal Democracy and the Limits of Democratization." In *Prospects for Democracy*, edited by David Held. Cambridge: Polity.

——. 1999. *Democracy and Human Rights*. Cambridge: Polity.

Bell, Daniel A. 2000a. "Teaching in a Multicultural Context." *Dissent* (spring).

——. 2000b. *East Meets West: Human Rights and Democracy in East Asia*. Princeton, N.J.: Princeton University Press.

Bell, Daniel A., et al. 1995. *Toward Illiberal Democracy in Pacific Asia*. London: Macmillan.

Benewick, Robert. 1998. "Towards a Developmental Theory of Constitutionalism: The Chinese Case." *Government and Opposition* 33.

Benhabib, Seyla. 1996. "Toward a Deliberative Model of Democratic Legitimacy." In *Democracy and Difference*, edited by Seyla Benhabib. Princeton, N.J.: Princeton University Press.

Bergere, Marie-Claire. 1989. *The Golden Age of the Chinese Bourgeoisie, 1911–37*. Cambridge: Cambridge University Press.

——. 2003 [1992]. "Tiananmen 1989: Background and Consequences." In *Twentieth-Century China: New Approaches*, edited by Jeffrey Wasserstrom. London: Routledge.

Berlin, Isaiah. 1969. *Four Essays on Liberty*. Oxford: Oxford University Press.

——. 1998. *The Proper Study of Mankind: An Anthology of Essays*. New York: Farrar, Straus and Giroux.

Berman, Marshall. 1983. *All That Is Solid Melts into Air: The Experience of Modernity*. New York: Simon and Schuster.

Bernstein, Richard, and Ross Munro. 1997. "The Coming Conflict with America." *Foreign Affairs* (March/April).

Bernstein, Thomas, and Lu Xiaobo. 2003. *Taxation without Representation in Contemporary Rural China*. Cambridge: Cambridge University Press.

Bettelheim, Charles. 1974. *Cultural Revolution and Industrial Organization in China*. New York: Monthly Review Press.

Bhabha, Homi. 1990a. "The Third Space: Interview with Homi Bhabha." In *Identity: Community, Culture, Difference*, edited by Jonathan Rutherford. London: Lawrence and Wishart.

———. 1990b. "The Other Question: Difference, Discrimination, and the Discourse of Colonialism." In *Out There: Marginalization and Contemporary Cultures*, edited by Russell Ferguson et al. Cambridge, Mass.: MIT Press.

Bhalla, A. S. 1995. *Uneven Development in the Third World: A Study of China and India*. London: Macmillan.

Blackburn, Robin. 1991. "Fin de Siecle: Socialism after the Crash." In *After the Fall: The Failure of Communism and the Future of Socialism*. London: Verso.

Blecher, Marc. 1989a. "Structural Change and the Political Articulation of Social Interests in Revolutionary and Socialist China." In *Marxism and the Chinese Experience*, edited by Arif Dirlik and Maurice Meisner. Armonk, N.Y.: M. E. Sharpe.

———. 1989b. "China's Struggle for a New Hegemony." *Socialist Review* 19:2 (April–June).

———. 1991. "The Contradictions of Grass-Roots Participation and Undemocratic Statism in Maoist China and Their Fate." In *Contemporary Chinese Politics in Historical Perspective*, edited by Brantly Womack. Cambridge: Cambridge University Press.

———. 1996. "Hegemony, Class, and State Socialism: Toward a Theoretical Approach to Cultural Change, with Application to the Chinese Case." In *Adaptation and Transformation in Communist and Post-Communist Systems*, edited by Sabrina Ramet. Boulder, Colo.: Westview.

———. 1997. *China against the Tides: Restructuring through Revolution, Radicalism and Reform*. London: Pinter.

Bloom, Irene. 1998. "Fundamental Intuitions and Consensus Statements: Mencian Confucianism and Human Rights." In *Confucianism and Human Rights*, edited by Wm. T. de Bary and Tu Weiming. New York: Columbia University Press.

Blue, Gregory. 1999. "China and Western Social Thought in the Modern Period." In *China and Historical Capitalism: Genealogies of Sinological Knowledge*, edited by Timothy Brook and Gregory Blue. Cambridge: Cambridge University Press.

Bobbio, Norberto. 1988. "Gramsci and the Concept of Civil Society." In *Civil Society and the State: New European Perspectives*, edited by John Keane. New York: Verso.

Bourdieu, Pierre. 1977. *Outline of a Theory of Practice*. Cambridge: Cambridge University Press.

———. 1998. "At the Heart of Any Political Battle: On Male Domination." *Le Monde Diplomatique* (October).

Bowles, Paul, and Xiaoyuan Dong. 1999. "Globalization, 'Chinese Walls' and Industrial Labor." *IDS Bulletin* 30:4.

Bramall, Chris. 1993. *In Praise of Maoist Economic Planning: Living Standards and Economic Development in Sichuan since 1931*. Oxford: Clarendon.

Brandt, Conrad, Benjamin Schwartz, and John K. Fairbank, eds. 1967. *A Documentary History of Chinese Communism*. 2nd ed. New York: Atheneum.

Braudel, Fernand. 1977. *Afterthoughts on Material Civilization and Capitalism*. Baltimore: Johns Hopkins University Press.

Brook, Timothy. 1999. "Capitalism and the Writing of Modern History in China." In

China and Historical Capitalism: Genealogies of Sinological Knowledge, edited by Timothy Brook and Gregory Blue. Cambridge: Cambridge University Press.

Brook, Timothy, and B. M. Frolis, eds. 1997. *Civil Society in China*. Armonk, N.Y.: M. E. Sharpe.

Brown, David, and D. M. Jones. 1995. "Democratization and the Myth of the Liberalizing Middle Classes." In *Towards Illiberal Democracy in Pacific Asia*, edited by Daniel A. Bell et al. London: Macmillan.

Brubaker, Rogers. 1996. *Nationalism Reframed: Nationhood and the National Question in the New Europe*. Cambridge: Cambridge University Press.

Brugger, Bill, and David Kelly. 1990. *Chinese Marxism in the Post-Mao Era*. Stanford, Calif.: Stanford University Press.

Bulag, U. 2000. "Ethnic Resistance with Socialist Characteristics." In *Chinese Society: Change, Conflict and Resistance*, edited by Elizabeth Perry and Mark Selden. New York: Routledge.

Bunce, Valerie. 1996. "Socialism and Underdevelopment." In *Adaptation and Transformation in Communist and Postcommunist Systems*, edited by Sabrina Ramet. Boulder, Colo.: Westview.

Burnheim, John. 1985. *Is Democracy Possible? The Alternative to Electoral Politics*. Cambridge: Polity.

Burns, John. 1984. "Chinese Interest Articulation." In *Groups and Politics in the PRC*, edited by David Goodman. Armonk, N.Y.: M. E. Sharpe.

———. 1988. *Political Participation in Rural China*. Berkeley: University of California Press.

Calhoun, Craig. 1994. *Neither Gods nor Emperors: Students and the Struggle for Democracy in China*. Berkeley: University of California Press.

Cammack, Paul. 1994. "Democratization and Citizenship in Latin America." In *Democracy and Democratization*, edited by Geraint Parry and Michael Moran. London: Routledge.

Cao, Tian Yu, ed. 2005. *Chinese Model of Modern Development*. London: Routledge.

Carr, E. H. 1946. *The Soviet Impact on the Western World*. London: Macmillan.

———. *The Bolshevik Revolution, 1917–23*. Vol. 1, 2 and 3. London: Macmillan, 1950, 1966, and 1985.

———. 1978. "The Russian Revolution and the West." *New Left Review* 111 (September/October 1979).

CASS (Chinese Academy of Social Sciences). 2001. *Report on Classes and Stratums*. Beijing: Social Science Publisher.

———. 2002/2003. *Blue Book of Chinese Society*. Beijing: Social Sciences Literature Publishing House.

CCP (Chinese Communist Party). 1985. "On the Questions of Party History: Resolution on Certain Questions in the History of Our Party since the Founding of the PRC" (27 June 1981). Reprinted in *China's Socialist Economy, 1949–84*, edited by Liu Suinian and Wu Qungan. Heilongjiang: People's Publishing House.

———, Central Committee, Documentary Research Office. 1996. *A Chronicle of Liu Shaoqi*. Vol. 2. Beijing: Central Archival Press.

———, Central Committee, Organizational Department. 2001. "Correctly Understanding and Handling Contradictions among the People under New Conditions." *Marxism and Reality* (Beijing) 2.

Chakrabarty, Dipesh. 2000. *Provincializing Europe: Postcolonial Thought and Historical Difference*. Princeton, N.J.: Princeton University Press.

Chan, Anita. 1993. "Revolution or Corporatism? Workers and Trade Unions in Post-Mao China." *Australian Journal of Chinese Affairs* 29 (January).

——. 2001. *China's Workers under Assault: The Exploitation of Labor in a Globalizing Economy*. Armonk, N.Y.: M. E. Sharpe.

Chan, Anita, Stanley Rosen, and Jonathan Unger, eds. 1985. *On Socialist Democracy and the Chinese Legal System: The Li Yizhe Debates*. Armonk, N.Y.: M. E. Sharpe.

Chan, Sin Yee. 2003. "The Confucian Conception of Gender in the 21st Century." In *Confucianism for the Modern World*, edited by Daniel A. Bell and Hahm Chaibong. Cambridge: Cambridge University Press.

Chan, Wellington. 1977. *Merchants, Mandarins, and Modern Enterprise in Late Ch'ing China*. Cambridge, Mass.: Harvard University Press.

Chang, H. J., and Peter Nolan, eds. 1995. *The Transformation of the Communist Economies: Against the Mainstream*. New York: St. Martin's Press.

Chang, Xiaohong. 2004. "The Shake Up of Township Government." *Caijing* (Beijing) 19 (October).

Chatterjee, Partha. 1986. *Nationalist Thought and the Colonial World*. London: Zed.

——. 1989. "The Nationalist Resolution of the Women's Question." In *Recasting Women: Essays in Colonial History*, edited by Kumkum Sangari and Sudesh Vaid. New Delhi: Kali for Women.

Chauhan, Shivdan. 1976. *Nationalities Question in USA and USSR*. New Delhi: Sterling.

Cheek, Timothy. 1998. "From Market to Democracy in China: Gaps in the Civil Society Model." In *Market Economics and Political Change: Comparing China and Mexico*, edited by Juan Lindau and Cheek. New York: Rowman and Littlefield.

Chen, Erjin. 1986. *Crossroads Socialism: An Unofficial Manifesto for Proletarian Democracy*. London: Verso.

Chen Guidi, and Chun Tao. 2003. "An Investigation of China's Peasants." *Dangdai* (Beijing) 6.

Chen, Man, and Yue Jianyong. 2003. "An Analysis of the Efficacy of China's Appropriation of FDI." *Horizons (Shijie)* (Beijing) 8.

Chen Yung-fa. 1994. "The Futian Incident and the Anti-Bolshevik League: 'Terror' in the CCP Revolution." *Republican China* 19:2 (April).

Cheng, Tiejun, and Mark Selden. 1994. "The Origins and Social Consequences of China's Hukou System." *China Quarterly* 139 (September).

Chesneaux, Jean. 1969. "The Federalist Movement in China, 1920–23." In *Modern China's Search for a Political Form*, edited by Jack Gray. Oxford: Oxford University Press.

China Statistics Year Book. 1985–2003. Beijing: State Statistics Publishers.

Christiansen, Flemming. 1990. "Social Division and Peasant Mobility in Mainland China: The Implications of the Hu-kou System." *Issues and Studies* 26.4.

——. 1994. "Democratization in China: Structural Constraints." In *Democracy and Democratization*, edited by Geraint Parry and Michael Moran. London: Routledge.

——. 1998. Untitled book review in *Political Studies* 46:5 (December).

Ci, Jiwei. 1994. *Dialectic of the Chinese Revolution: From Utopianism to Hedonism*. Stanford, Calif.: Stanford University Press.

Claude, R. P., ed. 1976. *Comparative Human Rights*. Baltimore: Johns Hopkins University Press.

Coates, David. 2000. *Models of Capitalism: Growth and Stagnation in the Modern Era*. Cambridge: Polity.

Cohen, Myron. 1993. "Cultural and Political Inventions in Modern China: The Case of the Chinese 'Peasant.'" *Daedalus* 122:2 (spring).

Cohen, Paul. 1984. *Discovering History in China: American Historical Writing on the Recent Chinese Past*. New York: Columbia University Press.

———. 2003. "Reflections on a Watershed Date: The 1949 Divide in Chinese History." In *Twentieth-Century China: New Approaches*, edited by Jeffrey Wasserstrom. New York: Routledge.

Cohen, Robert S. 1965. "Socialism and Democracy." In *Marxism and Democracy*, edited by Herbert Aptheker. New York: Humanities Press.

Coleman, James. 1988. "Social Capital in the Creation of Human Capital." *American Journal of Sociology* 94.

Coleman, Janet. 2005. "Pre-Modern Property and Self-Ownership before and after Locke: Or, When Did Common Decency Become a Private rather than a Public Virtue?" *European Journal of Political Theory* 4:2 (April).

Colletti, Lucio. 1972. *From Rousseau to Lenin: Studies in Ideology and Society*. New York: Monthly Review Press.

Comninel, George. 1987. *Rethinking the French Revolution: Marxism and the Revisionist Challenge*. London: Verso.

Confucius. 1992. *The Analects*. 2nd ed. Translated by D. C. Lau. Hong Kong: Chinese University Press.

Connor, Walker. 1984. *The National Question in Marxist-Leninist Theory and Strategy*. Princeton, N.J.: Princeton University Press.

Conroy, Annabelle. 1999. "Localities against the State: The Decentralization Process in Bolivia." Manuscript. London School of Economics.

Cook, Sarah. 1999. "Creating Wealth and Welfare: Entrepreneurship and the Developmental State in Rural China." *IDS Bulletin* 30:4.

Crick, Bernard. 1962. *In Defense of Politics*. Harmondsworth, U.K.: Penguin.

Croll, Elizabeth. 1978. *Feminism and Socialism in China*. New York: Schocken.

———. 1983. *Chinese Women since Mao*. London: Zed.

Croll, Elizabeth, Delia Davin, and Penny Kane, eds. 1985. *China's One-Child Family Policy*. Basingstoke, U.K.: Macmillan.

Cui Zhiyuan. 1998a. "Whither China? The Discourse on Property Rights in the Chinese Reform Context." *Social Text* 55 (summer).

———. 1998b. "The Mixed Constitution and a Three-Layer Analysis of Chinese Politics." *Strategy and Management* (Beijing) 3.

———. 2000. "Introduction to Tang Tsou's 'Interpreting the Revolution in China.'" *Modern China* 26.2 (April).

———. 2003. "Liberal Socialism and the Future of China: A Petty Bourgeois Manifesto." Unpublished conference paper available at http://zhiyuancui.ccs.tsinghua.edu.cn.

———. 2004. "The Lang Xianping Debate: Robbery by the Owners and a 'Good Market Economy.'" *Dushu* (Beijing) 11.

Cumings, Bruce. 1983. Introduction to *China from Mao to Deng: The Politics and Economics of Socialist Development*, edited by the Bulletin of Concerned Asian Scholars. Armonk, N.Y.: M. E. Sharpe.

———. 1997. "The Deng Xiaoping Era." *Monthly Review* (December).

———. 1999. "China through the Looking Glass." *Bulletin of the Atomic Scientists* 55.5 (September/October).

Dahl, Robert. 1961. "The Behavioral Approach in Political Science: Epitaph for a Monument to a Successful Protest." *American Political Science Review* 55:4 (December).

———. 1985. *A Preface to Economic Democracy*. Cambridge: Polity.

———. 1986. *Democracy, Liberty, and Equality*. Oslo: Norwegian University Press.

———. 1989. *Democracy and Its Critics*. New Haven, Conn.: Yale University Press.

Davin, Delia. 1976. *Woman-Work: Women and the Party in Revolutionary China*. Oxford: Oxford University Press.

Davis, Debra, and Ezra Vogel, eds. 1990. *Chinese Society on the Eve of Tiananmen*. Cambridge, Mass.: Harvard University Press.

de Bary, Wm. T. 1998a. *Asian Values and Human Rights: A Confucian Communitarian Perspective*. Cambridge, Mass.: Harvard University Press.

———. 1998b. *The Liberal Tradition in China*. New York: Columbia University Press.

Deng Xiaoping, 1994. *Selected Works of Deng Xiaoping*. Vol. 3. Beijing: Foreign Language Press.

Deng Yingtao, Cui Zhiyuan, and Miao Zhuangzhuang, 1994. *Reflections on Nanjie*. Beijing: Contemporary China Publisher.

Deng Yingtao, Wang Xiaoqiang, and Cui Heming. 1999. *Recreating China*. Shanghai: Wenhui Publishing House.

———. 2001. *The Strategies for Developing the West*. Shanghai: Wenhui Publishing House.

Dernberger, Robert. 1975. "The Role of the Foreigners in China's Economic Development, 1840–1949." In *China's Modern Economy in Historical Perspective*, edited by Dwight Perkins. Stanford, Calif.: Stanford University Press.

———, ed. 1980. *China's Development Experience in Comparative Perspective*. Cambridge, Mass.: Harvard University Press.

Derrida, Jacques. 1994. *Spectres of Marx*. London: Routledge.

Desai, Meghnad. 1990. "Birth and Death of Nation States: Speculations about Germany and India." In *The Rise and Decline of the Nation State*, edited by Michael Mann. Oxford: Blackwell.

———. 2002. *Marx's Revenge*. London: Verso.

Diamond, Larry. 1996. "Three Paradoxes of Democracy." In *The Global Resurgence of Democracy*, 2nd ed., edited by Larry Diamond and Marc Platter. Baltimore: Johns Hopkins University Press.

Diamond, Larry, Juan Linz, and Martin Lipset, eds. 1990. *Politics in Developing Countries: Comparing Experiences with Democracy*. London: Lynne Rienner.

Dikotter, Frank. 1992. *The Discourse of Race in Modern China*. London: Hurst.

Dikotter, Frank, Lars Laamann, and Zhou Xun. 2004. *Narcotic Culture: A History of Drugs in China*. Chicago: University of Chicago Press.

Dillon, Michael. 1994. "Muslim Communities in Contemporary China: The Resurgence of Islam after the Cultural Revolution." *Journal of Islamic Studies* 5:1.

Dirlik, Arif. 1978. *Revolution and History: The Origins of Marxist Historiography in China, 1919–37*. Berkeley: University of California Press.

———. 1982. "Spiritual Solutions to Material Problems: The 'Socialist Ethics and Courtesy Month' in China." *South Atlantic Quarterly* 81:4.

———. 1989a. *The Origins of Chinese Communism*. New York: Oxford University Press.

———. 1989b. "Postsocialism? Reflections on 'Socialism with Chinese Characteristics.' " In *Marxism and the Chinese Experience*, edited by Arif Dirlik and Maurice Meisner. Armonk, N.Y.: M. E. Sharpe.

———. 1994. *After the Revolution: Waking to Global Capitalism.* Middletown, Conn.: Wesleyan University Press.

———. 1997. "Modernism and Antimodernism in Mao Zedong's Marxism." In *Critical Perspectives on Mao Zedong's Thought*, edited by Arif Dirlik, Paul Healy, and Nick Knight. Atlantic Highlands, N.J.: Humanities Press.

———. 1998. "Socialism and Capitalism in Chinese Thinking: The Origin." *Studies in Comparative Communism* 21:2 (summer).

———. 2000. *Postmodernity's Histories: The Past as Legacy and Project.* Lanham, Md.: Rowman and Littlefield.

Dirlik, Arif, and Maurice Meisner, eds. 1989. *Marxism and the Chinese Experience.* Armonk, N.Y.: M. E. Sharpe.

Dittmer, Lowell. 1977. " 'Line Struggle' in Theory and Practice: The Origin of the Cultural Revolution Reconsidered." *China Quarterly* 72 (December).

———. 1987. *China's Continuous Revolution: The Post-Liberation Epoch 1949–81.* Berkeley: University of California Press.

Dittmer, Lowell, and Samuel Kim, eds. 1993. *China's Quest for National Identity.* Ithaca, N.Y.: Cornell University Press.

Dowdle, Michael. 1997. "The Constitutional Development and Operations of the NPR." *Columbia Journal of Asian Law* 11:1 (spring).

Dower, John. 1999. *Embracing Defeat: Japan in the Wake of World War II.* New York: Norton.

Dreyer, June. 1976. *China's Forty Millions: Minority Nationalities and National Integration in the PRC.* Cambridge, Mass.: Harvard University Press.

—— 1999. "China, the Monocultural Paradigm." *Orbis* (fall).

———. 1993. *China's Political System: Modernization and Tradition.* London: Macmillan.

Du Runsheng. 1998. *Selected Writings.* Taiyuan: Shanxi Economics Publisher.

Duara, Prasenjit. 1995. *Rescuing History from the Nation: Questioning Narratives of Modern China.* Chicago: University of Chicago Press.

Duggan, Lisa. 1989. "Vive la Difference: Joan Scott's Historical Imperatives." *Voice Literary Supplement* 71.

Dunn, John. 1989. *Modern Revolutions: An Introduction to the Analysis of a Political Phenomenon.* 2nd ed. Cambridge: Cambridge University Press.

Eastman, Lloyd. 1974. *The Abortive Revolution: China under Nationalist Rule, 1927–1937.* Cambridge, Mass.: Harvard University Press.

Eberhard, Wolfram. 1973. "Problems of Historical Sociology." In *State and Society: A Reader*, edited by Reinhard Bendix et al. Berkeley: University of California Press.

Eckstein, Alexander. 1977. *China's Economic Revolution.* Cambridge: Cambridge University Press.

Edmonds, Richard, ed. 2000. *Managing the Chinese Environment.* Oxford: Oxford University Press.

Edwards, Louise. 2000. "Women in the PRC: New Challenges to the Grand Gender Narrative." In *Women in Asia: Tradition, Modernity, and Globalization*, edited by Louise Edwards and Mina Roces. Ann Arbor: University of Michigan Press.

Eisenstadt, S. N. 1978. *Revolution and the Transformation of Societies: A Comparative Study of Civilizations.* New York: Free Press.

———. 2000. "Multiple Modernities." *Daedalus* 129:1 (winter).

Eley, Geoff, and Keith Nield. 2000. "Farewell to the Working Class?" *International Labor and Working-Class History* 57 (spring).

Ellman, Michael. 1979. *Socialist Planning*. Cambridge: Cambridge University Press.

Elster, Jon, Claus Offe, and Ulrich Preuss. 1998. *Institutional Design in Post-Communist Societies: Rebuilding the Ship at Sea*. Cambridge: Cambridge University Press.

Elvin, Mark. 2004. *The Retreat of the Elephants: An Environmental History of China*. New Haven, Conn.: Yale University Press.

Engels, Friedrich. 1978 [1895]. "Preface to Marx's 'Class Struggle in France.'" In *The Marx and Engels Reader*, edited by Robert Tucker. New York: Norton.

Escobar, Arturo. 1995. *Encountering Development: The Making and Unmaking of the Third World*. Princeton, N.J.: Princeton University Press.

Esherick, Joseph. 1995. "Ten Theses on the Chinese Revolution." *Modern China* 21:1 (July).

Esherick, Joseph, and Jeffrey Wasserstrom. 1990. "Acting Out Democracy: Political Theatre in Modern China." *Journal of Asian Studies* 49:4.

Esherick, Joseph, and M. B. Rankin, eds. 1990. *Chinese Local Elites and Patterns of Domination*. Berkeley: University of California Press.

Evans, Harriet. 1995. "Defining Difference: The 'Scientific' Construction of Sexuality and Gender in the People's Republic of China." *Signs* 20:2.

Evans, Peter. 1979. *Dependent Development*. Princeton, N.J.: Princeton University Press.

———. 1995. *Embedded Autonomy: States and Industrial Transformation*. Princeton, N.J.: Princeton University Press.

Evans, Peter, Dietrich Rueschemeyer, and Theda Skocpol. 1985. *Bringing the State Back In*. Cambridge: Cambridge University Press.

Fairbank, J. K. 1979. *The United States and China*. 4th ed. Cambridge, Mass.: Harvard University Press.

Falkenheim, V. 1978. "Political Participation in China." *Problems of Communism* 27:3 (May–June).

Fanon, Frantz. 1967 [1952]. *Black Skin, White Masks*. London: Pluto.

Feenberg, Andrew. 1995. *Alternative Modernity: The Technical Turn in Philosophy and Social Theory*. Berkeley: University of California Press.

Feher, Ference, Agnes Heller, and Gyorgy Markus. 1983. *Dictatorship over Needs*. New York: St. Martin's Press.

Ferdinand, Peter. 1991. *Communist Regimes in Comparative Perspective: The Evolution of the Soviet, Chinese and Yugoslav Systems*. London: Harvester Wheatsheaf.

———. 1994. "Xinjiang: Relations with China and Abroad." In *China Deconstructs: Politics, Trade and Regionalism*, edited by David Goodman and Gerald Segal. London: Routledge.

Fewsmith, Joseph. 1991. "The Dengist Reforms in Historical Perspective." In *Contemporary Chinese Politics in Historical Perspective*, edited by Brantly Womack. Cambridge: Cambridge University Press.

Finer, S. E. 1999. *The History of Government*. 3 vols. Oxford: Oxford University Press.

Fitzgerald, John. 1996. *Awakening China: Politics, Culture, and Class in the Nationalist Revolution*. Stanford, Calif.: Stanford University Press.

———. 1999. "In the Scale of History: Politics and Culture in the Twentieth Century China." *Twentieth-Century China* 24:2 (April).

Foley, Michael, and Bob Edwards. 1996. "The Paradox of Civil Society." *Journal of Democracy* 7:3.

Forbath, William. 1996. "A Critique of Habermas's Understanding of Law, Politics, and Economic Life." *Cardozo Law Review* (March).

Foucault, Michel. 1980. *Power/Knowledge: Selected Interviews and Other Essays, 1972–77.* New York: Pantheon.

Frank, Andre Gunder. 1969. *Latin America: Underdevelopment or Revolution? Essays on the Development of Underdevelopment and the Immediate Enemy.* New York: Monthly Review Press.

Fraser, Nancy. 1997a. "After the Family Wage: A Postindustrial Thought Experiment." In *Justice Interruptus: Critical Reflections on the "Postsocialist" Conditions*, edited by Nancy Fraser. New York: Routledge.

———. 1997b. "Rethinking the Public Sphere: A Contribution to the Critique of Actually Existing Democracy." In *Hannah Arendt and the Meaning of Politics*, edited by Craig Calhoun and John McGowan. Minneapolis: University of Minnesota Press.

Fraser, Nancy, and Axel Honneth. 2003. *Redistribution or Recognition? A Political-Philosophical Exchange.* London: Verso.

Fraser, Stewart, ed. 1971. *Education and Communism in China: An Anthology of Commentary and Documents.* London: Pall Mall.

Frazier, Mark W. 2002. *The Making of the Chinese Industrial Workplace: State, Revolution and Management.* Cambridge: Cambridge University Press.

Friedman, Edward. 1974. *Backward toward Revolution: The Chinese Revolutionary Party.* Berkeley: University of California Press.

———. 1982. "Maoism, Titoism, Stalinism: Some Origins and Consequences of the Maoist Theory of the Socialist Transition." In *The Transition to Socialism in China*, edited by Mark Selden and Victor Lippit. Armonk, N.Y.: M. E. Sharpe.

———. 1983. "The Societal Obstacle to China's Socialist Transition: State Capitalism or Feudal Fascism." In *State and Society in Contemporary China*, edited by Victor Nee and David Mozingo. Ithaca, N.Y.: Cornell University Press.

———. 1987. "Maoism and the Liberation of the Poor." *World Politics* 39:3 (April).

———, ed. 1995. *National Identity and Democratic Prospects in Socialist China.* Armonk, N.Y.: M. E. Sharpe.

———. 1999. "Asia as a Fount of Universal Human Rights." In *Debating Human Rights: Critical Essays from the United States and Asia*, edited by Peter Van Ness. London: Routledge.

———. 2000. "Immanuel Kant's Relevance to an Enduring Asia-Pacific Peace." In *What If China Doesn't Democratize? Implications for War and Peace*, edited by Edward Friedman and Barrett McCormick. Armonk, N.Y: M. E. Sharpe.

Friedman, Edward, and Mark Selden, eds. 1971. *America's Asia: Dissenting Essays on Asian-American Relations.* New York: Vintage.

Fujita, Masahisa, Paul Krugman, and Anthony Venables. 1999. *The Spatial Economy.* Cambridge, Mass.: MIT Press.

Fukuyama, Francis. 1993. *The End of History and the Last Man.* London: Penguin.

———. 1995. *Trust: The Social Virtues and the Creation of Prosperity.* London: Hamilton.

Furet, François. 1998. "Democracy and Utopia." *Journal of Democracy* 9:1.

———. 1999.*The Passing of an Illusion: The Idea of Communism in the Twentieth Century.* Chicago: University of Chicago Press.

Gan Yang. 2003a. "Towards a Political Nation." *Dushu* (Beijing) 4.

———. 2003b. "The Citizen and the Constitution." In *One China, Many Paths*, edited by Chaohua Wang. London: Verso.

Gao Mobo. 1999. *Gao Village.* London: Hurst.

Gao Xiaoxian. 1994. "China's Modernization and Changes in the Social Status of Rural Women." In *Engendering China: Women Culture, and the State*, edited by Christina Gilmartin et al. Cambridge, Mass.: Harvard University Press.

Gardner, John. 1969. "The Wu-Fan Campaign in Shanghai: A Study in the Consolidation of Urban Control." In *Chinese Communist Politics in Action*, edited by A. Doak Barnett. Seattle: University of Washington Press.

Garside, Roger. 1981. *Coming Alive: China after Mao*. New York: McGraw-Hill.

Gellner, Ernest. 1983. *Nations and Nationalism*. Oxford: Blackwell.

———. 1994. *Encounters with Nationalism*. Oxford: Blackwell.

———. 1995. "The Importance of Being Modular." In *Civil Society: Theory, History, Comparison*, edited by John Hall. Cambridge: Polity.

Gerschenkron, Alexander. 1962. *Economic Backwardness in Historical Perspective*. Cambridge, Mass: Harvard University Press.

Giddens, Anthony. 1990. *The Consequences of Modernity*. Cambridge: Polity.

Gills, Barry, Joel Rocamora, and Richard Wilson, eds. 1993. *Low Intensity Democracy: Political Power in the New World Order*. Boulder, Colo.: Pluto.

Gilmartin, Christina. 1995. *Engendering the Chinese Revolution: Radical Women, Communist Politics, and Mass Movements in the 1920s*. Berkeley: University of California Press.

Gittings, John. 1967. "The Origins of China's Foreign Policy." In *Containment and Revolution: Western Policy towards Social Revolution: 1917 to Vietnam*, edited by D. Horowitz. London: Blond.

———. 1968. *Survey of the Sino-Soviet Dispute: A Commentary and Extracts from the Recent Polemics, 1963–1967*. New York: Oxford University Press.

———. 1974. *The World and China, 1922–1972*. London: Eyer Methuen.

Gladney, Dru. 1991. *Muslim Chinese: Ethnic Nationalism in the People's Republic*. Cambridge, Mass.: Harvard University Press.

———. 1994. "Representing Nationality in China: Refiguring Majority/Minority Identities." *Journal of Asian Studies* 53:1 (February).

Gold, T. B. 1993. "Taiwan's Quest for Identity in the Shadow of China." In *In the Shadow of China: Political Development in Taiwan since 1949*, edited by Steve Tsang. London: Hurst.

Goldman, Merle. 1994. *Sowing the Seeds of Democracy in China: Political Reform in the Deng Xiaoping Era*. Cambridge, Mass.: Harvard University Press.

Goldstein, Melvyn. 1990. "The Dragon and the Snowlion." In *China Briefing 1990*, edited by Anthony Kane. New York: Asia Society.

———. 1998. "The Dalai Lama's Dilemma." *Foreign Affairs* (January/February).

Goldstein, Melvyn, and Cynthia Beall. 1991. "China's Birth Control Policy in the Tibet Autonomous Region: Myths and Realities." *Asian Survey* 31:3.

Goodman, David. 1981. *Beijing Street Voices: The Poetry and Politics of China's Democracy Movement*. London: Boyars.

———. 1986. *Centre and Province in the People's Republic of China: Sichuan and Guizhou, 1955–65*. Cambridge: Cambridge University Press.

———, ed. 1997. *China's Provinces in Reform: Class, Community and Political Culture*. London: Routledge.

———. 2000. *Social and Political Change in Revolutionary China: The Taihang Base Area in the War of Resistance to Japan, 1937–45*. New York: Rowman and Littlefield.

Goodman, David, and Gerald Segal, eds. 1994. *China Deconstructs: Politics, Trade and Regionalism*. London: Routledge.

Goodman, Roger, Gordon White, and Huck-ju Kwon, eds. 1998. *The East Asian Welfare Model: Welfare Orientalism and the State*. London: Routledge.

Gould, Stephen Jay. 2002. *The Structure of Evolutionary Theory*. Cambridge, Mass.: Harvard University Press.

Graham, A. C. 1992. *Unreason within Reason: Essays on the Outskirts of Rationality*. LaSalle, Ill.: Open Court.

Gramsci, Antonio. 1971. *Selections from the Prison Notebooks of Antonio Gramsci, 1929–35*, edited and translated by Quintin Hoare and Geoffrey Nowell-Smith. London: Lawrence and Wishart.

Gray, John. 1995. *Enlightenment's Wake: Politics and Culture at the Close of the Modern Age*. London: Routledge.

——. 1998. *False Dawn: The Delusions of Global Capitalism*. London: Granta.

——. 2000. *Two Faces of Liberalism*. Cambridge: Polity.

——. 2002. *Straw Dogs: Thoughts on Human and Other Animals*. London: Granta.

Gregor, A. James. 2000a. *A Place in the Sun: Marxism and Fascism in China's Long Revolution*. Boulder, Colo.: Westview.

——. 2000b. *The Faces of Janus: Marxism and Fascism in the Twentieth Century*. New Haven, Conn.: Yale University Press.

Grunfeld, A. T. 1987. *The Making of Modern Tibet*. Armonk, N.Y.: M. E. Sharpe.

——. 1999. "The Question of Tibet." *Current History* 98 (September).

Gu Xin. 1993–94. "A Civil Society and Public Sphere in Post-Mao China? An Overview of Western Publications." *China Information* 8:3 (Winter).

——. 1998. "Unit Welfare Socialism and China's 'Systematic Unemployment.'" *Comparative Economic and Social Systems* (Beijing) 4.

Gurley, John. 1969. "Capitalist and Maoist Economic Development." In *America's Asia*, edited by Edward Friedman and Mark Selden. New York: Random House.

Habermas, Jürgen. 1987. *The Theory of Communicative Action. Vol. 2*. Boston: Beacon.

——. 1989. *The Structural Transformation of the Public Sphere: An Inquiry into a Category of Bourgeois Society*. Cambridge, Mass.: MIT Press.

——. 1992. "Citizenship and National Identity: Some Reflections on the Future of Europe." *Praxis International* 12:1 (April).

——. 1996. "Between Facts and Norms: Contributions to a Discourse Theory of Law and Democracy" and "Further Reflections on the Public Sphere." In *Habermas and the Public Sphere*, edited by Craig Calhoun. Cambridge, Mass.: MIT Press.

——. 2000. *The Philosophical Discourse of Modernity: Twelve Lectures*. Cambridge, Mass.: MIT Press.

——. 2001. *The Postnational Constellation*. Cambridge, Mass.: MIT Press.

Haggart, Stephen. 1995. *Developing Nations and the Politics of Global Integration*. Washington, D.C.: Brookings Institution.

Hall, David, and Roger Ames. 1998. *The Democracy of the Dead: Dewey, Confucius, and the Hope for Democracy in China*. Chicago: Open Court.

Hall, John. 1986. *Powers and Liberties*. Harmondsworth: Penguin.

Hall, Peter, and David Soskice, eds. 2001. *Varieties of Capitalism: The Institutional Foundations of Comparative Advantage*. Oxford: Oxford University Press.

Halliday, Fred. 1999. *Revolution and World Politics: The Rise and Fall of the Sixth Great Power*. Durham, N.C.: Duke University Press.

Hamilton, Gary. 1999. *Cosmopolitan Capitalists: Hong Kong and the Chinese Diaspora at the End of the Twentieth Century*. Seattle: University of Washington Press.

Harding, Harry. 1986. "Political Development in Post-Mao China." In *Modernizing China: Post-Mao Reform and Development*, edited by A. Doak Barnett and Ralph Clough. Boulder, Colo.: Westview.

——. 1987. *China's Second Revolution: Reform after Mao*. Washington, D.C.: Brookings Institution.

——. 1993. "The Concept of 'Greater China': Themes, Variations and Reservations." *China Quarterly* 136 (December).

——. 1994. "The Contemporary Study of Chinese Politics: An Introduction." *China Quarterly* 139 (September).

Hardt, Michael, and Antonio Negri. 2000. *Empire*. Cambridge, Mass.: Harvard University Press.

Harrell, S. 1990. "Ethnicity, Local Interests, and the State: Yi Communities in Southwest China." *Comparative Studies in Society and History* 32:3 (July).

Harris, Jerry. 2005. "Emerging Third World Powers: China, India and Brazil." *Race and Class* 46:3.

Hart-Landsberg, Martin, and Paul Burkett. 2004. "China and Socialism: Market Reforms and Class Struggle." *Monthly Review* (July–August).

Hartford, Kathleen, and Steven Goldstein, eds. 1989. *Single Sparks: China's Rural Revolutions*. Armonk, N.Y.: M. E. Sharpe.

Harvey, David. 2000a. *Spaces of Hope*. Berkeley: University of California Press.

——. 2000b. "Reinventing Geography." *New Left Review* 4 (July/August).

Haug, Hrigga. 1995. "The Quota Demand and Feminist Politics." *New Left Review* 209 (January/February).

Hayden, Patrick. 2001. *The Philosophy of Human Rights: Paragon Issues in Philosophy*. St. Paul: Paragon House.

Hayek, Friedrich A. von. 1946. *The Road to Serfdom*. London: Routledge.

He Qinglian. 1998. *Modernization's Pitfall*. Beijing: China Today Publisher.

Heberer, Thomas. 1979. *China and Its National Minorities: Autonomy or Assimilation?* Armonk, N.Y.: M. E. Sharpe.

Hedin, Astrid. 2004. "Stalinism as a Civilization: New Perspectives on Communist Regimes." *Political Studies Review* 2:2 (April).

Held, David. 1987. *Models of Democracy*. Cambridge: Polity.

——. 1995. *Democracy and the Global Order: From the Modern State to Cosmopolitan Governance*. Cambridge: Polity.

——, ed. 1999. *Global Transformations*. Cambridge: Polity.

Henderson, Callum. 1999. *China on the Brink: The Myth and Realities of the World's Largest Market*. New York: McGraw-Hill.

Hernes, Helga M. 1987. *Welfare State and Woman Power: Essays in State Feminism*. Oslo: Norwegian University Press.

Hershatter, Gail, Emily Honig, and Randall Stross, eds. 1996. *Remapping China: Fissures in Historical Terrain*. Stanford, Calif.: Stanford University Press.

Herzen, Alexander. 1956 [1851]. "The Russian People and Socialism." In *From the Other Shore*, translated by Moura Budberg. London: Weidenfeld and Nicolson.

Hessler, Peter. 1999. "Tibet through Chinese Eyes." *Atlantic Monthly* (February).

Hill, Christopher. 1972. *The World Turned Upside Down: Radical Ideas during the English Revolution*. London: Temple Smith.

Hinton, William. 1972. *Fanshen: A Documentary of Revolution in a Chinese Village*. Harmondsworth: Penguin.

———. 1983. *Shenfan*. New York: Random House.

———. 1990. *The Great Reversal: The Privatization of China*. New York: Monthly Review Press.

———. 1994. "Mao, Rural Development, and Two-Line Struggle." *Monthly Review* 9 (February).

Hirschman, Albert. 1970. *Exit, Voice, and Loyalty: Responses to Decline in Firms, Organizations, and States*. Cambridge, Mass.: Harvard University Press.

Hobsbawm, Eric. 1990. *Nations and Nationalism since 1780: Programme, Myth, Reality*. Cambridge: Cambridge University Press.

———. 1994. *The Age of Extremes: The Short Twentieth Century*. London: Weidenfeld and Nicolson.

———. 1997. "Can We Write the History of the Russian Revolution?" In *On History*. London: Weidenfeld and Nicolson.

Hodgson, Marshall. 1993. *Rethinking World History*. Cambridge: Cambridge University Press.

Honig, Emily. 1985. "Socialist Revolution and Women's Liberation in China—A Review Article." Journal of Asian Studies 44:2.

Honneth, Axel. 1996. *The Struggle for Recognition: The Moral Grammar of Social Conflicts*. Cambridge: Polity.

Horkheimer, Max, and Theodor Adorno. 1972. *Dialectic of Enlightenment*. New York: Herder and Herder.

Howell, Jude. 1993. *China Opens Its Doors: The Politics of Economic Transition*. London: Harvester Wheatsheaf.

———. 1996. "The Struggle for Survival: Prospects for the Women's Federation in Post-Mao China." *World Development* 24:1.

———. 1998. "An Unholy Trinity? Civil Society, Economic Liberalization and Democratization." *Government and Opposition* 33:1.

———, ed. 2004. *Governance in China*. New York: Rowman and Littlefield.

Hu Shaohua. 2000. *Explaining Chinese Democratization*. Westport, Conn.: Praeger.

Hu Teh-wei. 1980. "Health Care Services in China's Economic Development." In *China's Development Experience in Comparative Perspective*, edited by Robert Dernberger. Cambridge, Mass.: Harvard University Press.

Huang, Philip. 1993. " 'Public Sphere'/'Civil Society' in China? The Third Realm between State and Society." *Modern China* 19:2.

———. 1995. "Rural Class Struggle in the Chinese Revolution: Representational and Objective Realities from the Land Reform to the Cultural Revolution." *Modern China* 21.1 (January).

Huang Ping. 2000. "Notes on 'Developmentalism.' " *Tianya* (Beijing) 1.

Huang Yasheng. 2003. *Selling China: Foreign Direct Investment during the Reform Era*. Cambridge: Cambridge University Press.

Hughes, Christopher. 2000. "Post-Nationalist Taiwan." In *Asian Nationalism*, edited by Michael Leifer. London: Routledge.

Hughes, Neil. 1998. "Smashing the Iron Rice Bowl." *Foreign Affairs* 77:4 (July/August).

Hunt, Diana. 1988. *Economic Theories of Development: An Analysis of Competing Paradigms*. London: Wheatsheaf.

Huntington, Samuel. 1968. *Political Order in Changing Societies*. New Haven, Conn.: Yale University Press.

——. 1991. *The Third Wave: Democratization in the Late Twentieth Century*. London: University of Oklahoma Press.

Isaacs, Harold. 1951. *The Tragedy of the Chinese Revolution*. Stanford, Calif.: Stanford University Press.

Jacka, Tamara. 1997. *Women's Work in Rural China: Change and Continuity in an Era of Reform*. Cambridge: Cambridge University Press.

Jacobs, Bruce. 1991. "Elections in China." *Australian Journal of Chinese Affairs* 25 (January).

Jacobs, J. B. 1997. "Shanghai: An Alternative Center?" In *China's Provinces in Reform: Class, Community and Political Culture*, edited by David Goodman. London: Routledge.

Jameson, Fredric. 1988. "Cognitive Mapping." In *Marxism and the Interpretation of Culture*, edited by Cary Nelson and Lawrence Grossberg. Chicago: University of Illinois Press.

——. 1993. "In the Mirror of Alternate Modernities." In *Origins of Modern Japanese Literature*, edited by Karatani Kojin. Durham, N.C.: Duke University Press.

——. 1994. *Postmodernism, or, The Cultural Logic of Late Capitalism*. Durham, N.C.: Duke University Press.

——. 1996. "Actually Existing Marxism." In *Marxism beyond Marxism*, edited by Saree Makdisi, Cesare Casarino, and Rebecca Karl. New York: Routledge.

Jayawardena, Kumari. 1986. *Feminism and Nationalism in the Third World*. London: Zed.

Jenner, W. J. F. 1992. *The Tyranny of History: The Roots of China's Crisis*. London: Penguin.

Jiang Linxiang. 1998. *A History of Confucianism*. Vol. 7. Guangzhou: Guangdong Education Publisher.

Jin Yihong. 2000. "Changes in Gender Structure during the Process of De-agriculturalization in Rural Areas South of the Changjiang River." *Social Sciences in China* 2.

Johnson, Chalmers. 1982. *MITI and the Japanese Miracle: The Growth of Industrial Policy, 1925–75*. Stanford, Calif.: Stanford University Press.

——. 1995. *Japan: Who Governs?* New York: Norton.

——. 1999. "In Search of a New Cold War." *Bulletin of the Atomic Scientists* 55:5 (September/October).

Johnson, Kay Ann. 1983. *Women, the Family, and Peasant Revolution in China*. Chicago: University of Chicago Press.

Jones, Gareth Stedman. 2002. Introduction to the *Communist Manifesto*. London: Penguin.

Joseph, William, Christine Wong, and David Zweig, eds. 1991. *New Perspectives on the Cultural Revolution*. Cambridge, Mass.: Council on East Asian Studies, Harvard University.

Judge, Joan. 1998. "The Concept of Popular Empowerment (*minquan*) in the Late Qing: Classical and Contemporary Sources of Authority." In *Confucianism and Human Rights*, edited by Wm. T. de Bary and Tu Weiming. New York: Columbia University Press.

Kang Youwi. 1994 [1902]. *The Book of Datong*. Selected and annotated by Kuang Bolin. Shenyang: Liaoning People's Publishing House.

Kant, Immanuel. 1991. *Political Writings*. Introduced and annotated by Hans Reiss. 2nd ed. Cambridge: Cambridge University Press.

——. 1991 [1784]. "An Answer to the Question: What Is Enlightenment?" In *Political Writings*. Introduced and annotated by Hans Reiss. 2nd ed. Cambridge: Cambridge University Press.

Karl, Rebecca. 2002. *Staging the World: Chinese Nationalism at the Turn of the Twentieth Century*. Durham, N.C.: Duke University Press.

Karmel, Solomon. 1995–96. "Ethnic Tension and the Struggle for Order: China's Policies in Tibet." *Pacific Affairs* 68.

——. 2000. "Ethnic Nationalism in Mainland China." In *Asian Nationalism*, edited by Michael Leifer. London: Routledge.

Kasfir, Nelson. 1988. " 'No-Party Democracy' in Uganda." *Journal of Democracy* 9:2.

Keddie, Nikki, ed. 1995. *Debating Revolutions*. New York: New York University Press.

Keith, Ronald. 1994. *China's Struggle for the Rule of Law*. New York: St. Martin's Press.

Kelliher, Daniel. 1992. *Peasant Power in China: The Era of Rural Reform, 1979–89*. New Haven, Conn.: Yale University Press.

——. 1997. "The Chinese Debate over Village Self-Government." *The China Journal* 37 (January).

Kelly, David, and Anthony Reid, eds. 1998. *Asian Freedoms: The Idea of Freedom in East and Southeast Asia*. Cambridge: Cambridge University Press.

Kent, Ann. 1993. *Between Freedom and Subsistence*. Hong Kong: Oxford University Press.

Khan, Azizur, and Carl Riskin. 1998. "Income and Inequality in China: Composition, Distribution, and Growth of Household Income, 1988 to 1995." *The China Quality* 154 (June).

Kirby, William. 2000a. *State and Economy in Republic China: A Handbook for Scholars*. Cambridge, Mass.: Harvard University Press.

——. 2000b. "The Internationalization of China: Foreign Relations at Home and Abroad in the Republican Era." In *Reappraising Republican China*, edited by Frederic Wakeman and Richard Edmonds. Oxford: Oxford University Press.

Kotkin, Stephen. 1995. *Magnetic Mountain: Stalinism as a Civilization*. Berkeley: University of California Press.

Krasner, Stephen. 1984. "Approaches to the State: Alternative Conceptions and Historical Dynamics." *Comparative Politics* 16.

Kraus, Richard. 1977. "Class Conflict and the Vocabulary of Social Analysis in China." *China Quarterly* 69 (March).

——. 1981. *Class Conflict in Chinese Socialism*. New York: Columbia University Press.

——. 1983. "The Chinese State and Its Bureaucrats." In *State and Society in Contemporary China*, edited by Victor Nee and David Mozingo. Ithaca, N.Y.: Cornell University Press.

Kristeva, Julia. 1974. *About Chinese Women*. New York: Marion Boyars.

Kwok, D. W. Y. 1998. "On the Rites and Rights of Being Human." In *Confucianism and Human Rights*, edited by Wm. De Bary and Tu Weiming. New York: Columbia University Press.

Lampton, David. 1987. "Chinese Politics: The Bargaining Treadmill." *Issues and Studies* 23:3.

Landes, David. 1998. *The Wealth and Poverty of Nations: Why Some Are so Rich and Some so Poor*. New York: Norton.

Lange, Oskar, and Fred M. Taylor. 1938. *On the Economic Theory of Socialism*. Edited by Benjamin Lippincott. Minneapolis: University of Minnesota Press.

Lardy, Nicolas. 1980. "Regional Growth and Income Distribution in China." In *China's Development Experience in Comparative Perspective*, edited by Robert Dernberger. Cambridge: Harvard University Press.

———. 1992. *Foreign Trade and Economic Reform in China, 1978–90*. Cambridge: Cambridge University Press.

———. 1998a. *China's Unfinished Economic Revolution*. Washington, D.C.: Brookings Institution.

———. 1998b. "China and the Asian Contagion." *Foreign Affairs* (July/August).

Latour, Bruno. 1993. *We Have Never Been Modern*. Cambridge, Mass.: Harvard University Press.

Lattimore, Owen. 1951. *Inner Asian Frontiers of China*. 2nd ed. New York: Capitol.

Lawrence, Susan. 1995. "Democracy, Chinese Style." *Australian Journal of Chinese Affairs* 32 (July).

———. 2002. "The Sickness Trap." *Far Eastern Economic Review*, 13 June.

Lee Ming-Kwan. 2000. *Chinese Occupational Welfare in Market Transition*. Basingstoke: Macmillan.

Leftwich, Adrian. 1995. "Bringing the State Back In: Towards a Model of the Developmental State." *Journal of Development Studies* 31:3 (February).

———. 1996. "On the Primacy of Politics in Development." In *Democracy and Development*, edited by Adrian Leftwich. Cambridge: Polity.

Leifer, Michael, ed. 2000. *Asian Nationalism*. London: Routledge.

Lenin, Vladimir. 1969 [1912]. "Democracy and Nationalism in China." In *Collected Works*. Vol. 18. Moscow: Progress Publisher.

———. 1932 [1918]. *State and Revolution*. In *Collected Works*. Vol. 25. New York: International Publishers.

———. 1969 [1918]. "The Proletarian Revolution and the Renegade Kautsky." In *Collected Works*. Vol. 28. Moscow: Progress Publisher.

Levenson, Joseph. 1967. "The Province, the Nation, and the World: The Problem of Chinese Identity." In *Approaches to Modern Chinese History*, edited by Albert Feuerwerker, Rhoads Murphey, and Mary C. Wright. Berkeley: University of California Press.

———. 1970. *Liang Ch'i-ch'ao and the Mind of Modern China*. Berkeley: University of California Press.

Lewin, Moshe. 1975a. *Political Undercurrents in Soviet Economic Debates: From Bukharin to the Modern Reformers*. London: Pluto.

———. 1975b. *Russian Peasants and Soviet Power: A Study of Collectivization*. New York: Norton.

Lewis, John. 1961. *Socialism and the Individual*. London: Lawrence and Wishart.

Lewis, W. John. 1963. *Leadership in Communist China*. Ithaca, N.Y.: Cornell University Press.

Leys, Colin. 1994. "Confronting the African Tragedy." *New Left Review* 204 (March/April).

Li Changping. 2002. *Speaking Honestly to the Premier*. Beijing: Guangming Daily Press.

Li, Linda. 1998. *Centre and Provinces, China 1978–97: Power as Non-Zero-Sum*. Oxford: Clarendon.

Li Peilin, et al. 1995. *Classes and Stratums in China's New Era*. Shenyang: Liaoning People's Publishing House.

Li Shi. 2003. "Current Conditions of China's Working Class." socialist_asia@ yahoogroups.com.

Li Xiaojiang. 1994. "Economic Reform and the Awakening of Chinese Women's Collective Consciousness." In *Engendering China: Women Culture, and the State*, edited by Christina Gilmartin et al. Cambridge, Mass.: Harvard University Press.

——. 1995. *Toward the Woman: An Empirical Report on Women's Studies in the New Era*. Kaifeng: Henan People's Publishing House.

——. 2003. "Recasting the Legacy of Our Forefather." *Dushu* 8.

——. 2005. "In Search of a New Approach for Gender Studies in Mainstreaming." *National University of Yunnan Academic Journal* 2.

Li Zehou, and Liu Zaifu. 1995. *Farewell to Revolution*. Hong Kong: Tiandi Books.

Lieberthal, Kenneth. 1992a. "The 'Fragmented Authoritarianism' Model and Its Limitations." In *Bureaucracy, Politics, and Decision Making in Post-Mao China*, edited by Kenneth Lieberthal and David Lampton. Berkeley: University of California Press.

——. 1992b. "The Collapse of the Communist Worldland: Mainland China's Foreign Affairs." *Issues and Studies* 28:9 (September).

——. 1995. *Governing China: From Revolution through Reform*. New York: Norton.

Lieberthal, Kenneth, and Michael Oksenberg. 1988. *Policy Making in China: Leaders, Structures, and Processes*. Princeton, N.J.: Princeton University Press.

Lifton, Robert. 1961. *Thought Reform and the Psychology of Totalism*. New York: Norton.

Lijphart, Arend. 1999. *Patterns of Democracy: Government Forms and Performance in Thirty-six Countries*. New Haven, Conn.: Yale University Press.

Lieven, Dominic. 2000. *Empire: The Russian Empire and Its Rivals*. London: Murray.

Lin Chun. 2000. "Participation and Recognition: The Transforming of (Un)Employment in China." *New Political Science* 22.4.

——. 2001. "Human Rights and Democracy: The Case for Decoupling." *International Journal of Human Rights* 5:3.

——. 2002. "Wither Feminism: A Note on China." *Signs* (July).

——. 2005. "What Is China's Comparative Advantage?" In *The Chinese Model of Modern Development*, edited by Tian Yu Cao. London: Routledge.

Lin Yusheng. 1979. *The Crisis of Chinese Consciousness: Radical Antitraditionalism in the May Fourth Era*. Madison: University of Wisconsin Press.

Lin Zili. 1982. "On the Contract System of Responsibility Linked to Production: A New Form of Cooperative Economy in China's Socialist Agriculture." *Social Sciences in China* (Beijing) 3.

——. 1983. "On the Distinctively Chinese Path of Socialist Agricultural Development." *Social Sciences in China* (Beijing) 3.

——. 1984. "More on the Distinctively Chinese Path." *Social Sciences in China* (Beijing) 1.

Lindau, Juan, and Timothy Cheek, eds. 1998. *Market Economics and Political Change: Comparing China and Mexico*. New York: Rowman and Littlefield.

Lindblom, Charles. 1977. *Politics and Markets: The World's Political-Economic Systems*. New York: Basic Books.

——. 2001. *The Market System: What It Is, How It Works, and What to Make of It*. Yale University Press.

Linz, Juan. 2000. *Totalitarian and Authoritarian Regimes*. Boulder, CO: Lynne Rienner.

Linz, Juan, and Alfred Stepan. 1996. *Problems of Democratic Transition and Consolidation: Southern Europe, South America, and Post-Communist Europe*. Baltimore: Johns Hopkins University Press.

Lipset, Martin. 1950. *Agrarian Socialism: The Cooperative Commonwealth Federation in Saskatchewan, A Study in Sociology*. Berkeley: University of California Press.

———1963. *Political Man*. New York: Doubleday.

Little, Daniel. 1989. *Understanding Peasant China: Case Studies in the Philosophy of Social Science*. New Haven, Conn.: Yale University Press.

Liu, Lydia. 1995. *Translingual Practice: Literature, National Culture, and Translated Modernity: China, 1900–37*. Stanford, Calif.: Stanford University Press.

———. 1997. "Translingual Practice: The Discourse of Individualism between China and the West." In *Formations of Colonial Modernity in East Asia*, edited by Tani Barlow. Durham, N.C.: Duke University Press.

Liu Shaoqi. 1993. "The Nature and Developmental Strategy of New China's Economy." In *Liu Shaoqi on New China's Economic Construction*. Beijing: Central Documentary Publisher.

Lo Chung-Sho. 1947. "Human Rights in the Chinese Tradition." In *Human Rights: A Symposium Prepared by UNESCO*. London: Allan Wingate.

Lo Dic. 1997. *Market and Institutional Regulation in Chinese Industrialization, 1978–1994*. New York: St. Martin's Press.

———. 1999. "Re-Appraising China's State-Owned Industrial Enterprises, 1980–96." *Cambridge Journal of Economics* 23.

Louis, W. Roger. 2002. "The Dissolution of the British Empire in the Era of Vietnam." *American Historical Review* 107:1.

Lu Aiguo, and Manuel Montes, eds. 2002. *Poverty, Income Distribution and Well-Being in Asia During the Transition*. Basingstoke, U.K.: Palgrave.

Lu Hsiao-po, and Elizabeth Perry. 1997. *Danwei: The Changing Chinese Workplace in Historical and Comparative Perspective*. Armonk, N.Y.: M. E. Sharpe.

Lu Xueyi. 2000. "Rural-Urban Separate Administration: One Country, Two Policies." *Dushu* 5.

Lu Zhoulai, 2004. "Let Labor Hire Capital." Paper presented at the Conference on Labor's Property Rights, Central Compilation and Translation Bureau, Beijing (July).

Lubman, Stanley. 1999. *Bird in a Cage: Legal Reform in China after Mao*. Stanford, Calif.: Stanford University Press.

Luckham, Robin. 1998. "Are There Alternatives to Liberal Democracy?" In *The Democratic Developmental State: Politics and Institutional Design*, edited by Mark Robinson and Gordon White. Oxford: Oxford University Press.

Luke, Timothy. 1997. "Localized Spaces, Globalized Places." In *The Rise of East Asia: Critical Visions of the Pacific Century*, edited by Mark Berger and Douglas Dorer. London: Routledge.

Luxemburg, Rosa. 1961. *The Russian Revolution, and Leninism or Marxism?* Ann Arbor: University of Michigan Press.

MacFarquhar, Roderick. 1974. *The Origins of the Cultural Revolution. Vol. I: Contradictions among the People 1956–57*. New York: Columbia University Press.

MacFarquhar, Roderick, and John King Fairbank, eds. 1987. *The Emergence of Revolutionary China: 1949–65*. Cambridge: Cambridge University Press.

Mackerras, Colin. 1994. *China's Minorities: Integration and Modernization in the Twentieth Century*. Hong Kong: Oxford University Press.

Macpherson, C. B. 1966. *The Real World of Democracy*. Oxford: Oxford University Press.

——. 1977. *The Life and Times of Liberal Democracy*. Oxford: Oxford University Press.

Mann, Michael. 1995. "Sources of Variation in Working Class Movements in Twentieth Century Europe." *New Left Review* 212 (July/August).

Mann, Susan. 1987. *Local Merchants and the Chinese Bureaucracy, 1750–1950*. Stanford, Calif.: Stanford University Press.

Mao Zedong. 1958. "Introducing a Cooperative." *Red Flag* (Beijing) (15 April).

——. 1977 [1959]. *A Critique of Soviet Economics*. New York: Monthly Review Press.

——. 1990 [1974]. "Chairman Mao's Main Points on Theoretical Questions." *Mao's Writings Since 1949*. Vol. 13. Beijing: Zhongyang Wenxian Publisher.

——. 1991 [1927]. "Report on an Investigation of the Peasant Movement in Hunan." In *Selected Works. Vol. 1*. Beijing: People's Publishing House.

——. 1991 [1937]. "Conversation with the British Journalist James Bertram." In *Selected Works*. Vol. 2. Beijing: People's Publishing House.

——. 1991 [1938]. "The Role of the Chinese Communist Party in the National War." In *Selected Works*. Vol. 2. Beijing: People's Publishing House.

——. 1991 [1940]. "On New Democracy." In *Selected Works*. Vol. 2. Beijing: People's Publishing House.

——. 1991 [1943]. "Some Questions Concerning the Methods of Leadership." In *Selected Works*. Vol. 3. Beijing: People's Publishing House.

——. 1991 [1945a]. "On Coalition Government." In *Selected Works*. Vol. 3. Beijing: People's Publishing House.

——. 1991 [1945b]. "The Foolish Old Man Removes the Mountains." In *Selected Works*. Vol. 3. Beijing: People's Publishing House.

——. 1991 [1948]. "On the Question of the National Bourgeoisie and the Enlightened Gentry." In *Selected Works*. Vol. 4. Beijing: People's Publishing House.

——. 1991 [1949]. "On the People's Democratic Dictatorship." In *Selected Works*. Vol. 4. Beijing: People's Publishing House.

——. 1996 [1962]. "Talk at the Enlarged Central Work Conference." In *Mao's Writings since 1949*. Vol. 10. Beijing: Central Documentary Publisher.

——. 1999 [1956]. "On the Ten Major Relationships." In *Selected Writings*. Vol. 7. Beijing: People's Publishing House, 1999.

——. 1999 [1957]. "On Correctly Handling Contradictions among the People." In *Selected Writings*. Vol. 7. Beijing: People's Publishing House.

March, James, and Johan Olsen, 1989. *Rediscovering Institutions: The Organizational Basis of Politics*. New York: Free Press.

Markovic, Mihailo. 1975. "Philosophical Foundation of the Idea of Self-Management." In *Self-Governing Socialism: A Reader*, edited by Branko Horvat, Mihailo Markovic, and Rudi Supek. White Plains, N.Y.: International Arts and Sciences Press.

Markovic, Mihailo, and Gajo Petrovic, eds. 1979. *Praxis: Yugoslav Essays in the Philosophy and Methodology of the Social Sciences*. London: Reidel.

Marshall, T. H. 1973. *Class, Citizenship and Social Development*. New York: Doubleday.

——. 1981. *The Right to Welfare and Other Essays*. London: Heinemann Educational.

Marx, Karl. 1963 [1844]. "Economic and Philosophical Manuscripts." In *Karl Marx: Early Writings*, edited by T. B. Bottomore. New York: McGraw-Hill.

——. 1966 [1871]. *The Civil War in France*. Beijing: Foreign Language Publisher, 1966.

——. 1967 [1864]. *Capital*. Vol. 1. New York: International Publishers, 1967.

——. 1969. *Marx on Colonialism and Modernization: His Dispatches and Other Writings on China, India, Mexico, the Middle East and North Africa*, edited by Shlomo Avineri. New York: Anchor Books.

——. 1978 [1875]. *Critique of the Gotha Program*. Moscow: Progress Publishers.

Marx, Karl, and Friedrich Engels. 1998. *The Communist*. London: Verso.

Mason, J. H. 1989. "Individuals in Society: Rousseau's Republican Vision." *History of Political Thought* 10:1 (spring).

Mayall, James. 2000. "Nationalism: the Asian Experience." In *Asian Nationalism*, edited by Michael Leifer. London: Routledge.

Mayer, Arno. 2000. *The Furies: Violence and Terror in the French and Russian Revolutions*. Princeton, N.J.: Princeton University Press.

Mazur, Mary. 1997. "The United Front Redefined for the Party-State: A Case Study of Transition and Legitimation." In *New Perspectives on State Socialism in China*, edited by Timothy Cheek and Tony Saich. Armonk, N.Y.: M. E. Sharpe.

McClelland, J. S. 1996. *A History of Western Political Thought*. London: Routledge.

McCormick, Barrett. 1990. *Political Reform in Post-Mao China: Democracy and Bureaucracy in a Leninist State*. Berkeley: University of California Press.

Meisner, Maurice. 1967. *Li Ta-chao and the Origins of Chinese Marxism*. Cambridge, Mass.: Harvard University Press.

——. 1982. *Marxism, Maoism, and Utopianism: Eight Essays*. Madison: University of Wisconsin Press.

——. 1986. "The Wrong March: China Chooses Stalin's Way." *Progressive* (26 October).

——. 1989. "Marx, Mao and Deng on the Division of Labor in History." In *Marxism and the Chinese Experience*, edited by Arif Dirlik and Maurice Meisner. Armonk, N.Y.: M. E. Sharpe.

——. 1996. *The Deng Xiaoping Era: An Inquiry into the Fate of Chinese Socialism, 1978–94*. New York: Hill and Wang.

——. 1999a. "China's Communist Revolution: A Half-Century Perspective." *Current History* (September).

——. 1999b. "The Significance of the Chinese Revolution in World History." London School of Economics, Asia Research Centre Working Papers, no. 1.

——. 1999c. *Mao's China and After: A History of the People's Republic*. 3rd ed. New York: Free Press.

Melotti, Umberto. 1977. *Marx and the Third World*. London: Macmillan.

Miliband, Ralph. 1977. *Marxism and Politics*. Oxford: Oxford University Press.

Mill, John Stuart. 1956. *On Liberty*. Edited by Currin Shields. New York: Bobbs-Merrill.

——. 1962. *Essays on Politics and Culture by John Stuart Mill*. Edited by G. Himmelfarb. New York: Anchor Books.

Miller, David. 2000. *Citizenship and National Identity*. Cambridge: Polity.

Milwertz, Cecilia. 1997. *Accepting Population Control: Urban Chinese Women and the One-Child Family Policy*. Richmond: Curzon.

Mirsky, Jonathan. 1999. "Nothing to Celebrate." *New Republic* 11 (October).

Misra, Kalpana. 1998. *From Post-Maoism to Post-Marxism: The Erosion of Official Ideology in Deng's China*. New York: Routledge.

Mitchell, Juliet. 1984. *Women: The Longest Revolution*. New York: Pantheon Books.

Mohanty, Chandra, Ann Russo, and Lourdes Torres, eds. 1991. *Third World Women and the Politics of Feminism*. Bloomington: Indiana University Press.

Molyneux, Maxine. 1985. "Mobilization without Emancipation? Women's Interests, the State and Revolution in Nicaragua." *Feminist Studies* 11 (summer).

——. 1998. "Analysing Women's Movements." In *Feminist Visions of Development: Gender Analysis and Policy*, edited by Cecile Jackson and Ruth Pearson. London: Routledge.

Montinola, Gabriella, et al. 1995. "Federalism, Chinese Style: The Political Basis for Economic Success in China." *World Politics* 48:1.

Moody, Peter. 1977. *Opposition and Dissent in Contemporary China*. Stanford, Calif.: Hoover Institution.

Moore, Barrington. 1966. *Social Origins of Dictatorship and Democracy: Lord and Peasant in the Making of the Modern World*. Boston: Beacon.

——. 1987. *Authority and Inequality under Capitalism and Socialism*. Oxford: Clarendon.

Morgan, Edmund. 1988. *Inventing the People: The Rise of Popular Sovereignty in England and America*. New York: Norton.

Mouzelis, Nicos. 1995. "Modernity, Late Development and Civil Society." In *Civil Society: Theory, History, Comparison*, edited by John Hall. Cambridge: Polity.

Murphey, Rhoads. 1977. *The Outsiders: The Western Experience in China*. Ann Arbor: University of Michigan Press.

Myers, Ramon. 1980. *The Chinese Economy: Past and Present*. Belmont, Calif.: Wadsworth.

Nairn, Tom. 1977. *The Breakup of Britain: Crisis and Neo-Nationalism*. London: New Left Books.

Nandy, Ashis. 1983. *The Intimate Enemy: Loss and Recovery of Self under Colonialism*. Delhi: Oxford University Press.

——. 2003. *The Romance of the State: And the Fate of Dissent in the Tropics*. New York: Oxford University Press.

Nathan, Andrew. 1985. *Chinese Democracy*. New York: Knopf.

——. 1994. "Human Rights in Chinese Foreign Policy." *China Quarterly* 139 (September).

——. 1997. *China's Transition*. New York: Columbia University Press.

Naughton, Barry. 1988. "The Third Front: Defence Industrialization in the Chinese Interior." *China Quarterly* 115 (autumn).

——. 1991. "Industrial Policy during the Cultural Revolution: Military Preparation, Decentralization, and Leaps Forward." In *New Perspectives on the Cultural Revolution*, edited by William Joseph, Christine Wong, and David Zweig. Cambridge, Mass.: Council on East Asian Studies, Harvard University.

——. 1991. "The Pattern and Legacy of Economic Growth in the Mao Era." In *Perspectives on Modern China: Four Anniversaries*, edited by Kenneth Liberthal et al. Armonk, N.Y.: M. E. Sharpe.

——. 1993a. "Deng Xiaoping: The Economist." *China Quarterly* 135 (September).

——. 1993b. *Growing Out of the Plan*. Oxford: Oxford University Press. 1993.

Nee, Victor. 1989. "A Theory of Market Transition: From Redistribution to Markets in State Socialism." *American Sociological Review* 54:5 (October).

——. 1991. "Social Inequalities in Reforming State Socialism: Between Redistribution and Market." *American Sociological Review* 56:3 (June).

——. 1992. "Organizational Dynamics of Market Transition: Hybrid Forms, Property Right and Mixed Economy in China." *Administrative Science Quarterly* 37 (March).

Nee, Victor, and Raymond Liedka. 1997. "Markets and Inequality in the Transition from State Socialism." In *Inequality, Democracy, and Economic Development*, edited by Manus Midlarsky. Cambridge: Cambridge University Press.

Nee, Victor, and David Mozingo, eds. 1983. *State and Society in Contemporary China*. Ithaca, N.Y.: Cornell University Press.

Newman, Michael. 2002. *Ralph Miliband and the Politics of the New Left*. London: Merlin.

Nivison, David, and Arthur Wright, eds. 1959. *Confucianism in Action*. Stanford, Calif.: Stanford University Press.

Nolan, Peter. 1988. *The Political Economy of Collective Farms: An Analysis of China's Post-Mao Rural Reforms*. Boulder, Colo.: Westview.

———. 1996. "Large Firms and Industrial Reform in Former Planned Economies: The Case of China." *Cambridge Journal of Economics* 20:1.

———. 1997. *China's Rise, Russia's Fall: Politics, Economics, and Planning in the Transition from Stalinism*. New York: St. Martin's Press.

———. 2001. *China and the Global Business Revolution*. New York: Palgrave.

———. 2004. *China at the Crossroads*. Cambridge: Polity.

Nolan, Peter, and J. Sender. 1992. "Death Rates, Life Expectancy and China's Economic Reform: a Critique of A. K. Sen." *World Development* 20:9.

Nolan, Peter, and Wang Xiaoqiang. 1999. "Beyond Privatization: Institutional Innovation and Growth in China's Large State-Owned Enterprises." *World Development* 27:1.

North, Douglas. 1990. "A Transaction Cost Theory of Politics." *Journal of Theoretical Politics* 2:4 (October).

Northrop, F. S. C. 1946. *The Meeting of East and West: An Inquiry concerning World Understanding*. London: Macmillan.

Nove, Alec. 1983. *The Economics of Feasible Socialism*. London: Allen and Unwin.

Nussbaum, Martha. 2000. *Women and Human Development: The Capabilities Approach*. Cambridge: Cambridge University Press.

O'Brien, Kevin. 1990. *Reform without Liberalization: China's NPC and the Politics of Institutional Change*. Cambridge University Press.

———. 1994. "Chinese People's Congress and Legislative Embeddedness: Understanding Early Organizational Development." *Comparative Political Studies* 27:1.

O'Brien, Patrick. 1982. "European Economic Development: the Contribution by the Periphery." *Economic History Review* 35 (February).

———. 1993. "Political Precondition for the Industrial Revolution." In *The Industrial Revolution and British Society*, edited by Patrick O'Brien and R. Quinault. Cambridge: Cambridge University Press.

———. 1999. "Imperialism and the Rise and Decline of the British Economy, 1688–1989." *New Left Review* 238 (November/December).

O'Connor, James. 1973. *Fiscal Crisis of the State*. New York: St. Martin's Press.

O'Donnell, Guillermo. 1992. *Delegative Democracy?* Notre Dame, Ind.: Kellogg Institute for International Studies, University of Notre Dame.

———. 1998. "Horizontal Accountability in New Democracies." *Journal of Democracy* 9:3.

O'Donnell, Guillermo, and Philippe Schmitter. 1986. *Transitions from Authoritarian Rule: Tentative Conclusions about Uncertain Democracies*. Baltimore: Johns Hopkins University Press.

Offe, Claus. 1996. *Modernity and the State: East, West*. Cambridge: Polity.

Offe, Claus, and Ulrich Preuss. 1991. "Democratic Institutions and Moral Resources." In *Political Theory Today*, edited by David Held. Stanford, Calif.: Stanford University Press.

Oi, Jean. 1989. *State and Peasant in Contemporary China: The Political Economy of Village Government*. Berkeley: University of California Press.

———. 1995. "The Role of the Local State in China's Transitional Economy." *China Quarterly* 144 (December).

———. 1999. *Rural China Takes Off: Institutional Foundation of Economic Reform*. Berkeley: University of California Press.

Oi, Jean, and Andrew Walder, eds. 1999. *Property Rights and Economic Reform in China*. Stanford, Calif.: Stanford University Press.

Oksenberg, Michael. 1993. "The American Study of Modern China: Toward the Twenty-first Century." In *American Studies of Contemporary China*, edited by David Shambaugh. Armonk, N.Y.: M. E. Sharpe.

Ollman, Bertell, ed. 1998. *Market Socialism: The Debate among Socialists*. London: Routledge.

Olson, Mancur. 1982. *The Rise and Decline of Nations: Economic Growth, Stagflation, and Social Rigidities*. New Haven, Conn.: Yale University Press.

Ong, Aihwa, and Donald Nonini, eds. 1997. *The Cultural Politics of Modern Chinese Transnationalism*. New York: Routledge.

Parayil, Govindan, ed. 2000. *Kerala, The Development Experience: Reflections on Sustainability and Replicability*. London: Zed.

Parekh, Bhikhu. 1993. "The Cultural Particularity of Liberal Democracy." In *Prospects for Democracy: North, South, East, West*, edited by David Held. Cambridge: Polity.

Parry, Geraint, and Michael Moran, eds. 1994. *Democracy and Democratization*. London: Routledge.

Pearson, Margaret. 1997. *China's New Business Elite: The Political Consequences of Economic Reform*. Berkeley: University of California Press.

Pei Xiaoling. 2002. "Collective Land System: The Root Cause for China's Rural Industry and Gradual Transition." *Economic Management Digests* (Beijing) 5.

Perkins, Dwight, ed. 1975. *China's Modern Economy in Historical Perspective*. Stanford, Calif.: Stanford University Press.

———. 1986. "The Prospects for China's Economic Reforms." In *Modernizing China: Post-Mao Reform and Development*, edited by A. Doak Barnett and Ralph Clough. Boulder, Colo.: Westview.

Perry, Elizabeth. 1994. "Trends in the Study of Chinese Politics: State-Society Relations." *China Quarterly* 137 (March).

———. 1999. "From Paris to the Paris of the East—and Back: Workers as Citizens in Modern Shanghai." Speech delivered at the Fairbank Center, Harvard University, October.

———. 2002. *Challenging the Mandate of Heaven: Social Protest and State Power in China*. Armonk: M. E. Sharpe.

Perry, Elizabeth, and Mark Selden, eds. 2000. *Chinese Society: Change, Conflict and Resistance*. New York: Routledge.

Peters, Guy. 1999. *Institutional Theory in Political Science: The "New Institutionalism."* London: Continuum.

Phillips, Anne. 1997. "From Inequality to Difference: A Severe Case of Displacement?" *New Left Review* 224 (July/August).

Pierson, Paul. 2000. "Increasing Returns, Path Dependence and the Study of Politics." *American Political Science Review* 94:2 (June).

Pocock, J. G. A. 1975. *The Machiavellian Moments*. Princeton, N.J.: Princeton University Press.

———. 1999. *Barbarism and Religion*. Cambridge: Cambridge University Press.

Polanyi, Karl. 1957 [1944]. *The Great Transformation: The Political and Economic Origins of Our Time*. Boston: Beacon.

Pomeranz, Kenneth. 2000. *The Great Divergence: Europe, China, and the Making of the Modern World Economy*. Princeton, N.J.: Princeton University Press.

Postiglione, Gerard. 1992. "China's National Minorities and Educational Change." *Journal of Contemporary Asia* 22:1 (February).

Potter, Sulamith, and Jack Potter, eds. 1990. *China's Peasants: The Anthropology of a Revolution*. Cambridge: Cambridge University Press.

Pretty, Dave. 1998. "Review of Orlando Figes, *A People's Tragedy: A History of the Russian Revolution*." H-Russia: http://www.h-net.org/~russia.

Price, R. F. 1970. *Education in Communist China*. London: Routledge.

Prime, Penelope. 1989. "Socialism and Economic Development: The Politics of Accumulation in China." In *Marxism and the Chinese Experience*, edited by Arif Dirlik and Maurice Meisner. Armonk, N.Y.: M. E. Sharpe.

Przeworski, Adam. 1991. *Democracy and the Market: Political and Economic Reforms in Eastern Europe and Latin America*. Cambridge: Cambridge University Press.

———, et al. 1995. *Sustainable Democracy*. Cambridge: Cambridge University Press.

Przeworski, Adam, and Michael Wallerstein. 1988. "The Structural Dependence of the State on Capital." *American Political Science Review* 82:1 (March).

Putnam, Robert. 1993. *Making Democracy Work: Civil Traditions in Modern Italy*. Princeton, N.J.: Princeton University Press.

———, ed. 2002. *Democracies in Flux: The Evolution of Social Capital in Contemporary Society*. Oxford: Oxford University Press.

Pye, Lucien. 1968. *The Spirit of Chinese Politics: A Psychocultural Study of the Authority Critics in Political Development*. Cambridge, Mass.: MIT Press.

———. 1985. *Asian Power and Politics: The Cultural Dimensions of Authority*. Cambridge, Mass.: Harvard University Press.

———. 1992. "Social Science Theories in Search of Chinese Realities." *China Quarterly* 132 (December).

———. 1996. "How China's Nationalism Was Shanghaied." In *Chinese Nationalism*, edited by Jonathan Unger. Armonk, N.Y.: M. E. Sharpe.

Qian Yung-xiang, and Wang Zhen-huan. 1995. "Toward a New State? The Formation of Popular Authoritarianism and the Question of Democracy." *Taiwan: A Radical Quarterly in Social Studies* 20 (August).

Qin Hui. 2002. "On the Question of the Gini Coefficient and Social Polarization." In *Economic Transition and Social Justice*, edited by Jin Yan and Qin Hui. Kaifeng: Henan People's Publishing House.

———. 2003. "Dividing the Big Family Assets." *New Left Review* 20 (March/April).

Ramet, Sabrina, ed. 1996. *Adaptation and Transformation in Communist and Post-Communist Systems*. Boulder, Colo.: Westview.

Ramo, Joshua Cooper. 2004. *The Beijing Consensus*. London: Foreign Policy Center.

Randall, Vicky. 1997. "Why Have the Political Trajectories of India and China Been Different?" In *Democratization*, edited by David Potter et al. Cambridge: Polity.

Rapp, John. 1987. "The Fate of Marxist Democrats in Leninist Party-States: China's Debate on the Asiatic Mode of Production." *Theory and Society* 16.

Rawls, John. 1993. "The Law of Peoples." *Critical Inquiry* 20:1 (fall).

Rawski, Thomas. 1980a. *Economic Growth and Employment in China*. New York: Oxford University Press.

——. 1980b. "Choice of Technology and Technological Innovation in China's Economic Development." In *China's Development Experience in Comparative Perspective*, edited by Robert Dernberger. Cambridge, Mass.: Harvard University Press.

Redding, Gordon. 1990. *The Spirit of Chinese Capitalism*. Berlin: Walter de Gruyter.

Resnick, Stephen A., and Richard D. Wolff. 2002. *Class Theory and History: Capitalism and Communism in the USSR*. London: Routledge.

Richter, Frank-Jurgen. 2000. *The East Asian Development: Economy, Growth, Institutional Failure and the Aftermath of the Crisis*. London: Macmillan.

Riskin, Carl. 1973. "Maoism and Motivation: Work Incentives in China." *Bulletin of Concerned Asian Scholars* 5.

——. 1987. *China's Political Economy: The Quest for Development since 1949*. New York: Oxford University Press.

——. 1990. "Food, Poverty and the Development Strategy in the PRC." In *Hunger in History*, edited by L. F. Newman. Oxford: Blackwell.

——. 1991a. "Neither Plan nor Market: Mao's Political Economy." In *New Perspectives on the Cultural Revolution*, edited by William Joseph, Christine Wong, and David Zweig. Cambridge, Mass.: Council on East Asian Studies, Harvard University.

——. 1991b. "Feeding China: The Experience since 1949." In *Hunger: Economics and Policy*, edited by Jean Dreze and Amartya Sen. Oxford: Oxford University Press.

——. 1997. "Behind the Silk Curtain." *The Nation* (10 November).

——. 1998. "Seven Questions about The Chinese Famine of 1959–61." *Chinese Economic Studies*, Special Issue.

Robinson, Joan. 1972. *Economic Management: China*. London: Anglo-Chinese Educational Institute.

Robinson, Mark, and Gordon White, eds. 1998. *The Democratic Developmental State: Politics and Institutional Design*. New York: Oxford University Press.

Roemer, John, and Pranab Bardhan, eds. 1993. *Market Socialism: The Current Debate*. Oxford: Oxford University Press.

Rofel, Lisa. 1999. *Other Modernities: Gendered Yearnings in China after Socialism*. Berkeley: University of California Press.

Rona-Tas, Akos. 1994. "The First Shall Be Last? Entrepreneurship and Communist Cadre in the Transition from Socialism." *American Journal of Sociology* 100:1.

Rong Jingben, et al. 1997. "Reform of the Political System at County and Township Levels: How to Establish a Democratic, Cooperative New System." *Comparative Economic and Social Systems* (Beijing) 4.

Rosemont, Henry. *A Chinese Mirror: Moral Reflections on Political Economy and Society*. LaSalle, Ill.: Open Court, 1991.

Rosenberg, Justin. 1996. "Isaac Deutscher and the Lost History of International Relations." *New Left Review* 215 (January/February).

Rousseau, Jean-Jacques. 1968. *The Social Contract*. Harmondsworth, U.K.: Penguin.

——. 1987. *Complete Correspondence of Rousseau*. Vol. 24. edited by R. A. Leign. Oxford: Oxford University Press.

——. 1988. *Rousseau's Political Writings*, edited by Alan Ritter. New York: Norton.

——. 1993. *The Social Contract and Discourses*. London: Dent.

Rowe, William. 1994. "The Search for Civil Society and Democracy in China." *Current History* 93 (September).

Rozman, Gilbert. 1985. *A Mirror for Socialism: Soviet Criticisms of China*. London: Tauris.

Rupnik, Jacques. 1999. "Eastern Europe after Ten Years: Postcommunist Splits." *Journal of Democracy* 10.1 (January).

Safran, William, ed. 1998. *Nationalism and Ethnoregional Identities in China*. London: Frank Cass.

Saich, Tony. 1984. "Workers in the Workers' State: Urban Workers in the PRC." In *Groups and Politics in the People's Republic of China*, edited by David Goodman. Armonk, N.Y.: M. E. Sharpe.

———. 2004. *Governance and Politics of China*. 2nd ed. London: Palgrave.

Saich, Tony, and Hans van de Ven, eds. 1995. *New Perspectives on the Chinese Communist Revolution*. Armonk, N.Y.: M. E. Sharpe.

Salecl, Renata. 1997. "The Postsocialist Moral Majority." In *Transitions, Environments, Translations: Feminism in International Politics*, edited by Joan Scott, Cora Kaplan, and Debra Keates. London: Routledge.

Sartori, Giovanni. 1962. *Democratic Theory*. New York: Praeger.

———. 1987. *The Theory of Democracy Revisited*. Chatham, N.J.: Chatham House.

———. 1994. "Compare Why and How: Comparing, Miscomparing and the Comparative Method." In *Comparing Nations: Concepts, Strategies, Substance*, edited by Mattei Dogan and Ali Kazancigil. Oxford: Blackwell.

Schmitt, Carl. 2004. *Legality and Legitimacy*. Translated by Jeffrey Seitzer; introduced by John P. McCormick. Durham, N.C.: Duke University Press.

Schmitter, Philippe. 1974. "Still a Century of Corporatism." In *Social-Political Structures in the Iberian World*, edited by Frederick Pike and Thomas Stritch. Notre Dame, Ind.: University of Notre Dame Press.

———. 1996. "Dangers and Dilemmas of Democracy." In *The Global Resurgence of Democracy*, 2nd ed., edited by Larry Diamond and Marc Platter. Baltimore: Johns Hopkins University Press.

Schram, Stuart. 1966. *Mao Tse-Tung*. Harmondsworth, U.K.: Penguin.

———. 1969. *The Political Thought of Mao Tse-tung*. New York: Praeger.

———, ed. 1973. *Authority, Participation, and Cultural Change in China*. Cambridge: Cambridge University Press.

———, ed. 1987. *Foundations and Limits of State Power in China*. London: Sage.

———. 1989a. *The Thought of Mao Tse-Tung*. Cambridge: Cambridge University Press.

———. 1989b. *The Political Thought of Mao Tse-Tung*. Cambridge: Cambridge University Press.

Schumpeter, Joseph. 1947. *Capitalism, Socialism, and Democracy*. 2nd ed. New York: Harper.

Schurmann, Franz. 1960. "Organizational Principles of the Chinese Communists." *China Quarterly* 1.1.

———. 1968. *Ideology and Organization in Communist China*. Berkeley: University of California Press.

Schwarcz, Vera. 1986. *The Chinese Enlightenment: Intellectuals and the Legacy of the May Fourth Movement of 1919*. Berkeley: University of California Press.

Schwartz, Benjamin. 1958. *Chinese Communism and the Rise of Mao*. Cambridge, Mass.: Harvard University Press.

———. 1964. *In Search of Wealth and Power: Yan Fu and the West*. Cambridge, Mass.: Harvard University Press.

Schweickart, David. 1998. "Market Socialism: A Defense." In *Market Socialism: The Debate among Socialists*, edited by Bertell Ollman. New York: Routledge.

——. 2002. *After Capitalism*. Lanham, Md.: Rowman and Littlefield.

Scott, James. 1990. *Domination and the Arts of Resistance: Hidden Transcripts*. New Haven, Conn.: Yale University Press.

——. 1998. *Seeing Like a State: How Certain Schemes to Improve the Human Condition Have Failed*. New Haven, Conn.: Yale University Press.

Scott, Joan W. 1988a. "Gender: A Useful Category of Historical Analysis." In *Gender and the Politics of History*, edited by Joan W. Scott. New York: Columbia University Press.

——. 1988b. "The Sears Case." In *Gender and the Politics of History*, edited by Joan W. Scott. New York: Columbia University Press.

——. 1996. *Only Paradoxes to Offer: French Feminists and the Rights of Man*. Cambridge, Mass.: Harvard University Press.

——. 2000. "The 'Class' We have Lost." *International Labor and Working-Class History* 57 (spring).

Selden, Mark. 1971. *The Yenan Way in Revolutionary China*. Cambridge, Mass.: Harvard University Press.

——, ed. 1979. *The People's Republic of China: A Documentary History of Revolutionary Change*. New York: Monthly Review Press.

——. 1982. "Cooperation and Conflict: Cooperative and Collective Formation in China's Countryside." In *The Transition to Socialism in China*, edited by Mark Selden and Victor Lippit. Armonk, N.Y.: M. E. Sharpe.

——. 1988. *The Political Economy of Chinese Socialism*. Armonk, N.Y.: M. E. Sharpe.

Selden, Mark, and Victor Lippit. 1982. *The Transition to Socialism in China*. Armonk, N.Y.: M. E. Sharpe.

Sen, Amartya. 1990. "Individual Freedom as a Social Commitment." *New York Review of Books* (14 June).

——. 1997a. *Development Thinking at the Beginning of the Twenty-First Century*. London: London School of Economics. Development Economics Research Program, Working Paper no. 2.

——. 1997b. "Human Rights and Asian Values." *New Republic* (July).

——. 2000a. *Development as Freedom*. New York: Knopf.

——. 2000b. "Population and Gender Equality." *Nation* 24/31 (July).

——. 2002. "How to Judge Globalism." *The American Prospect* 13:1 (January).

Seymour, James. 1987. *China's Satellite Parties*. Armonk, N.Y.: M. E. Sharpe.

Shakya, Tsering. 2002. "Blood in the Snows." *New Left Review* 15 (May/June).

Shambaugh, David. 1991. *Beautiful Imperialist: China Perceives America, 1972–90*. Princeton, N.J.: Princeton University Press.

Shanin, Theodore. 1983. *Late Marx and the Russian Road: Marx and the Peripheries of Capitalism*. New York: Monthly Review Press.

Shaw, Victor. 1996. *Social Control in China: A Study of a Chinese Work Unit*. Westport, Conn.: Praeger.

Shirk, Susan. 1993. *The Political Logic of Economic Reform in China*. Berkeley: University of California Press.

——. 1994. *How China Opened Its Door: The Political Success of the PRC's Foreign Trade and Investment Reforms*. Washington, D.C.: Brookings Institution.

Shue, Henry. 1980. *Basic Rights: Subsistence, Affluence, and U.S. Foreign Policy*. Princeton, N.J.: Princeton University Press.

Shue, Vivienne. 1980. *Peasant China in Transition: The Dynamics of Development toward Socialism*. Berkeley: University of California Press.

———. 1988. *The Reach of the State: Sketches of the Chinese Body Politic*. Stanford, Calif.: Stanford University Press.

Skinner, Quentin. 1998. *Liberty before Liberalism*. Cambridge: Cambridge University Press.

Skinner, William, ed. 1977. *The City in Late Imperial China*. Stanford, Calif.: Stanford University Press.

Simon, Herbert. 2000. "Public Administration in Today's World of Organization and Markets." *Political Science and Politics* 33:4 (December).

Skocpol, Theda. 1979. *State and Social Revolution: A Comparative Analysis of France, Russia, and China*. Cambridge: Cambridge University Press.

———. 1994. *Social Revolutions in the Modern World*. Cambridge: Cambridge University Press.

Smil, Vaclav. 1993. *China's Environmental Crisis: An Inquiry into the Limits of National Development*. Armonk, N.Y.: M. E. Sharpe.

Smith, Anthony. 1998. *Nationalism and Modernism: A Critical Survey of Recent Theories of Nations and Nationalism*. London: Routledge.

———. 1999. *Myths and Memories of the Nation*. New York: Oxford University Press.

Solinger, Dorothy. 1999. *Contesting Citizenship in Urban China*. Berkeley: University of California Press.

Song Yongyi. 2002. Preface to *The Chinese Cultural Revolution Database, CD-ROM*. Hong Kong: Chinese University Press.

Sovensen, Georg. 1993. *Democracy and Democratization: Processes and Prospects in a Changing World*. Boulder, Colo.: Westview.

Spence, Jonathan. 1999. *The Search for Modern China*. 2nd ed. New York: Norton.

Stacey, Judith. 1983. *Patriarchy and Socialist Revolution in China*. Berkeley: University of California Press.

Staniszkis, Jadwiga. 1991. *The Dynamics of the Breakthrough in Eastern Europe: The Polish Experience*. Berkeley: University of California Press.

Starr, John. 1972. "Revolution in Retrospect: The Paris Commune through Chinese Eyes." *China Quarterly* 49.

———. 1979. *Continuing the Revolution: The Political Thought of Mao*. Princeton, N.J.: Princeton University Press.

State Council of the PRC. 2001. "Progress in China's Human Rights Cause in 2000." Beijing.

Stavis, Benedict. 1983. "The Dilemma of State Power: The Solution Becomes the Problem." In *State and Society in Contemporary China*, edited by Victor Nee and David Mozingo. Ithaca, N.Y.: Cornell University Press.

Stedman Jones, Gareth. Introduction to *The Communist Manifesto*. London: Penguin, 2002.

Steinfeld, Edward S. 2004. "Market Visions: The Interplay of Ideas and Institutions in Chinese Financial Restructuring." *Political Studies* 52:4 (December).

Strand, David. 1989. *Rickshaw Beijing: City People and Politics in 1920s China*. Berkeley: University of California Press.

——. 1990. "Protest in Beijing: Civil Society and Public Sphere in China." *Problems of Communism* 39:2/3 (May–June).

Sun Yan. 1995. *The Chinese Reassessment of Socialism, 1976–92*. Princeton, N.J.: Princeton University Press.

Sun Zhongshan. 1956. *Selected Writings of Sun*. Beijing: Chinese Publishing House.

Sun Zhongfan, An Miao, and Feng Tongqing, eds. 1997. *An Outline and Commentaries on the Theories of Trade Unions in the Transformation toward a Socialist Market Economy*. Beijing: People's Publishing House.

Supiot, Alain. 2002. "Ontologies of Law." *New Left Review* 13 (January/February).

Szelenyi, Ivan. 1978. "Social Inequalities under State Redistributive Economies." *International Journal of Comparative Sociology* 1.

Szelenyi, Ivan, and Robert Mannchin. 1987. "Social Policy under State Socialism." In *Stagnation and Renewal in Social Policy*, edited by Gosta Esping-Anderson et al. Armonk, N.Y.: M. E. Sharpe.

Talmon, Jacob. 1952. *The Origins of Totalitarian Democracy*. New York: Secker and Warburg.

——. 1960. Political Messianism: The Romantic Phase. New York: Praeger.

Tang Wenfang, and William Parish. 2000. *Chinese Urban Life under Reform*. Cambridge: Cambridge University Press.

Tanner, Murray. 1999. *The Politics of Lawmaking in Post-Mao China*. Oxford: Oxford University Press.

Tao, Julia. 2000. "Two Perspectives on Care: Confucian *Ren* and Feminist Care." *Journal of Chinese Philosophy* 27:2 (June).

Taylor, Charles. 1979. *Hegel and Modern Society*. Cambridge: Cambridge University Press.

——. 1999a. "Two Theories of Modernity." *Public Culture* 11:1.

——. 1999b. "Comment on Jürgen Habermas: 'From Kant to Hegel and Back Again.'" *European Journal of Philosophy* 7.2.

Therborn, Goran. 1995. *European Modernity and Beyond, 1945–2000*. London: Sage.

——. 2000. "Reconsidering Revolutions." *New Left Review* 2 (March/April).

Tilly, Charles. 1992. *Coercion, Capital, and European States, AD 990–1992*. Oxford: Blackwell.

——, ed. 1996. *Citizenship, Identity and Social History*. Cambridge: Cambridge University Press.

Tocqueville, Alexis de. 1955 [1856]. *The Old Regime and the French Revolution*. New York: Doubleday.

——. 1968. *Democracy in America*. Vol. 1. London: Fontana.

Townsend, James. 1967. *Political Participation in Communist China*. Berkeley: University of California Press.

——. 1974. *Politics in China*. Boston: Little, Brown.

——. 1992. "Chinese Nationalism." *Australian Journal of Chinese Affairs* 27 (January).

Toynbee, Arnold. 1954. *A Study of History*. Vol. 1. London: Oxford University Press.

Trimberger, Ellen. 1977. "State Power and Modes of Production: Implications of the Japanese Transition to Capitalism." *Insurgent Sociologist* 7 (spring).

——. 1978. *Revolution from Above: Military Bureaucracy in Japan, Turkey, Egypt, Peru*. London: Transaction.

Trotsky, Leon. 1959. *The Russian Revolution: The Overthrow of Tzarism and the Triumph of the Soviets*. Edited by F. W. Dupee. New York: Anchor.

———. 1966 [1938]. *Their Morals and Ours: Marxist versus Liberal Views on Morality*. New York: Merit.

Tsou Tang. 1963. *America's Failure in China: 1941–50*. Chicago: University of Chicago Press.

———. 1983. "Back from the Brink of Revolutionary-'Feudal' Totalitarianism." In *State and Society in Contemporary China*, edited by Victor Nee and David Mozingo. Ithaca, N.Y.: Cornell University Press.

———. 1988. *The Cultural Revolution and Post-Mao Reforms: A Historical Perspective*. Chicago: University of Chicago Press.

———. 1991. "The Tiananmen Tragedy: The State-Society Relationship, Choices, and the Mechanisms in Historical Perspective." In *Contemporary Chinese Politics in Historical Perspective*, edited by Brantly Womack. Cambridge: Cambridge University Press.

———. 1995. "Chinese Politics at the Top: Factionalism or Informal Politics? Balance-of-Power Politics or Game to Win All?" *China Quarterly* 34 (July).

———. 2000. "Interpreting the Revolution in China." *Modern China* 26:2 (April).

Tu Weiming. 1991. "The Enlightenment Mentality and the Chinese Intellectual Dilemma." In *Perspectives on Modern China: Four Anniversaries*, edited by Kenneth Lieberthal et al. Armonk, N.Y.: M. E. Sharpe.

Tucker, Robert. 1967. "The Deradicalization of Marxist Movements." *American Political Science Review* 61 (June).

Twiss, Sumner. 1998. "A Constructive Framework for Discussing Confucianism and Human Rights." In *Confucianism and Human Rights*, edited by Wm. de Bary and Tu Weiming. New York: Columbia University Press.

UNDP (United Nations Development Program). 1998. *China: Human Development Report. Human Development and Poverty Alleviation, 1997*. Beijing: UNDP.

———. 2003. *Human Development Report 2002*. New York: Oxford University Press.

Unger, Jonathan. 1994. " 'Rich Man, Poor Man': The Making of New Classes in the Countryside." In *China's Quiet Revolution: New Interactions between State and Society*, edited by David Goodman and Beverly Hooper. New York: St. Martin's Press.

———, ed. 1996. *Chinese Nationalism*, Armonk, N.Y.: M. E. Sharpe.

Unger, Jonathan, and Anita Chan. 1995. "China, Corporatism, and the East Asian Model." *Australian Journal of Chinese Affairs* 33 (January).

Unger, Roberto. 1987. *False Necessity: Anti-Necessitarian Social Theory in the Service of Radical Democracy*. Cambridge: Cambridge University Press.

———. 1996. *What Should Legal Analysis Become?* London: Verso.

———. 1997. *Politics: The Central Texts*. Edited by Zhiyuan Cui. London: Verso.

———. 1998. *Democracy Realized: The Progressive Alternative*. London: Verso.

———. 2004. "The Transformation of Experience." The Boutwood Lectures, Corpus Christi College, Cambridge University.

Unger, Roberto, and Cui Zhiyuan. 1994. "China in the Russian Mirror." *New Left Review* 208 (November/December).

United Nations. 1988 [1948]. *Universal Declaration on Human Rights*. New York: United Nations.

van de Ven, Hans. 1991. *From Friend to Comrade: The Founding of the CCP, 1920–1927*. Berkeley: University of California Press.

Van Ness, Peter. 1984. "Three Lines in Chinese Foreign Relations 1950–80: The Development Imperative." In *Three Visions of Chinese Socialism*, edited by Dorothy Solinger. Boulder, Colo.: Westview.

———. 1993. "China as a Third World State: Foreign Policy and Official National Identity." In *China's Quest for National Identity*, edited by Lowell Dittmer and Samuel Kim. Ithaca, N.Y.: Cornell University Press.

Vanhanen, Tatu. 1997. *Prospects of Democracy: A Study of 172 Countries*. London: Routledge.

Vashney, Ashutosh. 1998. "India Defies the Odds: Why Democracy Survives." *Journal of Democracy* 19:3.

Veblen, Thorstein. 1990. *Imperial Germany and the Industrial Revolution*. New Brunswick, N.J.: Transaction.

Villa, Dana. 1997. "Hannah Arendt: Modernity, Alienation, and Critique." In *Hannah Arendt and the Meaning of Politics*, edited by Craig Calhoun and John McGowan. Minneapolis: University of Minnesota Press.

Village Self-Government Research Group. 1997. *A Study on the Election of Villagers Committees in Rural China*. Beijing: Chinese Society Publisher.

Wachman, Alan. 1994. *Taiwan: National Identity and Democratization*. Armonk, N.Y.: M. E. Sharpe.

Wade, Robert. 1990. *Governing the Market: Economic Theory and the Role of Government in East Asian Industrialization*. Princeton, N.J.: Princeton University Press.

———. 2001. "Winners and Losers." *Economist* 26 (April).

———. 2004. "The Ringmaster of Doha." *New Left Review* 25.

Wakeman, Frederic. 1991. "Models of Historical Change: The Chinese State and Society, 1839–1989." In *Perspectives on Modern China: Four Anniversaries*, edited by Kenneth Lieberthal et al. Armonk, N.Y.: M. E. Sharpe.

———. 1998. "Boundaries of the Public Sphere in Ming and Qing China." *Daedalus* 27:3 (summer).

Wakeman, Frederic, and R. L. Edmonds, eds. 1999. *Reappraising Republican China*. New York: Oxford University Press.

Walder, Andrew. 1982. "Some Ironies of the Maoist Legacy in Industry." In *The Transition to Socialism in China*, edited by Mark Selden and Victor Lippit. Armonk, N.Y.: M. E. Sharpe.

———. 1986. *Communist Neo-Traditionalism: Work and Authority in Chinese Industry*. Berkeley: University of California Press.

———. 1991. "Cultural Revolution Radicalism: Variations on a Stalinist Theme." In *New Perspectives on the Cultural Revolution*, edited by William Joseph, Christine Wong, and David Zweig. Cambridge, Mass.: Council on East Asian Studies, Harvard University.

———. 1994. "Corporate Organization and Local State Property Rights: The Chinese Alternative to Privatization." In *Changing Political Economies: Privatization in Post-Communist and Reforming Communist States*, edited by Vedat Milor. Boulder, Colo.: Rienner.

Waldron, Arthur. 1990. "Warlordism vs. Federalism: The Revival of a Debate?" *China Quarterly* 121 (March).

Walicki, Andrzej. 1969. *The Controversy over Capitalism: Studies in the Social Philosophy of the Russian Populists*. Oxford: Clarendon.

Wallerstein, Immanuel. 1991a. "The Construction of Peoplehood." In *Race, Nation, and Class*, edited by Etienne Balibar and Immanuel Wallerstein. London: Verso.

———. 1991b. *Unthinking Social Sciences: The Limits of Nineteenth Century Paradigms*. Cambridge: Polity.

——. 1999. *The End of the World as We Know It: Social Science for the Twenty-first Century*. Minneapolis: University of Minnesota Press.

Walzer, Michael. 1977. *Just and Unjust Wars: A Moral Argument with Historical Illustrations*. New York: Basic Books.

——. 1980. *Radical Principles: Reflections of an Unreconstructed Democrat*. New York: Basic Books.

——. 1994a. "A Day in the Life of a Socialist Citizen." In *Legacy of Dissent: Forty Years of Writings from Dissent Magazine*, edited by Nicolaus Mills. New York: Simon and Schuster.

——. 1994b. *Thick and Thin: Moral Argument at Home and Abroad*. Notre Dame, Ind.: University of Notre Dame Press.

——. 1998. "Intellectuals, Social Classes, and Revolutions." In *Democracy, Revolution, and History*, edited by Theda Skocpol. Ithaca, N.Y.: Cornell University Press.

Wang Chaohua, ed. 2003. *One China, Many Paths*. London: Verso.

——. 2005. "The Tale of Two Nationalisms." *New Left Review* 32 (March–April).

Wang Fei-Ling. 1998. *Institutions and Institutional Change in China: Premodernity and Modernization*. London: Macmillan.

Wang Gungwu. 1996. "Openness and Nationalism: Outside the Chinese Revolution." In *Chinese Nationalism*, edited by Jonathan Unger. Armonk, N.Y.: M. E. Sharpe.

Wang Hui. 1998. "Contemporary Chinese Thought and the Question of Modernity." *Social Text* 55 (summer).

——. 1999. " 'Modernity' and 'Asia' in the Study of Chinese History." Manuscript.

——. 2002. "The Genealogy of Asia." Manuscript.

——. 2003. *China's New Order: Society, Politics and Economy in Transition*. Cambridge, Mass.: Harvard University Press.

——. 2004. *The Rise of Modern Thought in China*. 4 vols. Beijing: Sanlian Publishing House.

Wang Huning. 1987. "A Comparative Analysis of Political Development in a Post-Revolutionary Society." *Fudan Xuebao* (Shanghai) 4.

Wang Jing. 2001. "The State Question in Chinese Popular Cultural Studies." *Inter-Asia Cultural Studies* 2.1.

Wang Lixiong. 2002. "Reflections on Tibet." *New Left Review* 14 (March/April).

——. 2004. *Dijin Democracy: China's Third Way*. Hong Kong: Social Science Publisher.

Wang Mei, et al. 1997. "The Implication of Redistribution on the Health of the Population." Manuscript.

Wang Ruoshui. 1998. "A Reappraisal of 'On the Correct Handling of Contradictions among the People': How Mao Gave Up an Opportunity for Political Reform." Manuscript.

Wang Shaoguang. 2003. "Public Health Is also an Indisputable Principle." *Dushu* (Beijing) 7.

Wang Shaoguang, and Hu Angang. 1999. *The Political Economy of Uneven Development: The Case of China*. Armonk, N.Y.: M. E. Sharpe.

Wang Xiaoqiang. 1980. "A Critique of Agrarian Socialism." *Wei Ding Gao* (Chinese Academy of Social Sciences). Beijing.

Wang Ying. 1994. "New Collectivism and a Market Economy with Chinese Characteristics." *The Twenty-first Century* (Hong Kong) 10.

Wang Zheng, 2000. "Gender, Employment and Women's Resistance." In *Chinese Society:*

Change, Conflict and Resistance, edited by Elizabeth Perry and Mark Selden. New York: Routledge.

Wasserstrom, Jeffrey. 1991. *Student Protests in Twentieth-Century China*. Stanford, Calif.: Stanford University Press.

———, ed. 2003. *Twentieth-Century China: New Approaches*. New York: Routledge.

Watson, James, ed. 1984. *Class and Social Stratefication in Post-Revolutionary China*. Cambridge: Cambridge University Press.

Weber, Max. 1951. *The Religion of China*. Glencoe, Ill.: Free Press.

———. 1994. *Political Writings*. Edited by Peter Lassman and Ronald Speirs. Cambridge: Cambridge University Press.

———. 1994 [1958]. "Politics as a Vocation." In *Weber: Selections in Translation*, edited by W. G. Runciman. Cambridge: Cambridge University Press.

Weil, Robert. 1995. *Red Cat, White Cat: China and the Contradiction of Market Socialism*. New York: Monthly Review Press.

Weitzman, Martin, and Xu Chenggang, 1994. "Chinese Township and Village Enterprises as Vaguely Defined Cooperatives." *Journal of Comparative Economics* 18.2 (April).

Wen Tiejun. 1999. "The Questions of Rural China, Agriculture and the Peasantry: A *fin-de-siecle* Reflection." *Dushu* (Beijing) 12.

Wertheim, Wim. 1995. "Wild Swans and Mao's Agrarian Strategy." *Australia-China Review* (August).

Westad, O. R., ed. 1999. *Brother in Arms: The Rise and Fall of the Sino-Soviet Alliance, 1945–63*. Washington, D.C.: Woodrow Wilson Center Press.

White, Gordon. 1981. *Party and Professionals: The Political Role of Teachers in Contemporary China*. Armonk, N.Y.: M. E. Sharpe.

———. 1983. "The Postrevolutionary Chinese State." In *State and Society in Contemporary China*, edited by Victor Nee and David Mozingo. Ithaca, N.Y.: Cornell University Press.

———, ed. 1988. *Developmental State in East Asia*. London: Macmillan.

———. 1993. *Riding the Tiger: The Politics of Economic Reform in Post-Mao China*. Stanford, Calif.: Stanford University Press.

———. 1996a. "Development and Democratization in China." In *Democracy and Development*, edited by Adrian Leftwich. Cambridge: Polity.

———. 1996b. "The Chinese Developmental Model: A Virtuous Paradigm?" *Oxford Development Studies* 24:2.

White, Lynn. 1989. *Policies of Chaos: The Organizational Causes of Violence in China's Cultural Revolution*. Princeton, N.J.: Princeton University Press.

White, Lynn, and Li Cheng. 1993. "Coast Identities: Regional, National and Global." In *China's Quest for National Identity*, edited by Lowell Dittmer and Samuel Kim. Ithaca, N.Y.: Cornell University Press.

White, Stephen, John Gardner, and George Schopflin. 1982. *The Communist Political System: An Introduction*. London: Macmillan.

Whiting, Susan. 2001. *Power and Wealth in Rural China: The Political Economy of Institutional Change*. Cambridge: Cambridge University Press.

Whyte, Martin. 1973. "Bureaucracy and Modernization in China: The Maoist Critique." *American Sociological Review* 38:2 (April).

———. 1986. "Social Trends in China: The Triumph of Inequality?" In *Modernizing China:*

Post-Mao Reform and Development, edited by Anthony Barnett and R. N. Clough. Boulder, Colo.: Westview.

Wilber, Charles, ed. 1978. *The Political Economy of Development and Underdevelopment.* New York: Random House.

Williams, Raymond. 1979 [1966]. *Modern Tragedy.* London: Verso.

Winnington, Alan. 1986. *Breakfast with Mao: Memories of a Foreign Correspondent.* London: Lawrence and Wishart.

Wolf, Eric. 1982. *Europe and the People without History.* Berkeley: University of California Press.

———. 1999. *Envisioning Power: Ideologies of Dominance and Crisis.* Berkeley: University of California Press.

Wolfe, Margery. 1985. *Revolution Postponed: Women in Contemporary China.* London: Methuen.

Womack, Brantly. 1982. *The Foundations of Mao Zedong's Political Thought, 1917–1935.* Honolulu: University of Hawaii Press.

———. 1989. "Party-State Democracy: A Theoretical Exploration." *Issues and Studies* 25.

———. 1991a. "Transfigured Community: Neo-traditionalism and Work Unit Socialism in China." *China Quarterly* 126 (June).

———. 1991b. "In Search of Democracy: Public Authority and Popular Power in China." In *Contemporary Chinese Politics in Historical Perspective*, edited by Brantly Womack. Cambridge: Cambridge University Press.

Wong, R. Bin. 1997. *China Transformed: Historical Change and the Limits of European Experience.* Ithaca, N.Y.: Cornell University Press.

Wong, Christine. 1991. "The Maoist 'Model' Reconsidered: Local Self-Reliance and the Financing of Rural Industries." In *New Perspectives on the Cultural Revolution*, edited by William Joseph, Christine Wong, and David Zweig. Cambridge, Mass.: Council on East Asian Studies, Harvard University.

Wong Tianzhen, et al., 1995. *Profit Sharing and Labor Dividend.* Beijing: China Labor Publisher.

Woo, Margaret Y. K. 1994. "Chinese Women Workers: The Delicate Balance between Protection and Equality." In *Engendering China: Women Culture, and the State*, edited by Christina Gilmartin et al. Cambridge, Mass.: Harvard University Press.

———. 2003. "Shaping Citizenship: Chinese Family Law and Women." *Yale Journal of Law and Feminism* 15:75.

Wood, Ellen. 1990. "The Uses and Abuses of 'Civil Society.'" *Socialist Register*.

World Bank. 1994. *China: Long Term Problems and Countermeasures in the Transition of Health Care Patterns.* New York: World Bank.

Worseley, Peter. 1969. "The Concept of Populism." In *Populism: Its Meanings and National Characteristics*, edited by Ghita Ionescu and Ernest Gellner. London: Weidenfeld and Nicolson.

Wright, A. 1960. "The Study of Chinese Civilization." *Journal of the History of Ideas* 21.

Wright, Mary, ed. 1968. *China in Revolution: The First Phase.* New Haven, Conn.: Yale University Press.

Wu Changhua. 1999. "The Price of Growth." *Bulletin of the Atomic Scientists* 55:5 (September/October).

Xian Han. 2001. "Correctly Understanding Certain Paradoxes of Modernization." *Theoretical Fronts* (Beijing) 17.

Xiao Shu, ed. 1999. *Heralds of History: Solemn Promises over Half a Century Ago.* Shantou: Shantou University Press.

Xin Wang. 2003.*The Historical End of the Sunan Model.* Kaifeng: Henan People's Publishing House.

Xu Jilin. 2000. "Liberalism in the First Half of the Century." *Dushu* (Beijing) 5.

Yahuda, Michael. 2000. "The Changing Faces of Chinese Nationalism: The Dimensions of Statehood." In *Asian Nationalism,* edited by Michael Leifer. London: Routledge.

Yang, Long. 2003. "Research in China's Regional Development and Politics." *Study and Exploration* (Beijing) 4.

Yang, Mayfair. 1989. "Between State and Society: The Construction of Corporateness in a Chinese Socialist Factory." *Australian Journal of Chinese Affairs* 22 (July).

Ye Xianming. 2000. "A Reading of Marx's Conception of Modernity." *Philosophical Research* (Beijing) 2.

Young, Alfred. 1993. *We the People: Voices and Images of the New Nation.* Philadelphia: Temple University Press.

Young, Marilyn, ed. 1973. *Women in China: Studies in Social Change and Feminism.* Ann Arbor, Mich.: Center for Chinese Studies.

Yu Guangyuan, ed. 1984. *China's Socialist Modernization.* Beijing: Foreign Language Press.

Yu Jianrong. 2001. *The Politics of Yue Village: The Changes of Rural China's Political Structure in China's Transformation.* Beijing: Shangwu.

Yu Zuyao. 1997. *A Study of Individual Income during China's Economic Transformation.* Beijing: Economics Science Publisher.

Yue, Jianyong, and Chen Man. 2003. "Why Has China Striven so Hard to Attract FDI?" *Modern China Studies* 3.

Zakaria, Fareed. 1997. "Democratic Tyranny." *Prospect* (December).

——. 2004. *The Future of Freedom: Illiberal Democracy at Home and Abroad.* New York: Norton.

Zhang Ming. 2003. "Resources from the Traditional World." *Dushu* (Beijing) 1.

Zhang Rulun. 2000. "The Third Road." *Dushu* (Beijing) 5.

Zhang Xudong, ed. 2001. *Whither China? Intellectual Politics in Contemporary China.* Durham, N.C.: Duke University Press.

Zhao Xiuling. 1999. "Current Conditions and Prospects for Research on the Ancient Grassroots Administrative System in China." *Social Sciences in China* 4.

Zheng Zhongbing. 1995. "The Concept of Freedom in Chinese Ancient Culture." *Eastern Culture* (Beijing) 3.

Zhu Di. 1995. *A Factual Account of Rectification and Anti-Rightist Campaigns.* Taiyuan: Shanxi People's Publishing House.

Žižek, Slavoj. 2002. "Revolution Must Strike Twice." *London Review of Books* (25 July).

Zuo Dapei. 2005. "We Must Settle this Account." http://boxun.com (21 August).

Zweig, David. 1989. *Agrarian Radicalism in China: 1968–81.* Cambridge, Mass.: Harvard University Press.

INDEX

Danwei (work unit) model, 86–87
Davin, Delia, 114
Decentralization, 106–107
Decollectivization, 81–82
Democracy: China's version of, 133, 137–138, 249; choosing, over neoliberalism, 16; and civil society, 206; and the collective will, 190–197; and the Cultural Revolution, 170; defining, 132–133, 169, 201, 203–204; and dictatorship, 139–140; and ideology, 188–189, 239–242; institutional dimensions of, 178–201; and legality, 185–186; and legitimacy, 13, 246–249; and liberalism, 207–224; and local elections, 180–183 (*see also* Elections); and management of the workplace, 151–156; Marxian model of, 139; and the "mass line," 143–148, 188–189; moral dimensions of, 178–201; representation in, 190–197; republican, 221–228; and revolution, 133–156; and self-management, 151–156; self-understanding of, 199; social, 7; socialist vs. Western, 201–202; "totalitarian," 172–178; traditions influencing, 142–143. *See also* Liberal democracy; Liberalism; "People's democracy"; Rights
"Democracy Wall," 208–209
Demographic challenges, 273–274
Deng Xiaoping: on development, 74; and foreign capital, 26; reform model of, 96–97
Dernberger, Robert, 92
Derrida, Jacques, 177–178
Desai, Meghnad, 109, 171
Development, economic. *See* Economic development
Development, national: and independence, 49; as state-led project, 69–74 (*see also* Nationalism; State [PRC]); trajectory of, 275–280. *See also* Reform
Developmentalism: criticism of, 274–275; and modernization, 15, 60–131, 128; and "socialism and backwardness," 15; state-centered framework of, 61–74
Diamond, Larry, 188

Dictatorship, and democracy, 139–140
"Dictatorship over needs," 159–162
Dikotter, Frank, 36, 47
Dirlik, Arif, 17, 25, 42, 46, 53, 57, 97, 286
Disources on Livy (Machiavelli), 227
Dittmer, Lowell, 44, 76, 168, 170
Djilas, Milovan, 255
Dong, Xiaoyuan, 282
Dowdle, Michael, 185
Dreyer, June, 100
Du, Runsheng, 43
Duara, Prasenjit, 20, 107
Du Fu, 235
Duggan, Lisa, 120
Dunn, John, 52

Eastman, Lloyd, 42
Eckstein, Alexander, 51
Economic democracy, and self-management, 151–156
Economic development: advantages and disadvantages of, 72–73; of "backward" countries, 27–28; Chinese model of, 3–5; conditions of, 258–268; disparities of, 7–8; and globalization, 18–35; international context of, 62–65; and investigation of politics, 15; problems with, 272–275; and reform failures, 14, 270–271; social organization engaging issues of, 29–30; socialist vs. capitalist, 68; socialization of, 91–92; successes of, 2; trajectory of, 54–55; views on, 1–4. *See also* Capitalism; Reform; Reform, economic
Edmonds, Richard, 47, 272
Edwards, Louise, 117, 217
Egalitarianism, and class politics, 74–98. *See also* Class politics; Equality
Eisenstadt, S. N., 22
Elections, 180–183, 192–193, 275. *See also* "People's democracy"; Representation
Eley, Geoff, 219
Ellman, Michael, 154
Elster, Jon, 281
Engels, Friedrich, 9
Entrepreneurs, conditions for, 258–268

Khrushchev, Nikita, 67
Kwok, D. W. Y., 225

Land reform, 43–45
Landes, David, 39
Lang, Larry, 257
Lange, Oskar, 266
Lardy, Nicolas, 86, 105
Lattimore, Owen, 107
Lawrence, Susan, 8
Lee, Ming-Kwan, 87
Leftwich, Adrian, 73
Legality: vs. centrality of people, 179; and democracy, 185–186; and morality, 183–187
Legitimacy, 10–11; and democratization, 13, 246–249; and ideology, 236–249; of the PRC, 81; sources of, 206; and workers' participation, 88–89. *See also* "People's democracy"; Representation; State (PRC)
Lenin, Vladimir, 24, 66, 100, 134; on democracy, 139–140; state capitalism of, 91
Leninism, 169
Levenson, Joseph, 34
Lewis, John, 235
Lewis, W. John, 143
Leys, Colin, 40
Liang Qichao, 46
Liang Shuming, 151
Liberal democracy, 221–228; feasibility of, 207–208; and social welfare, 226–227. *See also* Democracy
Liberalism: Chinese version of, 206, 207–236; debate over, 213–221; and democracy, as concepts, 223–224; and imperialism, 236–249; without democracy, 208–213
Liberation, 205–250. *See also* Revolution, Chinese
Li Changping, 84, 106
Li Cheng, 109
Lieberthal, Kenneth, 29, 70, 144, 158, 176
Liedka, Raymond, 96
Lifton, Robert, 173, 174
Lijphart, Arend, 175

Lin Chun, 14, 126, 264, 277
Lindau, Juan, 214, 236
Lindblom, Charles, 71, 148, 232, 244
Lin Yusheng, 37
Linz, Juan, 168, 231
Lippitt, Victor, 98
Lipset, Martin, 209, 222
Liu, Lydia, 113, 236
Liu Shaoqi, 68, 79, 91, 232
Liu Zaifu, 46
Li Xiaojiang, 120
Li Yizhe, 199
Li Zehou, 46
Lo, Chung-Sho, 85
Locke, John, 190, 229
Lubman, Stanley, 185
Lu Hsiao-po, 87
Luke, Timothy, 19
Luxemburg, Rosa, 51, 160
Lu Xiaobo, 268
Lu Xueyi, 94, 267

MacFarquhar, Roderick, 160
Machiavelli, Niccolò, 227–228
Mackerras, Colin, 101, 102
Macpherson, C. B., 168
Mann, Michael, 112
Mao era: the moral and the institutional in, 15–16; political participation during, 167–168; social and economic destruction during, 50–51. *See also* Post-Mao era
Maoism, 69, 96–97, 169
Mao Zedong: and the Angang constitution, 153–155; on capitalism, 199; on the collective will, 191; and the Cultural Revolution, 171; death of, 69, 207; and "dictatorship over needs," 159–162; on egalitarianism, 77–78; and Krushchev, 67; "mass line" of, 143–148; on morality and legality, 184; and Nixon, 63; on peasants, 80; and the "people's democracy," 137–138; on people's sovereignty, 189; self-reliance of, 26; on ten major relationships, 101; on the "united front," 150–151; on urban-rural divide, 164; working with disad-

vantages, 65. *See also* Mao era; Post-
Mao era

Markovic, Mihailo, 235

Markus, Gyorgy, 160

Marriage Law, 115

Marshall, T. H., 222, 226

Marx, Karl, 19, 24, 39, 100, 139–140, 152–
153, 234

Marxism: and Chinese traditions, 140; and
the Cultural Revolution, 165–166; and
democracy in China, 199

Mason, J. H., 224

"Mass line," 143–148, 188–189

Mass movements, 187–190

Masses, vs. people, 150

Mayer, Arno, 134, 181

Mazur, Mary, 151

McClelland, J. S., 136

McCormick, Barrett, 158

Meiji Japan, 23–26

Meisner, Maurice, 6, 28, 42, 46, 146, 157,
159, 166, 212, 256–257, 262

Mencius, 140–141, 190

Middle class, 89–93. *See also* Bourgeoisie;
Class

Migrants, population of, 83–84

Miliband, Ralph, 162, 171, 219

Mill, John Stuart, 148, 234

Miller, David, 224

Milwertz, Cecelia, 124

Mirsky, Jonathan, 47

Mitchell, Juliet, 121

Mobilization, and participation, 162–172

Modernity: alternative, 17–59, 32–33, 55,
57–58; and Asia, 52–57; and Chinese
revolution, 45–46; colonial, 52–57; revolutionary, 35–57; singular, 18, 28–35; as
a social construct, 28–35; socialist, 35–
57

Modernization: framework of, 15, 60–131;
integration of projects for, 35–36; and
NICS, 64–65; shift from globalization to,
253–254; and "socialism and backwardness," 15; state-led, 28 (*see also* State
[PRC]); as striving to surmount capitalism, 33. *See also* Reform, economic

Mohanty, Chandra, 127

Molyneux, Maxine, 117, 169

Mongolia, 110

Montes, Manuel, 51

Montinola, Gabriella, 106

Moody, Peter, 146

Moore, Barrington, 32, 53, 89, 92, 157, 168,
209, 225

Morality: and institutionalism, 15–16, 178–
201; and legality, 183–187

"Mourning the Coal Miners" (Shao Yanxiang), 9

Muslims, Chinese, 98–100. *See also* Ethnic
relations

Nairn, Tom, 55

Nathan, Andrew, 141, 190, 197, 215, 244

National bourgeoisie, 89–93. *See also*
Bourgeoisie; Class

Nationalism: blending with communism,
41–42; Chinese vs. European, 37–38;
and the colonial period, 37–41; and cultural China, 36–41; ethnic, 102–103;
European vs. Chinese, 37–38; function
of, 60–61; as response to foreign threat,
64; and "socialism and backwardness,"
15; and socialist modernization, 15,
60–131; state-centered framework of,
61–74

Nationalist projects, integration of, 35–36

"Nationality question," 61, 99–105. *See also*
Ethnic relations

Natural resources, depletion of, 272–273,
275–276

Naughton, Barry, 69, 79, 80

Nee, Victor, 31, 96

Negri, Antonio, 22, 282

Neoliberalism, choosing democracy over,
16. *See also* Democracy; Liberalism

Newman, Michael, 171

NICS (newly industrialized countries), 19–
20, 64–65, 70–71

Nield, Keith, 219

Nixon, Richard, 63

Nolan, Peter, 6, 85, 94, 259, 262

Noncapitalist development, 18–35. *See also*
Capitalism; Economic development

Nonini, Donald, 93

North, Douglas, 281
Nove, Alex, 172

O'Brien, Kevin, 185
O'Donnell, Guillermo, 73
Offe, Claus, 194, 195, 217
Oi, Jean, 31, 106, 217
Oksenberg, Michael, 47, 70, 158
Ollman, Bertell, 253
Olson, Mancur, 175
Ong, Aihwa, 93
Open history, Eurocentrism in context of, 20–24
Opium Wars, 36
Organizations, state, 148, 215–216, 218–221. *See also* Institutionalism; State (PRC)

Parekh, Bhikhu, 223
Paris Commune, 139–140, 166, 199. *See also* Communes
Participation, and mobilization, 162–172
Path-dependence, 280–284
Patriarchy, "public," 118–124
Pearson, Margaret, 216, 218
Peasants: exploiting, 66–67; as second-class citizens, 80. *See also* Class; Rural-urban divide
Pei Xiaoling, 32
"People": in Chinese version of democracy, 137–138; and the collective will, 194–195; vs. "masses," 150; vs. "subjects," 135–138
"People's democracy," 15–16, 132–204, 249; Chinese version of, 137; and communism, 200–201; and the Cultural Revolution, 170–171; idea of, 138–143; institutional infrastructure in, 148–151; legality in, 183–187; and the mass line, 143–148; morality in, 183–187; and ownership of, 197–201; and self-management, 151–156; timeline of events related to, 198; and the totalitarianism of the state, 172–178. *See also* Democracy; Rights
"People's democratic dictatorship," 133
People's Republic of China (PRC). *See* State (PRC)
"People's sovereignty," 133, 135–136; as col-

lective, 189; and institutions, 202–203; institutions vs. idea of, 179; and Mencius, 140–141
Perkins, Dwight, 69
Perry, Elizabeth, 87, 140, 214
Peters, Guy, 281
Phillips, Anne, 122
Pocock, J. G. A., 227
Political nationalism, and cultural China, 36–41
Political opposition, absence of, 174–175
Political participation, during Mao years, 167–168
Politics, class, 74–98; comparative assessments of, 93–98; and "internal accumulation," 61. *See also* Class
Politics, spatial, 105–113
Polyani, Karl, 254
Post-Mao era: increased equality in, 95; the moral and the institutional in, 15–16. *See also* Mao era; Mao Zedong
Poverty, 43–44, 49, 97–98, 221, 378; alleviation, 7–8, 82, 94, 129, 244–245; global, 13, 44, 242; and human rights, 245; rural, 75; in Tibet, 101–103; urban, 7, 235
Power, state monopoly of, 70–71, 81, 94–98, 138, 198
PRC (People's Republic of China). *See* State (PRC)
Prebisch, Raul, 274
Pretty, Dave, 48
Preuss, Ulrich, 195, 217
Price, R. F., 155
Price system, 266–267
Prime, Penelope, 69
Prince, The (Machiavelli), 227
Przeworski, Adam, 162, 180, 242
"Public good regime," 65, 74, 149, 203, 243; dismantling of, 269; and socialist paternalism, 158
"Public patriarchy," 118–124
Public services, decline of, 53. *See also* Welfare, social
Pye, Lucien, 38, 39, 161, 176, 179

Qin Hui, 257

Race rhetoric, invoking of, 36–37
Randall, Vicky, 72
Rapp, John, 199
Rawls, John, 117
Rawski, Thomas, 51
Redding, Gordon, 93
Red guards, 166–167. *See also* Cultural
    Revolution
Reflections on the Revolution in France
    (Burke), 190
Reform, Chinese model of, 1–3, 232–234;
    as continuation of Chinese socialist
    model, 59; contradictions with eco-
    nomic growth, 14; crisis of, 269–272;
    making, unmaking, and remaking of,
    16, 253; misconceptions about, 3–4;
    obstacles to, 12–13; rethinking, 251–287;
    and social emancipation, 12–13; trajec-
    tory of, 268–269. *See also* Socialism,
    Chinese model of
Reform, economic: assessment of experi-
    ences from, 85–88; crisis of, 269–272;
    and dismantling of state monopoly, 94–
    98; and globalization, 263–264; institu-
    tionalization of, 258–268; and land
    reform, 43–45; mid-course turn of, 271–
    272; and path-dependence, 280–284;
    periods of, 15; post-Mao, 95–96; views
    on, 1–4. *See also* Economic development
Regional relations, 15, 61, 98–113
Reid, Anthony, 225
Religious matters, handling of, 110–111
Representation, 190–197. *See also* Democ-
    racy; Elections; "People's democracy"
Republican democracy, 221–228
Resnick, Stephen A., 256
Revisionism, of Chinese revolution, 46–48
Revolution, Chinese, 41–52; achievements
    of, 44; and bureaucracy, 156–178; and
    democracy, 133–156; goals of, 205; and
    the "mass line," 143–148; and the "mod-
    ern," 45–46; as national, 40; "people"
    vs. "subjects" after, 135–138; questions
    on necessity of, 52; revisionist scholar-
    ship on, 46–47; role of conscious
    actions in, 49–50; as social, 40; unin-
    tended consequences of, 51–52

Revolutionary modernity, 35–57
Rights, 228–236, 234–235; protection of,
    206; and public welfare, 242–246; rec-
    ognition of, 206
Riskin, Carl, 6, 51, 68, 75, 86, 262, 263, 284
Robinson, Mark, 73, 154
Roemer, John, 253
Rofel, Lisa, 127, 176
Rona-Tas, Akos, 96
Rosemont, Henry, 225
Rosenberg, Justin, 25
Rousseau, Jean Jacques, 190–194, 196, 197,
    217, 225, 234
Rowe, William, 216
Rupnik, Jacques, 136
Rural bias, 152–153
Rural development, 66–67
Rural reform, 94–98
Rural-urban divide, 75, 78–83, 164. *See also*
    Inequality; Peasants; Poverty

Saich, Tony, 87, 144, 152
Salinger, Dorothy, 129
Sartori, Giovanni, 139, 160, 169, 201, 204
Schmitt, Carl, 206
Schmitter, Phillippe, 73, 149, 188
Schram, Stuart, 76, 141, 154, 171
Schumpeter, Joseph, 180, 247
Schurmann, Franz, 145
Schwarcz, Vera, 36
Schwartz, Benjamin, 42, 236
Schweickart, David, 5, 263
Scott, James, 178
Scott, Joan, 120, 122, 196, 277
Segal, Gerald, 20
Selden, Mark, 30, 80, 98, 145, 182
Self-determination, 111–112
Self-management, and economic democ-
    racy, 151–156
Sen, Amartya, 116, 246, 248
Seymour, James, 151
Shakya, Tsering, 105
Shambaugh, David, 160
Shao Yanxiang, 9
Shaw, Victor, 87, 197
Shirk, Susan, 106, 145, 259
Shue, Henry, 30, 171

Wong, Bin, 81, 267
Woo, Margaret Y. K., 119
Workers, 84–86; participation of, and state legitimacy, 88–89; women as, 115–116
Work unit, 83–89
Working class, and "class struggles," 129. *See also* Class
World Trade Organization (wto), 11–12, 83
Worseley, Peter, 146
Wu Changhua, 272

Xian Han, 58
Xiaokang socialism, 16, 253, 268–287
Xinjiang Uygur Autonomous Region, 101–102
Xu Chenggang, 31

Yahuda, Michael, 38
Yan'an model, 65–66, 143–148. *See also* Mao Zedong
Ye Xianming, 58
Young, Marilyn, 114, 133
Yue Jianyong, 10, 261
Yu Zuyao, 94

Zakaria, Fareed, 247
Zhang Ming, 14, 30
Zhang Zuoji, 273–274
Zheng Zhongbing, 225
Zhou Enlai, 164–165, 203
Zhu Di, 161
Žižek, Slavoj, 166
Zuo Dapei, 85